To

ARNOLD ROSE
1918–1968

scholar, co-worker, friend

Preface

THIS is a study of Europe in the mid-sixties and a look into the seventies, prepared by a group of scholars from the University of Minnesota. Its goal is to explore both from an interdisciplinary standpoint and from that of their respective disciplines the major economic, educational, political, military, and social issues of the era.

The research team spent 1966–67 in Europe, ranging widely in the process of inquiry and visiting, in the person of one or more of its members, every European country with the exception of Albania. Three of its five members returned in the summer of 1968, spending most of their time in Eastern Europe and the Soviet Union during a period which saw the Soviet intervention in Czechoslovakia.

The focus of the analysis is indicated in the introduction which follows and need not be spelled out here. It should be noted, however, that this is a summary volume, written essentially for the nonspecialist and greatly compressing the more specific analyses of the respective contributors; specialized monographs by several of them are in press or nearing completion.

Before the formulation of this project members of the group had spent a total of some twenty years in Europe in studies involving aspects of the contemporary international scene. The more immediate genesis of the project lies in several years of discussions and seminars which they undertook in the period 1963–66. From these it became clear that it would be most profitable for the group to spend a period of time in Europe itself to explore the many issues which had arisen in such discussions. The field work was made possible through grants provided by the office of International Programs of the University of Minnesota from funds made available by the Ford Foundation and by the Louis W. and Maude Hill Family Foundation. To these organizations we are deeply indebted for making this study possible.

We are likewise most grateful to the scores of Europeans and members of American embassy staffs who generously gave of their time and knowledge in exploring with us the problems in which we were interested. We also owe particular gratitude to the Bibliothèque Royale, Brussels, and to director Pierre Michel and Mme. Guy Lercangée of the Institute of American Studies for providing us with office space, assisting us in many other ways during the course of our research, and helping us to stage a symposium in the Belgian capital in June 1967 in which we could discuss with specialists from northwestern Europe many problems of major concern. Our work in our Paris headquarters was greatly facilitated by the possibility of making extensive use of the facilities of Reid Hall, operated by Columbia University. The Center for Northwest European Language and Area Studies of the University of Minnesota under its director, Alrik Gustafson, provided assistance in a number of ways.

Jean Belden Taber served as research assistant to the group during the European phases of the inquiry and provided assistance in preparing several chapters. Her language skills and knowledge of the European scene were invaluable. Jean Schleh of the Graduate Research Center of the University of Minnesota contributed greatly to the development of the manuscript. To other officers of the Graduate School we are indebted for assistance in staging an interdisciplinary seminar in 1967–68 and a series of educational television presentations, each of which aided us materially in drawing together our material and formulating conclusions. Mrs. Jeanne Forsberg and Mrs. Diana Hays were most helpful in the typing of the manuscript.

This volume is dedicated to the memory of Arnold M. Rose who died shortly after completing his chapter. He was an indefatigable worker, perceptive analyst, and helpful critic. But, more than that, he was a friend with whom we shared many a happy moment on the Continent.

These chapters were already in the hands of the publisher when, on April 27, 1969, President Charles de Gaulle announced his resignation. The authors, who had of course speculated upon such a possibility in their writing, subsequently made some revisions to take account of de Gaulle's action and to make further conjectures on the shape of things to come, given this change. But they could not begin to anticipate all the possible ramifications, nor could they foresee the changes following the German elections in the fall of 1969. The writing has to stop at some point.

ROBERT H. BECK
HAROLD C. DEUTSCH
PHILIP M. RAUP
JOHN G. TURNBULL

University of Minnesota
December 1969

Contents

THE CHANGING STRUCTURE OF EUROPE

Abbreviations Used in This Volume

Benelux	Belgium, the Netherlands, and Luxembourg
Comecon	Council for Mutual Economic Cooperation
ECSC	European Coal and Steel Community
EEC	European Economic Community (Common Market), the "Six"
EFTA	European Free Trade Association, the "Seven"
Euratom	European Atomic Energy Community
EAT	European Association of Teachers
FAO	Food and Agriculture Organization
FDP	Free Democratic party
GATT	General Agreement on Tariffs and Trade
ILO	International Labor Organization
NATO	North Atlantic Treaty Organization
OECD	Organization for Economic Cooperation and Development
OEEC	Organization for European Economic Cooperation
SDP	Social Democratic party
SED	Socialist Unity party
SHAPE	Supreme Headquarters, Allied Powers, Europe
UNESCO	United Nations Educational, Scientific, and Cultural Organization

CHAPTER *1*

Introduction

DESPITE two world wars and the many lesser conflicts of the early twentieth century which pitted European nation against European nation, there was considerable in the way of integration on that continent before 1945.

First of all there was a common heritage, a similarity of outlook and material culture that characterized nearly all European peoples in contrast to those in many other parts of the world. Second, there were the varied technical agreements, many worked out in the nineteenth century, that were resumed after each war as though they had never been interrupted: agreements for cross-national services (rail, bus, and air transportation; mail; telephone and telegraph); agreements on ways of coping with such problems as river pollution; and so on. Third, there was tourism, along with the many international events that brought Europeans of differing national backgrounds into personal interaction: conventions of scientists and other professionals; trade fairs; festivals. While national languages were retained, there was an ever-expanding training in other European languages. Fourth, there was a rapidly growing cross-communication through the mass media: in peacetime, newspapers and magazines from all over the Continent could be purchased in any large city; and in the 1930's the radio sharply reduced communication barriers, with television in the offing. Fifth, and not least, there were the cross-national ideological and social movements and their organizations — religious (particularly the Roman Catholic Church); political (especially the Socialist internationals); behavioral (such as the temperance movement) — and the exchanges among European peoples in the fields of art, literature, music, and science.

But more than this, there was a long history of efforts to fashion Europe into a unity in one way or another. In the Middle Ages there was the almost successful movement to make Europe entirely Roman Catholic under the hegemony of the pope, and there was the less successful but not insignificant effort to create a feudal political hegemony under the Holy Roman emperor. Napoleon came close to making a political entity out of

Europe and might have succeeded had he not overextended himself into Russia. Several of those who assumed political leadership in the wake of Napoleon's defeat had something of the same idea of greater political co-operation among the sovereign states: Metternich, Talleyrand, and others pursued the idea of a "Concert of Europe" that did much to keep the Continent at peace for fifty years. In the meantime, the British — while not politically oriented toward the Continent — led in a movement for international free trade that could not be said to have been wholly unsuccessful. No passports were needed to cross many frontiers.

Yet despite all this, there were wars that tore Europe into pieces and almost destroyed it, and there was a reversion to economic autarky which by the 1930's reduced national standards of living to points much lower than the level of technological knowledge and skill of the population justified.

So it was that a significant number of European and American political and intellectual leaders (Jean Monnet, Paul-Henri Spaak, Robert Schuman, Dean Acheson, among others) after World War II set fuller integration of Europe as an important goal for the Continent and some looked beyond that to integration of the "North Atlantic community." A series of European and Euro-American conferences were undertaken, many of which were successful in creating new and powerful cross-national political, military, and economic organizations — such as the European Coal and Steel Community (ECSC), the North Atlantic Treaty Organization (NATO), the European Economic Community (EEC, popularly called the Common Market), and the European Free Trade Association (EFTA) — as well as lesser cross-national entities.

The operations of these deliberately created organizations and their efforts in fostering or limiting the cross-national integration of Europe and the North Atlantic area form the central theme of the discussion and analysis in this book. All five of the authors center on this theme. Harold Deutsch treats political and military relations and institutions; John Turnbull deals with economic structures and policies; Philip Raup analyzes agricultural and related developments and institutions; Robert Beck discusses educational establishments; and Arnold Rose concerns himself with the social funds and the free movement of labor. The integrational developments in each of these areas in the postwar period are dealt with in selective detail, but the focus is upon the years 1966–68 and, more broadly, 1963–68, believed by many to include the "watershed" period in the pattern of European and Atlantic developments.

But integration can be analyzed in a more uniform context than such terms as "agreements," "institutions," and "organizations," used so frequently in the paragraphs above, would suggest. The unifying thread of this volume is to be found in the uniform framework within which each of the authors presents his discussion and analysis. Each inquired into a different subject area, though of course there was overlap. And varying approaches and methods were used: Rose posed a series of hypotheses which he sought to appraise; Raup and Turnbull applied the methodology of the institutional economist; Beck and Deutsch took the view of the comparative analyst. But there was a common framework within which these varying approaches were employed. This framework includes the following basic considerations.

In the first place, integration involves a setting in which values and attitudes are important and have a significant impact upon the process and extent of integration. Thus attitudes toward a common political entity as against separate national bodies or toward the acceptance of nationals of other countries are pertinent factors. It would seem obvious that the more these attitudes and values are favorable to integration, the more successful the process is likely to be.

There is more to this issue, however, than the above might indicate. Common attitudes and values which are not in themselves negative as respects integration may nevertheless require modification if integration is to bear its full fruits. Thus the European view toward, for example, entrepreneurship cannot itself be viewed as inhibiting integration. But competition from the world outside may require an attitudinal change on the part of all within the integrated entity: in this illustration the development of a more positive view toward entrepreneurship. What is so far-reaching about integration, then, is not only that a common set of attitudes and values may have to develop, but if such does develop (or exists), a major change of the common pattern may still be necessary. In a sense, society may have to reshape itself.

Given the setting of existing attitudes and values, integration involves structures, policies, and peoples. Several examples will clarify what we mean by this. A single legislative body replaces (or supplements, as in a federal-state relationship) those of the separate nations; a single central bank is created; a cross-national professional society is formed. These illustrate structural integration. (To escape from the tyranny of words it should be noted that the authors use "structure," "organization," "institution," "enterprise," "entity," and "body" as synonymous terms unless otherwise specified.) Even in the absence of a formal structural change, policy integration may occur. Separate central banks may coordinate their behavior so that a common pattern of action is followed. Separate educational institutions may maintain their identities but develop common policies for the transfer of students and the exchange of faculty. "Harmonization" is a term one frequently finds in the literature when such policy coordination is under discussion.

Thus an important component in integration is the development of common political, economic, social, and ideational entities in which people can interact with one another in a meaningful way and be dependent on each other. These common structures and policies may not develop primarily out of deliberate agreements of statesmen, although such agreements may hasten their development just as common structures and policies may make possible the successful agreements of the statesmen. How the evolution of the political and military structure in Europe has progressed or faltered is of particular concern to Deutsch. How the economic structure has progressed is of underlying interest in the chapters by Raup and Turnbull. How the common social structure has developed is of primary concern in the discussions of Beck and Rose. In a limited volume such as this, none of the authors deals, however, with common ideational structures — religious, intellectual, or artistic.

The third facet of integration is what might be called "international group consciousness" or the "integration of people." By this we mean the acceptance by nationals of a given European country of people from other European countries as "interchangeable" for most purposes with people of their own country. It consists of a set of attitudes — or a public opinion — affirming that one is a citizen of Europe just as much as he is a citizen of France, Germany, or the United Kingdom, but it also embraces all those policies and programs which enable easy mobility to occur. It is probably true all over the world that people feel closer to their neighbors than they do to those who live at greater distances, but a Nebraskan will recognize the right of a Californian or a New Yorker to move next door to him as much as that of a fellow Nebraskan, and to vote in local elections, to take a job on an equal basis in local industry, and otherwise to participate in local society. Do the Germans or the French accept each other — or accept Italians, Greeks, and Spaniards — in the same way? This is the main question which is posed and partially answered in the chapter by Rose. It is also an underlying theme in the chapter by Beck, who deals with the ways in which the schools of Europe are now training young people to think in European terms, and not merely in French, German, or other national ways.

Structural integration, policy integration, and the integration of people have progressed at different speeds in Europe and have reached different levels. These differences have inevitably affected the degree of optimism or, conversely, pessimism which infuses each author's estimation of probabilities for the future integration of Europe and the North Atlantic area. Thus Deutsch, though underlining the number and complexity of international cooperative agreements and the fact that some of them in operation may be approaching the point of no return, also emphasizes the half-finished business and the barriers that remain to be surmounted. In the category of half-finished business he would place the incorporation of a formerly disruptive Germany into a European and Atlantic structure from which it would be difficult to break out, as well as the expansion of NATO from a military alliance of convenience into a meaningful nucleus for a closer political, economic, and cultural association of the states of the West. He would assign Gaullism to the category of barriers, and he considers whether it is a transitory phenomenon or a long-range inhibitor of the integration of Europe, not to speak of the North Atlantic world.

Raup considers the great economic potential created by the release in recent decades of millions of low-productivity agricultural laborers for work in more productive occupations, but questions how much farther this can go in Europe as compared to the United States; he also worries about the acceptance of such myths as "economies of large scale" when, in agriculture, decision making on a regional scale may make more economic sense than community-wide decision making at EEC headquarters in Brussels. Turnbull is impressed with the expansion of output and trade within the EEC and EFTA and the probable consequence of this for the growing productivity of Europe, although he recognizes that many components of economic integration have not proceeded as rapidly as was hoped when these organizations were formed.

Beck stresses the importance of the educational activities of such organizations as the Council of Europe and the Organization for Economic Cooperation and Development (OECD). A European *baccalauréat* is being developed and it will make a reality of pan-European higher education. Beck notes the common European commitment to equality in educational opportunity, a commitment which has put pressure on barriers to equal access to education. In all European countries, he has found, there is a desire to extend the years of compulsory education and to meet the increasing expectancy among young people for continuing education.

Rose reflects upon the relatively slow pace of "people integration" and he would call attention to these facts: that Europe is regrouping into four blocs not less divided than the 25 or so countries of Europe were before 1933; that the remarkable agreements in the Treaty of Rome in 1957, under which the EEC was formed, have not been followed by significant new political agreements (except those — like the EEC agricultural accord of 1966 — which were already envisioned in that treaty); that despite NATO, the Kennedy Round of trade talks, and the various monetary conferences of 1965–68, the United States and the various blocs of Europe are moving in different directions; and that the "new nationalism" inspired partly by de Gaulle will not die with him because it has tended to reduce the idealism that some years earlier gave so much force to the movement toward European integration.

Such is the diversity — as well as the unity — of this volume. One final item by way of introduction. This is intended to be only a summary volume on the research of the five contributing scholars, and it is addressed primarily to the interested lay reader, not the specialist. It may, however, prove useful to the specialist in its analysis of developments in areas other than his own and in providing insight at points of interrelation among fields of study.

CHAPTER *2*

Anniversaries and Balance Sheets

BY JOHN G. TURNBULL AND JEAN BELDEN TABER

THE pattern of relationships among the nation-states of the North Atlantic community is many-dimensioned: cultural, diplomatic, economic, educational, military, technological, to mention but a few. The year 1967 saw anniversaries of two events which were critically important in shaping these relationships. The first of these was the twentieth anniversary of the launching of the idea for the Marshall Plan, a plan which enabled a war-devastated Europe to get back on its economic feet. The second was the tenth anniversary of the signing of the Treaty of Rome which brought into existence the European Economic Community, one of the boldest multi-country economic moves ever made. Therefore, it was a year of celebration, but even more a year of inventory taking, on both the European level and the level of the North Atlantic community.

The story begins in 1947 with an Atlantic relationship not at all like the one which exists today. That relationship could not be thought of as a "community" in the sense that word was used in 1967. It featured instead a European continent finding it difficult to rise by its own effort from the ashes of war, and in contrast an economically prosperous United States of America newly conscious of the need to use its wealth to aid its former wartime allies and enemies.

As the goals of the Marshall Plan for reconstruction of Europe were attained, as the European nations recovered and their economies surged ahead, and as these separate nations organized themselves economically in a variety of ways to be discussed later, the relationship changed. The United States, which initially played a role of overwhelming dominance, gradually found that she was no longer able to dictate according to her own interests. Although this was not necessarily true in all cases, it certainly must be admitted, for example, in the economic realm. One can cite the example of British bids for membership in the EEC. Those bids were

strongly supported by the United States in 1961–63, but effectively
blocked by the French in January 1963 and several times subsequently.
Another such example would be that of the Organization for Economic
Cooperation and Development which the United States had hoped would
play a role in more justly distributing the burden of aid to the developing
countries, but which has not succeeded — at least not to the extent anticipated — in awakening its more affluent member nations to the need for
augmenting the quantity of aid given.

There can be no doubt that by 1967 the European nations had recovered individually and were capable of exercising even greater economic
power collectively. Thus, 1967 was a good time, in light of the goals of the
Marshall Plan and of the Treaty of Rome, to take stock of the accomplishments of these twenty-year and ten-year periods. What was the status of
economic and political affairs in Europe and the North Atlantic community? A review here of this stocktaking will serve several purposes: provide a historical backdrop useful in setting the stage for the discussion and
analysis of ensuing chapters, acquaint the reader with the organizations
subsequently considered, and outline unresolved problems to be examined.

The Marshall Plan

Secretary of State George C. Marshall at Harvard University on June
5, 1947, assessed the contemporary situation in Europe: "The truth of
the matter is that Europe's requirements for the next three or four years of
foreign food and other essential products — principally from America —
are so much greater than her present ability to pay that she must have
substantial additional help or face economic, social, and political deterioration of a very grave character." Marshall's "plan" embodied three essential points: ". . . the United States Government can proceed much further in its efforts to alleviate the [grave European economic] situation and
help start the European world on its way to recovery . . ."; ". . . the
initiative . . . must come from Europe . . ."; and "The program should
be a joint one, agreed to by a number, if not all, European nations." [1]

Americans had earlier begun to equate postwar reconstruction of Europe with the idea of integration. Even before the Marshall idea was enunciated, individuals such as John Foster Dulles and Walter Lippmann, as
well as State Department officials and the Congress, voiced support for
some kind of "United States of Europe." It was doubtless both undesirable
and unrealistic to have hoped for the creation of a mirror image of the
United States of America on the eastern coast of the Atlantic Ocean. But
it was understandable that Americans should feel their experience with
federalism might well be drawn on and followed by the European states.

At any rate, officially, and unofficially, the United States encouraged

European integration as the best way to promote economic recovery and political stability and to ensure continued peace on the European continent. The unwillingness of some of the European states to set up an organization with strong central decision-making and decision-enforcing powers to handle the Marshall Plan aid was a disappointment to the United States. But American officials continued to promote the idea of integration. In the autumn of 1949, the United States administrator of the Marshall Plan, Paul Hoffman, in a speech to the Council of the Organization for European Economic Cooperation (OEEC — the entity created in Europe to organize mutual aid) proposed a setup strikingly like the present EEC.

By 1952 when the Marshall Aid funds ceased flowing to Europe, its economic recovery was assured. At this time there had developed a kind of euphoria concerning the progress that had been made and the steps which seemed to be forthcoming. The European Coal and Steel Community was just getting underway, projects for a European Defense Community and a European Political Community were under consideration, and ideas were being offered for agricultural as well as other types of sectoral economic communities. The hope existed that they would all come into being gathered under the "umbrella" of an organization such as the Council of Europe, the ten-nation organization created in 1949 (since expanded to fifteen members) to foster intergovernmental cooperation and coordination on common problems (defense excepted).

At that moment, Americans may not have realized what a potentially powerful economic entity might be spawned in Europe through the kind of aid and encouragement the United States was providing. Or realizing this, they may have felt that the political benefits of a united Europe were so great as to offset any economic disadvantage that might accrue to the United States in the future. In any case, the goals of the Marshall Plan seemed to have been quickly and fully realized.

The Economic Organization of Western Europe

There have been both economic and political motives for the postwar efforts toward economic cooperation in Western Europe. The economic rationale for this kind of cooperation was based upon both theory and example: upon classical economic theory suggesting, for instance, that a common market of 200 million people was more desirable than one of some fraction of that number; and upon the example provided by the United States with its extended tariff-free market. Supplementary economic arguments for economic cooperation have also been advanced: the gains to be achieved from additional resource specialization (a basic principle in the classical theory of international trade); gains from increased competition; gains from enterprises of more efficient size (i.e., "larger" enterprises); gains from new patterns of investment and technology. The political rationale was, of course, that economic cooperation would lock nations together in such a way as to make military conflict much less likely.

The Organization for European Economic Cooperation, which was formed in April 1948, was the first extended effort toward economic cooperation. But as set up it was no more than a type of classical intergovernmental agency. Despite efforts from some quarters to turn it into an organization resembling a customs union, the "right of independent action" was strongly adhered to by other members — especially Great Britain and the Scandinavian countries. The OEEC achieved the goal of getting Europe back on her economic feet — and this was an excellent accomplishment — but no concrete steps toward integration were taken under the guidance of this organization.

On a much smaller scale, the Benelux Customs Union (Belgium, the Netherlands, and Luxembourg) came into being gradually, based primarily upon monetary and customs conventions signed during World War II. By January 1, 1948, a customs union with no internal tariffs but a common external tariff had become effective. A further step was taken in 1958 when the treaty for a Benelux Economic Union was signed, to be effective from November 1, 1960. Benelux became what might be called "economic union within an economic union" (since the EEC, to which it belongs, aspires also to be an economic union). Thus in these first two organizations there were two extremes in economic organization: simple cooperation and full economic integration.

THE EUROPEAN COMMUNITIES

With the failure of the OEEC to move toward integration, it became evident that a more limited approach would be more likely to prove successful: an organization including a smaller number of nations, ones which were more committed to the idea of integration, and concerning itself with a smaller area of the economy, i.e., a "sectoral" approach rather than a "global" approach.[2] The European Coal and Steel Community, created in 1952, embodied these two elements: an organization of only six members (although the original appeal was to all those nations of Europe who wished to take part), and concerned only with the coal and steel sectors of the economy. The six countries who formed the community were Belgium, France, West Germany, Italy, Luxembourg, and the Netherlands.

The outstanding characteristic of the ECSC was the sharply defined nature of its economic goals. Its charter specifically called for the establishment of conditions which would assure the most rational distribution of production at the highest possible level of productivity. The ECSC had as its mandate removal of intracommunity barriers to coal and steel trade (the "fusion of markets"), expansion of the community economy, and improvement of living standards in the member states.

But the ECSC had two explicit political goals as well: the "negative" goal of forever preventing war between the member states and the "positive" goal of laying "the bases of institutions capable of giving direction to their common destiny." [8] This explicit goal of creating institutions which would be the precursors of the institutions of government in a unified Europe was given form in a High Authority which could make decisions binding on participating governments and which had at its disposal revenues independent of action by those governments; a Council of Ministers which, although composed of representatives of the national governments, was in some cases bound by majority decision; a Common Assembly to which alone the High Authority was accountable and which had the power to turn out the High Authority; and a Court of Justice to try cases which arose in the context of the community. Whatever the difficulties later to be encountered by the ECSC, a first step had finally been taken toward political unification via the route of economic integration.

A variety of elements prevented the immediate creation of additional sectoral communities of the ECSC type, although several such projects were proposed. The next bold step, culminating in the Treaty of Rome signed in March 1957, brought into existence the European Economic Community, or Common Market, composed of the same six member states as the ECSC. It embraced a global approach to economic integration and, once again, was an entity replete with political hopes. The preamble of the Treaty of Rome begins with the words "Determined to establish the foundations of an ever closer union among the European peoples . . ." And it was Walter Hallstein, the first president of the EEC Commission, the organization's executive body, who made the oft-quoted statement: "We are not in business — we are in politics." [4] On the economic side, the Treaty of Rome spoke of a "customs union": a free-trade area in the sense of zero intracommunity tariffs with the added characteristic of a common external tariff. But the EEC aspired to be a good deal more than this as it sought to achieve harmonized policies in various areas including commerce, social security, legal systems, patents, transport, taxation. It has proceeded toward its goals by a series of transitional steps, the last of which is scheduled to be effective by 1970. [5]

Institutions similar to, although not identical with, those of the ECSC were established for the EEC, with a Commission instead of a High Authority. One might suggest that the ECSC was given a "supranational" authority beyond that accorded the EEC, although this would be debatable. In addition, the ECSC treaty may be called "law-establishing" in that it specifies exhaustively the regulations to be applied within the sector, while the EEC treaty is more of an "outline" treaty, providing general guidelines for action.

One additional sectoral community was established at the same time as the EEC — that of the European Atomic Energy Community, or Euratom. This community, with the same membership as the EEC and almost identical institutions, was given the function of developing peaceful uses for atomic energy, in which work in Europe was either in its infancy or nonexistent. The hope was to head off the creation of vested national interests in this area. It is interesting to note that before the signing of the treaties which brought into being the EEC and Euratom, one group concerned to bring about the integration of Europe stressed the importance of the atomic energy community. This was Jean Monnet's Action Committee for the United States of Europe.[6] It felt that in the field of atomic energy a truly "European" industry could be created, unencumbered by the problems of long-existing industries like coal and steel. The Action Committee regarded Euratom rather than the EEC as potentially the real kernel of a European community.

THE "OUTER SEVEN"

The next organizational step followed an attempt by those countries outside the EEC to arrange some kind of free-trade agreement between themselves and the Common Market — an attempt which began, in fact, even before the Treaty of Rome was concluded. When these "Maudling negotiations" (named for Reginald Maudling, the British chairman of the negotiating team) failed, the "outer seven" countries (Austria, Denmark, Great Britain, Norway, Portugal, Sweden, and Switzerland) set up their own free-trade area. The treaty establishing it, signed in Stockholm in November 1959, includes a commitment to a schedule of tariff reductions and quota liberalizations; escape clauses in cases where such reductions might be damaging to a given country; "rules of origin" on the production of goods, designed to control the diversion of trade; bans on actions designed to offset the treaty concessions; and a minimal administrative bureaucracy (that is, nothing equivalent to major commissions or committees was visualized).[7]

This treaty setting up the European Free Trade Association was, like the Treaty of Rome, global in approach, with the exception that agriculture was omitted. EFTA was, however, intended to be a free-trade area and no more: its convention envisaged no common external tariff, nor was there the intention to harmonize policies or create common policies in monetary, social, commercial, legal, or other areas. In a very real sense, EFTA was established in business to go out of business, a major goal of its members (stated in the preamble to the Stockholm Convention) being to reach some kind of arrangement with the EEC.

THE OECD

The pattern of development continued with the metamorphosis, in 1960, of the original OEEC into the Organization for Economic Cooperation and Development which included at its formation the non-European countries of the United States, Canada, and Japan, as well as the members of the EEC, the members of EFTA, and Greece, Iceland, Ireland, Spain, and Turkey. Yugoslavia is an associate member. As already noted, the United States hoped that through this agency its members would be encouraged to shoulder more equitably the burden of providing aid to developing countries. The EFTA countries hoped that it would facilitate the task of "building bridges" from EFTA to the EEC. Both hopes remain largely unfulfilled.

The OECD contribution, valuable as it has been, may more properly be termed "consultation and coordination" than "integration," if for no other reason than that its organizational structure, again along classical intergovernmental lines, gave it no mandate to require a country to follow certain actions. There has been no question, for example, of a country being bound by the vote of the majority.

The OECD operates principally in the following ways: (1) In various problem areas (manpower, balance of payments, education, science and technology, to mention but a few) the OECD has put study groups to work. Technical papers or reports are published with policy prescriptions designed to assist in resolution of the problems. Other reports, such as those involving projections of economic growth, are also issued. (2) Representatives of member countries may serve as channels of communication to their governments on particular problems or on general developments. Insofar as the OECD reaches a "consensus" on an issue, such communication may serve a useful purpose in furthering international cooperation. Since there is considerable interlocking representation (a given country's representative to the EEC may have a similar role in the OECD) the process of communication is facilitated. The usefulness of this process is illustrated by the development of the grades and standards system in international trade; the final implementation of this system was largely a product of OECD activity. (3) The agency gathers comprehensive statistics. (4) Particularly in the area of economic development, where, for example, education has been an important component, the OECD has sought to become a primary force in fostering improvements. But in all of these functions, the OECD is without the kind of "authority" possessed by the ECSC High Authority or the EEC Commission.

European Economic Integration as It Appeared in 1967–68

THE OECD, BENELUX, EFTA: THREE DIVERSE ENTITIES

It is evident that the OECD, which emphasizes consultation, coordination, and cooperation, and whose membership includes non-European and even non-Western countries, has played an important role in the economic life of Europe. And to the extent that working together has had the result of bringing countries closer, the contributions of the OECD to integration may by no means be discounted. But this agency has had neither the goal of integration nor the means to bring it about. In this respect it is significant to note that during the times of French (or Gaullist) "obstructionism" toward any action which would impinge further on France's economic or political "sovereignty," France has remained quite willing to cooperate within the framework of the OECD. The French government sees in it no threat to sovereignty of the kind posed by the EEC or NATO.

The Benelux Economic Union, which operates as a sub-community within the EEC (with express recognition in the Treaty of Rome), need not be detailed further. Suffice it to say that free movement for persons and services exists; there is, in effect, a common labor market and also unrestricted movement of capital inside the union. The net impact is that factor markets are characterized by easy mobility. In product markets this goal was achieved on July 1, 1968, with the removal of tariffs within the EEC. All three countries "coordinate" their economic and social policies, consulting on monetary and fiscal policy, prices and wages policy, labor and social security, and so on.

As for EFTA, its future is very much in a state of flux. By December 31, 1967, the elimination of selective internal tariffs was accomplished, three years ahead of schedule. In a decade of existence, EFTA generated a sizable increase in trade among its members and with the outside world.[8]

The major concern of EFTA is seeing that distortions are not encouraged or created which would undercut the free-trade-area concept. But no further steps are envisaged toward a customs union or an economic union. Furthermore since agriculture, an important sector of the economy for some of the member countries (Denmark in particular), does not fall within the scope of the organization, further action for EFTA is limited.

As of 1967–68 at least four of the seven EFTA countries — Denmark, Great Britain, Norway, and Sweden — had either made formal bids to enter the EEC or had exhibited strong interest in doing so; and Austria has for several years been negotiating an associate agreement with the Common Market. In the light of these developments, the remaining countries were contemplating what they would do. From the beginning of its existence, as indicated above, the ultimate aim of EFTA has been to form some kind of relationship with the EEC. The shape this relationship might take was still unclear in 1968. What was clear, however, was that a majority of the EFTA member countries were convinced that the desirable relationship should be full membership in the EEC rather than some sort of associate status.

A note of caution should be added to what would appear, from these requests for membership in the EEC, to be a clear trend toward more complete economic integration. The EFTA countries that have sought full or associate membership in the EEC may currently feel that the path toward further economic and, especially, political integration has been effectively blocked by the French government's reactions. It has been argued that French actions have covertly been welcomed by some of the other countries already in the Common Market. The danger of a loss of national "sovereignty" has diminished because of the French position. It was widely felt that this lessening danger was precisely the reason for the Swedish government's shift to a greater interest in joining the EEC. In their attempt to block the British, Danish, and other membership bids from moving forward, French government officials themselves stressed that the addition of members to the EEC would change it radically from an economic union to some sort of looser free-trade area.[9]

Another note of caution sounds loud and clear from the state in which the ECSC and Euratom found themselves in the summer of 1967. In a very real sense, the ECSC and Euratom were examples of two types of failures or near failures. And the period 1966–67 witnessed a kind of holding action by the two agencies, while waiting for the merger of the executives of the three communities (the ECSC, the EEC, and Euratom) on July 5, 1967, as specified in the Treaty of Brussels signed in April 1965. The complete fusion of the three communities was to follow within three years. The hope was that the newly merged executive could solve the problems with which the ECSC and Euratom were beset. Whether the hope will be realized remains to be seen.

ECSC: ECONOMIC NATIONALISM

In the ECSC, trade barriers were dismantled by 1953. Like the later EEC, its guiding principle was the maintenance of competition. The ECSC High Authority had no power to "direct industry" in the sense of expropriating or nationalizing coal or steel enterprises, or of itself planning new investment or withdrawing old (though it could make loans and has done so). It could require coal and steel enterprises to maintain competitive practices — to prevent monopolies, price rings, or other arrangements inimical to competition. In effect, what it has really done has been to assist large segments of uneconomical coal-mining enterprises to go out of business and to assist in a somewhat more orderly development of the iron and steel industry.

In the case of coal, competing and more economical sources of energy have increasingly entered the market at the same time that low-cost seams played out, particularly in Belgium and France. United States coal can be laid down, particularly at coastal ports, more cheaply than it can be produced on the Continent.[10] Increased technology has raised productivity, which has compounded the problem of falling demand. And the ECSC countries have been unable to work out a common and integrated energy policy which might have mitigated these problems. A comprehensive labor policy has not been developed either. Coal-mining employment in the ECSC countries has fallen markedly; if 1955 is used as unity (100), the number of faceworkers has dropped to 70, surface and ancillary workers to 75, and apprentices to 30. The ECSC has made available economic aids of various kinds to help coal miners left without jobs, but the resettlement of displaced workers has not been particularly successful.[11]

In this declining industry, worker unrest and agitation has developed, leading to strikes and riots in Belgium and France. This in turn led certain of these countries to adopt special national policies to meet the problems. The ECSC High Authority noted in 1964: "Meanwhile, the member Governments, faced as they are with difficult home problems in the coal sector and with serious social and regional issues, have tended to resort to independent action at the national level. . . . Such a trend is dangerous and undesirable. The more collieries have to operate on the basis of national arrangements, the less of a consistent, homogeneous whole the Common Market for coal becomes." [12] Yet one may suggest that the existence of the ECSC did make for a more orderly withdrawal of resources from coal mining than otherwise would have been the case.

Iron and steel on the contrary proved to be an expanding industry. The annual production of steel, for example, doubled over the fifteen-year period from 1952 (the first year of the ECSC) to 1967, and employment (production workers) increased by nearly 15 percent from 1952–53 to 1960–61, dropping back by the mid-sixties to slightly less than a 10 percent increase over 1952–53.

Yet here also problems developed. In 1967–68 world overcapacity existed in steel, and ECSC producers' costs were not low, in part because their size was less than optimal. Hence the High Authority was caught on the horns of a dilemma: on the one hand needing to seek the creation of large — and hence more efficient — units, but on the other doing this within the mandated competitive framework. Critics have suggested that greater emphasis upon rationalization would have served the community much better.[13]

As of 1967–68 the verdict was incomplete on the ECSC. What criteria does one apply in making a judgment? A single market has been created and intracommunity trade has increased. Resource allocation is undoubtedly more economical and competition has made for greater efficiency. And in the case of coal, a more orderly withdrawal probably resulted — but not orderly enough to prevent national governments from taking their own actions, this to the discomfort of the ECSC. The problems are by no means ended. News releases in late 1966 noted that coal producers had a record 44.5 million tons of surplus coal on their hands. This resulted in part from purchase of American and Russian coal for $11 to $12 a ton compared to European producers' prices of $14 to $17. One proposal advanced was that the ECSC countries cut back on their foreign coal purchases. But certain steel producers (as in Italy) rely heavily on the cheaper coal to remain competitive. A second alternative, to which the ECSC members agreed in February 1967, was to allow governments to provide subsidies to coking-coal producers so as to enable them to meet foreign competition. The same decision also created a joint subsidy fund to cover coal traded among the six countries. It may be, given the problems of a declining industry oriented to vested interests and national economies, that a supranational organization is not fully capable of managing liquidation.

In steel, the picture is not currently clear either. There seems to be considerable agreement that the problems will not be solved in the absence of further integration, as by the development of a community-wide company policy in the EEC. As *The Economist* pointed out: "For example, all the steel giants are faced with the need for big coastal capacity to exploit cheap overseas coal and ore. But how can a French steel company with big plants in Belgium and Germany decide on the best way to use the plant it has when each national government wants to get into coastal steel works, irrespective of the amount of overcapacity that such competition will produce?" [14] *The Economist* suggested further that the answer was to be found in a genuine "European company." But for reasons of company law, social security, taxes, and national ambition such a European company is not on the immediate horizon. A French proposal of late 1966 would permit quotas to be set on steel imports from other countries *within* the EEC. The French would thus be "protected" from imports from Belgium, Germany, Luxembourg. But one might ask if this would not spell the end of the ECSC dream.

Thus in 1967–68, the ECSC was confronted with growing anarchy and economic nationalism on the one hand, and the results of lack of rationalization on the other.

EURATOM: A PRESTIGE INDUSTRY

Euratom appears to have been the least successful of the various attempts at economic cooperation. In effect, its program never really got off the ground.[15] Again, nationalism loomed importantly on the horizon. True, here was an industry in which vested interests should not yet have had a chance to grow. Yet there was a "prestige" factor of incalculable proportions in being a nuclear nation and this took precedence over cooperation.

The French attitude toward Euratom was made quite evident in 1961 when the French government declined to renominate strongly political-minded and "European" Etienne Hirsch for the presidency of the Euratom Commission. Although Hirsch declared that "the French President of Euratom is not in the service of France,"[16] this did not prevent his replacement by a much less political-minded and less independent president in the person of Pierre Chatenet. Whether this was the cause of the failure of Euratom or simply a symptom of the problems which would beset the organization is debatable. Euratom has engaged in and continues to undertake a number of useful activities, such as the coordination of research and the provision of inspection services. But, in terms of the larger mission for which it was created, there has been little evidence of fulfillment.[17]

The spring of 1967 witnessed an interesting and typical dispute within Euratom over the proposed nuclear nonproliferation treaty. "Industrial espionage" and the slowing down of progress in areas of peaceful uses of nuclear energy were issues that caused fear in Euratom quarters. But a more important issue appeared to center on discrimination against the five member countries (i.e., all except France) who were not "nuclear powers" in the sense of possessing nuclear weaponry. "At stake, as far as Euratom is concerned, is the principle of integration of the Six and the terms of the treaty on which Euratom has been built . . . five Euratom countries would be subject to IAEA [International Agency for Atomic Energy] inspection and one would be inspection free — and this would be a violation of the Euratom treaty."[18] *The Economist* further suggested in April 1967 that "Deeper down . . . there have also been fears that the non-proliferation treaty would reinforce France's political hegemony in the Six."[19] Throughout the entire debate, the French remained conspicuously on the sidelines. It seemed that the Euratom organization was struggling to preserve what little unity it had left.

EEC: TENTH ANNIVERSARY

Since the EEC was without a doubt an outgrowth of the Marshall idea, one can look at its accomplishments as a kind of balance sheet within a balance sheet. What did this balance sheet look like when the EEC celebrated its tenth birthday in 1967?

It is necessary to judge the results of these ten years in terms of both its economic and its political goals. It was anticipated that economic performance in the member nations would be bettered through the reduction of trade barriers and the creation of a wider market, the free mobility of not only goods and services but also the factors of production, a more efficient allocation of resources, and increased competition. On the political side it was believed by the authors of the Treaty of Rome that somehow economic integration would bring in its wake ever-increasing political cooperation and ultimately unification.

In an operational sense, how were these economic goals to be reached? As a first approximation, one may say the program was to be implemented by the removal of barriers to the free movement of goods and services and of the factors of production. Excepting agriculture as a special case, intra-community tariffs (as barriers in the product market) have been lowered. Special measures also have been enacted concerning the movement of labor and capital.

But tariffs or no tariffs, markets had to be structured in some way. What way? The Treaty of Rome is clear on this point, as have been the interpretations of the EEC Commission: competitive markets. What type of competition was envisaged? The answer seems clear: it was to be "workable competition."[20] While "workable competition" may suffer from a lack of conceptual precision, it does allow for useful latitude in its application. The concept is best explained by an example. During the early years of the community, the Commission seemed to place emphasis on the prevention of combinations which might inhibit competition. In contrast, in more recent years there has been greater encouragement of larger industrial units and beneficial marketing arrangements, this in order to make possible better adaptation to the larger market and to enable European industry to compete effectively with the larger American firms.

"Distortions" inhibiting workable competition may be of two kinds: the specific, operating to the advantage or detriment of given industries or classes of firms; and the general, affecting the entire economy of a given member state.

Specific distortions include the following: (1) State aids and preferential fiscal and transport rates. Such cases arise when an industry is exempted from a tax, given subsidies, or accorded low transportation rates up to the frontier in one country but not in the neighboring member states. The Commission is seeking to eliminate such practices or, where this is not possible, to harmonize them. (2) Restraints of competition by firms. The Commission has sought to eliminate a wide pattern of such activities: cartels, collective and reciprocal exclusive-dealing systems, market sharing, and so on.[21] However, in March 1967, the Commission adopted a regulation on the block exemption of exclusive-dealing agreements between a manufacturer and a dealer under which the dealer may have the sole right of resale of products in a specific area of the EEC. It was felt that, given the present circumstances of the community, such exclusive-dealing agreements in international trade could actually improve the distribution of goods.[22] (3) Public undertakings and monopolies: customs duties, quantitative restrictions, limitations on the free movement of goods and factors as well as cases where the state is an entrepreneur. Here again various actions have been taken to reduce the impact of noncompetitive forces.

General distortions include these: (1) Economic and monetary disparities, such as currency overvaluation (which encourages imports and hinders exports) and undervaluation (with the converse effect); differing cost and price trends; and the like. Here the Commission has recommended varying proposals designed to alleviate this problem. (2) Disparities in tax systems. This is one of the most important current problem areas. European countries have made extensive use of the "turnover tax" which tends to be cumulative and hence to have a "cascade" effect. Given differing tax-rate structures, the cascade effect produces serious price distortions in the member countries. Thus in February 1967 the EEC Council of Ministers adopted two directives aimed at replacing the individual national tax systems with a common value-added tax system (known as TVA or "tax on the value added"). This new tax was to become effective not later than January 1, 1970. That highly important decision was necessary for the establishment of the greatest possible equality in competitive conditions within the community, and for the eventual elimination of tax frontiers. (3) Disparities in national economic legislation, as in food legislation, pharmaceutical products, industrial safety, bankruptcy, freedom of establishment. Here again the Commission has been seeking, piece by piece, to eliminate restrictive practices.

In effect, what is taking place is the substitution — gradual though it may be — of a "uniform" community-wide framework of regulation (in which maintenance of "competition" is the cornerstone) for the disparate, frequently noncompetitive policies and practices found in the member countries.

A brief digression may be useful here. How is the decision on a common policy — such as "value-added tax" — reached? While this is not the place for an extended discussion, it may be well to provide a brief résumé. The process begins with the EEC Commission itself which is, with a very few exceptions, the initiator of all proposals. The Commission collects information on which to base its suggestions for a common policy by calling in representatives from the national ministries, consumer bodies, employer groups, labor organizations, and other interested parties. At the same time EEC civil servants in Brussels study the pertinent questions. On the basis of the information gathered, the Commission formulates its proposal which is then sent to the Council of Ministers. After examination by national experts including the permanent representatives in Brussels and most of the same groups previously consulted, national viewpoints can be assumed to have been registered. Following this process, the proposal finally goes before the Council which may accept or reject it, but by itself cannot alter it. (The Council can, of course, ask the Commission to go back and try again, taking into account the Council's wishes.) Since any proposal is likely to benefit one country more and another less, a package of proposals involving a fair balance of concessions on all sides usually is presented at any one time.

Given the goal of workable competition as the framework in which economic activity has taken place, what have been the economic results over the decade in which the EEC has been in existence? The results are almost always discussed in terms of growth, growth of two kinds: as measured by a "trade" figure such as the increase in trade among the members or with the external community and by an "income" figure such as gross national product.

Table 1. Exports from Each Member Nation to the Rest of the EEC

Member Nation	Exports to Rest of EEC in 1965 (1958 = 100)	Exports to Rest of EEC as Percentage of Total Exports	
		1956	1966
Belgium-Luxembourg	287	45.1%	62.9%
Netherlands	268	41.6	55.6
France	361	22.2	42.3
Italy	473	23.6	40.6
Germany	263	27.3	36.3

SOURCE: Statistical Office of the European Communities, *Basic Statistics of the Community* (Brussels: EEC, 1967), p. 116.

On trade within the community, the data in Table 1 are illustrative of the increasing trade interdependence within the EEC. The data show clearly, for the decade 1956–66, the increasingly "self-contained" nature of the pattern of trade, i.e., that the Common Market is becoming a larger "common market" for the six countries concerned. For the EEC as a whole, 30.1 percent of total exports went to member countries in 1958; in 1966 it was 44.1 percent. Of imports, 29.6 percent came from member countries in 1958; 42.7 percent in 1966. Does this suggest that the increase meant a decrease in exports to and imports from nonmember countries? No, since between 1958 and 1965 exports to nonmember countries increased 53 percent, while imports from these countries rose by 66 percent. Whether exports to and imports from nonmember countries would have increased more in the absence of integration is impossible to say. One might suggest, however, that increased internal trade occurred at the expense of "some" external growth, though there is little evidence of major trade diversion.

During the period 1958–65, domestic national product for the combined six member nations grew at a rate in real terms of over 5 percent per annum, a rate higher than for the United States or the EFTA countries. For 1965–70, the rate is expected to average closer to 4 percent per annum, because of increasing labor shortages and the need for anti-inflationary actions. Lest, however, the figure of over 5 percent appear high, it should be noted that if one plots the increase on a percentage scale, the increase is about the same as took place in 1950–58, though there was a slight acceleration between 1958 and 1960.

Given these increases in trade and income one may ask: how much can be ascribed to what would have occurred anyway and how much to the effects of the formation of the community? The answer is not easy to come by; and most of the analysis that has been undertaken focuses upon trade itself rather than production, income, investment, and consumption, although some production inquiries have been undertaken.

With respect to production and trade two varying conclusions have appeared. One is that the community itself has contributed few, if any, generating impacts. The opposing viewpoint is that the very creation and operation of the community — and its policy of reducing trade barriers — increased activity over and above what would have occurred in the absence of integration. Without attempting to detail the argument here, one may suggest the following: The creation of the community did not produce negative economic results in the sense of lowered production or trade — absolutely or relatively; following the formation of the community the level of economic activity and trade did increase though one cannot say with precision how much was the result of the community's existence; but, much more important, integration has had significant positive behavioral and psychological effects, likely to continue to produce favorable results in the future.[23]

"Economic planning" has also been the subject of considerable study and discussion within the community. While the French had long used such a technique, Germany had been opposed to planning, holding the "free market" to be the more appropriate mechanism. The result, in the community, was a compromise which might best be described as "indicative programming." Such a program — the initial attempt — was worked out for the community [24] and was accepted by the Council of Ministers and the governments of the member states in February 1967. The program, as "projected" on a five-year basis, proposed goals for such items as population, gross national product, and trade for each country in the community. The countries were then left individually "free," in seeking to attain the projected goals, to pursue such policies as were compatible with their philosophies. The program, in other words, provided objectives and guidelines to reach the objectives, but it specified neither detailed nor mandatory methods.

A less obvious but equally important and perhaps more telling accomplishment for the future has resulted from application of what might be called the "Marjolin method." This has involved bringing together on a regular basis (institutionalized since 1964) the central bankers of the member countries for discussion of current developments and problems. This was largely the work of Commission Vice-President Robert Marjolin. In this way, although binding decisions were not made, closer collaboration occurred — the kind of collaboration which effectively ties the member countries closer together without giving the appearance of forcing them to relinquish economic "sovereignty." In view of the unsympathetic attitude toward the Common Market Commission of de Gaulle while he was president of France, this "method" may have been one of the more realistic and thus fruitful activities undertaken.

Another indication of EEC success might be evidenced in the desire of other nations to be associated with it. It may be that these nations see the EEC as a success and want to be part of "a good thing"; or they may simply be fearful of the detrimental effects to their own economies of being outside the common external tariff wall. In any case, the years 1966 – 68 saw bids for full membership, and new or continuing bids for associate status or trade agreements, by a variety of countries in both Eastern and Western Europe as well as farther afield.

All has not, however, been unbridled success. Despite the elimination of internal tariffs on July 1, 1968, "workable" competition has not been attained. The wide variations in price for the same article in different countries attested to this. These price variations may be due to a variety of reasons: local variations explainable in terms of local demand and supply factors, the size of the profit the retailer is accustomed to making, the number of middlemen involved, different tax structures and tax levels, restrictive agreements between manufacturers and distributors, and the remaining customs duties on goods. Only some of these factors ultimately will be subject to common regulation. Regulations cannot, for example, alter local tastes or buying habits which could enable a seller to charge a price higher than that which "perfect competition" would support.

There are specific areas in which the Treaty of Rome calls for action, but in which little forward movement has been evident. The most important are the following:

1. Commercial policy. This may be defined as the policy applied by member states toward the rest of the world as regards both imports and exports. It is one of the most important community policy areas, since it is the link between the Six and the outside world. The Treaty of Rome specifically states in Article III: "Member States shall co-ordinate their commercial relations with third countries in such a way as to bring about, not later than at the expiry of the transitional period, the conditions necessary to the implementation of a common policy in the matter of external trade." Progress in developing this policy has been slow and tortured. The *EEC Eighth General Report* noted: "The Commission cannot, however,

conceal its growing concern at the total lack of progress in commercial policy, where the first essential is to ensure that the Treaty is observed." [25]

2. Transport policy. This has been — and remains — one of the thorniest of all areas, since national interests, particularly those of the Dutch, are so much at stake. Dutch interest is based on the fact that trade accounts for some 50 percent of the national income of the Netherlands, and receipts from the transport industry amounted to about 12 percent of this total in the mid-sixties. The part played by the port of Rotterdam and the connecting inland waterways, especially the Rhine River, is of overwhelming importance. Dutch shippers depend on price competition to maintain their commanding position on the Rhine. Hence the Dutch have desired a transport situation in which there is free price competition rather than fixed tariffs (or fixed maximum and minimum tariffs) on Rhine traffic.

The Treaty of Rome requires that a common transport policy be instituted which will embody "(a) common rules applicable to international transport effected from or to the territory of a Member State or crossing the territory of one or more Member States; (b) conditions for the admission of non-resident carriers to national transport services within a Member State; and (c) any other appropriate provisions." [26] Discussions started in 1958, and while some agreements have been reached, the difficult issues — such as rate structures — were still under advisement in the late sixties.

3. "European company" policy, involving the formation of companies across country lines. In the entire life of the EEC only one multicountry company of significance has emerged: the Agfa-Gevaert merger, designed to compete with Eastman Kodak. And this liaison was accomplished only through the devious (and not altogether satisfactory) process of establishing two identical companies in Germany and Belgium. [27] Instead of multicountry companies, there appeared to be a tendency for larger units to develop within a country. In some respects this compounds the problem of economic nationalism. [28] A variety of company policy proposals — to be discussed in Chapter 4 — were under consideration at the time of writing.

4. Energy policy. A common energy policy to encompass the various sources of energy, including coal, oil, and atomic energy, ran into the obvious problem of the existence of three distinct communities: the ECSC which is responsible for coal, the EEC into whose realm fall problems concerning oil, and Euratom which is concerned with atomic energy. Although the three community executives had proposed a plan for a common energy policy as early as 1962, at the time of the fusion of the executives in 1967 this policy had not been implemented.

5. Community patent policy. Again there is as yet no common frame-

work; and although extended discussions have taken place, no immediate solution appears on the horizon.

6. Social policy. The lack of an over-all community social policy was due largely to the reluctance of the member states to have the EEC "meddle" in this area. As a result, progress in such areas as housing and training programs has been much slower than some, particularly the trade unions, would wish, notwithstanding accelerated activity in 1967.[29]

What appeared in 1965–68 to be a rising tide of national economic interests may partly explain the failures in these areas. Two other important elements must be noted, however. First, it was evident that as the EEC approached a higher degree of "sophistication," the problems to be solved and the decisions to be taken had a higher "political" content and thus were more difficult. It may be argued that the attainment of agreement on a common agricultural policy was not prevented by the highly political content of that issue. The answer to this argument is the second important element. The agricultural policy, because its adoption was of vital interest to the French, had the active *backing* of one of the strongest members of the EEC. In direct contrast, a common transport policy, a potential direct threat to the vital interests of the Dutch, was being actively *resisted* by that member country. In other words, it appeared that success in these more difficult areas would require the direct positive intervention of an interested member country.

In a broader spectrum, other problem areas remain. These do not flow as automatically from implementation of the Treaty of Rome as did those noted above; they have either evolved in a more independent manner or existed independently of integration. They include the basic organization of the six economies which has been characterized by an excess of small enterprises and of the self-employed, particularly in distribution; the existence of less than efficient size manufacturing enterprises unable to take adequate advantage of the newly enlarged market (which the already larger United States firms were immediately able to do); inadequate allocation of resources to research and development, which aggravated the much-talked-of "technological gap" between the United States and Europe; a relatively high degree of inflation; and quantitative and structural problems with regard to capital markets. These problems are merely noted here; they will be discussed at greater length in the ensuing chapters.

So much for the economic side of the coin. As for the political accomplishments of these ten years, *The Economist* on April 15, 1967, stated bluntly that "For the foreseeable future all hopes of closer political cooperation between the Six are stone dead." [30]

Quite obviously in the back of the minds of the signatories of the Treaty of Rome was the hope that economic integration would lead rather

automatically to political integration. Leon Lindberg's "spill-over" theory
of integration provided buttressing support for such hope.[31] The belief
that political integration would come prompted the rejection in 1962, especially by the Benelux countries, of the "Fouchet plan" for institutionalized meetings of foreign ministers and heads of government. Opponents
of the plan believed that its acceptance would lead ultimately to a water-
ing down and hence a weakening of the existing European communities.
They preferred to reject the plan completely rather than accept what they
considered "half a loaf" at best.

Rumblings were heard in Brussels in the spring of 1967 about a possible rejuvenation of the Fouchet "method" if not "plan." However, statements regarding the possibility of increased political unification flowing
from economic integration were pessimistic. Even Commission President
Hallstein wrote in a tenth-anniversary article in *Die Zeit* (March 17 and
24, 1967): "Economic integration does not of course automatically lead
to what is known as political union. In politics nothing happens of its own
accord, what is done is done by man; it is human will translated into action. And there is nothing in the Treaty of Rome which cannot be exe-
cuted should the Member States fail to agree on matters such as frontiers,
military strategy or their relations with other powers in the world. For the
foreseeable future, at least, economic integration can proceed without unification having to be tackled in the fields of foreign policy and defence." [32]

In the EEC "crisis" of 1965–66, the French flew their anti-political-
unification colors for all to see, and effectively halted further progress in
that direction. Ostensibly the French 7½-month walkout from EEC meetings was occasioned by the failure of the Council of Ministers to reach a
decision on agricultural pricing and financing policies by the agreed-upon
date of June 30, 1965. In fact, however, the French were objecting to the
apparent growing independent power of the Commission. This body had
proposed that all levies on agricultural imports go directly into a community budget to be dispensed by the Commission. Another element in
the walkout was the majority-vote principle which was due to come into
effect on January 1, 1966, covering a much wider range of issues than
had been subject to majority vote previously. And a third element was
President de Gaulle's desire to rid the Commission (when its term expired,
also on January 1, 1966) of its too "independent," too "European" members — notably President Hallstein.[33]

It is difficult to say who "won" when the French returned to the Council table in January 1966. In succeeding months three factors became evident, however: (1) The Commission now appears to be "less bold" in the
proposals it makes to the Council. Since the Commission is the initiator of
all proposals, this has a significant effect on what the EEC undertakes to
accomplish. (2) There appears to have been a weakening of the "com-

munity spirit" in which member states in the past had compromised on issues in the interest of the community as a whole. They now seem more quick and tenacious about defending national interests — a kind of "if France can get away with it, so can we" attitude. (3) Walter Hallstein was replaced in 1967 as president of the newly fused Commission. And it has been agreed that the position of president will be rotated. Thus no single man is likely to grow to the stature that Herr Hallstein did in his job. There will be no "president of Europe." The new Commission in the summer of 1967 was composed of many new and unknown faces and was headed by the Belgian Jean Rey. The role that this new body would play was an unknown quantity.

Does this mean that the political element has been entirely missing? As matters have evolved, economic integration has become more important and has outdistanced the political. But to suggest that there is no "political" integration is specious. It is true that the degree of integration some had hoped for has not been realized. And it is true that such facets of the political element as defense or foreign policy have remained well within national orbits. But if one views "political" as embracing a spectrum with, for example, foreign policy at one end and maintenance of competition at the other, then there has been much "political" integration at this latter end. If nations give up their sovereignty on such matters as setting agricultural prices, negotiating external tariffs, or regulating labor mobility, some "political" integration has, in fact, taken place. The cooperative approaches taken by EEC countries in the monetary crises of late 1968 illustrate, in a different way, the nature of "political" integration. The Common Market countries have given up considerable in the way of "sovereignty" over their monetary systems in order to achieve coordinated solutions to monetary problems. But it is true that there has been virtually no progress in the building of political institutions as this term is commonly used.

Educational Changes Related to Economic and Political Changes

Although one must still speak of national schools — French, German, and so on — rather than of a "European educational community" in any organized sense, great strides have been made toward educational harmonization in Western Europe. In education as in the economic and political spheres, European nations have common interests, common problems, and common goals, and they have all been touched by waves of American education theory and practice.

By the latter half of the 1960's there was widespread emphasis in Europe (as in the United States) on the social principle of educational opportunity for all. This was buttressed by increasing recognition of the need in each nation and in Europe as a whole for adequate numbers of people educated to meet the demands of modern industrialized society. But tradition-encrusted school systems moved slowly.

Some progress was made at the secondary level where the comprehensive high school, so familiar in the United States, has grown in popularity and where vocational and technical training has won improved status. On paper, promising guidance programs exist for the equivalents of the American seventh and eighth grades, but European schools still lag well behind the American (including Canadian as well as those in the United States) in the attention paid to individual differences and in the flexibility of programs to meet individual needs and interests.

In higher education the drive to provide more rounded training and opportunity for technological and applied-science studies has been handicapped by the entrenched organizational pattern of European universities. Instead of being free to take coursework in numerous subject-matter departments as in the United States, European students have been largely restricted to "institutes" in which the curriculum is narrow and the budget is committed to the principal professor's research. The rioting of French university students in the spring of 1968 was chiefly a protest against the overriding prestige accorded throughout Western Europe to liberal arts studies and a demand for the kind of stress on technological know-how at the university level that has contributed so importantly in the United States to economic progress. There is still a long way to go in the universities and colleges of Europe before this goal can be met.

One special educational problem faced by the economically highly developed countries has been that of schooling the immigrants who come to work in their industries. The most adequate instruction usually given these people has been in language. The least adequate has been "sensitivity training" to acquaint the migrants with aspects of the material and nonmaterial culture of the receiving country.

The development of "European" schools has long been a dream on the Continent. It would be imprudent to suggest that the 1960's saw the realization of this dream. But cooperative steps were taken in the utilization of educational testing, in the development of curriculums, in the easing of restrictions on transferring of students from one institution to another, even in the establishment of several institutions known as European Schools. Certainly a start has been made, and future movements will go forward toward greater integration, not backward.

Atlantic Community Ties

THE NORTH ATLANTIC TREATY ORGANIZATION

Up to this point we have dealt with institutions which, with the exception of the OECD, have been essentially or exclusively European. It is now time to expand that discussion to the North Atlantic Treaty Organization.

The origins of NATO are to be found on the one hand in the increasing European and also American concern about possible Soviet aggression and on the other in the precursor Brussels Treaty (signed March 17, 1948, by Belgium, France, Luxembourg, the Netherlands, and the United Kingdom) which pledged its members to establish a joint defensive system and also to strengthen their economic and cultural ties.

After World War II it was increasingly recognized that not only was a national response to possible aggression inadequate, but so also was any approach that was limited regionally. Hence the search began on both sides of the Atlantic for a more rational approach to the problem. Wide-ranging discussions followed, involving various European statesmen, Prime Minister Louis St. Laurent of Canada, and Secretary of State George C. Marshall and Senators Arthur Vandenberg and Tom Connally in the United States. After almost a year of negotiation, the North Atlantic Treaty was signed April 4, 1949, by Belgium, Canada, Denmark, France, Iceland, Italy, Luxembourg, the Netherlands, Norway, Portugal, the United Kingdom, and the United States. Greece and Turkey entered the organization in 1952, and West Germany in 1955.

The core of the treaty is found in Article 5, which binds the parties to mutual assistance in the event of an armed attack upon one or more of them, whether in Europe or North America. But the intent was broader than that: it can be viewed as a multilateral political alliance incorporating not only mutual defense but also economic cooperation.

The principal institution of NATO is the North Atlantic Council on which each of the parties is represented and whose function primarily relates to implementation of the treaty. The Council, in turn, has carried out its obligations by establishing various subsidiary bodies: a Military Committee, a Standing Group, various regional planning groups, and so on. Streamlining of NATO took place in 1951, by incorporating into the Council such units as the Defense Committee and the Defense Financial and Economic Committee. A further reorganization took place subsequent to meetings in Lisbon, Portugal, in February 1952. The NATO secretariat, headed by a secretary-general appointed by the Council, is primarily responsible for implementing the Council's decisions.

The political, economic, and cultural interaction within NATO that had originally been envisioned scarcely came to even partial fruition. On the diplomatic side, there was a tendency on the part of the British, who were for many years the strongest of the Western European states militarily, to conduct affairs as much as possible bilaterally with Washington; and others, so far as they were able to, tended to follow suit. There was never much working out of common Western positions within the NATO framework. Another reason for this trend was that some of the major participants had interests which far transcended the boundaries of both Europe and the North Atlantic, and it seemed unrealistic to try to deal with them within the NATO institutions. For example, the decolonization in Asia and in Africa of the British, the French, and the Dutch aroused only academic interest among other NATO countries. Most important, the advance of the United States to the role of a universal power, with heavy and costly responsibilities in many parts of the world that most Europeans were glad not to share, dictated much decision making outside NATO councils. Thus, though in theory the mandate of NATO was not confined to the Atlantic area, this turned out to be largely the case in practice. It is noteworthy that even a problem of such deep concern to NATO as Cyprus found the northern tier of NATO countries little interested.

It is not surprising, therefore, that diplomatic discussions within NATO largely dealt with the more specific military concerns of the Alliance. Even here there have been major limitations. For instance the communications of the United States to the NATO Council on the progress of arms control discussions always have had more the character of informing than consulting. For many years of the fifties there was no serious exchange of views or proposals on the vital subject, so disturbing to the Alliance, of a role for NATO and its non-nuclear powers in the control and use of strategic nuclear forces. American recognition of the imperative nature of this problem came very tardily. Between 1954 and 1962 the United States did push strongly for the creation of a multilateral force (MLF) of twenty-five vessels with crews from participating countries. The project was from the first strongly opposed by France and failed to arouse any real enthusiasm anywhere else. Many had grave doubts whether nuclear defense funds could most effectively be invested this way and the problems of administrative control threatened to split the Alliance rather than consolidate it.

Out of these discussions and proposals, however, came a greater appreciation that the main concern of the non-nuclear powers was not to get their hands on nuclear weapons but to be informed and have a voice on what would govern their use in the event of a war in Europe. The United States showed understanding of this concern when, in 1966, it cooperated in the establishment of two subgroups of the NATO Council, the Nuclear Defense Affairs Committee and the Nuclear Planning Group. But it is widely recognized that much in this whole area must await clarification of the future status of an independent French nuclear force.

In the history of NATO there have been a considerable number of changes in the relative roles of military and civilian agencies. During the most anxious days of the Cold War it was natural to let the urgency of the military problems of the Alliance determine the primacy of military personnel. The prominence in the command for many years of the powerful personalities who had emerged during World War II accentuated this. The most important personage in the NATO framework was the Supreme Allied

Commander Europe and the ability of successive American commanders to forge a truly integrated command structure was a great source of pride and élan to all who had a share in it. Especially General Lauris Norstad, who commanded from 1956 to 1963 and who was often called "the most trusted man in Western Europe," had a reputation for subordinating national loyalties to his international mission.

The recent years have seen so many changes from this situation that there is talk of a "civil revolution." The domination which Robert McNamara as United States secretary of defense succeeded in gaining over the military authorities in the Pentagon seemed to set an example emulated by some of his colleagues in the Allied countries and by the civil administrators of NATO itself. Military functions and activities were also severely curtailed because of cuts in defense expenditures by the European member countries and, insofar as its forces stationed in Europe were concerned, by the United States. Most important, no doubt, was the erosion of apprehension about a war in Europe. This was associated with such factors as the nuclear stalemate, the end of the second Berlin crisis in 1962, and the belief that the U.S.S.R. was increasingly preoccupied by fears about China. Also relevant has been the curtailment of many functions of the NATO apparatus and the forced departure from France of NATO agencies and installations. The Council was shifted to Brussels late in 1967 and the military headquarters had preceded it earlier to Casteau in western Belgium, where it is not even within convenient reach.

The late sixties were clearly a period of major overhaul of the Alliance; these years also witnessed a variety of debates concerned with continuance of NATO itself and with its membership. Many of the issues which are associated with this overhaul and especially with the consequences of the withdrawal of France will be dealt with more fully in the next chapter.

CHANGING UNITED STATES–EUROPEAN RELATIONS

The United States in the early postwar years was almost "more European than the Europeans" in actively working for European economic and political integration. In 1967–68 she saw a relatively healthy economic giant on the eastern seaboard of the Atlantic Ocean, this notwithstanding Great Britain's plight, turbulence in France, and a temporary recession in Germany. The Six, with a combined population of some 183 million people (in mid-1966), make up the world's number one trading unit in terms of the value of exports and imports.

Officially the United States is still a proponent of economic integration and still hews to the "partnership" policy line. But there are highly placed and influential Americans who today display a certain dismay over the current situation, who say that the United States should not continue to encourage further integrative attempts. These adversaries feel that strong economic and political integration in Europe is incompatible with closer economic and political ties between the United States and Europe. They would like nothing more than to see the EEC become a looser, free-trade type of agency with the addition of more outward-looking members from EFTA.

Whatever should be the direction of economic development in Europe, an important realization in 1967–68 was that the influence of the United States was not of the magnitude it had been twenty years earlier. Some might say that the goals of the Marshall Plan had been all too successfully accomplished. Be it for better or worse, the lessened influence of the United States is a fact.

The final months of negotiations in the Kennedy Round of trade talks, terminating in May 1967, exemplified Europe's (at least Europe-of-the-Six's) ability to deal with the United States as an economic equal. It should be emphasized that the very existence of the EEC was one of the central new facts in this round of tariff negotiations. Why? There appear to be three main reasons:

1. It was the growth of the Common Market that convinced President Kennedy to ask Congress for entirely new authority in the field of tariff negotiations. The Common Market was proving extraordinarily attractive for American investments, and the movement of capital from the United States to Europe tended to aggravate the American payments deficit. In view of the EEC's common external tariff, American industrialists felt the need to get inside the tariff wall by investing directly in Europe. Furthermore, the Kennedy administration wanted to ensure that products of United States industries would have access to this new and enticing European market. The American people no longer had a choice between wanting or not wanting Europe to unite, although the degree of unification was a different and still open issue. The Common Market was already in being, and the Trade Expansion Act was President Kennedy's answer to the question of how best to accommodate to it.

2. The Common Market as an entity initiated the idea of the Kennedy Round. During earlier tariff negotiations, the EEC had offered a reciprocal 20 percent across-the-board reduction in tariffs; the United States could not accept this offer because of the limitations in the existing Reciprocal Trade Agreements Act. The United States was thus forced to come up with entirely new legislation to take advantage of the EEC offer. And in March 1962, the EEC gave important tariff concessions in return for anticipated American concessions once the Trade Expansion Act was passed.

3. Bargaining by the Common Market as a unit was a central factor for both positive and negative reasons. On the positive side, one bargaining position in place of six necessarily simplified the actual negotiating

process in Geneva. This was, furthermore, a valuable experiment in inter-country relations and represented a significant breakthrough by the EEC. On the negative side was the obvious corollary to this: it was a tortuous process for the Common Market to come up with its negotiating position and to arrive at a point where the Commission could be given a mandate flexible enough to make true negotiation possible. Once the internal EEC "crisis" of 1965–66 was passed and a common grains price agreed upon within the context of the Common Agricultural Policy, the EEC Commission proved itself a politically mature bargainer with outside powers. Its chief negotiator, Jean Rey, was a man with enough political courage to go farther than he had been instructed, and then return to Brussels to defend what he had done.

The results of the Kennedy Round fell far short of those hoped for on both sides of the Atlantic when the Trade Expansion Act was passed. But tariff reductions of some 35 percent were achieved, with the two principal bargainers, the United States and the EEC, facing each other on an equal footing unimaginable in 1947.

A glance at the political and military spheres of Atlantic relations reveals, however, no such clearly emerging pattern as the Kennedy Round and the several monetary conferences have provided on the economic side. Here the John F. Kennedy designs of 1962 for fuller United States–European cooperation have for the time being no meaning, for the "partnership" offered by the late president presupposed a stage of advance toward European unity which is nowhere in sight. NATO is moving ahead at half speed into half-charted waters with a diminished crew and under a jury mast or two. Its course in 1969 was beset with debates by some of the member states on whether they should remain within the organization and indeed whether NATO should continue in existence, on the pace and extent of the reduction of military force levels, and on the downgrading effect of the possible appointment of a European (presumably British) commander-in-chief.

In a way that is without parallel in the economic field, the American politico-military relation to Europe is affected by liabilities and commitments outside the North Atlantic area. The catalogue of the ways in which this influences adversely the affairs of the Western Alliance is a bulky one. There is, for example, the immensely complicated problem of détente with the Soviet Union and thus also with much of Eastern Europe. How does one arrive at a *modus vivendi* in Europe when the motivations and calculations of the negotiators are so largely determined by concerns about problems that exist elsewhere in the world? It is small wonder so many Europeans feel that under such circumstances their interests are in danger of being used as trading stock.

A matured and vigorous economic Europe has had new problems to face in the relations between the European countries themselves and within the Atlantic world. These problems, in their varying dimensions, will be taken up in detail in the following chapters.

Conclusion

In 1967–68, what did one see on balance? The Atlantic economic scene might be divided into three sections: relations within Western Europe, relations between the West and Eastern Europe, and relations within the Atlantic community.

WITHIN WESTERN EUROPE

Undeniable economic successes were scored and have already been documented. Failures occurred as well and have been noted. In addition, a certain "jostling about" was going on.

At the level of the European communities — EEC, the ECSC, and Euratom — the fusion of the executives of these three communities took place officially on July 5, 1967. A score of unanswered questions remained. How would this new community be organized? Could it solve the problems of the coal and steel pool and of Euratom? Would it be able to put together a coherent energy policy now that all forms of energy were under the same roof? The answers to some of these questions would depend to a large extent on a more fundamental question: what would be the orientation of the new Commission under the leadership of Jean Rey, fresh from his success at the negotiating table in Geneva?

Monsieur Rey was known to be an advocate of British membership in the community. He was further known to be a "federalist" of the Madison-Hamilton stripe. As a realist, however, he also had to be aware that French President de Gaulle had in effect forced President Hallstein out of the presidency; that de Gaulle had even refused to allow Hallstein to speak at the tenth anniversary celebration in Rome in May 1967; and that the French members of the Commission were adamant in expressing de Gaulle's "long-held view that the Commission should be a technical body without political pretensions." [34]

Outside of the EEC, but within Western Europe, a number of countries had filed formal applications for membership in that organization. French objections to these memberships were clearly spelled out at the July 10–11, 1967, meeting of the EEC Council of Ministers. In contrast, the other five member countries were favorable to these additions to the community. On an unofficial but influential level, Jean Monnet's Action Committee — composed of party leaders of every political group in the Six except the French Gaullists and the Communists — had given its strong endorsement to the British, Danish, and Irish bids. The signatures of leading Germans (even those in high office) were conspicuously present on this resolution. Even after France's "second rejection" of Britain, the issues were by no means settled.

The possibility of an extended community raised a multitude of inextricably entwined political and economic questions. What would be the shape of this new community? Would it continue on the path toward economic union or would it be diverted into a more limited free-trade area? What would be the relationships among the community organs? Would the community become so unwieldy as to be less effective? (Consider the added difficulties posed by the addition of yet more official languages.) Would the Commission in its role of initiator of proposals become more powerful or less? Could the "community spirit" — if indeed it still remained among the Six — be extended to nine or ten nations? And what of the intergovernmental relations which are outside the institutions of the Six, but which have an obvious bearing on the EEC (for example, the opposing opinions of the French and German governments concerning the extension of the community contrasted with their attempt at developing a special relationship via the treaty of January 1963)?

LOOKING TOWARD EASTERN EUROPE

In 1967–68, one of the most important new topics was that of relations between East and West. In this context, 1967 was also the year for two other anniversaries: the twenty-first anniversary of Winston Churchill's famous speech at Fulton, Missouri, in which he said, "From Stettin in the Baltic to Trieste in the Adriatic, an iron curtain has descended across the continent"; [35] and the twentieth anniversary of the Economic Commission for Europe (a body created in 1947 within the United Nations for the purpose of fostering economic cooperation), one of the few forums for contact between Eastern and Western Europe on economic issues. While this volume focuses upon Europe and the West, it will not be inappropriate here to comment briefly upon Europe and interactions with the East.

During the period under discussion Eastern Europe had also organized itself economically in a number of ways. The most important of the organizations was Comecon — the Council for Mutual Economic Cooperation — which was created in 1949 by the Soviet Union as an Eastern European response to the Marshall Plan. It can currently be visualized as a forum for economic collaboration among the following countries: the U.S.S.R., Poland, East Germany, Czechoslovakia, Hungary, Bulgaria, Mongolia, and Rumania. [36]

Given varying economic organizations in Western and Eastern Europe — or irrespective of them — the late 1960's saw an abundance of evidence that a thaw was taking place in East-West economic relations. In Brussels in the fall of 1966, a Russian store was opened. In July 1967 West Germany and Czechoslovakia announced that by September they would exchange official trade missions with restricted consular functions. In February 1967 Yugoslavia formally requested the conclusion of a nondiscriminatory trade agreement with the EEC. By the summer of 1967, such an accord was under active study by the Committee of Permanent Representatives in collaboration with the Commission.

Poland, Yugoslavia, and Czechoslovakia had been granted or had asked for full membership in the General Agreement on Tariffs and Trade (GATT), while Hungary and Rumania had been given observer status. The topic "East-West relations" had appeared on agendas of the OECD, NATO, the Council of Europe, the EEC. President Lyndon B. Johnson made a major speech on the subject in October 1966 and went on to catalogue in his state-of-the-union message the growing list of steps taken to develop East-West ties. These few examples can only begin to indicate the intensity of thought and activity devoted to the question of tearing down the barriers between East and West that were the legacy of the early postwar period. A step backward seemed to be taken in the summer of 1968 with the Czechoslovakian invasion. Whether this implies a cooling of East-West relations remains to be seen.

WITHIN THE ATLANTIC COMMUNITY

The new relationships between the United States and Europe have already been discussed at length. The new problems thus posed have been noted and will be discussed in the chapters that follow.

What emerged in 1967–68 as a major new theme of American policy was the United States effort to awaken in Europe the realization that economic problems remained in the world and that the resolution of these problems could not be achieved without active European participation. This was the emphasis of speakers at the Marshall Plan Commemoration sponsored in June 1967 by Paul-Henri Spaak in Brussels. There, after the growth of European-American ties was documented, the chief thrust of the discussion was the obligations of Europe and the United States to the developing nations.

While Western European policies were increasingly influenced by a fear of American economic penetration, American policy was increasingly focused on the dangers of a growing European isolationism in the face of increasing world responsibilities. As stated by the American ambassador to the European communities, J. Robert Schaetzel: "The United States considers it has an obligation to help the developing countries help themselves, if for no other reason than the self-interest of solving a major political and, potentially, a security problem before it becomes unmanageable. Europeans have not, however, felt that obligation to the same degree." [37]

In other words, it was time to use the fruits and apply the principles of the Marshall Plan outside of the small world of Europe and the Atlantic community.

CHAPTER *3*

The Western Crisis of the Sixties

BY HAROLD C. DEUTSCH

SINCE the first stirrings after World War II of a drive toward combination among the lands of the traditional West, there have been successive phases of advance and retreat, of achievement and setback, of high hopes and discouragement.[1] On the broad goal of finding the most effective forms of association there has been wide agreement. Differences have involved the type and degree of cooperation, the selection of roads and the distances to be traveled on them, the pace of advance, and the relationships among the travelers as well as between them and those not numbered in their company.

In the "Western Alliance" — which is taken here to mean not only NATO but that infinity of bilateral and multilateral pacts of every description that have linked states of the North Atlantic world in the last two decades — the 1950's reveal a more even and wider range of development than do the 1960's. In fact, for some fifteen years after 1948 there was a steady growth and intermeshing of Western European and Atlantic relationships. Now in one, now in another area the march forward seemed to be more promising, the integrative trend more irresistible. In the picture as a whole, progress appeared fairly even. One integrative drive for which conditions were particularly favorable would usually help to stimulate and support the others. The interdependence of much that occurred in the political, economic, military, social, and cultural fields evidenced itself both in the general similarity in the curves of advance and in the oft immediate response in one field — by a surge or shift of direction — to that which went on in another.

The situation emerging in the mid-sixties offered a drastically altered aspect. This can be ascribed to fundamental changes in both internal developments and external influences. In the political and economic fields these transformations proved to be largely disruptive. Old ties became frayed and new ones in the process of formation failed of completion. As early as the turn of the sixties it had become common to speak of "disarray" in the Western Alliance. More sweeping and derogatory verdicts multiplied as the united front of the Atlantic powers continued to crumble in these areas.

Inevitably the setbacks suffered in the political and military spheres had repercussions in every other sphere of the Atlantic environment, in most cases acting as a brake on the integrative process. In some instances it was possible to hold past gains and even to utilize the momentum that had been generated in order to score further advances: the integration of peoples and the harmonization of educational institutions and practices that are covered elsewhere in this volume have been able to move ahead with but minor interruptions. More typical, perhaps, in the variety and contradictions they reveal are developments on the economic side. In some the line of advance has withstood the reassertion of national influences, whereas in others notable progress has been followed by repulse or retreat. The most significant example certainly is that of the European Economic Community, if only because of its importance as the core institution around which the wider European and Atlantic economic and, eventually, political unification appeared destined to take shape. On the purely economic side notable goals have been reached, such as the realization of the scheduled internal tariff reductions and the attainment of a common external tariff. The community has even exceeded what many dared hope for in the way of agreement on agricultural policy. Against this, it is necessary to record the continuance and extension of many practices by which the member states manage to thwart the aims of the EEC in such matters as achieving a common price structure and harmonizing, gradually, programs of social security. This has been made easier by the arrest of development of the EEC as a political institution. The EEC's administrative apparatus has been weakened, its élan impaired, and the boldness of its initiatives much inhibited by the lack of political unity.

In short, any bird's-eye view of the current state of Western integration surveys a tableau which, though it would be exaggerated and misleading to call it chaotic, reflects an amazing variety of moods, stages of advance, arrest, or retreat, and prospects for the future. The study of any major sector of this panorama must take place against the backdrop of what is going on in the others.

It is fashionable to say that the West is the victim of its own success in dealing with the situations that originally induced it to close ranks. Since 1948 no ground has been lost to Soviet control in Europe. Essentially the same may be maintained about the Communist cause as a political force anywhere within the free areas of the Continent. In fact, until the action in Czechoslovakia in August 1968, this failure to make advances in Western Europe was matched by a coincident slackening of grip in the lands of the Soviet sphere. Thus one may assert that, until 1968, Moscow either had been rebuffed or had lost ground in the entire area west of Soviet borders with the exception of East Germany.

Coincident with this, tensions elsewhere than in Europe seized the spotlight in Soviet-American relations. The Cuban crisis of 1962 still overlapped with one (Berlin) in Europe. There is no such link between the Old World and American involvement in Southeast Asia. Instead, the debate since October 1962 has dwelt largely on whether the Cold War has been all but ended or has shrunken to a purely Moscow-Washington affair. The cement of fear — the original and most consistent binding element in the Western Alliance — has cracked and at many points eroded. Eloquent evidence for this is the change of sentiment in the most exposed country in Europe — West Germany. There Allensbach polls taken four years apart recorded the responses shown in the tabulation on whether those queried felt menaced by the Soviet Union.[2]

	1962	1966
Felt menaced	66%	38%
Felt no fear	15	37

Related to this waning anxiety about Soviet designs and pressures are changes in attitude toward the hegemonial and federative roles of the United States in Europe. The most constant and dominant factor in European situations of the last twenty years is that the relationship of the European peoples with one another has been governed by their relations with the United States. On occasion this has been put categorically as a verdict that America was really the one thing Western Europeans could be said to have in common.

Given so vital an American function with respect to the integrative process in Europe, the concept of its nature depends in the first instance on how it evolved historically. Yet even on so elementary a point there is no complete Western consensus and all too frequently there is more confusion than in former years. Thus, though it is rarely put so bluntly, the more extreme attacks on current American policy seem to imply that the United States set about exploiting the infirmities of postwar Europe in order to launch an Atlantic imperialism. The claim that the United States was only responding to Soviet aggressive moves would in this view be reduced to a convenient cover for pursuit of American ambitions.

Important in the spreading of miscomprehension is the rapid coming to the forefront of a generation without mature experience of the terrors and miseries of earlier postwar years. In its ranks, where anti-American attitudes engendered by the war in Southeast Asia have gained much ground, such innuendos about the motivations of the United States find a measure of acceptance. Inevitably there follows from this a tendency to equate the nature of American hegemony in the West with that of the Soviet Union's in Eastern Europe. NATO and the Warsaw Pact have increasingly been put upon the same plane of discussion, especially in proposals for their simultaneous disbandment.

Much, then, that once seemed obvious about the precedent-shattering plunge of the United States into European affairs demands redefinition. Accordingly it is imperative to reiterate that the Soviet satellite system, from its origins, was a vehicle for crassly exploitive domination, with the Warsaw Pact little more than a device for internal control of its members by the superpower. The system also was characterized by prohibition of any combination among its subordinate members that was not initiated by the Kremlin's own fiat. Anything that made for regional autonomy was anathema to Moscow. One need recall only Stalin's harsh veto of the project entertained by Tito and Dimitrov for a close association of Yugoslavia with Bulgaria. In stark contrast to this stands the unfailing support by the United States of every Western European design for ties between two or more states that might enable them to stand more independently.

It was not so much what it had learned from the war but rather the lessons of the first postwar years that imposed on a reluctant United States a far-reaching commitment in Europe, and, for that matter, outside the Western Hemisphere. In 1945 Americans would have applauded Franklin D. Roosevelt had they known that he, in all seriousness, assured Stalin that he anticipated the withdrawal of their forces from Europe within a year and a half after the close of hostilities. In no small degree American enthusiasm about the formation of the United Nations was tinged with neo-isolationism — a pious hope to evade national involvement in world problems by consigning responsibility to an international agency. Forced by repeated painful lessons to recognize the utopian character of this dream, Americans replaced it by another which envisioned a progressive reduction of their commitment. Much that promised to be self-liquidating insofar as American predominance was concerned was built into the structure of the Western Alliance. In effect, the hegemonial power welcomed whatever could facilitate the eventual dismantlement of its own hegemony. In fact, a common and often justified charge of those days was that the United States still stood too much aside, was shirking the full responsibilities of leadership, and complacently expected its European friends to advance rapidly on paths limiting national sovereignty where it was prepared itself to take only faltering steps.

Much in the character of American relations with Europe in the late fifties would seem to belie such a delineation of American policies and objectives. But there was a reluctance to disturb convenient and, for the time being, adequate-looking patterns of procedure; this accounted largely for the American failure to push ahead with programs that would have

given the Alliance more the aspect of a transatlantic partnership. Perhaps
the most noteworthy example of this is the lack of serious proposals concerning the problem of nuclear sharing. The major historical indictment
of American policy that may some day be made will probably concern
the nonchalance with which the United States marked time while the implications of Europe's miraculous comeback clamored for attention. The
long period of unchallenged preeminence had had the effect of a political
tranquilizer. It was so much simpler to drift along in what had begun to
look like a perpetual game of "follow-the-leader" than to anticipate and
seek to forestall or minimize tensions that lay ahead. Despite a growing
awareness that things could not continue indefinitely as they were, action
was triggered only when the American hand was forced by developments
it could no longer control.

The Long Shadow from Paris

Future debate on the sixties in North Atlantic history may well center
on the extent to which developments might have taken different directions but for the intervention of a single masterful personality. Historians,
who during the last century have leaned so decidedly toward deterministic
interpretations, may discover much in the life of our times that will cause
them to revise upward their estimates of the role of the individual. No one
seems fated to compel such a reevaluation more insistently than Charles
de Gaulle. At several critical junctures in the course of Western affairs
his interjacence assuredly did much to determine the fork of the road to
be traveled. The compass of his influence may best be gauged from the
simple fact that on every such occasion his country stood by itself, and
that each time it was his iron will which imposed the particular policy
upon his country.

This accomplishment leaves little doubt that as a historic figure de
Gaulle will more than match his preeminence in physical stature among
contemporary statesmen. The particular niche that will be assigned to him
in the annals of our times will of course depend on the aims he will be
judged to have pursued and the wide-ranging impact of his statesmanship
on French and world affairs. Strangely but not without precedent in the
case of other leaders of our era, one could often judge his intentions by
taking him at his own word. On all vital issues — the role of France in the
world, the needs of Europe, the urgency of contracting the American
presence there, and East-West relations — the General put himself extensively on record and could usually be taken very seriously indeed.

De Gaulle was always most fervent when his subject was the place in
the world that should be occupied by France. All his life, he recounts in
his memoirs, he kept before him "a certain idea of France." He early

conceived that France, "like a princess in the fairy tale or a Madonna of the Frescoes, had an eminent and exceptional destiny." She could only be herself when in the front rank: "In short, France, as I see her, cannot be France without greatness." [3]

Spelling this out, de Gaulle proclaimed that France must remain free of ties that limited her ability to make all vital decisions herself or that restricted her disposition over her armed forces. "Any system," he said, "that would consist of handing over our sovereignty to august international assemblies would be incompatible with the rights and duties of the French Republic." [4] In matters of defense, he asserted, it was the right and obligation of every Continental power to have its own national establishment. "It is intolerable for a great state to leave its destiny up to the decision and actions of another state, however friendly it may be." [5]

So rigidly national an orientation automatically and irrevocably determined for Gaullist France the limits within which she could accommodate her policy to the demands of contemporary world currents. National blinders focused her outlook on a precisely laid-out segment of the world horizon. To many of de Gaulle's contemporaries his insights therefore appeared exceptionally keen in some areas and sadly lacking in others. The border line was not easy to determine. To what degree, for example, did he perceive a saving national interest in international institutions which, in their half-arrested state, fell short of the restrictions on national sovereignty that were originally intended? It is not surprising that the clarity and consistency of his view on the unique place of France in world affairs should have been coupled with nebulous and often contradictory conceptions of Europe.

A nationalist who usually did not hesitate to flaunt unmistakable nationalist garb, de Gaulle did at times cover it with a European cloak he kept always at hand. As far back as the war years he fully perceived that some sort of confederate order within a substantial segment of the Continent was imperative if Europe was to continue to be a factor in global affairs. Even then, when French power had sunk to its lowest point in modern history, he claimed for her as of right the role of *fédérateur*. To a Swiss visitor in London in the mid-war years he unburdened himself to the effect that France had been entrusted by Providence with the task of advancing the unity of Europe. The first of her sons to undertake this charge, he said, had been Charlemagne and the second Napoleon. The third, he said meaningfully, did not need to be mentioned. [6]

Thus, well before the triumphant day of liberation, Charles de Gaulle dreamed of a future European mission for France and for himself personally. His most strident critics would hardly impugn his sense of reality so far as to ascribe to him a vision of French empire. On the other hand, any conception of a European order in which France functioned as leader dictated certain inevitable corollaries. It ordained severe limitations on both the American and the Soviet presence. Also, since even a loosely confederate order would threaten to submerge French influence if it involved too large a grouping, a basically "little Europe" concept was inescapable. The sweeping de Gaulle slogan "Atlantic to the Urals" no doubt signified some notion of a wider European concert; in part it also was one of the "keep off" signs for Britain and the United States.

To a man so accustomed to think in traditional terms, the unprecedented role of the United States in the postwar world could offer little to inspire enthusiasm. He could hardly have failed to magnify any hegemonial aspect of the massive American materialization on the European stage. A contributory element was a considerable, some feel a prodigious, overestimate of American power and influence. It is logical that, encountering and contending with them as he felt compelled to do at every turn, he should be obsessed with their omnipresence. Members of his entourage frequently quoted him to the effect that the United States really was the only world power, a conviction that was apparently further enhanced by the Middle East crises of June 1967. Addressing an assemblage of French and German ministers at Bonn a few weeks later (July 13), he put it thus: "One fact dominates present reality, and that is the enormous power of the United States. . . . By virtue of this fact there are two alternatives. One can accept things as they are: this is the easiest course and means that one must be a part of a whole dominated by American power. And there is the other alternative, that of safeguarding our national personality." [7]

Seen in this light, American commitments in so many areas of the world could only look like so many fingers in regional pies. The United States, appearing heretofore mostly absorbed with the problem of empire in the Atlantic, seemed in the mid-sixties to concentrate on consolidating its position in the Pacific. Cherishing the aims he did for France, de Gaulle naturally felt compelled to intervene against the American game in every sector of the globe.

It would seem out of line to imply, as some did, that Charles de Gaulle merely sought ways to rationalize an anti-American bias of a quarter century. Yet few doubted the depth and enduring quality of the resentments springing from the slights which he felt, not without justification, he had suffered at the hands of such Americans as Roosevelt and Hull. Twenty years after the landing in Normandy he refused to attend commemorative ceremonies and described how he had never forgiven his former allies for not informing him of the invasion until the day before it occurred.[8] The impressions of men who stood close to him during the 1960's differed considerably on how much he was swayed by such emotional factors. One political figure who knew him well discounted them, remarking grimly that what he really resented about the United States was that he was not privileged to rule it.[9] Instead he was the master of a country which, as he saw it, could expect to assert itself in Europe only in some proportion to the measure in which it could reduce American influence. Assuming that Britain also could be held at arm's length politically, the diminution of the American presence ordained a power vacuum into which France could hope at least partially to insert herself. Under French guidance Western Europe could then emerge as a "third force" that might balance American and Soviet influence.

Such a calculation would seem to break down on the obvious contradiction that a loose grouping of Continental states — a "Europe of fatherlands" confined politically and militarily to little more than the traditional Alliance ties — could not effect a concentration of power necessary to such a role. Difficult as it is to believe that de Gaulle could fail to have been aware of this, he persistently chose to ignore it. A Europe equipped to muster its fullest potential, he knew, meant the fading of French identity. He also dreaded the emergence of such a Europe as a step toward an Atlantic community. "A supranational Europe," he said, "is a Europe under American command."[10] The argument that it might work in the opposite sense, tending to slam the door on Atlantica, either did not seem convincing to him or failed to outweigh with him the price of French submersion as an independent power factor.

Over the years, observers of the French scene were faced with such perennial and closely related questions as the degree to which Charles de Gaulle personified genuine forces in his own country and in Europe, how much his impact on affairs served to further invigorate such forces, and what it would signify for French policy when he left the political scene. At those critical junctures when the ties of the Western Alliance have been most seriously disrupted, France, as has been noted, both acted by herself and pursued a policy imposed solely by his inflexible determination. Few would hold otherwise than that, save for his masterful direction, France would hardly have taken a single one of the escalating steps which first emasculated and in the end repudiated her relationship with the NATO military organization. She would not have ventured, and might have been disinclined, to veto Britain's entry into the Common Market, and she would, at the very least, have proved more flexible on the issue of implementing the Treaty of Rome by introducing majority rule and extending its political structure.

Despite the pronounced and decisive role of de Gaulle in these matters, he obviously could not have scored so heavily without a considerable spirit of accommodation at various levels of the French nation. It is scarcely necessary to dwell on the vitality of the French national tradition and its increased sensitiveness since the disaster of 1940. If anything, the liberation by Anglo-American arms made the tutelage of Washington more painful. This explains one's frequent experience over recent years with French friends of decided pro-American and anti-Gaullist leanings, who confessed wryly that they could not resist a tingle of elation when the General "stood up" to the United States. Though such purely psychological factors should not be overrated, it would also be a mistake to discount them entirely.

Scarcely less than in dealings with the United States, the yearning to preserve French identity comes to the fore where there seems danger of "sinking France in Europe." To begin with, the French are lacking in experience with federal institutions; their political memories are restricted to a Republic "une et indivisible." Thus they are perhaps more prone than others to think of "Europe" in all-or-nothing terms and shrink from being swallowed by an all-devouring international Moloch. Though other considerations certainly also affected their decision, reluctance to sacrifice so much of their national sovereignty undoubtedly played a major part when, in the mid-fifties, they repudiated the European Defense Community they had themselves initiated.

What has been the impact of the experience of the 1960's and what force should be assigned to such sentiments at present? They can hardly fail to have been strengthened by the consecutive setbacks to European unity. The thrust toward "Europe" waned in prestige and in momentum. Beyond this, de Gaulle was able to backwater without incurring political shipwreck or visible damage to France. The polls showed that, as usual, nothing succeeds like success. Until the summer of 1967 there seemed to be a progressive growth of sentiment in his support. As has been noted, de Gaulle, however much he displayed his nationalist garb, never failed to carry on his arm or draped over his shoulder a European cloak. In his press conferences and other public pronouncements he habitually hitched obeisance to the concept of a united Europe with policy declarations of opposite implication. French proponents of the cause of "Europe" testify that in their activities, especially in areas less sophisticated than Paris, they often encountered genuine surprise when the General was classified otherwise than as a firm supporter of the cause.[11]

In any event, Gaullist rule did not strengthen French aptitude for democracy and it worked to stifle interest in public affairs, notably in foreign relations, where the personal policy of the head of state prevailed so uncontestedly. Short of some major international crisis, there was little stimulus to national debate. In France, as elsewhere, the citizen has become increasingly inclined to listen to rather than to read the news, so that the government's dominance of radio and television is a potent force for discouraging political diversity. The explosion of May 1968 was therefore all the more surprising and perhaps portentous, raising the question whether the constriction of the usual media of protest and criticism does not lead inevitably to violence. Authoritarian rule, in short, is inhibitive of democratic procedure in the conduct of both government and opposition. The last word on this problem was clearly not spoken in the disorders of the late spring of 1968.

To date the metamorphosis in France from seeming political apathy to violent display of feeling does appear to be confined to issues that are restricted to the domestic scene. In foreign relations, indifference was so evident in the spring of 1967 that no one tried to make a major issue of them in the parliamentary elections.[12] The same was, of course, true in the election of June 1968, though the preoccupation with the internal crisis did not make this a significant test.

Despite the climate of indifference in the spring of 1967, much that occurred shortly thereafter in the international arena did shake the complacency of many Frenchmen about their external affairs. The year 1967 was not one to foster illusions de Gaulle and his chief admirers may have cherished about the relative influence of France in world affairs. Commencing in June, a series of acts gave rise to a growing impression that the General, then seventy-six, had begun to conduct himself like "an old man in a hurry" and was increasingly inclined to overreach himself. The growth of a nationwide uneasiness about this could be noted by anyone who spent much time in France in the second half of 1967. The international fireworks set off by him during this period roused a response that ranged from discomfort to shock.

The first sign of a parting of the ways between him and public opinion related to his handling of the Arab-Israeli conflict. At a time when the switchboard of the Israeli embassy was swamped with the calls of well-wishers from cabinet ministers down, the president adopted a line which brought cheers only from the Communists. His own staff in the Elysée was reported fiercely divided on the issue. There was further head shaking when, on June 21, he cast the blame for the Middle East troubles on the wide-ranging influence of the American war in Vietnam. Meanwhile this time his policy failed to gain the justification that comes with success. Not only, as he later indignantly put it, had Israel failed to "heed the voice of France" and to desist from attack on the Arabs, but the Soviets would not be persuaded to deal with the problem on the proposed four-power basis.

Even greater unanimity of critical comment was voiced in regard to de Gaulle's Canadian fling. For the first time a national poll turned clearly against him on a foreign policy issue, 56 percent of the respondents voicing disapproval of his appeal to Quebec separatism. The reaction was scarcely more cordial to his strident reiteration of this and of his Middle Eastern position in his November press conference. It did not help his prestige at home that his statements on Quebec, enunciating what looked like a species of "French folkdom" and recalling Hitlerite concepts, should raise at least a flutter of uneasiness in Switzerland and Belgium, with their large French-speaking populations. Meanwhile he seemed to have overrated any disposition in Eastern Europe to loosen ties with Moscow or to balance them off in part by creating others with France. His visit to Poland, however dramatic, has usually been reckoned a disappointment. Quite aside from reluctance to compromise Poland's relationship with Moscow, the noncommittal attitude of the Poles was influenced by considerations which had to do with the United States. They feel uneasiness rather than elation about projects to eliminate American influence from Europe, and well know that their future will be determined not by France but by the course of Soviet-American relations. A dissolution of the blocs with a return to a pluralistic-nationalistic political structure carries new perils for them, particularly in relation to Germany. De Gaulle, in fine, seems to have appeared to them as the representative of outdated forces.[13] Yet it would be a mistake to discount too greatly the dramatic impact of his personality, the splendor of his oratory, and his keen sense of audience appeal. Both in Poland and in his visit to Rumania in May 1968 he may be assumed to have left an impression that would ease the tasks of French diplomacy in future undertakings in Eastern Europe.

Withal, the year 1967 not only served to shake confidence in specific moves of de Gaulle in the international realm, but raised questions about his mastery of foreign relations generally. Many who approved of or went along with his anti-American posture still deplored the tone and manner of his dealings with Washington. It became common in the French press to complain that a statesman should not structure his policy on hostility to another country. Perhaps more significant were signs here and there of a tendency to hedge on support of de Gaulle so as not to be caught unprepared in the event of a change of regime. A notable example of hedging was a real surge of financial backing for European and Atlantic causes from "smart money" Patronat (big-business) sources in the second half of June 1967. Equally noteworthy was a similar and apparently more enduring surge of support of such causes after the Soviet intervention in Czechoslovakia in August 1968.[14]

The Problem of "After de Gaulle"

All calculations based on the experience of the second half of 1967 required intense review in light of the developments of the late spring of 1968. The repercussions of the national crisis in the international sphere were bound to be far-reaching. Neither the French nor the world could ignore the fact that, for a time, the regime appeared shaken to its foundations; all over the globe there were people who looked for early answers to the perennial question "After de Gaulle what?" However superbly he mastered the situation, there was no erasing the impression that it was a near thing, that at bottom his regime was more vulnerable than once supposed. Against this, his personal prestige again took a leap upward and his previously precarious parliamentary position was changed to one of unprecedented dominance. Even more than hitherto, his word seemed to be law in the making of French policy.

That policy itself, however, had to be formulated under influences that afforded less elbowroom than at any time in the previous half decade. There was a threat of complications from his "opening to the Right" and from the compromises with lukewarm and formerly dissident army elements which he felt compelled or deemed it advisable to make. More significant were the domestic and foreign consequences of the unfavorable economic situation. Both the immediate direct damage to the French economy and the burdensome social, wage, and other obligations assumed in the "carrot and stick" approach to mastering the semi-revolutionary situation were bound to leave some impress on policy making. What had often been labeled arrogance in dealing with Common Market partners and outsiders gave promise of being replaced by more considerate treatment. There was much interest in the degree to which this might be reflected in across-the-board relations with Western Alliance members. On the domestic side, but with many external implications, observers were bound to wonder how far de Gaulle would succeed in securing the means for his existing nuclear defense program and for the more ambitious one he had announced for the next two decades; this will be discussed later.

From the summer of 1967 those who followed French affairs closely had been looking ahead to the budget session that was to open in the fall of 1968. At that time the government was scheduled to make its play for the first truly large appropriations for the *force de frappe*. It has often been overlooked in analyzing French political currents that the really expensive phases of French nuclear-power building remain to be faced, and that as they are confronted with them many Frenchmen will be stirred to second thoughts. Awareness of this was strong among the most expectant of the would-be inheritors of power at the turn of 1967 to 1968, the leaders of the Federation of the Left, whose mood at that time almost approached a certain complacency. Time, they were convinced, was on their side; they looked forward eagerly to the political pickings to be gleaned from the budget sessions of autumn 1968. Hope, if not yet confidence, rose at that time to a point where discussion of portfolio assignment was commencing on at least one level. The problem was whether an electoral alliance could be formed with the Communists without handing portfolios to such unsure political partners. Some leading figures of the Federation, notably on the Socialist side, believed that it should not and need not be done. The Communists were assumed to think in long-range terms and it was argued that they would not insist on this point if one were firm enough and the obvious alternative was a government of the Right and Center. Other leaders of the Federation, such as François Mitterand, doubted whether the Communists would be so accommodating or were less finicky about granting them minor portfolios. The subject is a good example of how political calculations had to be revised in view of events in late spring 1968. Assuredly if the Left had come to power at that time, the Communists could have exacted a far larger price for their collaboration.

The Gaullist electoral triumph of June 1968 eliminated any probability of a parliamentary crisis over the financing of the next stage of the long-range arms program or, for that matter, any other issue. The financial stringency of the second half of that year and the crisis of the franc also dictated a reduction of the first goals of the 360-degree perimeter defense system announced a year earlier, which will be discussed later.

The point of departure on the absorbing topic of what would follow de Gaulle naturally concerned the circumstances that would prevail at the electric moment when the answers began to come in. At his age and in his situation de Gaulle could conceivably have ceased to govern France because of death, physical or mental failure, a decision not to run again in 1972, or voluntary or forced retirement. His health continued excellent and there were no signs of declining mental vigor.[15] The toll that age exacts of all men appeared most evident with him in the hardening of his prejudices and his growing self-righteousness and impatience.

It was obviously important whether he departed in an unexpectedly or only briefly signaled manner, faded out by not running in 1972, or left amidst the turmoil of a national crisis. The lopsided Gaullist majority cast in his lap by the backlash to the riotous spring of 1968 considerably reduced the range of possibilities if the General left the scene during the life of that parliament. Without this unanticipated political turn the outlook would have been a very different one. An intensive unpublished survey made in the autumn of 1966 convinced one able observer familiar with French politics that de Gaulle's Union National Republicaine was a political agglomeration scarcely fated to outlive its maker.[16] The writer's own experience with varieties of political colorations parading under the Gaullist label at that period inclined him to the same estimate.[17] The unprecedented Gaullist majority, however, afforded a measure of political leeway which raised the odds in favor of a greater degree of continuity. Another factor was the success of de Gaulle in assembling a team of able lieutenants with considerable skill in executing policies, though it remained to be seen to what degree they could develop as policy makers or popular leaders in their own right. Their role as "brilliant seconds" was of somewhat mixed benefit in this regard. Though clearly identifying them as potential heirs apparent, it also earned them a measure of public disesteem because of the rubber-stamp label that became attached to them.

It proved something of a political accident that Georges Pompidou was enabled to emerge so decisively as de Gaulle's successor after the latter's resignation in the spring of 1969. The spring 1968 national crisis had provided him the opportunity to demonstrate capacities of independent leadership. Thrust back for that very reason from the political forefront by a master who would brook no rival however distant, he won his first measure of public sympathy as a result of this cavalier treatment. He was also favored by the form of de Gaulle's departure from power, which took place in an atmosphere so devoid of national crisis that it worked for political continuity.

As already noted, there had long been agreement within and outside of France that whatever government succeeded de Gaulle would be considerably weaker than his. It seemed likely to be one neither utterly committed to his policies nor bursting with eagerness to break with them. On the issue of "Europe," for example, a conservative coalition would shrink from a clear repudiation of his positions, whereas a Left government would find its Communist allies a brake against retracing the steps which took France so far in other directions. The most promising climate for some tendency toward compromise was expected under a regime which, though still basing itself largely on "Gaullist" support, depended also on a somewhat broader political grouping.

The Pompidou government has, in fact, emerged from an election which demonstrated Pompidou's awareness of the need for this kind of backing. Both the electoral campaign and the subsequent formation of his cabinet departed from the Gaullist pattern in the extent of appeal made to a variety of interest groups. Clearly the new president is a political pragmatist who does not strictly adhere to any dogma and is the prisoner of no set program. France, in effect, may be said to have approached the end of that road on which the political course seemed immutably set and to which all national goals were oriented. It seems safe to assume that both popular sentiment and the particular requirements of each situation that arises will have a greater impact on policy than at any time in the previous decade.

How should we assess the capacity of the French nation to form and express its sovereign will? On this de Gaulle showed himself a complete skeptic in conversations with French political figures. "The French will always be the same," he said to Pierre Abelin in 1962. "After I am gone they'll go back to what they used to be: Disunited, divided, victims of their internecine bickerings." And in the same year to Pierre Sudreau: "Without me this country will amount to nothing. Without me all this will collapse." [18]

It will be the task of history to judge in what measure such expressions reflected merely mood or fancy. Insofar as they may be taken to predict a reversal of many of his policies, they jibe with a wide assumption in France that basic changes may be anticipated. In a 1964 survey of elite groups, including many persons with whom the author two or three years later also conferred extensively, 96 percent of the respondents were of this opinion. Expectations on the future of particular policies varied from 7 percent indicating they thought the policy toward European integration would continue after de Gaulle to 48 percent forecasting continuance of Gaullist positions vis-à-vis the United States.[19]

To what degree did anticipations coincide with leanings? On the basis of conversations with many of those involved, it is the author's impression that this was very often the case but that no exact correlation may be assumed. There remains, of course, the vital question of just how far those who desired some change wished to move away from the Gaullist model. No doubt, many who believed de Gaulle had gone "altogether too far" in undermining "Europe" could by no stretch of the imagination be classed as federalists. The most persistent feeling in France, as elsewhere in Europe, is that what matters just now are the live and immediate issues. Confronted by the need to make a decision, the French naturally react differently from the way they would toward an issue, like their relation to NATO, that can be likened to water already over the dam. It remains to be seen whether the French nation "after de Gaulle" will generate more fervent foreign policy demands than it did under his aegis.

In analyzing American attitudes toward de Gaulle's rule, it is not easy to forget that in recent years the French president managed to lacerate every sensitive nerve he could reach in the American national body. Most Americans came to take for granted that they could only gain from his departure from the world scene. After the winter of 1963, when the first reaction in the White House and the State Department to the veto on Britain's entrance into the Common Market was shocked incredulity, frustration piled on frustration in dealing with de Gaulle. Clearly, it was impossible to strike at him without also striking at French pride or interests and thus rallying the country more firmly to him. There was also the peculiar political constellation in Western Europe which rendered France largely invulnerable to pressures. To mention just one feature, there was her geographic position behind the rampart of German territory which the Western Alliance had no choice but to defend. Preoccupation with non-European concerns also prevented the United States from making the best of situations where there was no alternative but to proceed without

French cooperation. This will be noted later in consideration of the NATO situation in particular.

Though it would be premature to assess with any confidence the role of Charles de Gaulle as director of the policies of the Fifth French Republic, it appears safe to assume that the verdict of history will be a mixed one. Those who have closely followed European affairs for the last decade cannot ignore the services which de Gaulle rendered both to the French and to the Western world generally. The excision of the cancer which was the problem of Algeria we owe to him alone. A sense of obligation for the overcoming of the political instability that had been the bane of the Third and Fourth Republics should extend beyond his own country. It is less easy to isolate the share he can claim for the economic stabilization and advance which France came to enjoy in common with her partners of the Six. It can be said that without his unfaltering determination it is questionable whether even now they would have reached a common agricultural policy. Whatever else may be said about his role in the Middle East crisis, his resolution to remain on good terms with the Arabs had the positive aspect that one major Western country retained a measure of their confidence. No other Western statesman of the last quarter century showed such an awareness as he that the eastern half of the Continent is also inalienably a part of Europe or voiced it so eloquently.

Thus, in manifold ways, we should count ourselves among de Gaulle's debtors. But to recognize such positive aspects of his role cannot obliterate the essential sterility of much that characterized Gaullism on the international stage. It is true that the General often had to deal with statesmen undistinguished for identifying the signs of a new era. Brought up on lend-lease, the Marshall Plan, and the Cold War, they may perhaps be accused of having failed to recognize some of the implications of the profound changes within and without their immediate world. At times de Gaulle could legitimately claim the keener insight in estimating current realities. Yet the fundamental framework within which he registered such perceptions was one that much predated their own. George Ball's devastating comment that the "bold new idea" to which de Gaulle had given birth was "to return Europe to its prewar anarchy" is no doubt too one-sided a judgment. But it is hard to escape the conclusion that the views he presented about the future of his continent remained largely vague generalities. Certainly no clear pattern of what he had in mind had emerged in the late sixties, and the wave of the future still seemed to mean to him the backwash of the past. Granting, for example, the credit he deserves for striving to reopen roads to Eastern Europe, the results even there lack substance. French penetration there has been largely cultural. For example, though French cultural contacts with Rumania are most impressive, outnumbering those of the United States perhaps fifty to one, trade, and with it much of what there may be of Western influence, flows more strongly in the direction of Germany.[20] Here, as elsewhere in Eastern Europe, it is sensed that, aside from the relationship between the United States and the Soviet Union, the future position of Germany will have the most significant impact on the fate of the area.

German Dilemmas

The recent years have seen momentous changes in all parts of the North Atlantic world. Next to the consequences of the shacklement of American power in Southeast Asia and the French disengagement from much of the Western Alliance, there is probably no situation so changed as that of Germany. In contrast to France and the United States, where all seemed to flow from the decision-making authority, the alterations in Germany's position have been dictated mainly by external circumstances. The government of Chancellor Erhard was one of the least dynamic and innovative recently seen on the European stage. Despite this, affairs were so shaped that the position of the Federal Republic in the fading days of Adenauer was often hard to recognize under Kiesinger.

The external relations of Germany during the present century have been dominated by her unique position among the nations west of Russia. She alone in Europe has had a heavy preponderance of population over each of the other powers of the West. Additional elements of her power potential have been her strategic position, her national dynamic, and her industrial capabilities. Together they account for her bent toward dominance and the fears among her neighbors which furnish much of the explanation for the two world wars.

The last quarter century has presented a greatly changed picture. Most important: the weight of Germany need no longer be reckoned in terms of military capabilities for possible offensive wars. This may not appear true to many who remain so overwhelmed by their experience in World War II that they fail to grasp the altered situation, a factor which must never be discounted in the analysis of attitudes toward Germany. As a contributor to Western defense, West Germany stands both geographically and militarily in the first rank. She also remains an international factor in other ways that require constant reassessment. Her central position continues to offer possibilities for playing off states or power groups to the east and west of her against each other. Every Western project for combination which considers including her must be mindful of the proper balancing elements.

Tragic experiences endured by neighbors on all sides of Germany bred after World War II an initially irresistible impulse to destroy or impose crippling conditions on her. The passage of time compelled recognition that the original prescription spelled self-mutilation, perhaps suicide, for Europe generally. The need to mobilize all Western resources to meet the Soviet threat produced this realization much sooner than would otherwise have been possible. What elementary logic dictated from the start was gradually recognized — that the only long-range solution of the German problem was total integration under conditions of complete equality within a grouping formidable enough to allay anxiety about excessive assertion of German influence. Support of this solution demands from Germany's late enemies a stern mental and emotional discipline; and there has been among them somewhat less than wholehearted acceptance of the full implications of integration. The Germans themselves required little conversion to the idea of integration. Here obviously lay the only road to rehabilitation and, insofar as could be humanly expected, a canceling out of the past. Admittance into a reconstituted and more closely knit European family offered everything to which Germans of that era could legitimately aspire. It meant for them a measure of security, the restoration of national dignity, economic and political stability, and the hope of support in the long uphill struggle for reunification of the two Germanys. But such self-seeking motivations did not stand alone. They were buttressed by much enthusiasm for the "European idea," which offered a special appeal to youth. The old ideological idols lay broken and nature abhors a vacuum as much in the spiritual as in the physical sphere. Seldom has history provided the occasion for so happy a wedding between realism and idealism.

The upshot of this fortunate conjunction was that West Germany of the fifties and sixties could always be reckoned among the supporters of European and Atlantic unity. The Bonn government, it was commonly understood, would proceed along this road as far and as fast as its prospective partners were themselves ready to go. A major role here was played by the "special relationship" with the United States, which contrasts with the Anglo-American one in that the less brawny associate was more protégé than junior partner. It was in the nature of things that in the Western Alliance there should be a gravitational pull between its most powerful and its most exposed member. Then, too, the whole West German defense system was geared to the massive American military presence on German soil.

As with German response to the appeal of "Europe," practicality and sentiment went hand in hand in the following by Bonn of the American lead. The Germans knew well that at every point and stage the United States had led the way among Western allies in letting bygones be bygones and in taking the positive steps that led to the reconstitution of much of their nation as an independent state. At all times America had been the vital guardian and defender of Berlin. The presence in Germany of millions of Americans, who had followed each other in relays for what approached a quarter of a century, though not without its elements of friction, had on the whole been a harmonizing experience. No other country in Europe offers such a profusion of plaques and monuments commemorating the American stay, reminding Germans of the many ways in which the United States stood at their side in days of crisis.

Small wonder that year after year Bonn seemed to fall automatically into the wake of the giant liner that dominated Atlantic waters. It became an axiom of international politics that it would respond to directional signals from Washington. Like so much else in the European and German picture, this is now much changed, though blandishments from Paris have had remarkably little to do with it. Decisive have been a whole new range of circumstances that have affected the American role in Europe generally and thus, as always, its most deeply involved associate particularly.

The intense and indefinite preoccupation of the United States in Southeast Asia has now for several years allowed only secondary attention to its concerns in Europe and inhibits any strong lead there for the foreseeable future. It is in the nature of things that the Germans should be the most anxious about this and that they should be among those most disturbed about one of its side effects — the American fever to demonstrate in dealings with the Soviet Union every eagerness to promote peace and world stability. To prove this and perhaps to gain a face-saving mediator in the Vietnam conflict, the Johnson administration abounded in moves toward détente with the Soviet Union, notably in the treaty for nuclear nonproliferation.

Europeans have always been of two minds about American inclinations toward détente. Though themselves eager for the relaxation of tensions, they are always apprehensive about some sellout of their interests. If anyone is to be sold out, German assets come most easily to mind as trading materials; when American-Soviet negotiations are rumored, one can always count on anxiety in Bonn climbing several notches higher than anywhere else. This alone can explain the virtual hysteria which swept Germany when the nonproliferation issue reached a high point of discussion in the winter of 1967. To cap matters, it coincided with new pressures in the United States for reducing the level of American forces in Germany because of budget exigencies and Vietnam military needs. Congressional discontent erupted in extreme demands, while the administration seemed to blow alternately hot and cold. Bonn never felt sure what results to expect from some unheralded turn of the wheel in Asia. There have also been exasperated complaints from German army leaders that American defense doctrine undergoes too many shifts — that there is scarcely time to accommodate to one line before another is under contemplation.[21]

Altogether, American policy attained in Bonn in the mid-sixties a repute for unpredictability that had not characterized it in earlier years. Some German leaders who were previously classed as staunch advocates of the closest links with Washington began to confess privately to second thoughts. Like other European friends of America, their anxieties over its commitment in Asia and its racial troubles at home were compounded by the domestic cleavages which flowed therefrom. They began to use terms like "a crisis of will" and expressed fears about the "enduring substance" of American power. Most serious, they suffered some loss of confidence about the wisdom of hitching the fate of Germany so closely to the pursuit of an "American line" in the affairs of Western Europe.

All this would have meant less if the "Atlanticist" cause to which Bonn had been so firmly attached had not become becalmed or, worse, begun to drift backward. NATO was beset by difficulties, the dollar suffered the humiliation of repeated attacks, and all of Germany's Western neighbors became manifestly more Europe-centered without the idea of "Europe" gaining anything in the process. Again and again voices in Europe and America in the second half of the sixties questioned whether the United States was not drifting toward a new isolationism. The least that could be anticipated from Bonn under such circumstances was a tendency to hedge its reliance on Washington by looking for other sources of support or, failing such, facing more frankly the compulsion to rely more fully on its own resources.

The most natural course would be to seek firmer backing from a collective European security system. In the early sixties such prospects appeared excellent. With American blessing but largely independent of American stimulus, a line of development had been mapped out by 1962 which, if it could have endured for half a decade, would have built a structure that could begin to lay claim to the title "United States of Europe." Without recounting the successive blows which made a shambles of these high hopes, it can be said that most German leaders came to recognize that the dream of federal union for Europe was, for the time being, dreamed out. The bonds which were to link West Germany to her neighbors and eliminate independent action have been left half tied or, where they already seemed substantial, loosened. To many, the most severe indictment of the policies of Charles de Gaulle is that they served to cast Germany loose from her Western moorings and throw her increasingly on her own in an international sea that resembles his "Europe des Patries."[22]

Neither Germany itself nor any nation which must share the world with her has anything to gain from a resurgence of German nationalism.

Yet her range of choice is being tragically narrowed by the events of the last five years. Despite being, after the Soviets, the strongest nation in Europe in terms of population, trade, industry, and foreign financial reserves, and making, after America, by far the biggest contribution to Western defense, she is condemned in many ways to impotence and frustration. Because of the pall which hangs over her from the all-too-recent past, she cannot aspire to leadership in any Western cause. On top of this, she suffers from an abiding inferiority complex that inhibits her from striking boldly ahead on any issue. Yet one could hardly count on her continuing to endure meekly a place of mediocrity in a Continental framework in which the watchword "everyone for himself" was staging a comeback.

Germany and Eastern Europe

For several years the Germans have been undergoing an intense self-appraisal. The process began under Erhard and was stepped up under Kiesinger. Into each of the major current issues — NATO, the French relationship, the offset-troop level problem, the Kennedy Round, the course of the Common Market, and especially the nonproliferation treaty — there was injected a new national sensitivity of which the United States was slow to become more conscious. In 1966, for example, the process was so vividly manifest that one could follow it almost week by week. Practically overnight the Germans rid themselves of clichés and dogmas which had been rigidities in their foreign policy. The Hallstein Doctrine — that Bonn should forgo diplomatic relations with states recognizing East Germany — was ready for burial the moment proper arrangements could be made with Yugoslavia.[23] For more than ten years every German with an ounce of realism has known that the ultimate recognition of the Oder-Neisse line was inevitable. Yet, until 1967, all in authority shrank from attacking the problem as one of practical politics. The increased willingness to do so was due not only to the entry into the government of Willy Brandt, who for years, as mayor of Berlin, had a kind of brain trust working on this and other problems of Eastern relations, but also to the fact that Eastern Europe was the one area where, up to a point, the Federal Republic could act by itself.

The relations of West Germany to Eastern Europe are inextricably intertwined with the complex problem of reunification, many significant facets of which cannot be outlined or even alluded to within the confines of the present study. Realistically, the areas in any consideration of reunification are the Federal Republic itself, the so-called German Democratic Republic, and Berlin. As noted, the regions beyond the Oder and Neisse and the Czechoslovak areas formerly known as the Sudetenland have long been written off in the minds of most Germans. They could be recovered only by war, which even die-hard extremists acknowledge as unthinkable. Why, then, were these realities not officially recognized years ago in order to clear the air and allow a "normalization" of relations with Eastern Europe? There has been a hope that official acceptance of the territorial status quo could be used for bargaining purposes, especially face-saving for the leaders who must take the political risks attached to this plunge. What people like Brandt and his research group had in mind were such token concessions from Poland as allowing a relatively small number of aged expellees to return "to die where they were born," perhaps also some small payments in extreme hardship cases.[24] Probably even such modest expectations are now outdated and the Federal Republic may have to content itself with little or nothing in the way of return.

Actually, the problem is now more one of securing something like a gracious acceptance of the German renunciation. Contrary to fables engendered by American wishful thinking, notably during the critical summer of 1961,[25] the Soviets could find nothing less welcome than allaying Polish and Czech fears of Germany. Much the same could be said of Poland's Gomulka government and the departed Novotny regime in Czechoslovakia. Such fears have been their best stock in trade in keeping their people in line. Hence the rude rejection by Warsaw and, less emphatically, by Prague in the winter of 1967 of the feelers extended by Willy Brandt — a rejection setting as the condition for further negotiation the, as yet, impossible term of unconditional recognition of the German Democratic Republic. As one leading Czech Communist then put it to the present writer, Prague had felt it "necessary to maintain the front of the Socialist countries," a euphemism for yielding to Soviet pressure. Significantly, the same person expressed the hope that "within a year or so" it would be possible to resume progress toward normal relations with West Germany. We can probably assume that the Dubček government would have moved ahead in this direction almost instanter if it had not wanted to avoid too many immediate actions displeasing to the Kremlin. As matters were, the present writer was told in Prague early in August of 1968 that the establishment of full diplomatic relations with the Federal Republic could be anticipated by the end of the year.

Except for establishing a better climate for reunification efforts generally, and putting one more crimp into the Soviet Union's perpetual propaganda about Bonn's supposed revanchism, improvement in the Federal Republic's relations with Eastern Europe can do little to reunite Germany under one political roof. As always, this depends on Soviet consent and is only conceivable if Moscow (1) is obliged to face a whole new constellation of power factors on the world plane, and (2) renounces those aims for world revolution in which the control of Germany is a key feature.

Arguments about what might have been possible in the early fifties will continue indefinitely, but there was probably nothing the Federal Republic could have done to gain Moscow's agreement short of resigning the country to Soviet domination. This is likely to hold for the future, though there will always be fears that the Germans, as they are thrown more on their own, will be tempted to diplomatic adventure with the Kremlin. As long as the Federal Republic is not completely integrated with the West, shades of the Treaty of Rapallo (1922) and the Hitler-Stalin deal (1939) will continue to haunt us. Western statesmen may deserve no better, having muffed so many chances to bind Germany more closely within the Atlantic world, but unless the Germans feel utterly rejected, it is difficult to imagine them gambling with their national fate in this manner.

So West Germany can only wait and hope that some turn of the wheel will persuade the Soviets to come round. Meanwhile, there have been two areas where they could hope to promote long-range reunification aims and currently make life more tolerable for themselves and their East German brethren. These involve their relations with the German Democratic Republic and with their present allies.

Well into 1966 the relationship with "the zone" was frozen along fairly rigid lines. It was essentially confined to the economic field and every move was scrutinized to exclude what might dignify the despised state and so advance its recognition. The Hallstein Doctrine stood guard against other countries moving in this direction. Late 1966 and early 1967 saw dramatic changes in both popular and official attitudes that betokened impatience with the self-imposed restrictions of the past. The essential goal now was how best to live with the problem, one of the most vital and hard-to-learn lessons of international life, where "solutions" are few and far between. Suggestions previously regarded as unthinkable, or at least unmentionable, began to find a hearing. Some spoke of exchanging consular representatives. Herbert Wehner, soon to be minister of all-German affairs in the new coalition government, put forward the concept of a customs union.[26] Willy Brandt, on becoming foreign minister, quickly made it clear that in Eastern European relations recognition of the Oder-Neisse line would be a negotiable item, though he did not come out for it in principle until March 1968 (and then only as head of the Social Democrats, the SDP, rather than as foreign minister). Perhaps the most startling proposals came from the ranks of the Free Democrats (FDP), often classed as the most national of the three parties in the Bundestag. In January 1967 Wolfgang Schollwer, its press chief, disclosed before a leadership conference at Niederbreisig a study advocating the outright recognition of East Germany, formal acceptance of the Oder-Neisse line, offering of diplomatic relations without strings attached to all Eastern European states, and abandoning of the Federal Republic's claim to be sole representative of the German people. Though there was some outcry against him, Scholl-wer does not seem to have been disciplined. Soon, in fact, the discussion of such ideas became too commonplace to cause sensation.[27]

Thus the problem of relations with East Germany is being dealt with in terms that promise more than enough leeway to meet the actualities of today's situation. It is doubtful, however, whether this will avail so far as to establish a better *modus vivendi* with the German Democratic Republic. It has been too much taken for granted that the Ulbricht regime would welcome every gesture heralding a more favorable attitude toward recognition. Down to 1961 this was probably a valid thesis. But in the same way as the Kremlin and Gomulka have lost interest in the formal acceptance of the Oder-Neisse line, Ulbricht and his Moscow backers may now be disinclined to pay any price whatever for what has become of uncertain value for them.

To trace their natural line of thinking one need only look at the Federal Republic's own motivations for revising its view of the problem. Primary is the anxiety about the long-term effects of the walled-off state of East Germany. There is fear of erosion of "the substance of the nation" behind Ulbricht's prison walls. The East Germans, however little they may relish life in the most satellized state in the Communist bloc, are each year somewhat more resigned to it, more and more take its continuance for granted, and try to make the best of things as they are. To reduce or eliminate barriers to movement and communication would certainly work against this, would again advertise the attractions of life in the Federal Republic, and enhance pressures for "liberalization." Whatever contributed to the interweaving of the two economies would also increase the pull toward reunification.

As shrewd a political manipulator as Walter Ulbricht should have no trouble recognizing the other side of these arguments. Of late years he has fared rather well in his roped-off political preserve. His one experience with taking chances backfired so badly as to make him doubly cautious. In 1966 he suggested oratorical tournaments in an East and a West German town. The political jousters were to be leaders of his Socialist Unity party (SED) and the West German Social Democrats. Ulbricht's original motive apparently coincided with the current Communist line of encouraging popular fronts in Western Europe. He perceived an opportunity to infiltrate the lower levels of the SDP and had already sent agents across the frontier in the summer of 1965 to work in this direction. Further, he may have wanted to be rid of some of the onus that clings to him as jailor-in-chief of the East German people.[28] The SDP leaders jumped at the opportunity (March 1966) and all kinds of preparations were made. Then, in June, Ulbricht suddenly reneged on the whole deal, cold shouldering a last-minute SDP offer to hold the show on television without physical confrontation. His lame protest was that the East German leaders had been insulted by a special West German law guaranteeing them safe-conduct. Actually, the climate in which the affair was developing showed that the idea had boomeranged, that the SDP was gaining great prestige thereby, and that there were risks in relaxing controls for the occasion.

For these and other reasons, Ulbricht is not likely to respond favorably to proposals which threaten to loosen his grip or entail the reduction of physical barriers. The latter would involve the danger that one or two million of his best young workers might immediately run away, dealing a shattering blow to his economy. Obviously there is much the Federal Republic can offer along economic and other lines that would be attractive. But he will pick and choose with great care. In effect, those West Germans who are ready to go far to regain contact with their East German brethren may in the end be like men who, lifting a foot to step onto a bridge, are startled to find there is none there. The resumption of pressures on Berlin in the late spring and autumn of 1968 and again in the late winter of 1969 was further indication that Ulbricht was far from minded to make easier the road to rapprochement with West Germany. The resatellization of so much of Eastern Europe in conjunction with the Soviet intervention in Czechoslovakia also gave him a new lift in all dealings with the West.

Since the final decision on German reunification rests with the Soviet Union, one usually thinks of the problem in East-West terms. It is, however, a problem which obviously also has purely Western aspects. The West, and with it the world generally, have a deep and abiding interest in ending the division of Germany by means that can allay rather than exacerbate international conflict. This division has symbolized and reflected that of Europe: the bridging of the two fissures cannot take place in isolation from each other. Each requires the departure of Soviet forces from the heart of Europe. Equally important, only reunification will remove the cancer of Berlin, which twice has brought us to the verge of another world war. And, finally, the division of Germany furnishes a focus for whatever politically destructive forces may still exist or yet arise in that country.

The basic premises for dealing with the German problem in the terms discussed here remain unchanged. Since it is inseparable from the fundamental issues of European and Atlantic integration, the arrested if not retrogressive state of these movements brings an academic quality to discussion of the topic. Therefore many Germans feel thrown back on themselves, have no hope of making progress for the time being on the international plane, and see their best course for the long pull in fostering renewed contact with their separated brethren. To all intents and purposes, the reunification issue has been put on the shelf. Nothing is more indicative of the recognition of this in Germany than the way in which the

younger generation, so wrought up about much (and naught?), finds
nothing to excite it in the subject of ending national division.

The middle and late sixties saw little discussion of the many schemes,
both before and after that of the Pole Rapacki, for dealing with Germany
by neutralizing the central core of the Continent. Such proposals encountered even more than the usual difficulties and complications that neu-
tralization plans for large areas meet everywhere in a sharply divided
world. New schemes may always be forthcoming, but they are not likely
to contain elements of greater promise and novelty. More important for
Germany is likely to be the special relationship with France, apparently
sealed in 1963, but experiencing varied ups and downs in the succeeding
years.

The Paris-Bonn Axis

During the last century no international rivalry in Europe has been
so fraught with tragic consequences as that of France and Germany. The
war of 1870–71 dominated the memories of a generation and left a heritage of apparently unrelieved antagonism. Only the terrible lessons of
World War I seemed to produce in both countries a widening appreciation of the fatal consequences of that rivalry for themselves and for Europe. After World War II, when the trend of the era appeared so clearly
European union and close Atlantic ties, Franco-German reconciliation
approached the status of a universal Western dream.

French subscription to the pacts at the turn of the fifties signaled acceptance of the need to restore Germany to Western family relations. It
was natural that this should not signify wholehearted adherence to all the
logical consequences, which perforce led to much hesitation and soul-
searching. Also, although the French, like others, saw the need of restricting autonomous action on the part of the Federal Republic, they
found it very hard to accept commensurate restrictions on their own sovereignty. It has already been noted that this was a factor which contributed
to their disowning of the European Defense Community. Another factor
was unwillingness to proceed without Britain, the French having reason
to fear being "left alone" with Germany, which might emerge in time as
the dominant member of the combination.

The year 1958 saw the political comeback of Charles de Gaulle. As
in his dealings with Algeria, the German policies he pursued were evidence of his capacity to alter his views to meet the realities of a situation.
He had started after the war as a straight traditionalist: documents published by the United States Department of State in 1967 reveal that he had
then demanded the French "natural frontiers" of the Rhine. He tried out
on Churchill the idea of a new Anglo-French alliance and, discounting
the ideological factor in Soviet policy, actually did make a twenty-year

alliance with Stalin in 1944. He then became disenchanted with the Soviets and began to regard Britain as an alien influence in Europe.

If only by elimination, Germany remained the sole possible close associate. As he put it to his Council of Ministers in 1961: "In Western
Europe only two countries matter: France and Germany. Of course Italy
tries to stay in the game. And there are Belgium, Holland, and Luxembourg. All that carries no weight at all." [29] He could count on the Germans going far to effect a full reconciliation, which would remove many
a psychological block that had hung on in relations with the West. For
them the most promising road to "Europe" had from the start led through
Paris. Their chief was a fading Adenauer to whom de Gaulle was a hero,[30]
and who had the laudable ambition of achieving an epitaph that would
crown him as the German architect of the reconciliation.

In the end, what had been envisioned as a modest "cooperative agreement" was blown up to almost absurd proportions in the final stages of the
negotiation. For this Adenauer rather than de Gaulle must take the responsibility before history. The *Spiegel* affair, in which his defense minister, Franz Josef Strauss, had badly compromised the government by his
arbitrary procedure against an offending periodical, forced him in December 1962 to regroup his coalition and pledge to step down himself the
following autumn. Deprived of any prospect of presiding over a lengthy
working out of the new Franco-German relationship, the old statesman
resolved to nail things down in as wide an area as possible. To the dismay of the German negotiators, he unwittingly conveyed to de Gaulle an
exaggerated impression of how far the Federal Republic was prepared to
go in arraying itself at the side of France.[31]

The result was a treaty which amazed world observers by the scope
and intensity of the relationship it delineated. Assuredly it far transcended
the realities of the outlook and intentions of the two governments. Having
gone too far too fast, there was no way to proceed except backwards.
Thus the beginning of the decline of Franco-German relations may be
said to date from the moment when the signatures were affixed to the
treaty. In Germany, where a less far-reaching instrument would have
claimed universal applause, the immediate and predominant reaction was
a registering of second thoughts. The treaty sharpened greatly the conflict
between "Euro-Gaullists" and "Atlanticists" and threw the latter into
such a panic that they thought only of backtracking. In consequence, to
get the treaty ratified, it was necessary to include preambular "Atlantic"
provisos which stressed that nothing had changed in German commitments to the United States. It fell to the new chancellor, Ludwig Erhard,
and his foreign minister, Gerhard Schröder, to make personally clear to
de Gaulle how far Germany was prepared to go, a task in which they did
not distinguish themselves by finesse. Schröder has never been famed for

tact, whereas Erhard, a man much swayed by sentiment and notoriously unable to hide anything, was too basically pro-American and anti-Gaullist to deal with a problem of such delicacy. Understandably annoyed, de Gaulle, in turn, humiliated the West German chancellor by informing him with brutal directness that Germany, "as a defeated country," should not expect equality in her relations with France.[32]

By the summer of 1963 the Paris Treaty of January was already covered with political and military question marks. In the latter area, Germans were brought up short by an article by French Defense Minister Messmer which appeared in the *Revue de Défense Nationale*. This set forth the most extreme nationally oriented defense doctrine, using such (to Germans) spine-chilling terms as "defense in depth" and a "second battle" west of the Rhine — clear notice of scant concern for defending Europe on West Germany's eastern frontier. The Germans struck back in August by announcing that they would build their new tank in collaboration with the Americans. For the next three years, it was only downhill for the Franco-German alliance. For many reasons, however, the Germans were eager to keep the special relation with Paris intact. They felt it of use in influencing the United States to be more considerate of Bonn, representing as it did an element of competition and also a means which the Americans could hope occasionally to utilize to improve their own relations with Paris. There was, further, deep anxiety that if the tie should break, it would be infinitely harder to repair than one between countries which carried a less burdensome heritage of traditional animosity.[33]

As for de Gaulle, his public statements and private comments make it possible to reconstruct some of his thinking on the accord. An allied France and Germany would dominate the affairs of the Six and cooperate to restrict the American influence in Europe. In return for this aid and for Germany's accommodating herself to the status of junior partner, de Gaulle would exert himself to promote German reunification, something which, quite rightly, he said could never be gained by American military pressure. France, which with the Federal Republic in support would be clearly the dominant influence in Western Europe, would take the lead toward effecting a détente between the two halves of the Continent. The price offered the Soviet Union would be the permanent denuclearization of Germany and the gradual elimination of American forces from Europe. France would be preeminent in the Western European defense system, furnishing, in effect, the nuclear knights while the Germans would provide the "conventional" foot soldiery.[34]

If this corresponds with de Gaulle's original concept, it impresses as the kind of program which had the best chance to achieve a Gaullist European order. His first post-treaty visit to Germany, however, undeceived him on the degree of cooperation he could expect from that country. "We are the only ones who can say no to the American protectorate," he said on his return home. "The Germans, the Italians, the Belgians, the Dutch will not say no. We alone can and must say it." [35] In effect, he seemed to be stating, France would somehow have to go it alone. If the Germans, he added in 1965, refused to be "good boys" and kept "running to Washington," he would forsake them. Then it would be "all over with their unification." [36]

Yet the General, though not accustomed to woo those with whom he was displeased, avoided presenting the Germans with anything like an ultimatum or giving them more than an occasional verbal spanking. The alliance was permitted to stand and to grind through its elaborate routines of consultations between heads of state, ministers, and generals. More significant, it is an example of how the integrative thrust in Europe can generate momentum in nonpolitical areas when politics does not stand in the way or actually provides a congenial framework. What has developed in the way of Franco-German cooperation and even coordination in the cultural and educational fields has evolved less from mere faithful implementation of the relevant clauses of the 1963 treaty than from the efforts of elements in both countries eager to grasp the opportunity to further the interchange of ideas, cultural values, and people. Each year a third of a million French young people and an equal number of young Germans visit each other's country. Cultural and youth organizations collaborate, savants, technicians, and businessmen forgather, tourism is fostered. Undoubtedly the French and Germans are getting to know each other as no other two peoples of Europe or, for that matter, anywhere.[37]

To return to the political area, the Franco-German relationship has meant little more than going through the motions of being allies. With the coming of the Kiesinger government, there arose the prospect of reviving a meaningful association. Completely apart from its coalition character, it gave evidence of being not merely a new cabinet but something of a new regime. Toward France its tone was immediately more cordial, its general demeanor in international affairs more sophisticated. Certainly Kiesinger wanted to avoid the needless unpleasantness which had come about in part as a result of Schröder's ineptitude in personal relations.[38] Equally, he was vexed about what many Germans thought was the cavalier treatment they had been receiving from the United States in the autumn of 1966, wanted to be less dependent on Washington, and desired more diplomatic elbowroom. It is questionable whether he seriously hoped to restore a real working basis with Paris. No doubt there was much to be gained by a constructive cooperation of the two lands in the EEC. France could also be important in making available to the Federal Republic her influence and channels in Eastern Europe for the critical diplomatic campaign Kiesinger, and especially Brandt, had in mind for that area.

If such were the thoughts of Kiesinger and his ministers when they took office, they were succeeded by sober second ones by the spring and summer of 1967. Though still receptive to the idea of binding the Federal Republic to his chariot wheels, de Gaulle showed no disposition to meet the Germans even part way in order to provide the basis for the limited team operation for which Kiesinger may have hoped.

The future of the Franco-German relationship provides ample scope for wide-ranging speculation. Some believe that Kiesinger was biding his time and keeping the bonds with Paris as intact as possible while awaiting events. As one of his most astute ministers put it to the writer in the summer of 1967, this was the only policy for a country which still pursued the image of a Europe with the supranational features de Gaulle would never accept. Only after de Gaulle had left the helm would it be feasible to revive the French entente with, it was hoped, a more significant role for Germany. She would deal then with a country which, whatever else might be the case, was bound (1) to follow less rigid policies, and (2) to have a weaker government.

It is intriguing to note how fatalistically the French themselves continued to believe that "after de Gaulle" Germany would be the stronger party in any combination restricted to the two countries. The study of elite attitudes cited earlier reveals that Germany was regarded as both actually and potentially more powerful than France; that if "Europe" were left to the care of France and Germany, the latter would assume the dominant role. The most recurrent criticism of Gaullist external policy is that in trying to make a Franco-German alliance the cornerstone of his European program to the exclusion of Britain and the United States, he was underwriting German power and French inferiority.[39] Along the same line, the most telling argument in France against de Gaulle's exclusion of Britain from the Common Market was that, in the long run, it would assure Germany the dominant role in Western Europe. It is noteworthy, however, that in the poll on expectations concerning the continuance of particular Gaullist policies after the General's departure, the strongest expression (49 percent) was of the likelihood of a continuing rapprochement with Germany.[40] This was spelled out in conversations the writer had with many of the respondents to that survey. Since Britain and the United States were likely to be held at arm's length for some time longer (as noted earlier, 48 percent of the respondents expected the continuance of de Gaulle's American policy), Frenchmen were clearly apprehensive about having to deal with a Germany to which France had no or only tenuous links. In other words, if "left alone with Germany" in Europe, it was much better to deal with a closely allied Germany than one operating as an independent power.

If at the current stage we were to evaluate the Franco-German alliance

by its fruits, there would obviously be little to record. One feature that deserves stress is that its proving so much a dud has put a brake not only on
its more beneficent but also on its adverse influences. At one time it promised to open wide the gates of Germany to Gaullism in all of its aspects.
An elaborate alliance structure, intertwining the lives of the two nations
in every area, seemed to assure unrestricted impact. As it turned out, the
alliance was so nearly stillborn and led to so much disenchantment that it
may in sum have worked in the opposite direction. Naturally the example
of the successful strong man next door has not been beneficial to German
democracy. At the same time, the spreading conviction that, except on the
more destructive side, his work may prove exceedingly fleeting has reminded many contemporaries of the weaknesses of authoritarian government.

What spectacular intransigence can gain in the way of attention and
even deference is a lesson that can hardly fail to spur a more national policy in Germany. De Gaulle undoubtedly impressed by giving the self-imposed isolation of France a "splendid" aspect, thus enhancing for Germans the temptation to make a virtue of necessity and take comfort in a
similar position of "independence." The adherents of Gaullism in France
are, of course, reluctant to recognize its implications for Germany. It is a
game no nation can play alone for long and thus automatically becomes
an article for export. Needless to say, this feature is glossed over by those
French news media which are government controlled. An example of
compelling interest and considerable significance occurred during the
spring elections of 1967, when a group of young German visitors were being interviewed over television. When asked about his own particular
dream for Germany, one of the youngsters piped up brightly: "Oh, of
course we want the same things for Germany that de Gaulle is seeking for
France." It was as if a dirty word had been spoken. At this point translation for French listeners came to an abrupt stop.

As a final judgment one can only hold that the Franco-German alliance will in the end go as Europe goes. It has languished mainly because
thus far the West Germans have hesitated to pay the price in terms of
loosening their "European" and "Atlantic" ties. Unfortunately, the Western Alliance, of which these two dreams are integrally a part, seems fated
to continue on a rocky road.

Whither Europe? Whither Atlantica?

"The strength of the Soviets is the weakness of the West." These words
of Fritz Reuter, Berlin's mayor in its most beleaguered days, have lost
much of their impact as the element of fear which originally solidified the
Western Alliance has been losing force. That the Soviets hold to the align-

ment of 83 percent of their forces against Europe and in 1967 announced a substantial increase in their defense budget is largely passed over in confidence that the nuclear stalemate strictly limits their freedom of movement. Moscow also seems to many to have learned that the atmosphere of crisis which it so often engendered boomeranged by uniting the West.

Against this, reminders of other things that should bind the states of the Atlantic area together have fallen more and more on deaf ears. They speak of long-range concerns to which it is easy to render obeisance, but not to the point of overriding the preoccupations of the moment. Paul-Henri Spaak's injunction that if the Soviet menace did not exist it would have to be invented finds all too few echoes.

How can one assess the degree to which Europeans will continue sympathetic to progress toward European integration when circumstances become more favorable? The setbacks of recent years have stalled the previous momentum, detracted from the prestige, and struck a blow at the élan of the movement. There is nothing more difficult than an estimate of the power of an idea which, for the moment, has no prospect of realization. Some have seen a barometer in Jean Monnet's Action Committee for the United States of Europe. Despite the return of de Gaulle to power, this group was riding high at the turn of the sixties. It could boast major achievements in pushing through the negotiation and ratification of the treaties on the Common Market and Euratom. In November 1959 it passed resolutions calling for the merger of the European communities in 1962 and the first direct elections to a European Parliament in 1963. "At that moment," it declared, "the Committee believes that its action should cease."

The Monnet committee had indeed lined up behind it forces which seemed equipped to stand against any opposition. Except for the Communists and Gaullists, it could claim the affiliation of every major party of Europe.[41] These controlled two-thirds of the electorate of the Six. In addition it could count on 70 percent of organized labor and a blue-ribbon list of political leaders in every country. Besides pushing energetically for the final surge toward all-out integration of the Common Market countries, the committee backed the entry of the other Western European nations as well as Atlantic partnership. In America Monnet personally carried such weight with the Kennedy administration that he has been called the most influential foreigner ever to move across the Washington stage.

The vista of a full political blossoming of the EEC and its extension to the outermost borders of Western Europe merged with the "grand design" of John F. Kennedy. The making of "Europe" would coincide with the first concrete step to Atlantica. In 1962 this appeared almost within reach. That a single man would dare to halt work on the edifice at this most critical moment seemed incredible. In Washington there was a tendency to ignore the irritation of European sensitivities caused by American actions, as in the arbitrary cancellation of the skybolt air-to-air missile project and the late 1962 meeting at Nassau between Kennedy and Macmillan with its renewed flaunting of the special Anglo-American relationship. But, as has been seen, there proved to be no effective pressure that could be brought on the man of iron in Paris. The last rear-guard action for "Europe" was fought in 1965 by Walter Hallstein's Common Market Commission, when it asked for increased authority for the European Parliament and a vast revenue, drawn from the common external tariff, to give financial sinews to the merged communities. Actually the merger, projected originally for 1962, did not come off until 1967 — after many compromises, the partial emasculation of the Commission, and the ritual sacrifice of Dr. Hallstein.

Meanwhile the Action Committee, though it still can command political task forces to promote its policies in every land, has been reduced to an exhortatory role. By the end of 1967 (it was established in 1955) it had passed six resolutions calling for the political union of Europe, nine pleading for British membership in the Common Market, and six championing Atlantic partnership. It continues to claim the loyalty of the great majority of the political helmsmen and parties of Europe. But these can hardly influence events more than the governments they command are able to do.[42]

What has been merged are communities which lack much that was embodied in the ambitious designs of a decade earlier. In particular, Euratom is but a shell of what had been conceived for it. As in most such cases, Gaullist France led the way in this enfeebling process, but it is only fair to emphasize that support for her position also came from other EEC quarters. Another of the more inauspicious accompaniments of the merger of the communities was the swiftly following second veto of Britain's entry and thus also of the Outer Seven. The European Free Trade Association, which in recent years had been regarded as little more than a transitional phase before Common Market entry for the Seven, thus was forced to carry on its own limited communal life. In some quarters the chief promise of EFTA lies in its potential as an ultimate haven for the EEC partners should they in desperation try at some juncture for a new economic grouping resigned to proceeding without France.

As matters stood at the end of the 1960's, the merged communities were in something of an impasse. The EEC, for one, in 1967 appeared poised to embark on programs in such areas as science and technology, fiscal reform, and the organization of capital markets. In such endeavors it found its way obstructed by France, always inclined to forestall what seems to her overly ambitious communal action, and the Dutch, fearful that vigorous advances in the EEC at this stage would imply resignation to not enlarging the community. There were also charges from Amsterdam that the French had not only eliminated some of the best "Europeans" from the Commission, or sidetracked them within it, but were well on the way to dominating the Commission themselves.

It should be noted that despite its vicissitudes the EEC continued to exercise much magnetic pull in all of Europe outside the Soviet sphere. No better evidence of this for the period under discussion could be cited than the case of Sweden. By her qualified application for EEC membership in June 1967 she took a significant step away from her uncompromising neutrality, the more impressive since it was the decision of a Social Democratic government that had seemed firmly wedded to neutrality. Clearly, the factors making for long-range coordination of the resources of the Continent continue to operate.

All too obviously, of course, the structural integration of Europe inaugurated by the Treaty of Rome in 1957 had been arrested by the late 1960's. European politics to the greatest extent in the decade were dominated by national states. The extensive 1964 study on elite attitudes in France and Germany demonstrated that nationality remained a stronger determinant than class, age, occupation, party affiliation, religion, and (in most cases) ideology.[43] Notably in the case of France a natural assumption was that the progressive devitalization of ties with her Western associates would further enhance this. Paradoxically, however, there seemed to be a steady decline of resigned acceptance of the predominant role of the individual state. An amazing aspect of the years of most pronounced Gaullist intransigency was the increased readiness to contemplate a "Europe" in which national sovereignties would be severely limited.[44]

Should France at some not too distant date reverse her policies more swiftly and drastically than anyone holds likely, it would obviously not be possible to take up where things had left off in 1963. National patterns have become more set, new interests have arisen and become vested, shaken faiths must be restored. The necessary input in the economic, political, and emotional areas would have to be much greater.

What are realistic expectations on repairing the sadly frayed Atlantic ties? Though some may hold that Europeans in the future are more likely to find their way to union on their own, the weight of argument still favors the view that their success, as heretofore, will depend largely on the support and encouragement afforded them by the United States. Those who have tried to pry themselves and others loose from Washington in recent years have thereby pried Europeans loose from one another. No one doubts that in every European country there is a conviction that its destiny is less closely linked with the United States than in the bad days of the Cold War. On the two sides of the Atlantic the peoples are more Europe-centered or North America-centered. What remains to be determined is the strength of this feeling.

On this issue there is a wide range of opinion on both sides of the water. It is interesting to note the confusion which existed even before Vietnam developments obscured the many other factors which bore on the problem. An apt illustration of this is the extraordinary ambivalence of French elite opinion in 1964 on future relations with the United States. Although nearly one-half the respondents expected the continuance of anti-American policies "after de Gaulle," the group opted three to one for the United States as "principal ally" over Britain and two to one over Germany. Eighty-seven percent believed that France would share a long-term common interest with the United States, the EEC countries collectively scoring only one percentage point more.[45]

It appears safe to assume that if, despite a steady diet of anti-American strictures, such a substantial core of sentiment favoring long-range alignment with the United States remains in France, the feeling in other countries would be correspondingly more favorable, though the Vietnam issue obliges us to be cautious. In Germany, for example, the sense of common interest with the United States scored nearly three to one over France or Britain and still more than two to one against the EEC nations collectively.[46] In the experience of the present writer, the belief in a long-term common interest with the United States finds expression in all parts of Western Europe, even among the most vocal railers against the American war in Vietnam.

The more fateful decisions on Europe which the United States must make in the years immediately ahead concentrate about (1) the measure of its continued support of European integrative trends, and (2) the extent and form in which it should further promote transatlantic ties. In view of American frustrations of recent years the unquestioned backing that formerly was forthcoming from the United States whenever European integration was on the march can no longer be taken for granted. Whatever judgment can be formed about continued support for integration must come largely from deduction based on long-term interests rather than from passing trends. It would help if one could measure the extent to which the absorption in Southeast Asia has distracted America from Europe. Then, if this incubus were removed, one could estimate the effect of reviving American concern in terms of contemporary realities in the Atlantic scene. There is every likelihood that in the economic, social, and cultural fields the interest of the Atlantic peoples in each other will continue to mount. The mid-sixties saw a stepped-up interchange in goods, ideas, habits of life and thought, educational experience, the products of science and scholarship, and the peoples of the West themselves in their tens of millions. The "American invasion" of Europe has reached unprecedented heights on innumerable fronts and movement of every type within the Continent itself is accelerating at a similar pace. At the very moment that old national barriers seem to be reappearing, barriers are crumbling away in other fields. Political institution building on the international plane has been left far behind, but it may have a more congenial climate in which to operate once progress can be resumed.

The Place of NATO

The fate of the Western Alliance will continue of necessity to be closely interwoven with that of NATO, which has suffered the worst blow accorded the existing instruments of Atlantic cooperation. There is no escaping the verdict that its prestige, membership, and efficacy as a defensive system have retrogressed during the last decade. Undeniably this was in some measure unavoidable insofar as its role as a purely military instrument was concerned. In that sense, as Pompidou has put it, "NATO was a child of the Cold War." But much that has occurred to its detriment since 1958 could not be classified as preordained. It was not inevitable that it should suffer the calamitous departure of France, which, after Germany, was its most vital European component. And it is at least conceivable that, given more fortunate circumstances, it could have become in other than military ways the principal medium for the evolution of Atlantic institutions. For both the disengagement of France and the failure to make progress toward attaining its potential as a political organism, it seems a safe guess that history will lay responsibility at the door of Charles de Gaulle. We need only let his own words speak for him. Referring to his 1958 memorandum to President Eisenhower in which he proposed a troika directorate for NATO of the United States, Britain, and France, he said a few months later (March 1959):

> The memorandum of 1958 was but an instrument of diplomatic pressure. I was looking for a way out of the Atlantic Alliance and a way to regain freedom which had been alienated by the Fourth Republic when the NATO Treaty was signed.
>
> So I asked for the moon. I knew I would not get it. . . . They [the Anglo-Americans] made it possible to take steps towards leaving the Atlantic Alliance and I could not have done this if, first, I had not been turned down. In fact that is what we have been doing since 1958. We are no longer there; we are present without being there.[47]

To pass over the painful story and view only the consequences, these include the downgrading of the integrated NATO command, the thinning out of the integrated forces due to economy drives in Britain, Germany, and the United States, and the somewhat anomalous continuance of non-integrated (i.e., French) forces in the front lines of Western defense. The departure of France also did much more than tear a hole in a previously solid geographic defense block. NATO lost a vital backup area and an important part of its flanking position on the Mediterranean, the latter almost coincidentally with the appearance of an increasingly more formidable Soviet naval presence in that previously Western sea. Despite continuing as nominally a member of the Alliance, de Gaulle built a position in which France had an option to be neutral or fight in the event of war in Europe. Thus it was impossible not only to use French territory in the development and maintenance of the Western defense system, but also to reckon on it in planning for an actual conflict. There was further the loss of over one billion dollars' worth of installations which, as General Lemnitzer pointed out to the writer, obviously would not have been put into France in the first instance if she had not appeared the most suitable place for them. One need think only of the forty-six airfields involved to gauge the impact of the NATO pullout.

France's falling out of line created a solid tier of unavailable territory (Austria, Switzerland, France) between the northern and southern blocks of NATO countries. The most serious consequence of this was the handicap it imposed on the "Ace Mobile Force," that body of elite troops formed to act as a fire brigade to be rushed to any endangered spot. Though de Gaulle late in 1967 again increased to one year the grant of overflight rights (he somewhat earlier had restricted them to one month at a time), these could not be depended upon in planning for a crisis or wartime situation — under such a condition, it had to be assumed, movement from northern to southern Europe might well require that planes make a leg out into the Atlantic and come in eastward via Gibraltar. This innovation was especially disconcerting in view of the Soviet appearance in the Mediterranean in the second half of 1967, creating thereby a whole new category of Western defense problems.

One cannot conclude this sober recital without some consideration of the effect on morale of French withdrawal. The fact that a major participant in the Western defense system could depart in so cavalier a fashion, and do so with apparent impunity, shook confidence and raised many doubts. Before French withdrawal the indefinite continuance of NATO had been pretty much taken for granted. The fact that debates on continued affiliation could start in a number of countries (notably Norway and Denmark) in 1966 and that there was a certain girding for wider discussion in 1969 speaks volumes for this. As one NATO administrator sadly put it, there is now just so much more possibility of other states at least hinting at leaving whenever they perceive some cause for discontent. It was, of course, bracing when the fourteen who remained after the French departure held firm in 1967 and when the move out of France, superbly handled by General Lemnitzer, took place with so much dignity and at a cost much below estimates.

Some will argue that these features should cause no excessive dismay in that NATO had by the mid-sixties gone well beyond achieving its military *raison d'être*, stability and security in Europe. They wonder whether the price of French withdrawal in military terms was not worth paying in order to achieve the removal of obstructions to much overdue repair and extension of the Alliance. Though there are many differences in definition, there has long been agreement that much about NATO has become outdated. Agitation for developing NATO along political, economic, and cultural lines is as old as the organization itself and such development did, in fact, form part of the original blueprint. There has been no lack of urging this goal or of specific proposals from within the NATO countries themselves.[48] The high point of such pressures was reached in December 1961, when delegates meeting under the chairmanship of former Secretary of State Christian Herter issued a "Declaration of Paris" listing far-reaching proposals of this order.

Unfortunately the unhappy conjunction of a low state of élan in NATO and the preoccupation of the United States elsewhere has inhibited an energetic attack on this problem. Though final judgments remain to be made, one of the brightest hopes of the NATO reformers, a committee formed at the initiative of Belgian Foreign Minister Harmel to probe all sides of this question, did not seem to promise very significant results when it reported late in 1967. Growls from Paris at a time when prospects looked bright in the autumn of that year and the desire to "keep the door open" to France played a part here. The fear of offending the French especially played a role in such countries as Denmark, concerned as it is with securing membership in or some association with the Common Market. Thus the long shadow from Paris continued to exercise its somber influence despite the fact that France no longer belonged to the organization.

French elite opinion, in 1964, was less than 23 percent expectant that the current policy toward NATO would continue without de Gaulle.[49] This, however, antedated events which in 1966–67 put more firmly the stamp of finality on matters. At that time the conversation of those who responded in 1964 betokened matter-of-fact resignation. The NATO issue looked like a closed book after the vast apparatus of the Alliance in France had been shut down or moved out. Perhaps least reconciled were the French soldiers, who retained nostalgic memories of the superb comradeship of their NATO experience and doubted the realism of de Gaulle's military policies. A sign of their eagerness not to lose touch was their assiduity in fostering the last links that remained to them — the ties, however formal, between them and the Germans in the special alliance relationship and in the presence of French forces in Germany.[50]

Was it wise to move the NATO Council to Brussels? Many in the NATO secretariat and in the foreign ministries scattered over Europe continue to doubt it. They argue that it eased de Gaulle's task of making the break appear complete, that Paris enjoys a very special prestige that rubs off on whatever is headquartered there, and that the United States was too concerned about the effect on its own prestige in staying under so inhospitable a roof. Critics of American NATO policies discover here additional evidence to substantiate the French charge that, when it comes to the vital decisions, Washington acts on the basis of its own national interests at the cost of those of the community.

There is much that has occurred in NATO affairs that deserves far more attention than can be given here. It is impossible to do more than allude to the perennial disputations over defense doctrine. A basic cleavage resulted from the reaction of the Kennedy administration to the second Berlin crisis. The building up of American ground forces in Europe enabled the United States to dispense with the doctrine of massive retaliation, which the nuclear stalemate had done much to outdate in any event, and to turn to the concept of a "measured" or "flexible" response. This approach led to part of the difficulties with France, which clung to the former doctrine. It also led to considerable uneasiness in Germany, which remains far from allayed. But with France out of the way the doctrine was given official NATO blessing in December 1967, ironically enough regarded by many as the eve of an era in which progressive reduction of American forces in Europe would gradually render it out of date.

From many soldiers is heard the charge that there has been a certain "re-nationalization" of spirit and decision making in NATO councils. Despite the admiration of most of them for the abilities of former Secretary of Defense McNamara, they accuse him of having acted to the detriment of NATO in transferring into Alliance affairs the "civil revolution" he had carried out with success in the Pentagon. The argument is that in shifting planning from the military to the civil side, more national views have come to prevail. American military leaders who had learned their lesson under Eisenhower in World War II and in SHAPE had succeeded in instilling into their international staffs a comradeship and esprit de corps that made them truly the "integrated men" of NATO. General Norstad in particular was credited by his non-American comrades-in-arms with having "Europeanized" himself to a point where he thoroughly understood the viewpoints of his NATO associates and did not hesitate to interpret and defend them before his own government. Such, it is charged, is not the attitude of the civilian representatives of the NATO states, who conceive of themselves essentially as ambassadors of their own countries and approach all decisions from a multilateral rather than an integrated standpoint. To their rising influence is ascribed the "internal decline" of NATO as an organization.[51]

France and the Defense of the West

After the great trek of NATO structural and intrastructural elements out of France in 1967, it would seem that de Gaulle for a time had run out of opportunities for springing sensations on his allies. Yet before the year was out he delivered a final one in the shape of an article by Chief of Staff Ailleret in the *Revue de Défense Nationale.*[52] It goes without saying that no such sweeping declaration of defense doctrine could come from any source other than de Gaulle himself.

In the past, said General Ailleret, France had, in turn, as her "preferred eventual enemies" the British, the Germans, and the Soviets. All influences, he argued, now inclined Moscow toward peace for the foreseeable future. No one could foretell what the world situation would be like in twenty years, but one thing certain was that all parts of the globe would be menaced by nuclear missiles. France, deprived until now by her membership in the American-dominated Western Alliance of a balanced defense system, clearly needed a nuclear deterrent under her own control. In effect, the article was another ringing declaration of independence for France in defense matters and an argument for global striking capabilities.

Though the American public was too preoccupied to take much notice, the appearance of this policy declaration was front-page news in the Federal Republic. If France was really moving in the direction of a 360-degree perimeter defense system, what remained of the common front against the Soviet Union which justified the continuance of French forces in Germany? There was already an obvious contradiction between such continuance and France quitting the NATO organization. This had been glossed over because of German eagerness to keep France as committed as possible; the presence of French soldiers also gave a reassuring feeling of continued good relations with Paris. Now it was just that much more difficult to find a logical way to reconcile so stark a repudiation of a United Western front with French forces east of the Rhine. For some days Bonn hummed like a hive of disturbed bees.[53]

Ailleret's first statement was quickly followed by a second in the same periodical in February 1968, by a speech by de Gaulle in late January at the Centre des Hautes Etudes Militaires, by sundry inspired articles in *Le Monde,* and by leaks on what Defense Minister Messmer was to say during a visit to Moscow. Thus the world was put on extensive notice that de Gaulle was dedicating his last years to this wide-ranging nuclear program. On his aims it had already been informed for the better part of a decade. In November 1959 he had proclaimed at Saint-Cyr that, since France could conceivably be destroyed from any quarter of the globe, her nuclear force must be capable of reaching every part of it.[54] Such words, spoken when the French were still up to the ears in their Algerian muddle, seemed then to have a quixotic ring. But it is scarcely necessary to review how much of the program has already approached reality.

But could it be labeled realistic? In terms of accomplishing the task he set for himself and for France, performance to the late sixties argued that the goal was attainable. The most serious doubts were on the financial side in view of increasing stringencies, the rising demands for the *force de frappe*, and the extra $1.5 billion a year the missile program would swallow (at current prices) throughout the seventies. Accomplishment, let it be granted, is but a matter of national will. But to what extent has de Gaulle bequeathed to others his own iron determination? Will the French accept the implications in the form of stark isolationism? Will future defense doctrine support such an imbalance of forces at the cost of the army and navy? Where are the empty spaces for the emplacement of ICBMs? [55] These are but a few of the infinity of prickly questions with which France is confronted in her long-range nuclear policy.[56]

Of greatest concern have been the implications of the Gaullist nuclear program for the existing Western and potential European security systems. There is no perceivable prospect of reconciling de Gaulle's plans with past concepts of how the West can best be defended. As for a purely European defensive order along Gaullist lines, the only possibility would lie in his own 1963 formula of a tight Franco-German association with a strict division of function along nuclear and conventional lines. To this the Germans seem even less inclined to reconcile themselves than they were at that time. There remains the hope of a future change of heart in Paris in the form of a return to the idea of a basically European security system in which the French and British establishments would form the core for a communal force. This solution, in the view of the present writer the only acceptable one for the long pull, depends, of course, on a vigorous resumption of the drive toward European political unity, such as does not appear in the offing for the foreseeable future.

Conclusion

Many times in recent years those who are dedicated to building "Europe" have sought ways to do so without the support of France, only to abandon such a thought in quick order. Not only is France indispensable as a participant; she is almost equally indispensable as a leader. By geography, history, and cultural tradition she is uniquely equipped for such a mission. If only by process of elimination, this role, if she would but accept it, would fall to her. Britain has been too diverted from the mainstream of Continental affairs by centuries of following the call beyond the oceans; Germany lies under the curse of the recent past; Italy is too peripheral and too lacking in dynamism and sinew. From the Duke of Sully to the Abbé de Saint-Pierre, from Léon Bourgeois to Aristide Briand, French names are linked with the European ideal. In the postwar period itself, France could point to the Schuman Plan, the European Defense Community (though finally repudiated by its makers), and the brilliant pioneering of the grandest "European" of all, Jean Monnet.

Charles de Gaulle, a man of extraordinary force and genius, would have had no difficulty assuming the role of federator. As Jacques Duhamel put it wryly, his quarrel with the General was that he was "too modest": the nations would have been delighted to hail him as the first president of the United States of Europe.[57] Had he been willing to become the voice of Europe rather than of France, no one could have contested this distinction with him. With the United States pursuing its goals in distant Vietnam and neglecting its European knitting, it would not have been much of a problem for him to be acknowledged also as the voice of the West.

This was not the path he elected to travel. Instead he strove to block the road at every point that promised to lead to significant institutional growth on either a European or an Atlantic level. In consequence, many resigned themselves to the belief that the best hope for the immediate future lay in the steady advance of integrative trends outside of the political and military arcas. They pointed to the harmonization of education and of social institutions, the progress of every type of cultural exchange, and, especially, the many forms of greater economic interdependence. Even de Gaulle appeared to become increasingly the prisoner of economic forces, a process accentuated by the situation created by the 1968 internal crisis. In effect, and there are many who believe this, he had reached in some areas a point of no return.[58] In evidence is cited the accommodation French policy had to make to circumstances during the Kennedy Round negotiations.

The degree of truth in this could not be determined unless someone was willing to take the risks involved in putting the matter to test. Instead it was de Gaulle who most often seemed to use economic and psychological levers against his Common Market partners. An illustration of this may be seen in German efforts to make progress toward British entry into the Common Market. In mid-February 1968 Chancellor Kiesinger, meeting with de Gaulle, secured acceptance in principle of the eventual enlargement of the EEC and an agreement to negotiate an interim tariff arrangement with the British that would be a move toward a free-trade area. In return, Kiesinger agreed to a Franco-German declaration stating that, though Britain had made a worthwhile beginning toward qualifying for membership, she was still far from eligibility. The emptiness of what de Gaulle had yielded became clear on February 29 in Brussels, when the foreign ministers of the Six met to take up the "interim arrangement." Couve de Murville, who presided, immediately stated that there was no question of eliminating industrial tariffs and that Britain would have to pay for even limited concessions by purchasing Common Market farm products. Couve later was quoted as remarking cynically that one could now begin work on a 10 percent tariff reduction on certain British products, "but even the negotiations alone will take three to five years." [59]

Thus up to the time of de Gaulle's departure from power, France had succeeded in circumscribing the scope and significance of Common Market activities to a far greater extent than the Common Market had been able to put restraints on France. The restriction in the development of the Coal and Steel Community and of Euratom dealt with elsewhere in this volume,[60] the sidetracking of the project for a European University, the fading hope for the fiscal independence of the Commission, and the interruption of progress toward the political development of the EEC are part of this story. It was symbolized in the petty treatment of Dr. Hallstein, the best claimant after Jean Monnet to the name of "Mr. Europe," when he was denied a role of dignity at the tenth-anniversary meeting in May 1967 commemorating the Treaty of Rome.

At the opening of 1969 there was no avoiding the hard fact that on issue after issue pertaining to the Western Alliance a stage of stalemate had been reached. In one of the most fluid periods of world history there existed the paradox of suspended animation in a state of flux. Thus, in an era so pregnant with events that one could almost feel the birth pangs, there was a kind of stabilization of uncertainties, with nothing much likely to happen before one or more of three major developments: the departure from power of the French president; the end, or something like it, of the American involvement in Vietnam; the appearance on the Western scene of a statesman of stature who was ready, like de Gaulle, to cut through to essentials and prepared, like him, to show an unbending will to prevail.

None of these developments had appeared anywhere in sight as 1968 became 1969. What occurred so soon thereafter emphasizes once more the uncertainty of the world in which we live; the most unheralded and unexpected train of events may suddenly confront us. To think only of France for the moment, no one dreamed in the early spring of 1968 that a semi-revolutionary situation could arise there in a matter of weeks. Almost exactly a year later came the departure of de Gaulle from power at a time and under circumstances that were even more surprising.

Despite exclamations of wonder and a general feeling akin to incredulous awe, this event, whose probable import had for years been the subject of universal debate, had few immediate international repercussions. One was almost inclined to say as had Talleyrand of the death of Napoleon: "This is not an event, it is news." The explanation is that the retirement of de Gaulle, though little expected, did not for the time being lead to unexpected results. In strict accord with predictions, French poli-

cy underwent no startling changes. Also, as could have been equally predicted, outside pressures for change proved less compelling than the ha-
bitual laments about de Gaulle's policies might have led one to anticipate.
Once he was out of the picture, other factors which had worked quietly in
line with his intentions had to be more fully acknowledged. In many quarters he had been a convenient alibi for not moving more vigorously in
areas where there were doubts and second thoughts.

In short, de Gaulle's political demise could not by itself provide the
new point of departure of which the West stands so much in need. At the
moment, no one is prepared to offer any larger European or Atlantic programs or conceptions, least of all in Washington. Yet, though the time is
hardly ripe for great initiatives, the United States need not confine itself
to marking time. It cannot afford to lose sight of the fundamental maxims
on which its policy in Europe must continue to base itself. The situation as
it was developing in the second half of 1969 offered much in the way of a
more favorable climate for American initiatives than had prevailed for
half a decade. In a number of ways American stock was once more rising
on the European bourse. The fading out of the Johnson administration,
the evidences of serious American efforts to end the involvement in Vietnam, and the shock of the Soviet action in Czechoslovakia all served to
reduce anti-American sentiment.

Other factors may assert themselves more fully or reveal themselves
more clearly. Much can change as the result of the expansion of the Soviet
presence in the Mediterranean. Within the southern tier of NATO, and not
only there, it could become a source of anxiety as serious as the threat on
the Elbe used to be.[61] And, as will be dealt with more fully in the final
chapter of this volume, there are many and continuing aspects of the Soviets' Prague adventure that have their echoes in the West.

Doubtless some of the major challenges to American policy in the
months and years ahead will continue to lie in the dealings of the United
States with France. Policy makers will now have more flexibility so far as
American popular sentiment is concerned. Americans forget easily and, to
whatever degree their resentments against de Gaulle turned also against
the French nation, no enduring impress seems to have been left. The immediate jump after de Gaulle's resignation in the consumption of French
wines and of French tour bookings is evidence of this.

In several ways the American problems with France may be most effectively attacked by indirection. As former President Gronchi of Italy
said to the writer, we should promote all developments that make it difficult for the French to stay by themselves. This will at times prove the exact
opposite of "going slow" to spare the prejudices of whoever rules at Paris.
Like other peoples, the French are most likely to feel attracted to Western
institutions which are going impressively forward.

On the French side, the realities of the international scene are likely to prevail more and more over programs which, however determinedly pursued under de Gaulle, never enjoyed more than hesitant national backing. It has been noted that grim economic necessities threatened to make a prisoner even of de Gaulle. These and other factors, in fairly short order, can make a shambles of the program of "defense in all directions" and thus of some of the basic conceptions on which French policy has been based. A methodical review of French policy can also restore awareness of what, under de Gaulle, was studiously ignored — that there is no greater service to the West than to promote the European idea in Germany. The measure in which he reacts constructively to this verity should be the supreme test by which any Western statesman of the present and future will deserve to stand or fall.

CHAPTER 4

The Course of Economic Integration

BY JOHN G. TURNBULL

A CAPSULE summary of the state of affairs in European economic integration, as they appeared in the years 1965–68, would include the following:

Formal organizations existed — the European Economic Community, the European Free Trade Association, the Benelux Economic Union, the European Coal and Steel Community, the European Atomic Energy Community, and, in the East, Comecon, all were in being. Europe *had* organized itself.

If the two primary organizations of Western Europe — the EEC and EFTA — are singled out, considerable accomplishments may be noted in the way of economic integration. To cite but two examples, EFTA reached its goal of selective tariff abolition by December 31, 1966, three years ahead of schedule; the EEC, with a much broader list of tariffs, did the same on July 1, 1968, a year and a half ahead of schedule.

Economic growth in Western Europe in the period 1950–65 had been at high levels — indeed higher than the United States for much of the period. Yet as 1965 passed, stresses developed and for both the short-term future and the longer run a variety of problems loomed on the horizon.

Notwithstanding accomplishments, a kind of psychological lassitude appeared within the various organizations in the late 1960's, the pace of development slackened, and there was a degree of concern about the future that did not exist in the early 1960's.

Given this backdrop, the analysis which follows will center on three topics: (1) What has been the nature and economic impact of Western European movements toward integration? (2) In evaluating the contemporary scene (1965–68) what problem areas should be viewed as important? Why? (3) What might be said about the pattern of future developments? What are the implications of European economic integration for other economies, particularly that of the United States?

While detailed consideration will be given in the pages that follow to certain relevant issues such as the technology gap and the capital markets problem, the discussion is not intended to provide an analysis in depth of these or other special issues; rather a synthesis of these developments will be sought.[1]

A Framework for Analyzing Economic Integration

Of the many dimensions in the process of integration, it is the economic that is under discussion in this chapter, and within that dimension primarily the structural component. EFTA and the EEC are examples, at the highest level, of structural integration; they are superstructures of integration. Within these superstructures, additional structural integration is required and it is at this level that attention will be focused.

Structural integration, as that concept is used here, may be viewed as consisting of two major types: integration of institutions and integration of policies. The following examples illustrate these two types. If a group of nations (say, members of the EEC) were to create a single central bank (in place of one for each country), a structural change would have taken place, a new and single institution (without much loss of precision one can visualize an organization, a bank, as an institution) would have replaced the old, individual entities. This is one type of integration. Or integration may come about in another way. Institutions like banks, in the day-to-day pursuit of their goals, devise and implement policies designed to attain these goals. Thus, the central bank of a given country adopts certain policies so as to maintain a stable price level. If several such central banks coordinate their policies, integration may be considered to have been achieved. Integration of policies can take place without institutional integration; the central banks in the illustration at hand can still maintain their separate organizational identities. But if the institutions themselves integrate, their policies are necessarily integrated. When speaking of policies, as noted earlier, "coordination" and "harmonization" are more commonly used terms than "integration." Reference herein, therefore, will be to the integration of institutions and the coordination or harmonization of policies.

If nations seek to integrate economically, what are the areas which require the development of integrated institutions and coordinated policies? The answer depends, of course, in large measure upon the degree to which they wish to integrate; upon the kind of accommodation they visualize. What is required of a free-trade area, such as EFTA, is much less than that demanded by an organization which seeks to go considerably farther: the EEC, for example. The latter will serve as a useful prototype for discussion here.

In a framework of integration such as the EEC is seeking to develop, cultural attitudes toward economic activity are basic: attitudes toward entrepreneurship and work, to mention but two specifics. Integration may not require harmonization of opposing attitudes; there may already be a common pattern. But, as already suggested in Chapter 1, the purposes, or consequences, of economic integration may necessitate a *change* in existing common attitudes. Thus, increasing business enterprise competition — a consequence of the formation of the EEC — appears to be a compelling force toward the development of a more favorable climate for entrepreneurship and managerial motivation.

When one turns to the integration of institutions, both the public and private sectors must be considered. One could visualize a spectrum along which institutions are arrayed in terms of the ease or difficulty of integration, given contemporary attitudes and convictions. "Complete" integration in the public sector would appear to call for, using the example noted previously, a single central bank and a common currency. Integration to this extent does not appear realizable in the near future in Western Europe. At the other end of the spectrum, one might visualize in the private sector a community "company" under Italian direction, using a German patent, and securing its capital in France. Such a situation does not yet exist either, but it is under active discussion and likely to be realized much sooner than, say, a single central bank. Additional examples of such types of institutional integration come easily to mind.

In the harmonization of policies, again there are both public and private sectors to be taken into account. In the public sector, policies often may be more aptly characterized as regulations; in the private sector this is less often the case. Policies (and regulations) cover the entire gamut of economic activity. In the public sector one finds, for example, government concern with monetary and fiscal policy, with the regulation of competition, with policies on patents and their issuance. In the private sector, business enterprises develop and apply policies on manpower use, on marketing, and on research, to cite but a few cases.

The need to harmonize such policies, especially in the public sector, arises for several reasons. For one, economic efficiency is lessened if, instead of a common code, each country in the integrated unit has its own rules and regulations with which cross-national business enterprises must comply. For another, an aim of integration is to minimize competitive distortions; this is not possible if there are differential advantages dependent upon the rules and regulations of the particular country in which the enterprise finds itself located.

In summary, then, economic activity involves institutions (organizations) adopting specified policies to achieve certain goals and existing in an environment in which cultural, social, and other mores are relevant. One purpose of integration is to alter institutions structurally and to harmonize policies, all with the intent of improving economic performance. In the process, the cultural setting may likewise (have to) undergo a transformation.

Against this background, selected descriptive and comparative statements may be made about the economies of Western Europe and the United States:

Cultural attitudes toward entrepreneurship, innovation, and competition appear more supportive of economic performance in the United States than in Europe. Whether American culture should be characterized as more materialistic, which in itself favors economic activity, is a matter for speculation.

In the United States economic institutions are integrated to a considerable degree. There is a single "central bank," a common currency, an integrated capital market (or at least interlocked markets), and so on. The same is not true for Europe.

The degree of policy harmonization in the United States is much higher than in Europe. Regulation of business enterprise, labor legislation, economic security programming, and regulation in a host of other areas provide examples. It is true, of course, that total harmonization (however that be defined) does not exist in the United States. Witness but one example: varying state tax policies as they affect business enterprise operation. But compared with Europe the level of harmonization is indeed high.[2]

(One should not infer, however, that this economic framework is the only or even necessarily the primary factor influencing economic performance. The availability of natural resources, including the man-land ratio, and the nature and extent of government policies are two of many additional factors that come to mind. Nevertheless the over-all framework is important and one that Europe is seeking to modify.)

Economic Organization and Economic Performance

Two conclusions appear from the foregoing discussion: First, economic principles suggest that the over-all framework within which economic activity takes place in the United States is more favorable than is that of Europe. Second, the thrust of European integration is toward the development of a framework more similar to that of the United States than to that of Europe of the past. The elimination of tariff barriers, the creation of common institutions, the harmonization of policies all attest to this.

Given these conclusions, one would infer that the differentials described would favor economic performance in the United States, and that, by a measure such as real income per capita, the United States would be better off than Europe. Such indeed is the case. This may be noted in several ways.

In 1960, per capita real national income in seven northwest European countries was 69 percent as large as that in the United States if U.S. price weights were used (or 54 percent, with European price weights). Were Europe set at unity, per capita real national income in the United States was 45 percent higher than in Europe using U.S. price weights; 85 percent higher using European weights.[3] (The technicalities of these price-weight elements need not blur the significance of the conclusions: the per capita real income of the United States is significantly higher than Europe's.) Another way of putting it is to say that in 1960 Western European national income per person employed was at a level which had been reached by the United States in 1925 — thirty-five years earlier.[4]

If, however, one looks at the data for the period 1950–65, one finds that increases in the production of goods and services, as measured by average annual increases in real output, were higher for the EEC countries than for the United States, and almost as high for EFTA countries as for the United States. These data lead to a series of questions, the discussion of which will constitute the major portion of this chapter.

Economic growth is a complex issue in terms of its nature and dimensions, its importance, and its causes.[5] First, it may be defined in various ways: increase in the flow of total economic output during a given period; increase in output per head or per worker; increase in consumption per head; increase in personal welfare; changes in economic structure; movement through the stages of economic development. Second, growth is desirable for many reasons, all of which relate, however, to the stability of an economy, to the economic well-being of its people, and to the ability of the economy to compete internationally and to discharge its responsibilities to other nations, particularly the developing economies. Finally, the causes of growth are many and diverse; those relevant to recent developments in Western Europe are examined below.

Table 1 summarizes the comparative growth patterns for Western Europe and the United States, 1955–65. The table indicates that for the decade 1955–65, Western Europe outperformed the United States (and the same would hold approximately true for the fifteen-year period 1950–65). It was earlier suggested that the American economic framework was innately more conducive to higher-level economic performance than was Europe's and, indeed, over the long run, the American performance has been superior to the European. Then why in the decade 1955–65 did output increase at faster rates in Europe than in the United States? And if

Table 1. Average Annual Percentage Increases in Gross National Product at
Constant Prices for Selected Countries

Country	Increase in Aggregate Gross National Product			Increase in Per Capita Gross National Product		
	1955–60	1960–65	1955–65	1955–60	1960–65	1955–65
Germany (F.R.)....	6.3%	4.8%	5.6%	5.1%	3.5%	4.3%
France	4.8	5.1	5.0	3.7	2.7	3.7
Italy	5.7	5.5	5.6	5.0	4.7	4.8
Netherlands	4.1	5.0	4.5	2.7	3.6	3.2
Belgium	2.5	4.9	3.7	1.9	4.2	3.0
Luxembourg	...	...	...	...	...	...
EEC	5.2ᵃ	5.1ᵃ	5.2	4.3	3.9	4.1
United Kingdom....	2.8	3.4	3.1	2.2	2.6	2.4
Norway	3.2	5.4	4.3	2.3	4.6	3.5
Sweden	3.3	5.0	4.2	2.7	4.3	3.5
Denmark	4.7	5.0	4.8	4.0	4.2	4.1
Switzerland	4.0	5.2	4.6	2.4	3.1	2.8
Austria	5.2	4.1	4.7	5.0	3.5	4.2
Portugal	4.5	6.3	5.4	4.0	5.5	4.8
EFTA	3.2	4.0	3.6	2.6	3.1	2.9
Greece	5.2	8.7	6.9	4.3	8.1	6.2
Turkey	5.2	4.3	4.7	2.2	1.3	1.8
Finland	4.1	5.1	4.6	3.1	4.3	3.7
United States.......	2.2	4.7	3.4	0.5	3.2	1.8
Canada	3.4	5.5	4.4	0.7	3.6	2.1
Japan	9.6	9.7	9.6	8.6	8.6	8.6

SOURCE: Statistical Office of the European Communities, *Basic Statistics of the Community* (Brussels: EEC, 1966), Table 14.
    ᵃ Subsequent figures indicate 5.3 and 4.9 respectively.

Europe did as well as it did, why the concern about European economies which seemed to be widespread in the period 1965–68 (during which this research was undertaken)? These issues merit further analysis.

"Growth," as that term is used here, refers to an increase in the economic capacity or potential that can generate increases in actual output. However, an increase in actual output may arise from two sources: the underlying growth rate may be the basis (that is, new capacity, such as new and more efficient plants, may be added); or unused capacity may be taken up and utilized (plants which were only partially used are more fully utilized). Both sources can, of course, contribute during any given time period. When an increase in output arises from an increase in the utilization of capacity it is customary to use the term "expansion." [6] Hence three concepts should be kept in mind: increases in output (the result), growth, and expansion (the causal factors leading to the result).

If one looks more closely at the European and American output patterns for 1950–65, the following become evident. For Europe, the increases in output closely approximated the underlying growth rate; there was little in the way of unused capacity and hence expansion was not a major factor. For the United States, unused capacity developed in 1955–60, and output increases in 1960–65 resulted in part from taking up that slack.[7] Therefore, a first explanation for the European performance arises out of the difference in the degree of utilization of capacity: Europe operating at close to full capacity during the period in question, the United States not so operating. This conclusion, however, needs to be interpreted with caution. It would appear possible, depending upon comparative technologies, for an economy operating consistently at less than full capacity still to maintain annual increases in output equivalent to or even greater than another economy operating at capacity levels. But if an economy which was operating at capacity moves to a stage in which the given unused capacity becomes larger, one could expect its output increases to become smaller. This is what happened in the United States in 1955–60, as Table 2 illustrates. In essence, the United States performance was as it was because after 1955 and through the early 1960's unemployment increased markedly and remained high, the level of utilization of resources declined, and hence so did annual increases in output. This was not true for Europe.[8] The Council of Economic Advisers in the United States was cognizant of this relationship between unused capacity and increases in output. For example, it noted: "The cumulative excess of potential output [that is, full-employment or capacity output] over actual output in the period 1958–62 totals $170 billions (1962 prices) or nearly $1,000 a person." [9]

But this explanation leaves unanswered two other questions: why did

Table 2. Average Annual Percentage Increases in Gross National Product at Constant Prices Compared with Unemployment Rates (Five-Year Annualized Percentage Averages)[a] for the EEC, EFTA, and the United States

Unit	1950–55	1955–60	1960–65
EEC			
GNP increase	6.7%	5.3%	4.9%
Unemployment	3.0	3.0	3.0
EFTA			
GNP increase	3.1	3.2	4.0
Unemployment	3.0	3.0	3.0
United States			
GNP increase	4.3	2.2	4.5
Unemployment	3.8	5.3	5.5

SOURCE: OECD, *Economic Growth, 1960–1970* (Paris: OECD, 1966), Table V.
    [a] Unemployment estimates were made by the author. For EFTA and the EEC the unemployment estimates are the most conservative he could develop given the difficulties of making comparisons. The GNP figures vary slightly from those in Table 1 because of a different source.

Europe operate closer to capacity and what other factors were relevant in the pattern of performance?

The answer to the first question is the more easily disposed of here. Western European economies appear to have operated closer to capacity for two reasons: "inherent" factors — to be examined shortly — which provided an impetus for high-level economic activity; and a willingness of governments to use policies designed to effectuate capacity performance.[10] (Why this willingness is a matter upon which the reader may wish to speculate: in no small measure the answer is to be found in the economic philosophy of the parties in power.)

The second question is much more complex; indeed, Edward F. Denison utilizes nearly 500 double-columned pages in his path-breaking analysis of the factors in European economic performance. Basically, however, two factors contribute to output increases: increases in the quantity and quality of inputs and increases in the quantity of output per unit of input. Increases in inputs imply increases in the quantity of the factors of production (land, labor, capital), as well as such increases in quality as the level of education of the worker and hence of the labor input. Output per unit of input may increase for a number of reasons: (1) advances in technological and managerial knowledge, (2) increasingly more efficient allocation of resources, (3) reductions of obstacles imposed by governments, business, and unions, so that efficiency is increased, (4) enlargement of markets and reductions of unit costs, (5) changes in the level of resource utilization.[11]

In comparing and analyzing European and American increases in output, 1950–65, two qualifications need to be kept in mind. The first is a technical point: annual percentage increases in output — as indicators of economic performance — have been subject to criticism by some on the basis that it is presumed to be less difficult to improve on a smaller base than on a larger; it is held to be less difficult to move from, say, 50 to 52.5 than it is from 100 to 105.[12] Second, as noted earlier, the factors giving rise to growth are many and varied, and they may differ greatly according to time and place. Hence, comparing the United States and Western Europe during such a short span as 1950–65 may not do justice at all to the longer-run and more pervasive underlying factors.

With these precautions in mind, it will still prove instructive to look at the output increase patterns for Europe and the United States from 1950 on. Denison estimates that for the period 1950–62 total national income grew at a rate of 3.32 percent for the United States and 4.76 for northwest Europe (the EEC minus Italy but plus Denmark, Norway, and the United Kingdom).[13] Of the figure for the United States, 1.95 percent arose from an increase in factor input (for example, in part an increasing labor force) and 1.37 percent from an increase in output per unit of input (example: advances in knowledge). For Europe, the figure breaks down into 1.69 and 3.07 percent respectively. Neither the variation between the terminal years used by Denison (1950–62) and those used here (1950–65) nor the difference between the measures of national income and gross national product is critical for the comparisons. What is pertinent relates to the factors giving rise to differential growth patterns. In essence, and apart from capacity influences, European growth was greater than that of the United States, from 1950 on, primarily because Europe profited from certain conditions not available to the United States (or available only on a lesser scale).

What were these factors? They included the following: (1) the contraction of agricultural labor inputs, which, among other things, made much-needed labor available to the rest of the economy as well as simultaneously increasing agricultural productivity, (2) the reduction in nonagricultural self-employment, (3) the reduction of trade barriers, and (4) the economies of scale associated with the growth of national markets and changes in the patterns of consumption. Denison calculates that for the United States these factors made up .61 percentage points of the aforementioned 3.2 percent output increase rate, whereas for Europe they amounted to 1.55 of 4.78 percent. Had the contribution of these particular factors in the United States been equal to that in Europe, the overall rate of increase in U.S. national income would have been 4.26 percent (compared to 4.78 percent for Europe) instead of 3.32 percent.[14] These advantages for Europe will tend to lessen as time passes. For example, the future gains from further reductions in agricultural inputs and self-employment will become less the smaller the residual number of persons in these activities becomes. Conversely, other factors may have more critical impacts upon increases in output — for example, labor supplies in Europe over the next decade.

In summary, the United States has over the long run exhibited an unmatched rate of increase in output. For the period 1950–65, however, European performance was better than that of the United States, in part because of operating closer to full capacity, in part because of certain options not as fully available to the United States. But, as noted above, over the longer run, various advantages and disadvantages tend to even out the more alike economies become.

Where does all this lead? Let us turn to the questions and problems that were of importance in 1965–68.

Questions and Problems: 1965–68

The discussion and data above suggest that the American cultural and economic setting has been conducive to high-level economic performance and over the long run such performance indeed has been exhibited; yet the Western European output record for 1950–65 was better than the American, and Europe, moreover, is moving ahead with economic adaptations designed to further improve its economic performance. One could reasonably suppose that on both sides of the Atlantic the situation would be viewed with some degree of satisfaction. Instead, as the decade of the sixties moved toward a close, both Western Europe and the United States were voicing fears about their economic future *and* about their economic roles vis-à-vis the opposite side of the Atlantic.

For Western Europe the problems giving rise to these concerns appear to be as follows:

Short-run (1965–68) economic instabilities troubled a number of European countries. These instabilities arose out of inflationary pressures and market imbalances of one kind or another, and they necessitated the imposition of stabilization measures which slowed down the rise in output. In addition to this slowing down, annual increases in output in recent years have been much more uneven than during 1950–65. There is no sign that these instabilities have ended; witness the French predicament of 1968, the 1969 resignation of de Gaulle and the devaluation of the franc, the 1969 German elections and the revaluation of the mark.

The following figures illustrate the slowing down. For 1955–60, the annual average growth rate of gross national product at constant prices for the EEC was 5.3 percent; for 1960–65, 4.9 percent. For the United States, on the contrary, the figures were 2.2 and 5.5 percent respectively. When such other combinations as 1962–67 or 1963–68 are used, the U.S. rates for the second half of the period remain higher than those of the EEC. What happened is that in the mid-sixties the United States forged ahead in terms of annual increases in output, after lagging behind in 1955–61. In particular, the years 1966–68 saw the lowest output increases in several decades for the EEC countries, though in 1968 some countries, such as West Germany, made major turnabouts.

For the period 1968–73, it also appears that European annual increases in output will be at levels lower than those of 1950–65, and also below those of the United States. Thus there will be a lower output increase rate for Western Europe, a higher one for the United States, with the implications that such shifts entail for economic interaction. Table 3 provides projections for 1965–70, along with selected past comparisons.

The special case of Britain is of concern to all her European neighbors: her bid to enter the EEC, the devaluation of the pound in late 1967, her critical economic situation, and the need for considerable readjustment to make her a viable economic entity. The rebuff of her second bid to join the Common Market by de Gaulle in 1967 compounded the problems. And the summer and autumn of 1968 saw France and President

Table 3. Average Annual Percentage Increases in Gross National Product at Constant Prices for the EEC, EFTA, and the United States

Unit	1950–55	1955–60	1955–65	1960–65	1965–70[a]
EEC	6.7%	5.3%	5.2%	4.9%	4.0–4.6%
EFTA	3.1	3.2	3.6	4.0	3.4–3.8
United States	4.3	2.2	3.4	4.5	4.0–4.5

SOURCE: 1950–65 data from Tables 1 and 2; 1965–70 estimates made by the author from EEC, OECD, and other data.

[a] The lower output expansion rate figures in the 1965–70 column are late 1968 estimates made by the writer and are based upon 1966–68 realized increases in output. Two factors are relevant in suggesting the realized rates for 1965–70 may be closer to the lower rather than to the higher figures. First, in Europe, marked unevenness has been exhibited in output increases. Although Germany made a major turnaround in 1968, the 1966 and 1967 rates were minimal. Likewise the 1968 difficulties in France have altered her short-term picture. A similar story holds for the United Kingdom. Second, in the United States rising prices in 1967 eroded much of the increase. See *The OECD Observer* (Paris), August 1968, for comments on the economic outlook.

Charles de Gaulle with problems of their own. What the April 27, 1969, resignation of de Gaulle portends is not immediately clear. It is not likely to produce an overnight change in attitude toward Britain's entry. Moreover, continuing French economic instability (witness the August 1969 devaluation of the franc) does not ease the situation.

Within the EEC one finds — along with a sense of accomplishment — an impatience to get on with the tasks of integration: to effectuate structural changes, in capital markets, for example; to develop common policies such as company, patent, transport; to bring about fundamental cultural and economic alterations, as with respect to the role of entrepreneurship or the rationalization of industry.

Finally, one senses in Western Europe concern about the role and impact of American direct investments. This concern relates not only to "national pride and foreign takeovers," but also to other impacts: American business practices and, most important, the competitive thrust of external enterprises.

The problems of concern to the United States include maintaining high levels of economic activity without price instabilities (while considerable improvement was made after 1961–62 in the rate of increase of annual output, as has been noted, by 1966–67 as much as two-fifths of the increase, in current prices, was a result of price increases); the balance-of-payments situation and the relation to it of U.S. direct investments abroad, particularly in Europe; and European competition in the American as well as world markets (an interesting parallel to the European concern noted above).

That these problems interact at points is clear. For example, the first item noted for both Europe and the United States, the concern for continued economic growth, is basically the same. The direct investment issue is seen from different viewpoints, but is of mutual concern; the same is true about the fears of foreign competition. The lower annual increases in output for Europe and the special case of Britain are not paralleled by American problems, but American concern about European stability is patent. That these problems are important is clear: they all relate to economic performance, to growth, to stability. While other objectives — the maintenance of peace, to mention but one — are also highly relevant, it is worth reiterating that a prosperous economy is a necessary condition for survival in this modern industrial age.

A comment may be made here about political economy and the politics of economics. The European and American problems noted above will not be solved by the Invisible Hand, that is, by economics alone. An analysis of the key issues within these problem areas and the approaches necessary for their resolution indicates why. In ensuing pages an examination will be made of four issues central to Western European economic integration and to the problems listed above. For the first three, use will be made of the analytical framework proposed at the beginning of this chapter; the fourth extends the analysis to interactions between Western Europe and the United States. These issues are technology and its impacts, typifying the importance of cultural influences upon economic activity; capital markets, an example of the structural integration of institutions; implementation of policies, exemplifying the harmonization issue; and the role of American direct investments, which provides an illustration of the interaction of economies with one another.

TECHNOLOGY AND CULTURAL ATTITUDES TOWARD ECONOMIC ACTIVITY

One of the most publicized topics in Western Europe in the period of 1965–68 was technology and the technological gap. Concern over this issue arose for a variety of reasons that merit attention: What is technology? Why is Western Europe concerned about it? Is there a technological "gap" between Western Europe and the United States? If so, what are the causes? What measures is Europe taking to narrow the gap?

In a narrow sense, technology can be viewed as the development of new products and processes flowing out of basic scientific inquiry and/or through the activities of the inventor and the engineer. Even in this narrow sense, there are many technologies, as a moment's reflection will indicate. However, in the context of the current discussion, this view needs to be broadened considerably. Technology in this context would certainly include new products and processes, but beyond that it includes, first, the attitudes of business enterprises toward technology (and research and development), and indeed their attitudes toward a broader spectrum of closely related philosophies and practices: enterprise size, competition, and the entire range of policies such as industrial engineering, manpower, marketing.[15] Second, institutional mechanisms for the transformation of abstract conceptualizations, discoveries, innovations into engineered techniques and thence to products and processes must be taken into account. The capital market provides one example of such a mechanism. A third element is cultural attitudes toward innovation and invention and the role of the scientist, inventor, engineer, among others. The first two items fit into and operate within this broader cultural context.

As to Western Europe's concern about technology, there appear to be four reasons behind it.

One factor involves economic growth. Growth, in the form of increases in the capacity to produce, can occur, as noted earlier, through two basic means: an increase in inputs, of which the labor input has been important historically, and an increase in output per unit of input.

Because of age gaps in the population caused by two world wars, Europe faces a situation over the next decade in which the rates of increase of the total population and, more important, of working population and of numbers employed will be lower than for the past ten to fifteen years. Tables 4, 5, and 6 illustrate this.[16] In the United Kingdom (not shown in the tables), working-age population growth will be considerably lower in 1965–70 than it was in 1960–65 (0.1 percent and 0.9 percent respectively). But higher participation rates will modify this somewhat and the projected annual increase in the labor force is expected to run about 0.3 percent per annum compared with 0.6 percent for the previous five years.

Hence, annual increases in output of magnitudes of the past fifteen years are less likely in the future if one takes into account only labor supply increases and their contributions to such output. EEC projections do not indicate migration will contribute significantly to labor supply increases; conversely such factors as increased length of schooling may reduce the

Table 4. Trend of Total Population in EEC

Country	Numbers (in Thousands)[a]		Annual Growth Rates		
	1960	1970	1955–60	1960–65	1965–70
Germany (F.R.)	55,430	60,700	1.1%	1.3%	0.6%
France	45,680	51,290	1.0	1.4	0.9
Italy	49,760	53,100	0.6	0.7	0.6
Netherlands	11,490	13,230	1.3	1.4	1.5
Belgium	9,180	9,780	0.6	0.7	0.6
Luxembourg	315	348	0.6	1.1	0.8
EEC	171,860	188,450	0.9	1.1	0.8

SOURCE: *Preliminary Draft of the First Medium-Term Economic Policy Programme* (Brussels: EEC Medium-Term Economic Policy Committee, March 25, 1966), p. 5.

[a] Except for Luxembourg, the figures are rounded to the nearest 10,000.

Table 5. Trend of Working Population in EEC

Country	Numbers (in Thousands)[a]		Annual Growth Rates		
	1960	1970	1955–60	1960–65	1965–70
Germany (F.R.)	26,520	27,300	1.1%	0.6%	0.0%
France	19,720	20,760	0.1	0.6	0.5
Italy	19,880	20,980	0.4	0.5	0.6
Netherlands	4,190	4,840	0.7	1.6	1.3
Belgium	3,530	3,760	−0.1	0.7	0.5
Luxembourg	131	137	0.1	0.7	0.2
EEC	73,970	77,780	0.5	0.7	0.4

SOURCE: *Preliminary Draft of the First Medium-Term Economic Policy Programme*, p. 6.
[a] Except for Luxembourg, the figures are rounded to the nearest 10,000.

Table 6. Trend in Numbers Employed in EEC

Country	Numbers (in Thousands)[a]		Annual Growth Rates		
	1960	1970	1955–60	1960–65	1965–70
Germany (F.R.)	26,250	27,150	1.7%	0.7%	0.0%
France	19,480	20,140	−0.1	0.8	0.5
Italy	19,010	20,360	1.3	0.6	0.8
Netherlands	4,140	4,780	0.7	1.6	1.2
Belgium	3,350	3,660	−0.1	1.1	0.6
Luxembourg	134	142	0.2	0.7	0.4
EEC	72,360	76,230	1.0	0.7	0.5

SOURCE: *Preliminary Draft of the First Medium-Term Economic Policy Programme*, p. 7.
[a] Except for Luxembourg, the figures are rounded to the nearest 10,000.

labor supply below projections. Moreover, other forces are likely to contribute less than in the past. For example, the exodus of labor from agriculture contributes to output increases, for it places manpower in economic activities in which productivity is higher and it tends similarly to increase productivity within agriculture. But this impact becomes less and less significant the more labor leaves agriculture (and hence the smaller the residue left to leave). Reducing unemployment (that is, increasing output through expansion — through a higher utilization of capacity) will not yield much, since Western European unemployment rates tend to be at the hard-core level (with some temporary exceptions from time to time in the past decade).

Whether one looks, therefore, at potential labor supply increases through population and labor force growth and immigration or through occupational shifts in labor supplies, one concludes that increases in such inputs will be relatively smaller in the next decade than in the past. The alternatives are those of substituting other types of inputs, such as capital, for labor and/or increasing output per unit of input. Insofar as capital can be and is substituted, it compensates for the "absent" labor — even if the additional capital merely replicates those forms already in existence. But — and this is where technology, as it relates to production methods and processes, becomes vital — if the substitution involves more efficient production, the gain is compounded.

This series of issues has been summarized concisely by the EEC Commission:

It seems probable that most of the Community countries will have two main problems to face the next five years.

The first is the slower rate of increase of the working population expected in several countries. The danger of shortage of labour is linked with problems arising from structural changes in the various economic sectors and with the need for better-qualified manpower.

It will therefore be necessary to encourage the development of a flexible apparatus of production which will be more capable of satisfying demand. Vocational training, scientific and technical research, and a policy to promote the adjustment of structures can play important parts here.

Another big problem which is likely to present itself in the next few years is that of the considerable additional investment, particularly public investment, which will be required to increase productivity and meet the rising need for public utilities and services in the fields of transport, education, health and town planning. A selection must be made, for needs are likely to exceed available resources and it is important that savings should be promoted and utilized to the best advantage.[17]

A second factor relevant to the importance of technology — and mentioned as frequently as growth — is competition. Europeans are concerned that competitors (and the American producer is frequently cited) will develop new products which will permit preemption of European markets, that is, Americans will be the only suppliers. Europeans are likewise afraid that the American producer will find ways to produce existing products more economically.

Third, and more psychological than economic in its impact, the national (and/or European) image is viewed as being tarnished by the apparent technical superiority of America. That is, on some kind of a world (or Western) technological rating scale, Europe views itself as ranking lower than the United States, and it finds this disturbing.

Fourth, and also psychological, the problem of adjustment to the "new" technology involves "major changes in a social hierarchy, disrupting deeply rooted, traditional methods of doing business . . . and . . . posing a challenge to deep-seated attitudes, forcing innovation in education and changes in other social institutions."[18] Thus Europe is caught on the horns of a dilemma: if she does not respond, her ranking in the technological hierarchy is not improved, her competitive position may be worsened, and her capability of generating output increases is lessened; if she does respond, this requires major changes in the underlying economic and social framework. Resentment also appears to arise because the problem is not entirely of Europe's own making but has been thrust upon her, principally by the United States.

Does a technology "gap" in fact exist? Qualitatively, if "gap" is viewed as "uneven distribution of technologically relevant resources," there seems to be agreement on its existence.[19] The "evidence" takes a variety of forms: Fields are cited in which the United States has taken a commanding lead, such as aerospace, computers, electronics, optical systems. Also cited are expenditures on research and development (R and D) where, for example, the United States spends nearly three times more of its gross national product than does the EEC.[20] Differences in such expenditures are sometimes expressed in a "research exchange rate" (which takes into account complex differences in research cost). By it, for the mid-1960's, the United States spent on research about 2½ times as much as did Western Europe. In military and space research, using this rate, the difference was on the order of 4 or 5 to 1; for civil research alone, it was 1½ to 1.[21] The number of "patented" inventions is another common item in documentation of a technology gap. Thus, in 1962, the United States registered some 4000 more patents than did all the EEC countries — and the disparity is increasing.[22] Between 1957 and 1961, of the total patents taken out in Western Europe, Americans contributed approximately 17 percent; in the same period Europeans contributed 10 percent to the U.S. total. Figures on the use of certain kinds of technological equipment are similarly adduced as evidence. Thus, for computers, the United States had (in 1966) 144 installed for each 1,000,000 population; the United Kingdom had 37, West Germany 48, France 31, the Netherlands 33.[23]

Now one might suggest that larger numbers alone (absolute or relative) do not "prove" anything more than that U.S. research expenditures are higher on an absolute basis, in per capita terms or as a percentage of GNP; or that the United States uses more technological equipment — for example, that more computers have been installed. Indeed one critic has concluded: "In truth there is no direct correlation between R and D expenditures and the rate of economic growth or trade expansion. Research expenditures do not explain why European economies have grown faster than the U.S. economy. Nor does it explain why the U.K. economy, with relatively higher R and D expenditures than other European countries, has advanced less rapidly than other countries on the continent." [24]

What is the Western European worry then? The European would say that, given its technological superiority, the United States could have performed as well or better than Europe in the period 1950–65 had it chosen to use policies to maintain high levels of employment (particularly dur-

ing 1955–60). The European would also say that for the future the tide
has turned: the United States *will* perform better, particularly given the
growth-dampening stabilization procedures that various Western European countries have found it necessary to apply. Beyond this, he would
argue that even if the United States operates at less than capacity, it still
has the technical capability of invading and dominating the markets in
which the European has a vital concern — of outcompeting Europe in
whatever markets it chooses.[25] Ultimately he feels it is the technology gap
(defined in the broad sense) which gives the advantage to the United
States.

If the existence of a gap is accepted, what factors are instrumental in
contributing to it?

One fundamental differential is to be found in the cultural attitudes
alluded to above. There is a difference in the values placed by Americans
and Europeans upon such factors as entrepreneurship, education, and the
status of engineers, inventors, technicians. The American scale of values
is presumed to be more favorable toward technological development.
Moreover, it is these values which so concern the European because
change *is* necessary, but change also involves many difficult readjustments
in the entire way of life. The European is no less creative in research (in
the "research" of research and development). But, for reasons inherent
in his culture, he has been less concerned with "development." This is the
core of the issue.

Within this cultural context, the businessman, in turn, behaves differently. One cannot help but evoke stereotypes here, but they are the char-
acterizations that were frequently cited by European businessmen in interviews undertaken on this project. American business enterprises and
businessmen tend to be regarded as the more "aggressive." The writer
takes this to mean that the American enterprise itself is more continuously
alert for potentially profitable operations; it does not, as is frequently
said of the traditional European businessman, prefer the "quiet life." Further, the American businessman is viewed as the more committed to his
enterprise and more willing to seek the achievement of enterprise goals.
(It is frequently suggested that the American system of pecuniary rewards and punishments aids and abets this process.) The American business is the more willing to undertake research and apply it, uses more
sophisticated manpower, marketing, and industrial engineering techniques, is more willing to grow.

The second fundamental differential is that this more "dynamic"
American enterprise functions in a larger market, relatively barrier free,
with "common" policies already existing: monetary, tax, company, transport, and so on. Hence, the conclusions are that the institutional environment for American business is more favorable to the development of

technology; that within that environment the business enterprise behaves more dynamically, operates more efficiently, and is more technologically committed; and that the culture encourages and sanctions this kind of performance.

Does enterprise size have any particular relation to technology and the technology gap? Are European and American differences relevant here? A business enterprise needs to reach a certain size before it is capable of engaging in research and development. There is a critical mass which must be reached as a necessary condition for R and D. An exact size is not easy to specify; in terms of, say, numbers of employees as a criterion of size, R and D cannot be done effectively by the firm with 1 to 9 employees and may even be difficult for the enterprise with 10 to 100.[26] This critical mass concept is simply a reflection of economies: R and D requires certain minimum inputs in terms of money and men, and the small firm does not possess these. It may contract out its R and D, but unlike U.S. practice, this is not common in Europe. The median size of American firms is over twice the European in terms of number of employees. Hence on this count alone the European firm is disadvantaged in respect to R and D. But while minimum size may be regarded as a necessary condition, it is not sufficient; it does not ensure that enterprise resources will be used for R and D. Two other factors merit attention.

The first is that increases in enterprise size come about in part as a consequence of the size of the market and competition. But market growth and competition force other changes: in the realm of products and processes they require changes in enterprise outlook toward developing new goods and services for the market and the methods through which the goods and services are produced. Failure to respond to market changes and competitive thrusts may result in a failure to survive. It is here that the American competitor is both praised and criticized in the same breath — praised because it is his competitive thrust that is forcing a change upon the European enterprises; criticized because the change alters a long-standing way of doing things, which change, moreover, is being imposed from the outside.

The second factor is that changes in markets and in the degree of competition have brought in their wake changes in the whole spectrum of managerial practices, manpower practices, and marketing practices. All of these are highly relevant to the efficiency of business enterprises and can be viewed as facets of technology defined in the broadest sense.

Hence, it is suggested that increases in the size of business enterprises (and the pressures which bring about an increase) are conducive to the generation of increased enterprise emphasis upon technology. The major concern of Europeans is that one dimension may still be missing and that is entrepreneurial awareness of the importance of these forces to the con-

tinued existence of business enterprises. The European exhibits some fear
that too many enterprises may go out of business — by default — before
entrepreneurs become fully alert to the dynamics of change. One may suggest this fear is overdrawn, but it is not uncommon to hear the European
say that by the time Europe wakes up the market will have been preempted by outsiders (Americans).

If one concludes that a technology gap exists and that from the European viewpoint it is desirable to close it, what steps should be taken? If
one looks at the array of suggestions that have been proposed the answer
appears to be that Europe should remake itself from top to bottom. This
is not said lightly, as will be indicated.

For example, one set of proposals includes the following. At the national level, it is recommended that there be an expansion and democrati-
zation of higher education, including encouragement by industry of continuing education in technological fields; that to facilitate research the mobility of scientists among European countries should be encouraged and
industry-university relations should be improved; that government should
improve the partnership between the state and industry and education, including particular emphasis upon computer technology. At the European
level, it is recommended that graduating engineers be encouraged to follow training courses in industry or in countries other than their own; that
a few European strong points be developed on an experimental basis; that
there be established a European institute of science and technology; that
industry take the lead in computerizing techniques, multinational companies provide leadership in furthering such organizations, and European
governments be more fully apprised of the aerospace gap; that governments develop an over-all strategy for science and technology, harmonize
their requirements, and undertake certain major joint European development projects, facilitate supranational corporate activities, and simplify
and harmonize patent procedures. At the Atlantic level, there should be
an interchange of information and know-how.[27]

This list can readily be fitted into the framework of discussion on
technology provided earlier in this chapter. The suggestions relate to
changing basic cultural attitudes, altering the economic and social framework of institutions, and modifying the policies and practices of business
enterprises as they operate within that framework. This is, of course, a
sizable order and one may legitimately ask if it conceivably can be done
except over the very long run. Modifying society in such a fashion not
only requires changes in the underlying sociocultural value system, but
demands resources (as for extended education) which simply may not be
available in the short run. Europe is faced with difficult choices!

But lest it be said that the list above consists of gratuitous recommendations in which non-Europeans had a hand, a roughly similar set of

proposals issued from the three European executives (the Euratom Commission, the ECSC High Authority, and the EEC Commission) in March 1967.[28] While these proposals are less specific on matters such as education, they are much more emphatic (as might be expected) on the need for further integration, without which technological endeavors are unlikely to progress. Western Europe *is* aware of the problem and what needs to be done. But modifying values and marshaling resources to do it is quite another matter.

In addition to the kinds of comprehensive proposals noted above, a host of more specialized or individualized ideas have been aired. Several of these, in particular, involve American cooperation. One of the most publicized suggestions was for a "Technological Marshall Plan." This was put forth in 1966 by Italian Foreign Minister Amintore Fanfani. Although this plan has received considerable attention and discussion, it has not developed in any concrete detail. Probably a major difficulty is to be found in the nature of technological aid. If generalized to, say, management practices, there is no particular problem, though how such might be "exported" is another question. But if technology in the narrow sense is at issue, sharing becomes difficult if not impossible since such technology is owned and controlled by private enterprise (and protected by patents) and the government could not "give it away."

A much more modest proposal recommends that U.S. industry "create more research laboratories under control of their European affiliates and see that substantial amounts of R and D work are assigned to them. A study made by the Stanford Research Institute states that of 200 American firms engaged in European operations, only 4 percent conducted any research in Europe. This situation should be redressed, for the economy of the whole Atlantic Community will profit from increased research in Europe, and the United States should encourage it." [29] This approach has merit and in fact was a form of cooperation many Europeans suggested in interviews and discussions.

These proposals may well be too simplistic in nature. The forces that generate technological leadership are deeply rooted in underlying cultural, social, and economic conditions — as has so frequently been mentioned in earlier pages. Hence much more than a mere "transfer of knowledge" may be involved in closing the technological gap. In certain respects the entire problem comes back to integration. As was aptly put, "If America really wants to do something [to close the technological gap] let it start introducing different currencies in all the fifty states and impose serious boundaries between them. If this experiment were tried, ten or fifteen years from now we might well bridge the gap." [30] The parts of the whole once again interlock, and integration becomes an important element in still another problem area.

CAPITAL MARKETS: A STRUCTURAL PROBLEM

The technology problem, discussed in the last section, is in large measure centered upon underlying attitudes toward and convictions about innovation. The capital markets issue also involves underlying cultural elements, but beyond that are more important structural components. It is upon the latter that this discussion focuses.

The importance of physical capital — whether as an equivalent substitute input for labor or in terms of new and technologically superior processes (the "technology" previously discussed) — is apparent in light of the relatively slower increase of labor inputs anticipated in the Europe of the next decade. But the importance of capital markets, as the institutional mechanism through which liquid funds are made available to business enterprises for investment in physical capital, is currently germane for two reasons.

First, the relative ability of industry to self-finance its capital needs has decreased in the last decade because of the "profit squeeze." In 1960, labor income as a percentage of national income ran between approximately 52 and 60 percent for varying Western European countries (the United Kingdom excepted, where it was 66 percent). By 1965, the figures ran between 60 and 68 percent, the latter for the United Kingdom. Conversely, there was a relative deterioration of profits. In the United States the increase in labor income has resulted in large part from a reduction in proprietor's income, not in profits. If self-financing is made possible through cash flows (the sum of depreciation allowances plus undistributed profits, plus miscellaneous items), then it becomes more difficult as proportionally increasing labor income reduces profits. If industry has difficulty in passing along rising wage costs, the problem is accentuated. This is the "Lamfalussy Hypothesis," and its importance for capital markets is evident.[31]

Second, the public sector has become increasingly important as a user of capital. For example, for the EEC countries, the increase in total security issues was $4.5 billion from 1961 to 1965, and the public sector — public authorities and state enterprises — proportion of the total rose from 18 to 36 percent.

Hence, at the very time that self-financing possibilities for business enterprise have been reduced, governments have increasingly been preempting such capital as is available.

Within the years 1966–67, three comprehensive reports by different agencies were made on the capital markets problem.[32] All three are highly similar in their statements and analyses of the problems, in their recommendations, and in their somewhat pessimistic conclusions about the possibilities of improvement.

The discussion of problems customarily starts with savings: their source, their quantity, their sufficiency. Household savings constitute the most important single source, outdistancing government and business sources. But having noted this, one study states: ". . . there appears to be no consensus among the experts in their qualitative appraisals [on household savings] except that there is no readily available way to increase the *aggregate supply* of household savings." [33]

No comprehensive data appear to exist on the problems of quantity and sufficiency, but two kinds of statements are commonly made. First, agreement exists on the desirability of "increasing the supply of capital as financial savings are attracted to the markets by the wider range of investment outlets." [34] The use of "increasing" suggests that additional savings would make a positive contribution to the economic process. Second, "Although the rates of saving differ appreciably from one country to another in the Community, they are in fact high and are unlikely to pose problems for the working of a future European capital market. On the other hand, the ways in which the financial surpluses of some sectors of the economies are adjusted to the financial deficits of others vary sharply from country to country; this fact has a direct impact upon the working of the domestic capital markets and thus on the process of integration of these markets." [35] This suggests a different problem, but it is not necessarily inconsistent with the previous statement.

Thus "more" savings (quantity unspecified) would be desirable but the adequacy problem is as much structural as it is a matter of the sheer magnitude of available funds. Given the need for increasing physical capital consequent upon slower labor force growth rates and hence labor inputs and the public sector demand for liquid capital, one would conclude that increasing the supply of capital *is* important.

A number of methods have been proposed or introduced for the purpose of increasing the savings of households. One involves increasing the range of savings forms and institutions, this in the belief that the greater the range of alternatives, the more likely will variety itself elicit response. This remains to be proved, however, for the fact that an economy with numerous alternatives has a higher ratio of household savings does not yield the conclusion that one causes the other. There may exist more important underlying factors.

Individual savers have a high preference for liquidity, resulting generally in the use of bank deposits. Several European countries have developed programs to encourage savings of a long-term nature as substitutes for short-term liquidity contracts. The Federal Republic of Germany has introduced long-term savings contracts; interest payments received thereunder are tax exempt. France recently instituted ten-year savings contracts utilizing subsidies rather than tax exemption.[36] Such inducements, however, are not without their costs since they may involve a loss of revenue to the state.

The two suggestions most commonly made with respect to the supply of capital are less concerned with its augmentation and more with the mechanisms of its use: the transformation of liquid funds into sources for longer-term investment, where there is a greater need; and increasing "institutional" saving, particularly the contractual variety.

On the transformation issue one study notes: "Savers generally prefer to hold cash or short-term assets and it would be difficult to alter this preference radically in the short term. . . . Savings which take the form of deposits will remain a major factor in the supply of capital. The financial institutions which collect this form of savings should therefore be able to offer medium- and long-term loans and to use their funds on the capital market." [37]

While there has been no marked shift in the pattern of institutional mechanisms for the conversion of short- to long-term savings (the study quoted indicates that this state of affairs does not seem likely to change spontaneously), there are some encouraging trends. For one thing, commercial banks and the *banques d'affaires* are moving closer, joining sources of funds with institutions concerned with meeting the long-term credit needs of business enterprises. For another, some EEC countries are stimulating the consolidation of savings and their use for longer-term investments.

"Contractual savings" represent the least liquid form of savings; they are typified by insurance, pension fund rights, and unit trusts. But they represent an extremely useful kind of savings for two chief reasons. First, as has been noted: "they are invariably capitalized . . . they collect savings in the present [and thereby reduce consumption] for ultimate distribution [waiting their payout as capital market investments]." [38] Second, from the viewpoint of actual experience, countries such as the United States, the United Kingdom, and the Netherlands, which are prime users of this form, have found it effective as a basis for providing long-term capital.

There are other reasons for the usefulness of the contractual form. The demand of households and banks for bond and share purchases exhibits wide swings, depending upon monetary policy, the rate of interest, the expectation of capital gains. There is, on the other hand, a very high degree of stability in contractual purchases and they provide a strong base of secondary market support. Contractual institutions make wholesale purchases with the resulting cost economies that are analogous to the economies that result from the marketing of group as against individual insurance. And by their very nature contractual institutions are long term in both assets and liabilities; there is no need for "transformation."

But even if individual countries in Western Europe were to improve their institutional frameworks and practices in the contractual and transformation spheres — as some have done, though to varying degrees — this says nothing for "integrated" capital markets, whatever it bespeaks for more effective operation in a given country. Integration is a different problem, involving different dimensions. If it is difficult to be optimistic about the trend and speed of capital market developments *within* a given economy, it is considerably more difficult not to be pessimistic about integration *among* countries.

Several problems stand in the way of an integrated European capital market. The demands of the public sector are increasing and one characterization is that "The key obstacle [to a European capital market] is that governments tend to demand an overriding priority for their own issues on capital markets. That leaves comparatively little room for industrial companies seeking to raise capital, and it hurts especially in the present profits squeeze. . . ." [39] If capital markets were integrated, the state could no longer use the market as its own domain: competition would be on more equal terms. Moreover, the advantages of priority, of favorable tax rates, and commission charges, of requiring institutional investors to purchase the issues, would disappear. The state, in effect, would be forced to reappraise the financial policies of its public authorities and public enterprises. Further, free movement of capital would, in effect, require free monetary convertibility. Two directives under the framework of the Treaty of Rome have been adopted providing for freedom of movement of capital in the fields of direct investment, listed securities, real estate, and some personal and commercial transactions. But restrictions remain in the issuance of securities, in financial loans, and in short-term capital movements of a purely financial character. These restrictions were originally intended to safeguard the balance of international payments; they now appear as devices to ensure the autonomy of domestic monetary policies. [40]

In essence, then, the technical adjustments, while difficult, are not the real stumbling block to integration. That block is political — once again noting the politics of political economy. Given the current economic instability in certain European economies, one may suggest that national approaches and policies will take precedence over movement toward integration, even though it appears that integration would increase stability. [41]

But the concern here is less with the details of European capital markets — which have been analyzed in depth in an expert way in the reports previously cited — than with the broader issue of their relevance to integration. The critical importance of an integrated capital market is readily apparent: (1) As a factor of production — and an increasingly important one — capital cannot be allocated most effectively in economies which seek to integrate unless it plays its role in an integrated market. This point need not be labored; merely consider six separate markets with capital in search of the most profitable outlets as against one common market with its efficiency in the balancing of supplies and demands. (2) There is an obvious relationship among the many elements in integration. Assume that a company policy is adopted which permits the development of true European enterprises. Those enterprises will not function most efficiently if they need to secure capital in fragmented markets. (3) If the fruits of technological development are to be enjoyed, liquid funds will be required to make the necessary investments in physical plant. And technology is likely to require large amounts of capital — witness that called for by computer development — which only an integrated market may be capable of supplying. (4) Moreover, the longer the delay in integration, the more likely national interests are to harden, given increasing state fundings and preemption of the markets. But, having said this, one should not be sanguine about the chances of integration in the near future; national positions seem simply too overriding.[42]

In sum, the integration of capital markets is highly important, but the likelihood of its development soon is doubtful, given both the underlying national politics and the technicalities — including the necessity of changing, within countries, fundamental structural patterns of financial institutions.

THE FRAMEWORK OF PUBLIC POLICIES: PROBLEMS OF HARMONIZATION

Thus far in this section on questions and problems, two issues have been examined: the cultural setting and its relevance to problems of technology, and structural factors and the capital market question. In keeping with the framework of analysis, attention is now directed to the topic of policies and their harmonization. Since it is the purpose and nature of such policies, not their detail, which is important, this issue can be treated in brief compass.

Why such policies? Why their harmonization? In the broadest sense because they are the very instrumentalities of integration, as visualized in the creation of the EEC, used here as the focus of discussion. For example, consider a business enterprise operating under the separate regulations of six nations as against one operating within a unified framework.[43]

These policies consist of two basic types, though the line between them is not hard and fast. One type is the "enabling" policy, the other "regulatory." There is overlap between the two, but that notwithstanding, the intent is quite different. Company policy provides an example of the enabling type. Were such a community-wide policy introduced, it would permit a business to become multinational. Such policy tends to be unique in its application: once the company has been created, the policy has served its purpose. (The company may have to conform subsequently to various requirements of the policy, but this does not negate the point of the illustration.) Competition policy affords an illustration of the regulatory type. Here behavior through time is controlled. An enterprise is not expected, for example, to engage in practices violative of the competition policy.

The development of such policies provides an interesting example of the art of negotiation. Frequently, important national interests of one kind or another are involved, and as a result implementation policies have been slow in evolving. Time and again the point was made in interviews with the author that this was because the negotiators had not reached the "right formula" for securing agreement, but that in due time this would be rectified.[44] Two specifics appear to be relevant in the negotiation of policies: the substantive nature of the proposals and the skill of the negotiators. While the latter is important, the former is regarded as the more critical. Unskilled negotiators may preclude acceptance of a proposal that has substantive merit, but even the most expert would have a difficult if not impossible time in getting agreement if the substance did not provide an "acceptable formula."

Two examples of implementation policies may be cited: company policy, which exemplifies politically oriented negotiating issues, and transport, in which the economic content is much higher.

The creation of a European incorporated company would provide many advantages "for the combination of various factors of production now dispersed throughout the Common Market."[45] The content of such a policy is not difficult to structure nor is there particular disagreement concerning it. What is at issue is the particular statutory dimensions it should have. Given the same content (and intent), three different approaches have been suggested. One would utilize the scope provided in the Treaty of Rome; a second would provide for a standard law introduced into the jurisdiction of each member state; a third would establish a European law (in effect, a community law).

The EEC Commission prefers the third alternative; the French favor the second. As is well known, the French have sought to limit movement toward "supranational" structures and policies and this is a case in point. Content itself does not appear at issue, but at the same time no amount of negotiating skill is likely to yield the third alternative unless the French position changes. "Economics" is not the issue; national "image" is. As long as the French do not choose to enhance the community image at the expense of what they believe is their own, a standoff exists.[46] And one may conjecture that the French view of their image is more pervasive than the personification of it in de Gaulle. Hence his resignation is not likely to produce an early shift in attitudes.

It is interesting to note how the EEC Commission and Council function in such cases. The principal approach appears to be that of avoiding inaction even if there is an impasse; to try instead other routes, to continue to analyze and discuss, and not to allow a vacuum to form. For example, the Commission records as follows its work on this problem:

In April 1966 the Commission laid before the Council a memorandum on the creation of a European incorporated company. The memorandum is at the same time a comment on the French Government's note of 15 March 1965 on the same subject. In its memorandum the Commission indicated the opportunities a European incorporated company would provide for the removal of the obstacles company laws still place in the way of amalgamations, and it pointed out the advantages presented by the European incorporated company for the combination of various factors of production now dispersed throughout the Common Market.

In December 1965 the Commission asked a group of independent experts to examine in detail the principle questions posed by the creation of the new legal form of a European incorporated company. This work led to the preparation of a draft memorandum and draft articles of association of such a company, which were submitted by Professor Sanders, chairman. The Commission passed on the draft and the accompanying comments to the Council. These documents were therefore available for study by the *ad hoc* working party — for which Professor Sanders is also chairman — set up in autumn of 1966 by the Council.[47]

The approach is then one which emphasizes flexibility; if the initial effort does not produce agreement on a suggested policy, the negotiating process does not stop but goes ahead with reanalysis, reformulation, resubmission, rediscussion. As important as any other factor for the strength of its negotiating position is the fact that the Commission is a full-time body operating from a consistent point of view.

Transport policy affords a quite different kind of example. Here "content," which is basically economic, is at issue. And here again the approach of flexibility is demonstrated. Transport policy discussions were among the earliest to be held after the formation of the community. While considerable agreement has developed over the years since then, the policy areas agreed upon were those, such as safety regulations or licensing requirements, not embodying what is regarded as vital national economic interest.

A common transport policy, if it is to be viable in terms of equalizing competition, cannot stop short of resolving the problems of rate structures. It is here that the difficulty has occurred, and it has occurred — as noted in Chapter 2 — because the national interests of the Dutch are threatened. Rotterdam is the most important port in the world in terms of tonnage handled. It is also an important entrepôt for the transshipment of goods laid down by liners in Rotterdam and sent to various areas by river or canal. Because of the Dutch transshipment rate structure based on the economical use of waterways, the Netherlands moves a high percentage of waterborne traffic reaching community countries. If designed to equalize competition, a transport policy must of necessity tackle rate structures. And presumably, such a policy must involve minimum rates. It is on this point that the Dutch have remained obdurate: minimum rates, if higher than current levels, would reduce if not eliminate the Dutch advantage. The result has been no agreement — at least on the larger issues involved.

As M. Lambert Schaus, then a member of the Commission, noted: "As a result of the last Council session of 19–20 October 1966 an impartial observer might have the impression that all discussions held since 1958 were to start all over again. Nevertheless, some satisfactory results could be recorded. Since 1960 as many as 12 Council regulations, directives, and decisions implementing common transport policy had become Community law. Seven more regulations and two directives were under consideration of the Council." [48]

How does one handle an impasse such as this? As noted earlier, one proceeds in other directions, and in this case utilizes an additional dimension, that of time. If resolution is not possible today, it may be tomorrow or the next day when the situation may have changed enough, or the views of the parties altered, so that accommodation is possible. Note this approach in the following:

Discussions in the Council in July and October 1966, led to the adoption of a resolution by which the rate system was no longer to be a matter of priority but which recommended that further steps should be taken throughout the field of transport in an endeavour to secure a balanced organization of transport. In response to this resolution the Commission submitted to the Council, in February 1967, a memorandum of the common transport policy containing the results of an examination of the divergent opinions in the Council and of how the differences could be resolved. In particular, it submitted to the Council a programme showing the various measures to be taken and a time-table for their execution. The Community organization would be set up in two phases, the first of which would last until 31 December 1969 (the transitional period). In this first phase, measures should be taken to regulate rates and the conditions of admission to the haulage trade between Member States, as well as most of the harmonization measures and a financial system governing the use of the infrastructures. During the second phase, ending on 31 December 1972, the arrangements on freight rates would be completed and their scope extended to traffic within Member States; the conditions of admission to the haulage trade, introduced during the first phase, would be applied to road haulage within Member States and to inland navigation within the Community; the conditions of competition would be harmonized; and a common financial system introduced to cover the use made of transport infrastructure.[49]

In summary then:

1. Policies implementing the Treaty of Rome are the means by which economic integration in the EEC is furthered: to transform a "halfway" house into a viable entity.

2. Policy formulation is a difficult process, involving as it does strong national interests, complex negotiations, and acceptable formulas.

3. Both economic and political factors have been relevant in cases where little progress has been made; transport illustrates the former; company policy the latter.

4. The weight of national interests as against imaginative proposals is difficult to evaluate in cases where policy development is at a standstill. Arguments are posed for both sides: (a) If one is on the inside (for example, a member of the community bureaucracy) and for some people on the outside, the substance of the proposal seems the more pertinent. That is, one needs an imaginative proposal if one is to be successful. (It has frequently been suggested, for example, that a transport policy could have achieved acceptance had it been packaged differently.) There is some sentiment to the effect that the imaginative fires of the Commission have cooled; that new ideas are needed. Those holding these views on the development of community policies tend to be optimistic, certain that re-thinking, reworking, and resubmission will eventually lead to success. (b) The opposing school – the pessimists, mostly on the outside – contends that national interest is much the more critical and that no amount of formulizing or negotiating will do the job. This point of view suggests that developments occur when the advantages of policy harmonization become glaringly obvious to all member states (as in the case of the value-added tax); that strong resistance by one member virtually blocks development (the Dutch and transport); conversely that heavy pressure by one government may be enough to advance a policy (France and agriculture). Thus, national position, not the proposal itself, is the critical element.

5. Yet, with or without agreement on certain policies, the Commission does not stand still as respects their development. New tacks are tried, new discussions held. Whether this is merely an operation in which the parties delude themselves or whether the continued makework of reformulation will be likely to yield results depends again upon one's point of view. The optimist would see success; the less sanguine would conclude as follows: "Conversely, where none of the member states has exerted real pressure for common policy decisions, or where at least one government has resisted such pressure as there was, the results of Commission proposals have been derisory. The Commission can go on producing draft regulations for transport, energy and social policies until it is blue in the face, but nothing will happen until there is some strong pressure

from at least one government — and one may be enough, if its methods are brutal enough as in the case of agriculture — to secure some forward progress." [50]

U.S. Investments in Europe: Problems of Interaction

With the exception of the technology gap, we have thus far viewed Western Europe as if it were virtually a closed economy, or two closed economies, EFTA and the EEC. Attention has been focused on the issues involved in integrating member nations into the larger organizational units. But just as these member nations relate not only to each other but to these larger units so in turn the EEC and EFTA (and their members) interact with the outer world. As a matter of fact, given the present incomplete stage of integration it is as accurate to specify individual country interaction with the outer world as it is to specify EEC or EFTA interaction. This is particularly true of outer-world investment in the member countries of EFTA and the EEC.

One of the currently most publicized instances of such outer-world interaction is that of direct investment by the United States in Western Europe.[51] Direct investments will be examined from two points of view: the nature of such investments and the reasons therefore; the problems that have arisen out of this development.

Attention centers here not upon short-term shifts of investable funds, but upon what is conventionally viewed as long-term investment. There are two basic types of such investment. One is the portfolio investment in which credit obligations or equities of a foreign enterprise are purchased. This type of investment is impersonal in nature in the same way as is the purchase of so many shares of a given company's stock in one's own country. It is perfectly true, of course, that one may purchase so large a number of shares that direct representation, such as on the board of directors, may be sought, but this is not a major issue at hand. The second type of long-term investment, and the critical one in the European context, is direct investment: a foreign interest goes into business in the other country. It is this type which is of relevance here. The two primary ways in which a direct investment is made are to take over, by purchase or other arrangement, an already existing firm in the other country or to open a foreign branch of the home country enterprise. In either case some degree of control or voice in management is involved.

Direct investments by American entrepreneurs in Europe are not new: F. W. Woolworth entered before World War I, General Motors in the 1920's, to cite but two examples. And there have been cases of investments that did not work out: the 1929 American Can Company entry into Britain, which terminated in 1931. Direct investment is not even as new as the above might indicate, for European capital played an important role in the development of American industry in the nineteenth century.[52] What is new, however, quantitatively speaking, is the magnitude of American direct investment and its recent growth and concentration. Table 7 highlights this.

Table 7. U.S. Direct Investment Abroad (in Millions of Dollars)

Area of Investment	1950	1957	1961	1962	1963	1964	1965
Total	11,788	25,394	34,667	37,225	40,686	44,386	49,217
Canada	3,579	8,769	11,602	12,133	13,044	13,789	15,172
Latin America.....	4,445	7,434	8,236	8,424	8,662	8,894	9,371
Europe	1,733	4,151	7,742	8,930	10,340	12,109	13,894
Common Market...	637	1,680	3,104	3,722	4,490	5,426	6,254
United Kingdom...	847	1,974	3,554	3,824	4,172	4,547	5,119

SOURCE: U.S. Department of Commerce, *Survey of Current Business.* See the September issues of the *Survey* for annual data.

The figures in the table underestimate the total, for they are based upon only those enterprises in which the American interest is 25 percent or more; and the fixed asset valuation tends to be more undervalued than overvalued. By 1967, "book value" figures showed $20.2 billion invested in Western Europe. If the data from Table 7 are used, the compounded annual rate of increase, 1958–65, is 8.8 percent for total direct foreign investment, but 18.5 percent for the EEC countries, and 16.0 percent for the EFTA nations.[53]

It is true that Western Europe's *total* investment was larger (1965 data) in the United States than vice versa: $34.1 billion (Europe in the United States) compared with $29.6 billion (United States in Europe). But of these totals over 47 percent of the U.S. investment in Europe is direct; only 18.5 percent of the European (in the United States) was direct. In 1965, the United States had approximately $6.3 billion of direct investment in EEC countries; they in turn had close to $2 billion (a surprisingly high one-third as much) in the United States. Significantly, much of the European direct investment in the United States is of older vintage; and the total has grown relatively slowly, while the U.S. total in Europe increased ninefold from 1950 to 1965.

The significance of U.S. direct investment in Europe is, however, more marked than the dollar totals would indicate. Such investments tend to be concentrated: in manufacturing, particularly in automobiles, chemicals (of which carbon black is an outstanding example — Europe has no enterprises of its own), computers, and certain personal and household items such as razors and sewing machines; in petroleum; and in food processing in the "other" industry category. There is concentration among firms also: in Britain, France, and West Germany, Chrysler, Esso, Ford, and General Motors accounted for over half of all U.S. direct investment.

American business enterprises have been keenly aware of what they visualize as profitable possibilities in Europe. By 1965, over 700 of the largest 1000 American corporations had established a bridgehead in Europe, and a large number of medium and small concerns had followed suit.[54] The writer made an analysis of twenty-one Minneapolis–St. Paul, Minnesota, companies that either were started or offered their stock to the public during the period 1955–60 (roughly the period of negotiation and creation of EFTA and the EEC). By 1967 five of these companies had entered the European market through the direct investment route and two more were contemplating so doing. A detailed — though far from exhaustive — examination made in Brussels, Belgium, in 1967 did not yield any indication of comparable investments made in the United States by companies of that country. Apart from whatever environmental factors may be relevant, the writer found a basically different outlook on the part of entrepreneurs in the United States as against those in Belgium.

Few data appear to be available on the percentage share American investment is of *total* (not new) investment in Western Europe. One study for the Federal Republic of Germany indicated that in 1965 approximately 3.4 percent of the capital of German public companies was owned by Americans.[55] Other estimates range between 1 plus and 5 percent. (These compare, for example, with U.S. ownership of 45 percent of the capital of Canadian industry.) Moreover, only in Great Britain are U.S. investments in the majority as compared with those of *other* foreign countries; on the Continent the stake of other foreign countries is higher than that of the United States for any country in question.

But even if the *total* ownership of European industry by Americans is small (a hazarded estimate is less than 6 percent at the outside) and ownership by other foreign countries is greater than that of the United States (except in Britain), the more important qualitative datum is the sizable increase in the rate of *new* direct investment. As Table 7 indicates, it grew by over 700 percent for Europe from 1950 to 1965 and nearly 900 percent for the EEC. In 1950, U.S. direct investment accounted for 2 percent of new investment in plants and equipment in Europe; by 1965–66 it was running approximately 6 percent.[56] It is this development, along with the kinds of fears that it has brought with it, which forms the basis of much of the current European concern.

Why did American investments in Europe increase? And why more than proportionately in terms of total U.S. investments being made abroad? The answer need not be belabored: the creation of EFTA and the EEC provided an impetus in and of itself.[57] (Differentiated reasons can be given: opening new markets, profit differentials, cost differences, and so on, but they all add up to the same fact, which is that of "economic opportunity" as afforded by the newly emerging entities.)

The new, integrated, markets generated increased American investment; in turn the rising tide of investments generated or at least accentuated a number of problem areas.[58] From the European viewpoint, these appear three in number: the political — the national "image" evokes a belief that foreign "domination" of one's economy should not be countenanced; the economic — there is a belief or fear that the efficiency of the foreign competitor (based in one's home country) will prove disastrous; and the operational — American methods of business enterprise frequently are at variance with the European.

Before looking at these in greater detail one needs to note that the European is also highly aware of the benefits of such investment: new industries, products, and processes, increased productivity, more efficient methods, higher exports, greater competition. But Western Europe is still concerned, concerned enough so that several shifts in policy toward U.S. investments have occurred in various countries.

In the period 1945–60, European countries, for readily apparent reasons, welcomed U.S. investment, and frequently made efforts to attract it.[59] But the flow became a flood tide in the eyes of some Europeans, and resistance began to develop, sparked by a number of trends and incidents including emerging national concern simply about the magnitude of "takeover"; individual resentment by competitors when an American firm took over an enterprise in a given field; specific instances of what were regarded as "malpractices": 1962 layoffs in France by General Motors and Remington Rand, an advertising "war" in Germany involving Proctor and Gamble, the 1963 Chrysler takeover of Simca in France, a 1964 bid by Socony Mobil to secure Aral (the remaining independent petroleum distributor in Germany). In general, one might suggest that a basic fear in Europe is that the American firms will behave as "patriotic" Americans, rather than "patriotic" Belgians, Frenchmen, Germans, and so on.

In the case of France, resentment was brought to a head in the well-known computer cases in which IBM was refused U.S. government permission to provide a computer to France (for nuclear programming) and in which General Electric had been seeking to buy into Machines Bull, the French computer manufacturer. No "anti-direct investment" laws have resulted from these incidents. But a screening process evolved in France which was applied to American investment after 1963. By 1965 this had crystallized to the point where American investments were to be sanctioned only if they brought in new technologies or assisted in regional development. France likewise pressed for a community investment policy that would be "selective" in its application. In 1966–67, some sentiment favorable to selectivity was to be found in other EEC countries; but no community policy has yet evolved nor have other countries adopted restrictions.[60]

Why no restrictions? One businessman explained, using an American phrase, "We are damned if we do [permit American investment] and damned if we don't." And the "don't" seems to carry more criticism at the moment. The advantages of such investment outweigh the disadvantages. Belgium, as a matter of fact, in April 1967, announced a drive to attract American capital and investment.[61] Individuals with whom this drive was discussed were most aware of the advantages of attracting U.S. industry. (A long stay in Belgium convinced the author, however, that that country is less "image-conscious" than is France.)

But even a receptive country such as Belgium differentiates between "desirable" (or more desirable) and "undesirable" (or less desirable) American investments. The desirable is one in which the U.S. firm (1) introduces a new product or service, (2) locates in an area of labor surplus (depressed area), and (3) brings its own capital with it. The less desirable is one in which the firm (1) enters a field already populated with European enterprises, (2) locates in or near an already crowded urban area, and (3) secures its capital locally.

The capital problem is of post-1965 origin; the others are of earlier vintage, but the capital issue added yet another dimension to earlier criticism. The European capital markets tightened considerably in 1965–67, this at the very time American "controls" on capital exports were causing U.S. firms seeking to locate abroad also to seek to raise more of their capital abroad. This put an added layer of demand on already tight markets.[62]

Even when an American firm makes a "good" investment in terms of the criteria noted, it is not always above criticism. Other of its policies and practices may be (and frequently are) at variance with local custom as the following examples indicate: (1) On takeovers, the American firm frequently feels it needs majority control, whereas the European frequently prefers some other form of sharing. (2) Basic decisions concerning the European subsidiary of the American firm may well be made in the United States, leading to the "remote control" criticism. The European *is* aware that the European branch is but a unit in the complex constellation and there may be considerable logic in the centralized decision-making procedure. But he is also likely to conclude — frequently with justification — that not enough consideration is given to local conditions or to local authority.[63] (3) The American firm will frequently utilize approaches (apart from competition itself) which upset the European since they disturb the pattern of Continental practices and give the U.S. firm advantages over local national firms: payment of higher wages; innovative collective bargaining (such as the Esso "productivity bargaining" at Frawley in Great Britain, through which sizable wage increases made possible the elimination of a wide range of restrictive practices); new techniques in management training; and so on. (4) The American enterprise is frequently more "European" than the individual European country enterprise. The U.S. firm may well have a marketing network throughout the Continent with its production facilities rationalized. While production and marketing facilities may have a high degree of local operation, they are tied together in a way that is easy to adapt to the community (or Continental) market.

Fundamental to any European answer to these problems, as well as to the problems of technology, company size, capital, and policies, is further integration. In the view of an American, though, one hopes, an unbiased one, it appears that Europe has no choice. One may not wish to go so far as to say "integrate or fail" as some have said. But the world is getting to be more and more of a unitary market. While there will remain, in many cases at least, home production for home consumption, the world market, let alone the Continental market, cannot be competed in by an overly large number of overly small firms. While intracountry mergers will help, it will take more than that. So company policy, patent policy, and all the rest of the array come again to the fore.

Not all Americans take the viewpoint outlined above about the relative attractiveness of American investment. Leo Model, an international banker in New York, concludes that there should be a moratorium on American investment abroad as one step in a major program to stop the rising tide of nationalism abroad. In his view, the large increase in U.S. direct investments has had the consequence not of fostering integration but of increasing nationalistic reaction. Moreover, he holds that the situation would be improved if American business itself took the initiative in curtailing investment rather than reacting to what he feels will be increasing foreign demands or increasing U.S. government pressures (arising, for example, out of balance-of-payments deficits). He also recommends a set of "good conduct abroad" practices for U.S. enterprises in order to lessen foreign criticism.[64]

One may ask whether there is a rising tide of nationalism abroad and, if so, what causal part American ventures play. There is evidence of some increase in nationalistic sentiment in Europe in recent years, but the conclusion that American investments have played an instrumental role is, on the basis of this study, not demonstrable. Nor can one be sanguine about "voluntary efforts" to curb such investment, for there is still too much interest in Europe in having such investments continue — witness the previously noted Belgian program to *attract* more U.S. investment; and there still is too high a level of economic opportunity in Europe for American firms voluntarily to cease their activities. Therefore, it is not likely that

European countries will shut the gates nor should a U.S. government embargo be anticipated.

From the point of view of the United States the direct investment issue is of a quite different order: namely its impact upon the balance of payments. This problem is well known, well analyzed and documented, and does not require extensive discussion here. Once the layers of detail relating to exports and imports, to military spending and aid, and to short-term capital movements are peeled away, the basic problem is that income received in the United States from investments in Western Europe is less than the capital outflow to Europe, and in recent years the absolute difference has been increasing. However, the bulk of the U.S. deficit accrues from other causal factors, and not from European relationships. And even in terms of European–United States interaction, some uncertainty exists about the relations between direct investments and the balance of payments.[65] It has been suggested that the balance-of-payments problem of the United States is akin to that of a wealthy man who has heavy short-term debts but who sees many profitable long-term investment outlets.

Nonetheless, a general belief exists that any reduction in investment would assist in closing the payments gap. Hence recent U.S. administrations have tackled the problem on a series of fronts: the Interest Equalization Tax; voluntary "restrictionism" by banks on loans and large corporations on investments abroad; and a direct appeal (December 1965) for a cut in the outflow for direct investment. Through 1965 the approaches yielded negligible results (in the first half of 1965 the outflow of $2.1 billion was nearly as large as the total 1964 figure of $2.4 billion). The 1966 and 1967 data do not show any marked improvement. Moreover, one side effect has been that the American business enterprise has increasingly entered European capital markets for funds; this in turn has provoked additional criticism abroad.[66] In January 1968, President Lyndon B. Johnson proposed additional "drastic" steps: direct controls on investment and the well-publicized "tourist tax."

In part the payments deficit problem should begin to correct itself in the not-too-distant future. The EEC in particular was assumed to be (and has proved to be) an area in which profitable investment could be undertaken by American business. There seems to be considerable agreement that the major thrust of direct investment has taken place, that opportunities are narrowing, and hence that if (new) direct investment does not actually decrease, it will increase at a slower rate. This is not to say that economic opportunity has disappeared, but it has diminished relative to, say, a decade ago. Moreover, the income from such investments is increasing and will continue to do so as the investments increasingly pay off.[67] Also, beginning about mid-1965 a change in American direct investment practices began to be felt. An American company opening a subsidiary on the Continent would equip the subsidiary with machinery shipped from the United States, thus saving dollars, and (as already noted) borrow the working capital required from Continental money markets, thus also conserving dollars. Hence, even given the current critical problem and the need for strong measures, the problem does have a self-correcting, longer-run tendency.[68]

For the United States, then, the direct investment problem is visualized as to all intents one-dimensioned, namely the issues it poses for balance of payments. There is recognition — as in the comments of Leo Model — that other factors may be of relevance. But with respect to these other factors there is no unanimity of thought or position.[69] And there is not likely to be.[70]

The Situation in European Integration at the End of the 1960's: Achievements, Problems, Outlook

The following are the reflections of one observer of the European scene; they are based upon a year's stay on the Continent, upon scores of interviews and discussions, and upon the foregoing discussion, but they, of course, reflect one man's outlook and prejudices.

The primary achievement in integration is that Europe has organized itself: EFTA, the EEC, Euratom, the ECSC, Benelux, and the other entities are proof of this. The author believes that these were monumental enough undertakings so that the fact of organization itself is significant.

But more important than creation has been survival, this in the face of severe strains from time to time. The EEC, for example, overcame the agricultural crises of 1961, the crisis involved in the two vetoes of United Kingdom membership, the agricultural-constitutional crisis (and the French walkout) of June 1965–January 1966. It is the conclusion of the author that the point of no return has been reached and that the costs of breaking up are too high.

In terms of treaty goals, the European organizations have moved ahead. As noted, EFTA reached its tariff-free goal on December 31, 1966, and the EEC reached the same point on July 1, 1968, a year and a half ahead of schedule. True, special exceptions were invoked by France in light of its economic difficulties of mid-1968. But the fact that the goal was reached even in the face of the French situation is, the author believes, remarkable.

In terms of the framework of analysis developed early in this chapter — the concepts of the cultural setting, structural integration, policy harmonization, and the integration of people — much also has been accomplished. It is the judgment of the author that the cultural setting is changing, is responding to the new forces, as of competition, occasioned by the creation of the integrated units. (How one views the desirability of this change, and the passing of the old order, is a matter of one's own value judgments. But the fact remains that the response to the challenge is taking place.) Structural accommodation has not proceeded very far; although the merger of the executives in the EEC is an important structural achievement, there is no single central bank, for example, and capital markets are far from being integrated. In contrast, harmonization in the EEC has been successful in important cases: the accord on agricultural prices, the agreement on the value-added tax, the creation of a common external tariff through the unified Kennedy Round negotiations. All this is not to deny that there have been certain failures thus far — the lack of a common transport policy being perhaps the outstanding example. Arnold Rose concludes elsewhere in this volume that the integration of peoples has not been a marked success; the reaction of the author of this chapter is surprise that there has been as much as there has.

In terms of economic performance the author would also conclude that the results have been positive. Annual increases in output have been high and sustained, even with the instabilities of the past few years. While one cannot say quantitatively and conclusively how much of a contribution to economic growth arose from the creation of EFTA and the EEC, the general consensus appears to be that it was positive and significant.

The major underlying problem, particularly relevant to the EEC, is that posed by the gap between expectations and realization. For one thing, little in the way of political integration, at least in the sense supported by many enthusiasts of integration, has taken place. This is not without its advantages, however, for this fact has made the EEC more attractive to certain prospective members — Sweden for example — who might not otherwise have made bids to enter. For another, again looking at problems in the EEC, internal developments such as policy harmonization have proceeded at a pace much less rapid than had been hoped for. The consequence is a kind of psychological lassitude which many believe is inimical to continued development.

A second problem, in some respects more pervasive and far-reaching than that just stated, is found in the stresses and strains of adjustment and accommodation that are taking place. Elsewhere in this volume Philip M. Raup deals with the ways in which life is changing in the agricultural sector and the problems that are arising therefrom. The business sector is likewise undergoing a major transformation as the pressures of increased competition not only make for structural change but also force a marked alteration in entrepreneurial outlook and in enterprise practices.

The American presence in Europe is not an unimportant factor in pacing the adjustments noted above and may have some influence on developing nationalism as discussed below. The American presence through direct investment poses problems for Europe in forcing the nature and pace of adjustments. But it also poses problems for America and the American in terms of interaction across the Atlantic. It is not likely that diplomatic relations will be ruptured by U.S. economic activity in Europe. But that it has created some tensions and evoked major discussion cannot be doubted.[71]

All the pressures noted above appear, in some respects, to be evoking an increase in nationalistic sentiments. While it is difficult to ascertain if this is, in fact, taking place and if so how much, the belief exists that the tide of nationalism is rising and this is detrimental to the progress of integration. The impacts are probably more noticeable with respect to the operations of Euratom and the Coal and Steel Community than to those of EFTA and the EEC, but even for these latter two, some effects appear to have occurred.

In the more narrowly economic realm two problem areas are evident. The first of these relates to the instabilities of the recent past. As market imbalances appeared and inflationary pressures developed, various stabilization measures were invoked. These had the result of slowing down the rate of increase in annual output and hence the rate of achievement as compared with the previous decade. The longer-run problem arises out of the slowing down of the rate of growth of labor inputs and the necessity of providing substitute inputs. The role of technology in this process becomes all the more important. Certain countries have had their own particular forms of economic distress: France in the summer and autumn of 1968 and in the spring and summer of 1969; the United Kingdom over a longer period.

A summing up and weighing of the achievements and problems cited yields the following observations:

1. That the integration of Europe is here to stay, and that it will widen in the future, probably through absorption by the EEC of various EFTA members as well as other nations. It would be foolhardy to set down a timetable, but the 1970's should see major changes. The resignation of President Charles de Gaulle is likely, this writer believes, to accelerate integration though not necessarily immediately or rapidly. But one strong figurehead of resistance has departed from the scene.

2. That integration has taken a particular, if not peculiar, path but this very path may well have been its salvation. It appears that economic integration can take place without political (in the broader sense of that term) integration or even without the integration of people; that the economic sector has provided the major thrust for integration; and that this sector has carried the whole integration movement along with it. In a sense, the real liberals in the integration process are the members — broadly defined — of the business community. Hence if the author had to state what force

provided the staying power for integration he would conclude it was not the politician or the ordinary citizen but rather the business enterprise in pursuit of profit in the best sense of the word.

3. That crises have been surmounted and will continue to be. Concentration upon crises in the EEC tends to blur the fact that each crisis has in some respects been followed by a new breakthrough: the agricultural accord, the unified Kennedy Round negotiations, the value-added tax. One may suggest with some safety that further cultural accommodation will take place — accommodation conducive to the changing patterns of economic activity; that structural integration and policy harmonization will evolve, albeit more slowly than some would wish. There will one day be a "central" central bank, a common currency, and a transport policy.

In all the preceding discussion two criteria have been implicit: that the basic purpose of economic integration is to create that kind of framework conducive to more effective economic performance and that any and all activities which facilitate the development of such a framework are therefore desirable. The underlying criterion is simply that the improvement of the economic well-being of the peoples of Western Europe is, in itself, a worthwhile goal. No attempt has been made to assess the costs that may be involved in integration, such as the dislocations brought about, though Philip M. Raup looks at those in agriculture in his chapter and in the conclusion. The qualitative impression brought back from Europe by the research group that prepared this volume was that the European believes the benefits outweigh the costs.

If one moves to the world outside of Europe several additional issues emerge. One fact of global importance may be mentioned first. Insofar as economic integration interlocks nations and makes armed conflict less likely, this consequence is of major importance. Up to the present, at least, this result has flowed from economic integration in Western Europe. This is a contribution of considerable significance.

As for the United States, European integration has had two opposing economic impacts. On the one hand, integration has created additional opportunities for American business enterprise, through direct investment in Europe as well as from additional U.S. exports to Europe, made possible by the expanding economies. On the other, integration has raised efficiency in Europe and made for increased U.S. competition in world markets. Witness the appeals by U.S. business enterprise in 1968 (following the Kennedy Round tariff reductions) for special protective measures of one kind or another. The steel industry in the United States provides a particular example of this competitive European thrust. But, challenge or not, economic integration in Europe is a fact, and the United States will need to accommodate to it. The qualitative conclusion reached here is that economic integration in Europe has yielded benefits to the United States which outweigh the costs.

With respect to the rest of the world, the chief criticism raised against European integration is that it has been too inward looking and not enough concerned with other nations, particularly the developing economies. These viewpoints are held notwithstanding the kind of relationship existing, for example, between the EEC and the Association with Certain African Countries and Madagascar (formally renewed by the Yaounde Convention of 1964), in which economic assistance played an important role. Whatever one believes should be the level of concern for other nations, one may suggest that Europe had a legitimate reason for primary preoccupation with internal affairs during the initial stages of integration and that over the long run she will assume her external responsibilities.

In conclusion, three comments. First, the main thrust of integration thus far has been economic in nature and in a very real sense this has carried forward the whole movement. But, second, integration in the economic sector cannot help but "spill over" into other sectors and hence it is likely that integrative developments in other areas will occur. Finally integration may not be an unmixed blessing — however one wishes to define these terms — but it is a fact and, on balance, an important contribution to global economic and political development and stability. Merely compare Europe after World War II with the situation that obtained after World War I.

CHAPTER *5*

Constraints and Potentials in Agriculture

BY PHILIP M. RAUP

EUROPEAN agricultural policy has been conditioned for centuries by lessons learned in past wars. One of the most fundamental of these lessons has been the necessity to preserve a food-supply base. Even France, with one of the most favorable potentials in all Europe for producing a food surplus, entered the Common Market era with its agriculture insulated from external competition and dependent upon an elaborate network of state support. Georges Pompidou, then prime minister, concluded a long interview in September 1967 with the prophetic observation that France "is practically ungovernable," leaving the clear implication that integration even within the boundaries of the French nation-state has usually involved the unifying force of a threat or a crisis.[1] This has typically included a threat to the agricultural sector and to rural lands and value systems.

A basic national policy of England since the repeal of the Corn Laws has been to keep open her food-supply lines. Beginning in the 1930's and accelerated by wartime controls, this policy has been amended by a complex system of support for domestic producers including marketing boards, guaranteed prices for fatstock, egg, and wool producers, deficiency payments to cereal growers, and some twenty different programs of grants to individual producers ranging from subsidies for fertilizing, plowing, and draining to hill-cow-and-calf subsidies and "grants to rabbit clearance societies."[2] The end result is a domestic agricultural economy that is increasingly insulated from the world market, in spite of the fact that England still imports about one-third of her temperate-zone food products, and nearly one-half of her total food.

Germany in the industrial era has been notoriously preoccupied with the guarantee of a food supply from internal resources or from contiguous territories, often to further war aims or render her immune to blockade. The Netherlands, with one of the best records in Europe in the pursuit of freer trade, has made massive investments in land reclamation at nominal cost-benefit ratios that would be rejected out of hand if proposed by a developing country applying for a World Bank loan. Sweden and Switzerland have in the past based their traditional neutrality on policies designed to supply as much of their food as possible from their own resources. A measure of the cost is provided by a retail price of butter in Geneva in recent years that has averaged roughly twice the United States price and three times the London price, and by a farm price of slaughter-weight beef cattle in Sweden in mid-1968 approximately 50 percent above the average United States farm price.[3]

These policy goals have generated a siege mentality that has dominated modern agricultural policy throughout much of Europe. The focus has been on production, and cost considerations have been secondary. This approach has been demonstrated in Eastern Europe as well, where the experience of the Soviet Union in the 1930's and again in the 1960's provided a repeated reminder of the extent to which socialism is dependent on its farm-policy base.

The twin threats of war and scarcity have thus been the principal generators of European agricultural policies in the industrial era. These basic policy determinants were supplemented in the depression of the 1930's by a new wave of protectionism, caused by the worldwide collapse of commodity prices and the resulting crisis among small-scale, high-cost European farm producers. The fragmented nature of land holdings in many parts of Europe retarded the adoption of cost-reducing agricultural technology, while the sheer number of farms and farm families guaranteed a political approach to their economic and social problems. With the notable exception of the Danes and the Dutch, Europe as a consequence entered the second half of the twentieth century with trade policies designed to provide high levels of protection for farm producers, a fixation on agricultural output expansion, and no experience with chronic domestic food surpluses. Prospects of peace and the appearance of food surpluses have been fundamentally disturbing to these patterns of thought.

To balance the picture, it must be added that the problem of food surpluses is almost uniquely a twentieth-century problem in any country. The novel idea of a planned limitation of agricultural production, or "agricultural adjustment," was first seriously considered in the United States in the reorientation of farm policy caused by the agricultural depression of 1919–23.[4] In Europe it appeared in serious form in the French wine areas in the 1930's. In the 1960's Sweden undertook a systematic study of the possibilities of an orderly reduction of the agricultural sector, but the idea remains suspect throughout most of Europe.[5]

The fact of surpluses remains to plague agricultural policy makers. This was unmistakably clear at the 5th Regional Conference for Europe of the Food and Agriculture Organization of the United Nations, at Seville, Spain, October 5–11, 1966. The opening address by FAO Director General B. R. Sen was an urgent plea that the developed countries of Europe provide more food and technical aid to developing countries. In the ensuing conference discussions it was clear that for southern and eastern Europe the main goal of agricultural policy is increased output. For northern and western Europe the emphasis shifts from output increases to productivity increases, particularly labor productivity. And farm policy makers in the most highly industrialized countries were preoccupied with the appearance of chronic surpluses in soft wheat, sugar, and milk.

This points up a seeming paradox. The European countries that have increased agricultural output most rapidly since 1950 include many of the most highly industrialized nations, in which decreases in the proportion of the labor force in agriculture have been greatest. In Germany agricultural labor was 20.0 percent of the total labor force in 1955, and 11.4 percent in 1964. Over this same period, the index of total agricultural production rose from 100 in 1955–56 to 126 in 1964–65.[6] Switzerland cut its agricultural labor force from 15.2 percent of the total work force in 1950 to 8.1 percent in 1964 while the index of physical output in agriculture rose from 112 in 1951–55 (1939 = 100) to 135 in 1964.[7] The United Kingdom, with the smallest proportion of its labor force in agriculture of any country, continued to reduce this proportion from 6 percent in 1950 to 3.3 percent in 1967, while the index of total output rose from 100 for the crop years 1954–55 through 1956–57 to 144 in the crop year 1967–68.[8] Even more striking changes have taken place in France and, especially, in Italy. Although 28.3 percent of the French labor force was in agriculture in 1950, this proportion declined to 21 percent in 1960 and to 17 percent in 1965. For Italy, comparable percentages were 41 percent in 1950, 31 percent in 1960, and 25 percent in 1965.[9] Despite large declines in both the relative and absolute size of the farm labor force, the index of total agricultural production (1952–56 = 100) had risen by 1965 to 136 in France and 127 in Italy.[10]

Sharp increases in self-sufficiency ratios have also been associated with reductions in the agricultural labor force in several countries. At the height of the 1935–39 period of preparation for war, the area that is today the Federal Republic of Germany was never more than 60 percent self-sufficient in foodstuffs. By 1965, with a larger population, it was 69 percent self-sufficient. If account is taken of value added in domestic production through the use of imported feeds, the figure becomes 74 percent.[11] In twenty-five years the United Kingdom doubled her self-sufficiency ratio in grains, from a prewar average of 31 percent to 62 percent in 1965–66. The ratio for all dairy products rose from 31 to 47 percent and for all meats from 47 to 69 percent.[12] The shift to cereal grains in the heavily industrialized countries of Europe has been especially noteworthy. The 1966 barley crop in the United Kingdom, 8,944,000 metric tons, exceeded that of the United States and in that year was second only to the Soviet Union.[13] While retaining her position as one of the world's largest importers of feed grains, the United Kingdom has also moved into the ranks of major exporters, with barley exports of 112,200 metric tons in 1964–65, 678,100 tons in 1965–66, 1,108,500 tons in 1966–67, and 797,000 tons in 1967–68.[14]

These data underline a phenomenon of the second industrial revolution: Industrialized nations have replaced agricultural labor with capital, chemicals, and biological technology at rates that increase food self-sufficiency ratios while drawing large quantities of labor out of agriculture. It is this ability of industrialized nations to excel in both primary production and manufacturing that creates new dimensions for agricultural policy in the 1970's. The basic causal forces are found in the accelerated rate of farm production increases, the relatively slow rate of population expansion, and the diminishing income elasticity of demand. The resultant falling real cost of producing a food supply from domestic resources has played a major role in determining the pace and direction of current trends in European integration. It is in this sense that the 1960's retaught an old lesson: the primacy of agricultural policy in the reformation of economic and political institutions.

A perspective is provided for this development by a review of revolutionary movements since the late eighteenth century. From the French Revolution to date, a strong case can be made for the argument that the principal characteristics of new institutional structures thrown up by the great revolutions were fixed by the solutions hammered out for the agricultural problems of the day. The tone, the characteristics, and the most distinguishing features of the French Revolution were heavily influenced by the reform in the land-tenure system. The new liberty and equality were typified by the individualistic philosophy of those segments of the Code Napoléon that concerned land ownership and the transfer of ownership to future generations. This was the principal issue involved in the American Civil War, a war ostensibly over property rights in Negroes, but more basically a war that reflected a conflict of attitudes toward rights in all forms of property, and especially in land. The theme was repeated in the Mexican Revolution of 1910 and in the subsequent identification of that revolution with land reform and policies for agricultural change.

The most dramatic example of this primacy of agricultural policy in institution building in our time has been the Russian Revolution of 1917 and the subsequent collectivization drive after 1928. If we take away from the Soviet Union those features of her economy that concern agriculture, the institutional structure is much less dramatically different from those of several European countries outside the Soviet bloc. Remove the collective and state farms, the procurement methods, the multiple-price system in agriculture, and the collectivization drive of the 1928–33 era, and the course of Russian history in the past fifty years would appear in a completely different light.

The pervasive role played by agricultural policy was repeated in Europe in the 1960's. Positive evidence is provided by the approach taken by the European Economic Community to its agricultural problems. How these have been resolved has formed and shaped the general EEC approach to problem solving. Agricultural policy negotiations have played a major role in determining the relations among different elements in its secretariat. These negotiations created political precedents that are guiding subsequent developments as other segments of economic policy are hammered out in Brussels.

Negative evidence is provided by the experience of the European Free Trade Association and by the Benelux union of Belgium, the Netherlands, and Luxembourg. It is precisely because the EFTA agreement omitted agriculture that it is widely regarded as "just a customs union," and not a bold or revolutionary step toward European integration. And the failure of the Benelux union to deal with agriculture had seriously reduced its effectiveness until remedied by the EEC agreement on a Common Agricultural Policy.

The steps by which the struggle for solutions to agricultural problems has molded Common Market institutions have been detailed by Theodor Dams in his inaugural lecture at the University of Freiburg. Between 1962 and mid-1966 some 900 ordinances and legally binding regulations were issued in the name of the EEC in the agricultural sector alone. Some 350 ordinances were subsequently needed in order to carry out the decision of July 27, 1966, to achieve a Common Agricultural Market by July 1, 1968.

Dams concludes that the achievement of a Common Agricultural Policy contributed basically to the creation of a body of law that is recognized as "Community Law." [15] Business and commercial interests in the member states wanted to get on with integration in the industrial sector, in order to gain the advantage of larger markets for their industrial products. It was this driving force that led them to overcome differences in the area of agricultural policy. "Industrial integration compelled agricultural integration," Dams observes, but at this point the Common Agricultural Policy began to live a life of its own; it became self-propelled. And the resultant "induction effect" of decisions regarding the Common Agricultural Policy contributed to a significant expansion of the area covered by community law.

This can be illustrated with the following examples: (1) A decision was taken in 1962 to expand the field of competence of the EEC to include the coordination of measures aimed at improvement of the agrarian structure. This was not expressly required by the Treaty of Rome. (2) A "Guidance and Guaranty Fund" was created, based on sections of the Treaty of Rome that dealt explicitly with market organization, not with structural change. This represented an expansion of the scope of the field of competence of the EEC, an expansion that was carried further by measures adopted to finance improvement of the agrarian structure.

There were also important consequences outside the agrarian sector: (1) A decision was taken to specify uniform grain prices as of July 1, 1967, in "Units of Account" (*Rechnungseinheiten*), based on gold dollars. This had the unanticipated effect of greatly restricting if not nullifying the explicit provision of the Treaty of Rome that permitted each member state to determine its foreign exchange policy independently but in the "common interest." Independent action was now hardly possible. (2) An agreement on common agricultural prices required an agreement to remove price distortions resulting from freight-rate structures that were not based on transport costs to central markets. This is leading to a reconstruction of transport policy of great significance for the nonagricultural sectors. (3) Decisions to promote improvement of the agricultural structure led to an increased interest in measures to develop regional economic policy, a goal mentioned in the Preamble of the Treaty of Rome, but not given any legal basis in the text of the treaty. Although there is still no explicit regional policy in the community, the urgent need for structural change in agriculture has unquestionably introduced aspects of regional policy into virtually all the community decisions. (4) The accelerated adoption of a Common Agricultural Policy before the end of the planned transition period was coupled with the requirement that a common market for industrial products should also be achieved before the end of the transition period. In effect, the Common Agricultural Policy, which had been regarded as a bottleneck, became the "motor" that drove forward the total integration process and significantly expanded the area covered by community law.

In this way, Dams concludes, agricultural policy strengthened and enlarged the EEC. What may prove to be more significant in the long run is that solutions achieved in conflicts over agricultural policy set the tone, the style, and the operating procedures for this new form of quasi-federal state. A future historian may well look back and conclude that this was the leitmotif-creating phase of the Common Market.

Historians in the future may also ask whether or not this dominance of agricultural policy was a beneficial influence in the formative years of the EEC. Policy decisions of far-reaching importance were taken under the influence of agricultural problems of the moment. The decisive example concerns the most basic price of all — the price of money. When the franc was devalued on August 10, 1969, the resulting crisis in the Common Market was centered on agricultural policy. To devalue the "unit of account" (the gold equivalent of a United States dollar) would have lowered farm prices for all members of the community while permitting French farm prices to remain unchanged. In effect, French farm prices would have been raised relative to the rest of the community. The alternative chosen was to isolate the French agricultural price structure from the Common Agricultural Policy of the EEC, completely for the crop year 1969–70 and partially for 1970–71.

The sequence in these events is ironic. It was France that had insisted upon a formalized agreement on a Common Agricultural Policy, effective for grains on July 1, 1967. It was France that repeatedly opposed British entry into the Common Market until final agreement could be reached on the financing of this policy. And it was France, by the unilateral devaluation of August 10, 1969, that brought about a breach in the Common Agricultural Policy, thus reopening the door to renewed efforts by Britain and her trading partners to enter the EEC. These instances dramatized the extent to which a common monetary policy was essential for any true community of economic interests. They reinforced the fact that no agreement on common agricultural policies could be enforced without a substantial compromise of national sovereignty. And they underlined the extent to which national sovereignty had already been restricted, as a price of common policies in the agricultural field.

For the short run, the price proved to be too high. The special concession of August 1969, isolating French agricultural prices from those of the rest of the EEC, was repeated for Germany in October 1969. If German farm prices had remained pegged to the EEC "unit of account," the upward revaluation of the mark would have lowered German farm prices relative to those of the rest of the community. The German solution was to impose a tax on farm imports from other members of the EEC roughly equivalent to the amount of the revaluation. To protect her farmers from a price drop, Germany chose to violate the policy of unrestricted trade in farm products. In effect, the Common Agricultural Policy was temporarily abrogated for the largest exporter (France) and the largest importer (Germany) of farm products within the community. The imperatives of national monetary and fiscal policy pointed up the degree to which the EEC members were not yet ready to subordinate national goals to the demands of a common market. Although a blow to the prestige of the EEC Commission, these unilateral actions were not without a positive dimension. The special arrangements for France and Germany made it much more plausible for Great Britain to press her request for major modifications in agricultural policies as a condition for entry. Although the immediate crises of 1969 underlined the weakness of agricultural agreements that were not founded on a common monetary policy, they provided dramatic evidence of the degree to which national economies were in fact linked by aspirations for common trade, a linkage that extended beyond the boundaries of the EEC.

How did it happen that this point was reached in European integration in the 1960's? The answer to this question must begin by paying homage to the men who dreamed and planned for European unity during the war and in the first chaotic postwar years.[16] But there have been men of wisdom and vision in earlier generations in Europe, and dreamers of great dreams. Why did dreams crystallize in the 1950's? Another part of the answer must be sought in the horror and revulsion that came with full realization of the awfulness of World War II. The combination of leaders of vision and people of determination was in part a direct outgrowth of the scale of the war and the extent to which it had touched the lives of people in almost all parts of Europe. So much of the answer must be given in terms of the nature of the war itself.

There are less heroic explanations that also go far to explain why European integration in the 1950's and 1960's was an idea whose time had come. Some of these are technical, and some of the most important pertain directly to the agricultural and food economy. It is the thesis of this chapter that the trends and processes of European integration since 1945 have evolved in a society whose agriculture is still dominated by a traditional culture. The resultant structural rigidities play a major — and in some cases a dominant — role in determining the path that integration is taking and the constraints that inhibit its further development. The traditions that served this society well in the past were focused on survival in a world of shortages. They are not well adapted to an age of abundance. And in the second half of the twentieth century they have been profoundly disturbed by change in modes of communication that erode a traditional society in its most basic dimension: its ability to insulate itself from the external world. The following sections will explore dimensions of this receding isolation that accelerate or retard the movement toward an integrated European community.

The Transport Revolution and the Integrating
Force of the Automobile

Problems of integration have a spatial dimension, and it is this dimension that has been fundamentally altered in the twentieth century. Europe entered the automobile age for the first time in the 1950's, and entered it suddenly. As a consequence, the transport, storage, and marketing revolutions that were spread over several decades in North America came hurriedly in Europe and with great force. They were experienced by a community whose principal lines of communication had been laid down in an era of waterborne or animal-powered transport. Up to the 1950's the location of industries and the siting of conversion capacity, of milling, of transshipment facilities, and of major markets in Western Europe were still largely those determined when transport was horse- or ox-drawn, or waterborne, by canals, rivers, and oceans. This is less true in Eastern Europe. Eastern Europe industrialized later, and the locations of many of its markets and conversion centers do reflect the railroad era. But in neither Eastern nor Western Europe does the locational matrix of major centers reflect the automobile era or the highway.

As a consequence, the sudden appearance of the motor car and the motor truck has demanded fundamental changes in the pattern of location of industry and agricultural processing facilities in Western Europe. John K. Fairbank has emphasized that the railway burst into China in the 1890's as a foreign intrusion, disruptive of trade relations based on transport by waterways.[17] Europe is not China, and the automobile in Europe is hardly a foreign intrusion. But in this different setting, the impact of the automobile in Europe after 1950 has been similarly profound.

Table 1. Automobiles per Thousand Persons in
Western Europe and North America

Country	1950	1960	1967
Western Europe			
Austria	6	61	132
Belgium	32	88	156
Denmark	28	86	182
Finland	7	41	117
France	39	123	206
Germany (F.R.)	13	82	175
Greece	1	5	15
Ireland	31	60	109
Italy	10	39	136
Luxembourg	31	86	217
Netherlands	15	48	135
Norway	20	55	150
Portugal	7	17	34
Spain	2	10	42
Sweden	42	161	251
Switzerland	32	93	178
United Kingdom	49	109	192
North America			
Canada	139	224	278
United States	268	344	413

SOURCE: Automobile Manufacturers Association, *Automobile Facts and Figures* (Washington, D.C., 1954, 1962, 1969).

Depression inhibited the demand for automobiles in the 1930's and war disrupted production in the 1940's. Prewar levels of production were reached in most Western European countries by 1949–51, and the boom began. As Table 1 shows, France had 39 cars per thousand people in 1950, 123 in 1960, and 206 in 1967. The Federal Republic of Germany went from 13 cars per thousand persons in 1950 to 82 in 1960 and 175 in 1967. Italy climbed from 10 cars per thousand people in 1950 to 39 in 1960 and 136 in 1967. Increases were similarly explosive in Finland and the Netherlands.

The contrast with Eastern Europe is dramatic. In Albania, Bulgaria, Hungary, Rumania, and the U.S.S.R. there was virtually no increase in automobiles per thousand of the population from 1950 to 1967 (see Table 2). Czechoslovakia and East Germany reached in 1967 the level that prevailed in northwestern Europe in 1950. Poland and Yugoslavia had automobiles in 1967 in about the frequencies that prevailed in Italy and the Netherlands in 1950.

These data provide background for an appreciation of the impact that tourism had on Europe in the 1960's. In search of his Black Sea holiday, the Western European motor tourist in Bulgaria or Rumania introduced more than hard currency to these Eastern European economies. The demonstration of his consumption level, and above all his car, are among the seminal political influences in contemporary Eastern Europe. There are cars enough in France or Germany to enable the entire populations (with a little squeezing) to be on wheels at any one time. In Bulgaria, Hungary, or Rumania the national stock of automobiles in 1967 would not hold the populations of Plovdiv, Szeged, or Cluj.

The explosive effect of this sudden mobility has affected much more than trade and transport. Until well into the 1950's the motor car in most of Western Europe remained the plaything of the wealthy. In the 1960's

Table 2. Automobiles per Thousand Persons in
Eastern Europe

Country	1950	1960	1967
Albania	0.4	1.3	1.3
Bulgaria	1.3	1.2	1.4
Czechoslovakia	9.2	14.0	27.0
East Germany	...	8.7	42.2
Hungary	1.2	2.1	4.4
Poland	1.2	4.0	9.8
Rumania	0.9	0.5	1.4
U.S.S.R.	3.2	3.1	4.6
Yugoslavia	0.4	2.9	17.6

SOURCE: Automobile Manufacturers Association, *Automobile Facts and Figures* (Washington, D.C., 1952, 1962, 1969).

it became a realistic goal of the working class. The resultant pressure for roads and for a fundamental replanning of cities has developed in a setting in which attitudes toward private cars were class-conscious ones, by those who had them and those who did not. Much of the most vocal resentment toward the automobile is traceable to the annoyance of those who have had private cars for a generation and who find suddenly that this status symbol has been sharply depreciated.

This revolution in attitudes has also been keenly felt in traditional working-class political parties. The late Hugh Gaitskell found it necessary in 1962 to warn Labour party workers in Britain that they must combat the notion that the motor car is incompatible with socialism.[18] And when Mrs. Barbara Castle was named minister of transport for the United Kingdom in 1966, she won political kudos from her Labour supporters for the fact that she could not drive. The Austrian government, with a long tradition of public construction of workers' housing, has come under recent fire from members of traditional labor parties for refusal to include garages for workers' cars. The conversion in class symbolism involved in the shift from villas with carriage houses to workers' apartments with garages has been telescoped into a few short years and conditioned political reflexes have been slow to adjust.

Colin Buchanan, whose now-classic report on *Traffic in Towns* is the most provocative effort to come to grips with the automobile, has estimated that Europe is still "less than one-third of the way to full satisfaction of the demand for cars."[19] The force of this demand in the 1960's did much to shape the urban scene in Europe, but its effects may be even more profound in the countryside.

The network of central places in Western Europe was established in the water-transport era. The rail grid was superimposed upon this network in the nineteenth century in a manner that energized it but did not basically alter the locational matrix. The railway boom that followed was the accelerator of European economic growth after 1848.[20] Great as were the indirect effects of railways on the pattern of European agricultural production in the latter half of the nineteenth century, they did not directly touch the individual farm. The highway and the motor truck do. It is this fact as much as any other that created after 1950 a basically altered market structure for European agriculture.

The most important consequence has been to reveal with unmistakable clarity the disadvantaged position of farms and villages in mountain and hill-farming areas. In a broad band reaching from the Pyrenees and the French Massif Central in the west to the Carpathian, Balkan, and Rhodope Mountains in the east, there are farms and rural people accounting for much of the cultural variety and economic poverty of Europe. Of all farms in Austria, one-third are mountain farms. Some 10 percent of all farms cannot be reached by motor truck or car.[21] Depopulation of hill towns was the major demographic fact in Italy and southern France in the 1960's. Hill farms are increasingly being abandoned or permitted to run down in Germany, in the United Kingdom, and in Scandinavia. It is too simplistic an explanation to attribute this exodus wholly to the motor car, but it is to the impact of the automobile era that we must look for the primary cause.

The contrast with the automobile era in North America is sharp and merits a closer look. West of the Appalachians and the Laurentian Shield, the settlement pattern in North America was dominated by the railroad. Agricultural development was directly dependent on access to markets, and the rail network dictated the demographic pattern. Interstitial areas between rail lines were slow to develop and sharply disadvantaged from the beginning of settlement. The automobile changed this dramatically. Campaigns for good roads to "get the farmer out of the mud" in the 1920's and 1930's were welcomed by these disadvantaged areas. The motor truck reduced dependence on local market towns and increased the relative value of lands lying outside the horse-and-wagon-trip radius of the railroad towns. Roads, cars, and trucks reduced local-market price differentials for farm products and upgraded the status of the lower-valued lands.

The motor car in rural Europe has had an opposite effect. There are a few "railroad towns" in Eastern Europe, but almost none west of a line running through Berlin, Prague, Vienna, and Trieste. The market status of rural service towns in this area was established long before the railroad era. The railroads redirected flows of goods, but railroads had not "made" the small towns of Europe and neither did they break them.

The road and highway network that existed by the 1960's is another matter. The motorways, autobahns, autoroutes, and autostrada are having an effect on Europe much like that of the railroads on the Mississippi Valley a century earlier. To be remote from access to key motor freight routes is a keenly felt disadvantage. Access to agricultural markets is being channelized. Freight-cost structures set by waterway and rail linkages are no longer realistic. The location of processing capacity is outmoded and the spatial dimensions of markets have shifted and expanded. It has been this promise of restructured market areas that has held out one of the most effective baits to those who might in an earlier era have opposed European integration. The automobile and motor truck are symbols of this promise.

The Revolution in Processing, Storage, and Materials Handling

The rise in volume of motor-freight transport has been paralleled by a supporting increase in refrigerated warehouse capacity, improved materials-handling techniques, and the more recent appearance of refrigerated motor trucks. This revolution in storage and materials handling broke over Europe like a huge wave in the 1950's. Some of the most impressive evidence is provided by the data in Table 3 on the expansion in public and semipublic refrigerated warehouse capacity, especially in Mediterranean Europe. In the decade 1957–66 this capacity more than doubled in France, more than tripled in Greece, and increased over five times in Spain.

Table 3. Public and Semipublic Refrigerated Warehouse Capacity (in Cubic Meters) for Selected European Countries in 1957 and 1966

Country	1957	1966[a]
Austria	94,000	126,220
Belgium	180,000	252,250
France	660,000	1,450,000
Germany (F.R.)	620,000	1,074,650
Greece	228,000	768,200
Spain	336,800	1,807,600
Sweden	278,000	484,240

SOURCE: For 1957, "International Survey on Refrigeration Equipment and Activities, 1957," *Bulletin of the International Institute of Refrigeration* (Paris), Vol. 39, Nos. 1 and 2 (1959); for 1966, data from interviews with the staff of the Institut International du Froid, Paris, 1968.
  [a] Data for 1966 refer to plants affiliated with the Association Européenne des Exploitations Frigorifiques and are not strictly comparable with the data for 1957.

In refrigerated transport, almost all the recent increase in capacity has been in refrigerated motor trucks. In France, for example, the number of refrigerated railway cars has not increased in recent years, while the number of refrigerated motor trucks rose from 275 in 1957 to 2120 in 1965.[22] The motor truck has eaten into rail-freight volume to an extent that has shocked the managers of Europe's nationalized rail systems. One of the most extreme reactions has been in Germany, where the minister of transportation, Georg Leber, laid before the Federal Parliament in 1967 a draft law that would tax truck transport and use the proceeds to reduce the mounting railway deficit. In addition, long-distance truck transport of certain classes of goods (wood, steel, stone) would be expressly forbidden. This has been sharply attacked as a direct threat to rational regional planning, and a discriminatory measure that would penalize remote and disadvantaged areas.[23]

The greater flexibility permitted by the motor truck has pointed up the outmoded nature of old freight-rate structures and transport traditions. The effects are clearly seen in livestock marketing. The traditional method was to transport live animals by rail or water, with slaughter facilities concentrated at ports or in the major cities. Modern refrigerated storage and transport techniques have shifted the advantage away from large central slaughterhouses and markets in favor of slaughter near major livestock-producing areas. This development in the United States has all but closed Chicago as a major livestock marketing or slaughter center and has shifted slaughter closer to the main meat-producing regions. A major part of the movement of fresh meat to market has been taken over by the motor truck.

These same forces are at work in Europe but are inhibited by institutional arrangements that attempt to support old centers of processing. These are well illustrated by recent trends in German-Danish trade relations. Northwest Germany, a meat-deficit area and a big importer, has major slaughtering plants located in the port cities of Lübeck, Kiel, Flensburg, Hamburg, and Bremen. These have been supplied traditionally with dairy cow beef from Denmark and other countries bordering the Baltic. In order to keep these outmoded slaughter plants in operation, trade agreements between Denmark and West Germany specify that all Danish exports of meat to Germany must be of live cattle and must move by seaborne freight. This has inhibited the growth of cheaper and faster movement of meat into the Ruhr by motor truck.[24]

This "slaughterhouse problem" is endemic throughout Europe, both Eastern and Western. A major reason is that livestock-slaughtering facilities have typically been operated by municipalities outright or taxed heavily. They have been major sources of local public revenues, and small and large cities have fought to retain these plants. This struggle, for example, did much to delay and complicate the decision to move Les Halles, the famous central food market, from Paris to suburban Rungis.

The striking feature of livestock slaughter in Europe is its small scale. In 1963 there were 4856 public slaughterhouses in the EEC, of which 2662 were in Italy and 1576 in France.[25] The only concentration of relatively large slaughterhouses is in densely populated and heavily industrialized areas of the Netherlands and adjacent areas of North Germany. Belgium and Italy had only one plant each that slaughtered over 20,000 tons in 1963, and there were only five plants of this size in France. The only relatively large slaughterhouse in the EEC is at La Villette in Paris, with an output of 109,400 tons in 1963.[26] And this is not an integrated plant but a congregation of small, almost medieval slaughtering rooms.

In order to provide some sense of scale for these figures, it may be noted that there are five slaughtering plants in small midwestern cities of the United States (Albert Lea and Austin, Minnesota; Estherville and Mason City, Iowa; and Huron, South Dakota), each one of which produced over 55,000 tons of meat in 1961, three of them over 80,000 tons. Located in livestock-producing areas, instead of in meat-consuming centers, these plants make it unnecessary to move live animals long distances and permit significant economies of both scale and location. This is made possible by refrigeration and the motor truck. Until European slaughtering plants are moved out of consuming centers to producing areas, and are greatly increased in size, it is difficult to see how the benefits of integration and wider markets can be achieved in the meat and livestock economy.

A similar restructuring is long overdue in grain milling and processing. Virtually all European countries (the Netherlands excepted) are oversupplied with old and outmoded mills that have been kept in operation long past their economic usefulness. The situation is worst, perhaps, in Germany, which was overbuilt with small mills as long ago as the 1930's. These were kept in operation in preparation for war, and during the war, on the ground that major milling centers in Atlantic coast and Rhine River cities were vulnerable to military action.[27] France, on the other hand, had developed major grain-handling and grain-processing facilities in port areas and the Paris region. Traditionally, there had been a relatively modest movement of French grain into the Ruhr, the greatest deficit area on the Continent.

Investments are thus needed in new mills and storage capacity, and at new locations. On the cost side, this represents a major European capital investment in the 1960's. On the benefit side, the promise of larger markets and lower costs through relocated processing facilities has reinforced the integrative tendencies in Europe that have been triggered by the revolution in transport and storage.

Supporting this have been several other revolutions that are hardly less significant. One of them is the statistical and computer revolution. This child of a larger communications revolution has made available information in quantity and quality that permits the manipulation of economic variables in integrating complex and nonsimilar economies in a way that was not possible a generation ago. Statistics in the 1920's and 1930's simply were not available on the scale used in creating the Common Market in the 1950's and 1960's. The quality of national statistics was not good, and capacity to integrate and interpret them was lacking. The statistical and data-processing revolution is of the greatest significance in accounting for the capacity to promote integration in Europe in the 1960's.

Underlying this statistical revolution is a more fundamental revolution in education and research. It has been said that we are in fact entering a university culture, and that it is no longer appropriate to describe our world as a technological culture. We have entered a world in which research and development are at the top of the status structure in business and industrial circles.

This change is particularly significant in agriculture. It was the rewards for publicly supported investment in research and development in agriculture that first dramatized the high rates of return on this form of investment. Significantly, it was agricultural economists who pioneered in the analysis of the significance of investments in research, experimentation, and public support for these activities. The benefits from socialized activities in the business world have nowhere been more apparent than in the socialization of investment in research and experimentation in agriculture. That this has occurred in agriculture is doubly significant. It is precisely that sector of the economy in many countries that is most conservative and most likely to react violently to any suggestion that it benefits from socialism. Yet it has been the agricultural sector that exhibits the most expanded and developed form of socialist activity in many capitalist countries, namely, public support for investment in agricultural research and development and distribution of the fruits of research without resort to the price system. There has typically been no charge for the benefits of agricultural research; they are available to the total community.

It is in this sense that technical revolutions have supported an approach to economic integration problems in Europe of the 1960's that was beyond the capacity of earlier generations.

The Inhibiting Effects of Traditional Beliefs: Rotations and Climaxes

While integration has been facilitated by these revolutions in processing, transport, storage, materials handling, data reporting, and the support of research and development, there have been other powerful inhibitors. Among them are the use of health and sanitary regulations as disguised barriers to trade, restrictions on the movement of people (see Chapter 7), refusal to accept another nation's certification of professional competence (the "freedom of establishment" problem discussed in Chapter 6), and, operating in more subtle ways, welfare and social security differentials, freight-rate structures, and tax-system vagaries. These are the partially visible signs of deep-seated attitudes and beliefs. To explore beneath the surface for forces that work against European integration it is necessary to examine first these implicit articles of faith.

In the field of agriculture, one of the most pervasive can be characterized as the concept of the climax crop. Although the most vigorous proponent of this theory in the twentieth century was an American botanist, F. E. Clements,[28] the elements of his theory had long been incorporated into the conventional wisdom of European farmers and had their parallels in post-Darwinian social thought.[29] In simplified form, the theory held that in a given location there was a unique configuration of plant associations that represented the optimum adaptation of site to climate. This theory of the climax crop, or monoclimax hypothesis, carried with it the clear corollary that in any given location there was a unique answer to the question: What use should be made of this land?

The agricultural response is found in concepts of appropriate rotation systems necessary to maintain fertility by natural means, using some combination of grasses, grains, root crops, animal manures, and fallow. This approach still dominates land-use policy in much of Europe. It is no longer dominant in North America. In a market economy rotations conceived in the sense of a climax crop or a unique and naturally determined land-use pattern are not an adequate guide to optimum use of a site with its rain and sun endowment.

In its policy implications, the climax-crop theory reduces to a land-management guide that is basically determined by climate. In this sense, it takes its place as one stage in the evolution of thought regarding the importance of climate for man and land. This evolution has recently been summarized by the climatologist Emmanuel LeRoy Ladurie, who raises serious questions about the validity of a theory of climatic determinism that seeks to explain economic behavior, migration of peoples, or secular trends in agricultural productivity in terms of the weather.[30] But he does present evidence that certain geographic regions, because of their climate, are peculiarly suited to specific crops and patterns of land use. Although he rejects climatic determinism, the implication remains that these climatic determinants of land use are sufficient to explain, for example, the persistence of wheat in the Paris-Chartres region.

The work of ecologists and paleobotanists has done much to undermine climax-crop theory, especially in areas of relatively cold climate and wet soil. Bog-pollen analysis in the Oslofjord region of Norway has demonstrated that over the millennia there have been successive climaxes, with birch dominant before 7000 B.C., giving way to pine in the 1500 years to 5500 B.C., followed by mixed elm-linden-oak-ash forests in the period to 500 B.C. and an overwhelming dominance of spruce after 500 B.C.[31] The introduction of agriculture and domesticated plants yielded new climaxes, but these take their place in a long history of successively dominant ground covers, with no one of the periods of dominance definable as optimum on ecological grounds.

Modern work in the field of synecology (the study of communities as parts of ecosystems) has further undermined the simplistic versions of climax-crop theories. They are largely useful today as expository devices in tracing the development of our understanding of the origins and distributions of plant systems.[32] This shifts the emphasis in land-use planning from site and climate to consumption patterns and markets. It was this transition that was being accomplished in Europe in the 1960's, and against it tradition exerted a powerful retarding force.

The anthropologist Pierre Bourdieu points out that the essence of a traditional society is its refusal to acknowledge the existence of alternatives that are excluded by traditional beliefs.[33] In this sense, attitudes toward the sanctity of crop rotations in major portions of Europe are evidence of the existence of traditional beliefs that inhibit the full consideration of possible alternatives. This is especially the case in Eastern Europe where heavy official stress has been placed on the identification of "natural zones" as determinants of the crop combinations to be employed.[34]

At the level of the individual farm operator, the force of traditional rotations is still strong in Western Europe. The authors of a recent study of French agricultural potentials were forced to conclude that even on the larger French grain farms (the ones most favored by the Common Agricultural Policy of the EEC) any increase in grain acreage "is limited by current rotation constraints which will probably continue to be respected over the next few years." [35] In England the shift to continuous cropping of barley has resulted in charges of bad husbandry and irresponsible propagation of crop diseases, leading one observer to the conclusion that "the tradition of rotations will not die until the risks of monoculture are grasped fully." [36]

It is not consistent to believe in unique solutions, the primacy of natural law, or the immutability of man's relation to nature, and at the same time accept the possibility of continuous cropping with chemical weed control and inorganic fertilizers. These are irreconcilable beliefs. The probable outcome is that continuous cropping will be accepted and traditional beliefs will be changed. The history of mankind is replete with circumstances in which this has been the outcome when cultural values run head-on into technological change coupled with economic opportunity. But it is clear that this change is more than an economic or an agricultural phenomenon. It is a very significant step in cultural evolution. And it underlines the point that constraints upon realization of the full potentials of larger markets and economic integration in Europe are profoundly cultural in some of their most important dimensions.

The Distorting Influence of the Search for Economies of Scale

A second traditional habit of thought with distorting consequences for European integration is the faith in economies of scale or size that has supported the desire for larger firms and wider markets. The appeal of this idea is especially strong in agriculture, where the small size of many farms has been a major barrier to technological advance. As Table 4 shows, the proportion of all farms under 5 hectares (12.35 acres) is very high in a group of countries that includes some of the least industrialized as well as the most highly industrialized in Europe.

Table 4. Farms under Five Hectares as a Percentage of the
Total Number of Farms and Area of Farmland for
Selected European Countries

Country	Year of Census	Percentage of Farm Units under 5 Hectares	
		In Total Number of Farms	In Total Farm Area
Portugal	1954	88%	22%
Norway	1959	65	...
Switzerland	1955	53	16
Germany (F.R.)...	1960	51	9
Austria	1960	42	5
Finland	1959	36	...
France	1963	29	...
England and Wales[a]	1963	29	2.6
Poland	1960	28	...
Denmark	1966	13	2

SOURCE: For Portugal, Norway, Switzerland, Austria, and
Finland, data are from *Agriculture in EFTA* (Geneva: EFTA,
1965); for West Germany, from *Statistisches Jahrbuch über
Ernährung, Landwirtschaft, und Forsten der Bundesrepublik
Deutschland* (Hamburg and Berlin: Paul Parey, 1967), p.
23; for France, from *Annuaire Statistique de la France 1966*
(Paris, 1966), pp. 71–72 (the data refer to farm units of
2–5 ha. only; units under 2 ha. are not enumerated as
farms); for England and Wales, from *Agricultural Statistics
1963/1964* (London: HMSO, 1966), pp. 66, 72; for Poland,
from *Concise Statistical Yearbook of Poland 1967* (Warsaw:
Central Statistical Office, 1967), pp. 115, 125 (data refer to
private farms only which in 1966 accounted for 84.9 percent of the total agriculturally used area); and for Denmark,
from *Landbrugsstatistik 1966, Statistiske Meddelelser* (Copenhagen), 1967, No. 4, pp. 7, 27.
   [a] Under fifteen acres.

Although most of the agricultural land is in farm-operating units of
over 10 hectares (24.7 acres) in all but a few European countries, the
large number of very small farms creates both social and political problems that defy solution by price or trade policies. The Common Market
countries, for example, have an arable land area only 21 percent as large
as that of the United States but four times as many people dependent upon
agriculture for a livelihood. Europeans, as a consequence, are very conscious of the limitations of small-sized farms.

The problem is not confined to agriculture. Small, uneconomic firms
are a major reason for the high cost of marketing and distribution. The
size problem is also endemic in European manufacturing, processing, and
service trades, including banking and finance. The dramatic conversion in
the attitude of the United Kingdom toward the EEC in the 1960's can be

traced to a belief in economies of scale as much as to any other single factor. Edward Heath for the Conservative party in 1962–63 and Harold Wilson as Labour prime minister in 1966–67 made effective use of the argument, at home and on the Continent. It has been coupled with an appeal to fears of takeovers by giant American firms, leading the editors of *The Economist* to warn that although "the proponents of bigness rest their case in the first instance on economies of scale . . . we should not be wafted away by a flood of enthusiasm for bigness." [37]

The potential role of economies of size in promoting productivity increases is tremendous, but the concept belongs to a class of explanatory principles that invite misinterpretation. In a strict production economics or input-output sense, the big farm or the big factory is not necessarily more efficient. One of the most dramatic trends of modern industry has been the miniaturization of production technology. This has, in effect, appreciated the worth of the small firm relative to the big firm, when measured in output per unit of input. We can see this in virtually every field of modern technology. In terms of equivalent work output, the first-generation computer that once filled a room can be matched by a modern unit the size of a table. The big tractors first available to European agriculture seemed to indicate that only big farms could mechanize. We know now that this is not true. The fuel conversion efficiency of the small tractor is almost as great as the efficiency of a large one. Cost-reducing advantages of the larger tractor are due primarily to capital and labor costs, not mechanical efficiency.

Among agricultural processing industries one of the phenomena of the 1950's and 1960's in the United States was the superior performance record of small- to medium-size livestock slaughter and meat-packing firms. The top four firms in meat packing accounted for 41 percent of value added in manufacture in 1947, but only 31 percent in 1963. The share of the top 20 firms fell from 63 percent to 49 percent in the same period.[38] It is this type of evidence that calls for a shift of attention away from strictly mechanical and physical dimensions of economies of size and toward market-oriented aspects. This offers a more promising key to the reshaping of thought with respect to larger European markets and the agricultural policies that can create them.

It is not only the small size of farms that condemns European agriculture to high-cost production. The defects of the ten- or twenty-hectare farm lie at least as much in the inadequate nature of its marketing organization as in its production organization. The structural characteristics of agricultural production and marketing are interrelated, with reinforcing feedback effects. A population of small farms tends to breed an inefficient market system made up of many small retailers. But it is necessary to separate the two structural systems. Simply enlarging farm size will not solve the agricultural problem unless there is a basic change in market structures.

A conceivable alternative, and in some countries a realistic one, is to change the market structure and retain relatively small-sized farms. This has been the case in Japan. Japanese economists complain that farms are too small, averaging only one to two hectares in major producing areas. But too small in the Japanese context means that if farms are enlarged to what is currently believed to be an economic size, they will still be far below the average farm size in Germany, which in 1966 was 10.3 hectares. And while small in area, many Japanese farms are not small in their volume of business. Japan exhibits a highly industrialized, highly efficient agricultural production plant with economies of size achieved through the market structure, permitting the maintenance of a group of small producing units.

This has been done at the cost of a degree of organization and market discipline that at present is rare in Europe. Apart from Scandinavia and the Netherlands, market discipline on this scale is resented and resisted in key agricultural areas and especially in the Common Market countries. The difficulty with size of farms in Western Europe lies not so much in the inefficient nature of small producing units. It lies primarily in the resistance of farmers to organization on the scale necessary to make the marketing structure efficient.

This is, in part, a non-farm responsibility. It is associated with the absurdly high number of retail outlets found in the most industrialized countries of Western Europe. As long as the housewife derives some satisfaction from spending a large fraction of her total available time in shopping for food, this preference will maintain an uneconomic stock of retail outlets and inhibit market structure reform. This is a reflection of the strong European insistence on product differentiation. It reflects limitations set up by barriers to efficient transportation, refrigeration, storage, and warehousing. Until the 1950's it was uneconomic to transport Italian vegetables to northwestern Europe or Dutch tomatoes to Milan. And each mountain valley had its own kind of cheese of which it was extremely proud. In this historical sense European taste preferences for differentiated products are a reflection of outmoded transportation and storage systems. The necessity now is to reorganize consumer preference scales.

Instead of marketing over 400 varieties of cheese, as is now the case in France, we can anticipate a reduction in the number of varieties to several dozen. Rationalization of this type is already taking place so rapidly in the wine industry that it is scarcely possible for business firms to keep up with trends. Investments are being made in large-scale plants in which the wine is pooled from entire regions and marketed by brand name, not identifiable by vintage year or necessarily by geographic origin.

This transition is also well underway in other food industries. It dramatizes the gains to be got from market-structure reform, and it calls for a reexamination of the sense in which economies of scale are offered as a justification for European integration. It is significant that Edward Denison, in searching for explanations for the superior growth rates in Western European economies after 1950, applies the economies-of-scale argument primarily to markets, rather than to producing firms.[39] The most telling implications of economies of scale have emerged in discussions of the scale of investments in research and development. It is difficult to measure the shock waves from an idea — there is no "Richter scale." But when the London *Times* reported in 1967 that the research budget of IBM exceeded the total turnover from gross sales of the entire indigenous European computer industry, a force-9 shock must have surged through the scientific and technical community.[40]

The economies-of-scale argument has been used in another context in a manner that may inhibit the investments in agriculture needed to realize the potentials of larger markets. Nicholas Kaldor has argued that economic growth brings with it efficiency because the demand that generates growth in developed economies is for the products of industries that experience economies of scale when output is expanded. These are especially the manufacturing industries, and not the service trades.[41] Although a high rate of growth in manufacturing results in productivity gains, Kaldor points out that they are not great enough to offset the need for more labor. The place to look for this labor is in "diminishing-returns" industries, particularly agriculture and mining. The prescription for growth, Kaldor concludes, is to move labor from diminishing-returns industries to economies-of-scale industries.

This argument obscures the facts. Agriculture in several European countries has reached a point at which levels of labor productivity are almost the same as in manufacturing and annual rates of increase are greater. In the United Kingdom, for example, "The rate of increase in labour productivity in agriculture is much higher than the average improvement in manufacturing industries and double the rate of improvement in the economy as a whole." [42] The relevant data are presented in Table 5. In Switzerland, labor productivity in agriculture in the decade of the 1950's rose at an average rate of 5½ percent per year; "in the history of [Swiss] agriculture no period is known in which the increase in labor productivity approaches this rate." [43]

In a highly industrialized economy possessing the internal capacity to supply capital to agriculture, it is strange indeed to argue for favored treatment for manufacturing on the grounds that economies of scale can contribute to productivity increases, when in fact productivity increases in agriculture have outpaced the rest of the economy. This does not nec-

Table 5. Average Annual Productivity Gains in Agriculture
and Industry in the United Kingdom (Actual for
1954–64 and Anticipated for 1964–70)

| Sector | Actual Gains | | Anticipated Gains for |
	1954–60	1960–64	1964–70 [a]
Industry	2.4%	2.7%	3.2%
Agriculture [b]	4.0	6.0	6.0+

SOURCE: *The National Plan*, Command 2764 (London: HMSO, September 1965), p. 24 for industry, p. 136 for agriculture.

[a] The actual rate of increase in labor productivity in agriculture in 1966–68 was just under 6 percent a year. *Annual Review and Determination of Guarantees, 1968*, Command 3558 (London: HMSO, March 1968), p. 8.

[b] "If measured on the usual basis adopted for agriculture the annual growth in labour productivity was about 5 per cent in 1954–60 and 7 per cent in 1960–64." *The National Plan*, p. 136.

essarily refute the economies-of-scale argument for manufacturing industries. It does suggest strongly that economies of scale can also be experienced in agriculture, and that too great a weight is placed on the characterization of agriculture as a diminishing-returns industry.

M. A. Adelman points out that "Manufacturing or service industries may have economies of scale plant by plant yet all together show diminishing returns after some point, as expansion presses harder on factors in tight supply." [44] And this points up a major weakness in Kaldor's argument. Diminishing returns are being attributed to agriculture as an industry, while economies of scale are being attributed to manufacturing plants or firms.

One final anomaly of Kaldor's argument deserves mention. He stresses the gains to be got through transfer of labor from diminishing-returns sectors to manufacturing, in the context of a paper that examines the causes of the slow rate of economic growth of the United Kingdom. The conclusion is that growth has been inhibited by the gradual disappearance of labor reserves in sectors with excess labor, particularly agriculture and mining. As we have seen, productivity growth rates in the United Kingdom are declining in manufacturing and rising in agriculture. With only slightly over 3 percent of the labor force in agriculture, and with little opportunity to squeeze more industrial labor out of this sector, it seems appropriate to suggest that a significant part of presumed economies of scale in manufacturing in the past were in fact a consequence of the supply of labor to manufacturing from agriculture at less than its true social cost.

It is these misuses of the economies-of-scale argument that lead to doubt about the weight it is being asked to carry in conventional arguments for European integration.

Zero-Sum Games and the Concept of Limited Good

A third pattern of traditional thought that inhibits European integration is reflected in what has been characterized as the concept of "limited good." Although enunciated by anthropologists and sociologists in studies of developing countries, it has application in developed countries and in economic sectors.[45]

The usefulness of this approach to economic analysis can be tested on two levels. In one formulation, the concept of limited good refers to the observation that a principal problem of people in lagging regions is not that they are poor, not that they are ignorant, not that they are remote from markets. It is that they themselves think nothing can be done to help them. This is explicitly Danilo Dolci's conclusion regarding Sicily. He has perhaps dramatized this more effectively than any other man in modern Europe.[46]

In farm interviews conducted in the course of this study of European integration in 1966–67, this attitude was demonstrated in Ireland, in hill-farming communities of Italy, in Greece, in the Balkans, and in parts of France. Many of the people who have chosen to remain in agriculture in disadvantaged areas do not believe they can be helped. More to the point, they do not believe they can do anything to help themselves. The hypothesis involved in the concept of limited good is that this resignation is symptomatic of a fundamental belief in a finite sum of good in their world.[47]

If the available good is redistributed in some fashion, the only way to get more is for someone else to have less. If one gets richer, another must get poorer. If religious beliefs dictate it is wrong to steal, and one can only get rich at the expense of someone else, there is religious sanction for remaining poor, and for being fatalistic. This provides a moral justification for remaining impassive in the face of any motivational structure that seeks to create an incentive for economic advancement.

If this is the belief, a rational approach to the development process emphasizes redistribution. This, of course, has been the advocacy that has characterized most of the political movements of Europe in the twentieth century. They have been redistributional in their basic dimensions. It is too simple to say that this characterizes Marxist theory, but it has been a major characteristic of applied Marxism. Most of the men who have been influential in leading the great European social movements of the twentieth century, in labor and in agriculture, have been men who were basically influenced by a belief that the only way their sector could be improved was by redistributing goods or wealth at the cost of some other sector. In economic jargon, they have rejected the possibility of Pareto-optimal solutions. In their world, the players play zero-sum games: if one is benefited, another must be hurt, and the sum of gains and losses is zero.

On another level, the concept of limited good can be used to throw light on attitudes toward economic power, military strength, and national sovereignty. The current French attitude toward gold and toward international monetary policy can be interpreted as a reflection of a concept of limited good. M. Jacques Rueff, one of the most influential monetary advisers to Charles de Gaulle, consistently warned that there is a finite sum of gold in the world and international liquidity must be related to that finite sum. A similar attitude is revealed by those who argue that national budgets must be "balanced." Consistent with this view is a belief that there is a fixed, or certainly finite, amount of revenue to be got, and no more than that can be obligated without inviting disaster.

In a more explicitly political setting, intense nationalism is one aspect of a concept of limited good when good is measured in loyalty or patriotism. To the pathologic nationalist, there can be no division in loyalties. "If you are not for us you are against us." Any expression of allegiance to another locus of sovereignty must diminish your attachment to your present sovereign. The attitudes of many of Europe's political leaders reflect a belief that national sovereignty is a finite sum. To them, any growth of power in Brussels must reduce power in Paris, or Milan, or Bonn. It is this belief that is challenged by the Common Market, by the rise of functional agencies of the United Nations, and by less overt examples of the growth of supranationalism in Europe. One of the most interesting of these trends concerns the growing internationalism of science and the reemergence of old loyalties to guild or profession. To the extent that you identify yourself with a discipline or a profession, you permit an expansion in your stock of loyalty. You can be a German, and an economist, and this yields a greater capital stock of loyalty and identification than is possible if you can be a German only. You are thus richer, in some sense, when you can identify your interests with those of more than one group. But this route to riches is closed if you conceive of loyalty as a limited good.

The most extreme version of this latter viewpoint in modern Europe was of course President Charles de Gaulle of France. Hoarding gold, obsessed with the protection of French sovereignty, trained in a nineteenth-century military tradition to play zero-sum games, exhibiting a flagrant case of retarded nationalism, he may well go down in history as the last great leader of France, and perhaps of all Europe, to base policy on a peasant concept of limited good. *Une France sans Paysans* is the title of a perceptive book reviewing recent trends in French agriculture.[48] The brunt of the argument here presented is that "a France without peasants" will have a significance that extends far beyond the agricultural sector.

This is a basic issue in any discussion of integration or of the potentials of a "new economics" in Europe. The significance of the new economics is that it provides a respectable theoretical base for the argument that, within limitations, it is possible to engage in redistributional policy without hurting some sector at the expense of another. In other words, the new economics is inconsistent with a world in which there is limited good and the only way to get more for yourself is to take it away from your neighbor.

Many of the political leaders in Europe in this generation have acted as if they believed in the concept of limited good. The concept has been urbanized. It is not necessarily a peasant characteristic, nor is it simply a characteristic of poor, backward, remote farm communities in Greece, Italy, Ireland, or France. Measured by responses to current political slogans, it is characteristic of the "urban peasants" of many industrial communities in Europe. Where it exists, it is one of the most serious limitations to the further development of European integration potentials.

An implicit climax-crop model as a guide to land use, a preoccupation with economies of scale, a concept of limited good as a constraint on the creation and more equitable distribution of new wealth — these are among the legacies with which Europe enters the affluent society. Together they form a pattern of thought that has been fundamentally disturbed by the potentials of European integration. The fabric of a society, Claude Lévi-Strauss is fond of repeating, constitutes an ordered whole.[49] It is precisely this ordered whole that was disrupted in Europe in the mid-twentieth century.

Food Surpluses and the Threat of Nonfunctional Trade

Economies of scarcity generate institutions and thought patterns designed to cope with deficits. The nations of Europe are richly endowed with this type of institutional equipment. They are poor in their stock of conditioned economic reflexes that can aid in struggles with surpluses. In the 1960's they encountered overproduction and unmarketable abundance in food. And it is virtually certain that this situation will grow worse. As Denis Bergmann has emphasized, this generalized problem of excess capacity in agriculture is only one aspect of a much larger problem of underdevelopment and mal-distribution of resources.[50] Although his analysis refers explicitly to France, the conclusion can be applied to virtually all countries of Western Europe, with the possible exception of Sweden and the United Kingdom.

There is a large measure of agreement among available output projections, with particular convergence on two points: (a) Western Europe will have surplus problems in cereal grains. (b) It will have an even more troublesome surplus in milk. There is also near-unanimous agreement among European economists that these will be generated in spite of the price system, and not because of it. The driving forces behind this output expansion are the uses of a developed agricultural technology to substitute capital for labor, in regions where nonfarm jobs are increasing, or to provide more nearly full employment on farms in regions where there are few nonfarm jobs.

A measure of the shift in relative costs of labor and capital in agriculture is provided by a comparison of trends in the cost of a tractor and in annual labor wages. Table 6 presents data from farm-accounting records in Soissons, covering an area of relatively large farms north of Paris. Between 1952–53 and 1965–66 the ratio of the price of a tractor to a year's labor wage was more than cut in half. In 1952–53 three men could be hired for the price of a tractor; in 1965–66, less than one and a half. In England, over a longer period, the trend has been similar. A prewar tractor of 20 horsepower cost roughly twice the annual wage of the driver. In 1967 a tractor of 35 horsepower could be had for the approximate equivalent of the driver's annual wage.[51]

These data underline the fact that, in modernizing agriculture, the simplest and easiest step is to shift land into grain crops, thus permitting the substitution of combine harvesters and tractors for labor. The technology is available and mature, the equipment is produced in Europe, is well developed over a wide range of scale, and is within the financial capacity of many existing farm units. There is general agreement that the first reaction of European farmers to rising costs will be to substitute capital for labor by expanding grain operations, even at the expense of cutting back other farm activities.

This process is now well underway. France in 1968 produced over 14.8 million metric tons of wheat, or some 545 million bushels, from

Table 6. Ratio of Agricultural Labor Wage to the Cost of a Tractor in France in 1952–53 and 1965–66

Item	1952–53 (Old Francs)	1965–66 (New Francs)
Wage of a full-time agricultural worker[a]	288,000	8,850
Price of a Renault tractor, Type 3043[b]	860,000	12,600
Ratio of tractor price/ man-year of labor	2.98	1.42

SOURCE: For wage figures, Office Central de Comptabilité Agricole de Soissons and Institut National de la Recherche Agronomique, Paris. For tractor figures, Syndicate Française de Constructeurs de Tracteurs et Machines Agricoles, Paris.

[a] Excludes employers' social security contribution.

[b] The 1953 tractor was 22–30 horsepower; the 1966 tractor was 30–35 horsepower. If quality differences are considered, the ratio in 1965–66 was much below 1.42.

slightly over 4 million hectares. This was 63 percent more wheat than was harvested on average in 1951–55, and from 8 percent fewer hectares.[52] Italy in 1955 produced only 94 percent of her domestic requirements for wheat. From fewer hectares in 1965 she produced 104 percent of domestic requirements, for a population that was 10 percent larger.[53]

For Germany and France, there is a consensus that no present or prospective range of allowable movements in agricultural prices in the EEC will prevent an increase in wheat output. Its magnitude will be dictated largely by technological and cost considerations, the most important being the rate of increase in rural labor wages. For Italy, the projection is for wheat production at a level that will meet domestic food requirements to 1975, although the deficit in feed-grain production is expected to increase.[54]

The performance of individual countries is even more revealing in terms of increases in self-sufficiency ratios for wheat since the formation of the EEC, shown in Table 7. These increases are especially remarkable for Germany, the Netherlands, and Belgium. It is difficult to believe that, in these most heavily industrialized and most densely populated countries of the EEC, the wisest use of land is to grow more wheat.

The production response obviously exceeded the expectations of those responsible for the agreement of December 14, 1964, on common prices for grains. It is also clear that, except in the Netherlands, this increased output has not to date been significantly affected by farmers' responses to grain prices. Technological considerations and structural characteristics appear to be exercising the most important influences on grain production.

Dairy production provides the clearest evidence that in determining supply response in the immediate future, the structural characteristics of European agriculture will be more important than farm-product prices. The northern latitudes in which much of European agricultural produc-

Table 7. Percentage of Self-Sufficiency in Wheat for EEC Countries in 1955–56 to 1958–59 and in 1963–64 to 1966–67 (Four-Year Averages)

Country	Average for 1955–56 to 1958–59	Average for 1963–64 to 1966–67
Germany	63%	79%
France	105	127
Italy	103	95
Netherlands	28	57
Belgium-Luxembourg	65	72
EEC	89	101

SOURCE: EEC, *Agrarstatistik, 1968* (Brussels), No. 1, p. 58.

tion takes place dictate that the most efficient tool for photosynthesis is grass, and the most efficient device for converting sunlight and rainfall into a product for human consumption is the dairy cow. When coupled with a history of rural population pressure and farmland parcelization over many generations, the result is a size of farm and a degree of capital intensity in many areas that only dairying or market vegetables can justify.

A persistent milk surplus seems guaranteed. West Germany was 96 percent self-sufficient in milk on average in 1961–64; 111 percent self-sufficient in 1965; and for 1975 the ratio is estimated at 116 percent.[55] The self-sufficiency ratio for French dairy products averaged 105 in 1964–66, if milk fed to calves is included in consumption. If milk fed to calves is excluded, production exceeded human consumption by 32 percent in 1966. An excess of 34 percent is projected for 1970 and 38 percent for 1975.[56]

In 1963 the EEC published a careful assessment of possible trends in agricultural production from 1958 to 1970. Table 8 summarizes the three possibilities that were foreseen for milk output. Increases have exceeded the highest estimates. Production in France in 1967 approached 30 million tons, a level not anticipated until 1970 under even the highest of the three alternative assumptions. Production increases to 1967 reflected a combination of trends that was not included in the 1963 EEC forecast for 1970: increasing dairy cow numbers, plus increasing output per cow in France.[57]

Outside of the Common Market the potential milk surpluses in northern Europe are equally threatening. Denmark in 1966 was 225 percent self-sufficient and searching for export markets. With over 60 percent of

Table 8. Estimated EEC and French Milk Production in 1970
(in Thousands of Metric Tons)

Assumption	EEC	France
No change in number of dairy cows between 1958 and 1970 and "low" output per cow in France (2600 kg. per year)	69,054	24,406
No change in number of dairy cows between 1958 and 1970 and "high" output per cow in France (2800 kg. per year)	70,932	26,284
Increases in number of dairy cows between 1958 and 1970 and "low" output per cow in France (2600 kg. per year)	78,650	30,160

SOURCE: "Der gemeinsame Markt für landwirtschaftliche Erzeugnisse, Vorausschau 1970," *EEC Studien, Reihe Landwirtschaft,* No. 10 (Brussels: EEC, 1963), pp. 36–40.

total farm receipts derived from milk and dairy products, Finland is producing 20 percent more milk than is consumed domestically, her exports of dairy products fell by 12 percent in 1966, and a major adjustment is underway.[58] The adjustment is already advanced in Sweden and Norway. Dairy cow numbers have gone down sharply, and still the milk surplus remains a critical agricultural problem.

The consequences for world trade in dairy products are already apparent. With a domestic wholesale price of butter of over 80 cents per pound, France in the spring of 1968 was reportedly delivering fresh butter in Lebanon at 29.5 cents per pound and storage butter as low as 13 cents per pound, which was virtually the cost of transport. Nonfat dry milk, with a wholesale price of 21 cents per pound in Paris, was delivered to Beirut for 10 cents per pound, and to Lima, Peru, for 13 cents.[59] France has replaced the United States as the principal supplier of dried skim milk to Mexico, the closest United States foreign market.

The use of export subsidies to permit penetration of world markets has done much to dim early hopes that the EEC would promote greater freedom in world agricultural trade. The subsidies are paid out of equalizing levies collected on imports, to bring the price of imported agricultural products up to the levels of internal EEC prices. By supporting high internal prices for food, both the import levies and the export subsidies constitute a disguised tax on consumers in the EEC. In the first years of the Common Agricultural Policy this complex system of levies and rebates has had some odd consequences.

It is abundantly clear, for example, that grain traders have been among the major beneficiaries. From 1957–60 to 1962–65 total cereal grain production in the EEC rose from 50 to 58 million metric tons, an increase of 16 percent. Consumption increased by about 15 percent, with the result that the self-sufficiency ratio for all cereals in the EEC was 84.5 percent on average for the three crop years 1957–58 to 1959–60, and 86.6 percent for the years 1962–63 to 1964–65. In actual tonnage, consumption of cereal grain was 58 million metric tons in 1958 and 68 million metric tons in 1965. Over the same period the total movement of grain across national boundaries of EEC countries (exports plus imports, for both member and nonmember countries) rose from 14 to 30 million metric tons, an increase of 114 percent.[60] In other words, from 1958 to 1965 grain production in the EEC increased by 8 million metric tons, consumption by 10 million metric tons, and total movement of grain across national boundaries by 16 million metric tons.

Depending upon world prices for wheat and feed grains, and the amounts set as export subsidies or denaturing payments, an incentive situation can result in which wheat that could have been fed to livestock is exported from the EEC and replaced with imported feed grain. Given the availability of the export subsidies, and since the EEC is currently more than self-sufficient in bread grains, with France over 125 percent self-sufficient, it has paid in recent years to export wheat in order to receive the export subsidy, and import feed grains, on which the variable levies are collected. This explains the fact that the EEC has become a net wheat exporter since 1965 while continuing to be a heavy importer of feed grain. And it also explains how an increase in consumption of 10 million metric tons could be associated with an increase of 16 million metric tons in the movement of grain across national frontiers. Not all of this increased movement of grain is nonfunctional. Some of it represents an increasing specialization within the EEC. But the conclusion seems inescapable that to date the operation of EEC grain trade regulations and of the Common Agricultural Policy has been of particular value to the grain traders.

Two countries have dominated recent increases in EEC grain trade with nonmember countries. In terms of EEC exports to non-EEC countries, France is the principal exporter and wheat is the principal product. French cereal grain exports in 1965 accounted for 76 percent of total EEC grain exports to nonmember countries. For wheat, the French share was 85 percent. The 3,294,000 metric tons of French wheat exported in 1965 accounted for 57 percent of total community exports of all cereal grains (5,827,000 m.t.). On the export side, France is clearly dominant. On the import side, the situation changes. Italy is the dominant importer in the EEC and fodder grains are the principal products. From 1958 to 1965 total EEC grain imports from nonmember countries increased by 6,752,-000 metric tons. Fodder grains accounted for 95 percent of this increase. Over this same period, the increase in total Italian grain imports of 5,494,-000 tons was 77 percent of the total EEC increase in grain imports. Even more impressive is the fact that Italian fodder-grain imports alone were 72 percent of the total increase in all EEC grain imports from nonmember countries.

In the Kennedy Round negotiations, EEC representatives stressed the fact that up to 1967 the EEC had been a good market for grains from non-EEC countries. Although grain exports from the EEC increased sharply after 1961–62, so too did grain imports, with no appreciable reduction in net imports through 1966–67. This apparent stability in import demand played a major role in the agreements of May 1967 that brought the Kennedy Round to a close. But the trend since 1967 has been sharply reversed. The EEC was a net importer of 11.9 million metric tons of grain in 1966–67 and 10.1 million tons in 1967–68, with a forecast for 1968–69 of 6.5 million tons and 5.9 for 1969–70.[61]

In retrospect, it is clear that the agricultural agreements of the Kennedy Round were concluded at a most opportune moment for the EEC. Nonmember countries that had anticipated a continuing EEC demand for grain imports have watched this market decline since mid-1967. Given the unexpectedly large increases in grain output in the EEC and the high export subsidies, there is every reason to believe that the decline will continue. This has played no small role in the growing mood of protectionism that has characterized the Western trading world in the aftermath of the Kennedy Round.

On the production side, an interpretation of trends in grain output within the EEC is made difficult by the fact that through 1967 farmers in Germany, France, and Italy had not yet felt the full effects of the price changes agreed upon in Brussels. A three-year schedule of degressive supplementary payments for grain in the Federal Republic of Germany cushioned the effects of the reduction needed to bring German grain prices to the agreed EEC levels. In France, governmental attempts to move to the higher EEC levels of grain prices in three steps held back grain prices during the crop years from 1964–65 through 1966–67.

Although the ultimate effect of the EEC agreement on common grain prices will be to lower the level of German prices for wheat (and for other grains), the average producer prices received for wheat by German farmers were actually higher in 1965–66 and 1966–67 than they had been in any of the preceding five years, 1960–61 to 1964–65. And although the long-run effect of the EEC grain price agreement will be to raise French grain prices, French farmers actually received lower average prices for their wheat in 1964–65 and 1965–66 than they had received in the three preceding years, 1961–62 through 1963–64. While common wheat prices went into effect on July 1, 1967, in all six EEC countries, Italy was granted an exception permitting special feed grain prices until 1972.

There is thus general agreement in France, Germany, and Italy that grain production through 1966–67 was relatively unaffected by the EEC agreements on grain prices. Only in the Netherlands did wheat prices have a clearly stimulating effect on production. The average price received by Dutch wheat farmers rose from $80 per ton in 1961–62 to $95 per ton in 1966–67, the largest increase experienced in any country in the EEC.[62] This underlines the fact, noted in Table 7 above, that the increase in the Dutch self-sufficiency ratio for wheat is the largest in the EEC, having doubled from the second half of the 1950's (crop years 1955–56 to 1958–59) to the mid-1960's (crop years 1963–64 to 1966–67). French and German farmers bear the brunt of much of the criticism of EEC agricultural surpluses, often ascribed to the high level of agricultural prices. Up to 1968 the evidence suggests that the principal beneficiaries of Common Market agricultural price policy were the Dutch.

European trends in agricultural output have been affected by another characteristic of the price system that is striking when viewed from outside. The land input in agricultural production is priced in two markets, a

private market and a public market. The private market for land was disrupted by two world wars and the consequent inflation and financial instability. Only in the latter part of the 1950's did land prices in the private
market begin again to play an important role in determining agricultural
land use and choices of crops. In the public market, the price of land
should be reflected in land taxes. When land becomes scarce and highly
desirable, this "public price" or tax should go up. It is this public market
price mechanism that is not functioning in major agricultural areas of
Europe. Taxes on agricultural land are extremely low, when measured by
land-tax levels in North America, Japan, and some other developed countries.

The effect of rising land taxes is to discourage relatively extensive uses
of land. If landowners are profit maximizers, the lure of greater profits
should lead them to intensify land uses as market opportunities emerge,
urbanization expands, and technology offers new production possibilities.
And even if they are not imaginative profit maximizers, a rising burden
of land taxes will force them to intensify. A different situation exists if
land is transferred primarily through inheritance, if commercial sales of
land are relatively infrequent, and if agricultural taxes are low. Landowners can look with gratification on rising land values that increase their
net worth without feeling any necessary compulsion to increase the intensity with which they use their land.

Wheat is a traditional crop in Europe. The techniques of its production are well developed and widely understood. It is particularly well
adapted to production on tenant-operated farms, in that it is easily measured, relatively standardized, readily stored and transported, and highly
divisible. And it ranks at the top of the list of farm products for which machines can be substituted for much of the labor traditionally required in
its production. As labor grows scarce in supply and dear in price, wheat
growing gains in attractiveness as a form of land use. If taxes are not rising, there are few forces to compel farmers to shift out of wheat, and many
incentives to hold them to their traditional crop. If at the same time the
price of wheat is rising (as in France and the Netherlands) or due to fall
slowly (as in Germany and Italy), the lure of possibly higher profits from
some more intensive form of land use is weak when measured against the
more readily comprehended benefits of a greater emphasis on grain crops.

This is the situation in Western Europe, particularly in the EEC, and
above all in France. Although the total wheat acreage has remained relatively unchanged, there has been a sharp increase in the area sown to
wheat in the north of France and in the Paris Basin. In the heart of this
wheat region labor is increasingly scarce and expensive, land is traditionally passed on by inheritance, a significant part of the land is operated by

tenants, the real burden of taxes on agricultural incomes is low, and land taxes are virtually nonexistent.

Tradition, economics, and institutions combine to permit the continuation of relatively extensive land uses in some of the most densely populated sectors of Western Europe. Where the carrot of higher profits in alternative land uses exists, the stick of rising land taxes is missing.

To summarize, migration of labor out of agriculture has created an incentive to mechanize, and this favors crop production over the production of animal products. This tendency is reinforced by low land taxes, which in most EEC countries are too low to provide an incentive for the more intensive use of scarce and valuable land. Trade patterns have been altered by a system of variable levies and export subsidies, and relatively high internal prices have created favorable incentive patterns for output expansion. The internal balance of agricultural production has thus been disturbed by forces that are the result of technological change and structural and institutional defects. Too much milk is being produced and not enough beef, grain production has increased more rapidly than anticipated, and there has been an expansion in nonfunctional trade.

Looking back, we can now see that the entry into force of the Common Agricultural Policy on July 1, 1967, marked the crossing of a great divide in European history, and not alone in the history of the EEC countries. Agricultural policy in the past had been dominated by the twin goals of increased production and national self-sufficiency. These policy goals are no longer valid. Europe must now face the unfamiliar problems of agricultural surpluses. And it must do so in a trading world in which policies that sufficed for nation states in the nineteenth century are no longer relevant.

It is unbecoming for an American observer to criticize these developments without acknowledging the painful adjustments required in reducing a nation's commitment of labor, land, and capital in agriculture. In spite of massive migrations out of farming, heavy support from public funds, and a concerted effort over three decades, the problem cannot be considered solved in the United States. It is only now being recognized in Europe. Intensive thought has been devoted to this problem in Sweden, the Netherlands, Denmark, and more recently France and Germany. Extensive programs to accelerate retirement by offering pensions to farmers in their fifties have been adopted in several countries. Pioneering work along these lines has been undertaken in Sweden and the Netherlands, elaborating upon earlier programs dating from the 1950's and designed to retire farm land, consolidate small farms, and accelerate the movement of farm families out of agriculture.[63]

The most dramatic proposals were those urged upon the EEC Commission by Sicco Mansholt, the commissioner responsible for agriculture, in December 1968. Funds would be made available to retrain farmers and encourage migration out of agriculture or early retirement; a premium of $300 per dairy cow was proposed for farmers who agree to slaughter their cows and quit dairying; a wide-ranging program of reforestation or recreational development would remove 12.5 million acres from agriculture; and a gradual program of cuts in support prices would be set in motion.

The costs of the program would be enormous, but must be judged against current costs to the Common Market of rapidly climbing surpluses. The budgeted costs for EEC agricultural support programs for 1969 were set originally at $2.1 billion and it is certain that they will go higher.[64] Including the amounts spent by national governments in addition to the support activities of the EEC, the total bill for farm support and structural change in 1968–69 was estimated at $4.3 billion.[65] As a percentage of the gross national product, this is well in excess of the highest levels of government expenditure on farm-support programs ever experienced in the United States. Only in 1959 did the total cost of farm-support and foreign-food-aid programs in the United States reach 1 percent of GNP; in 1966–68 it averaged one-half of 1 percent.[66] As a percentage of GNP, the projected costs of EEC agricultural support programs (EEC and national combined) for 1968–69 were over twice as high as in the United States, and with a GNP less than half as large. Even after allowance is made for price-level and purchasing-power differentials, the burden of EEC farm-support programs approximately doubled that of the United States in 1968–69, measured in percentage of the respective gross national products.

One of the most discouraging aspects of this problem of abundance is that the EEC is unable to exercise a leadership role in promoting freer trade. In terms of political realities, it has deprived itself of the use of price policy to guide readjustment. EEC agricultural prices are high, inflexible, and politically dangerous. Given inflexible prices, the production responses of farmers in the next few years will be dictated primarily by agrarian structural characteristics that include inadequately sized farms, defective market structures, land prices that are unrealistically high in relation to farm incomes, and a shortage of educational facilities to train surplus farm labor for nonfarm jobs.

This throws the emphasis with unmistakable clarity on the need for structural reform programs on a scale much larger than has been attempted to date. One of the greatest challenges to EEC leadership arises from the fact that funds that might have been used to accelerate these structural changes through the European Agricultural Guidance and Guaranty Fund (FEOGA) are increasingly diverted to finance price-support programs, storage costs, and export subsidies.

The Integrating Potential of Cheaper Food

Food costs as a proportion of private consumption expenditures in 1965 in Europe varied from a high in the 50 percent range for Bulgaria and the Soviet Union to a low of 21.9 percent in Denmark.[67] As Table 9 shows, these proportions have been falling slowly since 1955, but they are still high in comparison with the United States and Canada. Greece at 40.1 percent, Italy at 38.9 percent, and Ireland at 33.7 percent are high, among the countries of Western Europe, and these percentages have declined slowly in recent years. With the exception of Denmark, the range for the remaining Western European countries is from 30 percent for Austria and Finland to 25 percent for Sweden and the United Kingdom. These relatively high fractions of consumption expenditures "mortgaged" to food are a significant brake on the expansion of European demand for other consumer goods and services.

A measure of the significance of a fall in the fraction of total consumer disposable income spent on food is provided by the experience of the United States since 1952. Food expenditures were 23 percent of disposable personal income in 1952, and 17.7 percent in 1967.[68] In dollars, disposable income totaled $544.2 billion and food expenditures $96.4 billion in 1967. If the percentage spent on food in 1967 had been the same as that spent in 1952 (23.0 percent), the food bill would have been $125.2 billion, or $28.8 billion higher. In 1967, personal consumption expenditures included $29.3 billion on automobiles and parts, and $32.0 billion on household equipment and furniture.[69] Rising real incomes and the falling real cost of food from 1952 to 1967 reduced the fraction of consumer disposable income spent on food by an amount almost as great as total expenditures on automobiles and parts in 1967, and equivalent to 90 percent of the amount spent on household durable goods.

It is a common experience in Europe to be told that "France (or Italy, Germany, Austria) is striving for an affluent society, but not on the United States model." In one dimension, at least, the European affluent society is not likely to be "on the United States model" in any near future. Food costs are a relatively high fraction of consumer expenditures and exercise a pronounced restraining influence on the growth of consumer demand for durable goods and services. This is especially the case in the EEC. With the exception of those countries in which all trading is "state trading," EEC farm producers are more effectively insulated from the world market than are the producers in any other major countries of the trading world. With this degree of protection it seems unlikely that consumers in the EEC will benefit as they should from falling real costs of food made possible by agricultural modernization. The most likely way in which lower real food costs may be achieved is through price changes that raise other prices and

Table 9. Expenditures for Food as a Proportion of Private Consumption Expenditures for Selected Countries in Europe and North America in 1955, 1960, and 1965 [a]

Country	1955	1960	1965
North America			
Canada	23.1%	23.0%	20.7%
United States [b]	22.6	21.3	19.5
Western Europe			
Austria	38.5	34.1	30.4
Belgium	29.1	27.5	26.0
Denmark	27.6	23.4	21.9
Finland	34.0	33.3	30.0
France	34.0 [e]	31.6	29.3
Germany (F.R.) [d]	40.7 [e]	37.9	34.6 [e]
Greece	48.9 [e]	41.6	40.1
Ireland	38.3	36.4	33.7
Italy	41.0	39.9	38.9
Netherlands	33.7	31.0	29.1
Norway	31.6	30.0	28.5
Spain	34.3	37.5	...
Sweden	30.0	27.3	25.5
United Kingdom [b]	31.3	28.4	25.6
Eastern Europe			
Bulgaria [f]	...	58.7	57.6
Hungary	...	38.9	36.6
Yugoslavia	53.2	44.8	...
U.S.S.R.	50.1 [g]	...	...

SOURCE: *National Food Situation*, U.S. Department of Agriculture, NFS-124 (Washington, D.C., May 1968), p. 9. All data are derived from United Nations, *Yearbook of National Accounts Statistics, 1966*, except the figure for the U.S.S.R., which comes from A. Bergson and S. Kuznets, *Economic Trends in the Soviet Union* (Cambridge, Mass.: Harvard University Press, 1963), p. 361.

[a] Total expenditures, defined as those of households and private nonprofit institutions, include expenditures of residents abroad. Food expenditures, excluding beverages unless otherwise indicated, include amounts purchased by nonresidents. As a proportion of disposable personal income, U.S. food expenditures in 1965 equaled 18.2 percent.

[b] Includes nonalcoholic beverages.

[e] Not strictly comparable with data for later years.

[d] Includes beverages and tobacco.

[e] Includes expenditures on nonalcoholic and alcoholic beverages and tobacco, estimated at 8.1 percent of total expenditures in 1963. See EEC, Statistical Office of the European Communities, *Wirtschaftsrechnungen 1962/63, No. 5, Deutschland* (Brussels, August 1966), pp. 153, 160, 167.

[f] Percentage of "individual consumption," which excludes all services not contributing directly to material production (such as personal and professional services).

[g] Includes all beverages.

Table 10. Expenditure on Food as a Percentage of Total Consumer Expenditures, by Types of Household, for EEC Countries in 1963–64

Type of Household	Germany	France	Italy	Nether-lands	Bel-gium	Luxem-bourg
Workers (*Arbeiter*)..	42.9%	46.0%	50.4%	37.0%	40.7%	41.4%
Employees and officials (*Angestellte und Beamte*)	34.4	34.5	40.1	28.1	31.1	34.7
Farmers (*Landwirte*) Percentage of cash outlay	32.7	41.5	46.0	32.3	36.9	34.7
Percentage of total consumption	49.8	52.2	52.9	37.9	43.7	44.8

SOURCE: EEC, Statistical Office of the European Communities, *General Statistical Bulletin*, No. 1 (1967).

costs more rapidly than food prices. Even for meat, for which there is strong demand, the index of real prices received by EEC farmers is expected to decline from the 1965 level of 123 (1960 = 100) to a level of 119 in 1970.[70]

The tentative conclusion is that the principal way open to the EEC to benefit from technological advances in agriculture is through inflation. This is an unattractive prospect, in view of the orthodox financial theories that have dominated national government policies within the EEC, and particularly so in view of the desire of the EEC to remain competitive in world industrial export markets.

The magnitude of consumer expenditures on food in the EEC is set forth in more detail in the family budget studies conducted in the six countries for 1963–64, from which the data in Table 10 are taken. Food expenditures on this scale are a restraining influence on the potential expansion of the market for consumer durable goods, including household equipment, automobiles, and housing. It is significant that the first moves toward the creation of European-wide industries after the Treaty of Rome were in radio and electronic equipment and in household equipment, especially refrigerators.

Of all Italy's boom products, refrigerators have probably had the most astounding success. The industry, practically nonexistent before the war, began in humble workshops in the early 1950's. It now employs about 35,000 men, mostly in large new plants in northeast Italy. It is second only to the American industry in production, is top world exporter and has so far escaped the painful sales cycles that have plagued its longer-established competitors . . . It is perhaps the first truly European industry — so devastatingly so that the French have twice had to give their own makers emergency protection.[71]

The EEC has generated hopes for a European version of the affluent society, led by mass markets and a "consumer durable goods revolution."

These hopes must be moderated by the knowledge that the market expansion potential is distinctly limited by the present high cost of food.

The rising importance of consumer durable goods and automobiles in European consumption patterns is underlined by the experience in the United States since the turn of the century. Since 1899, net business capital formation in the United States has been declining, as a fraction of the gross national product, while the proportion devoted to net consumer capital formation has been rising. Through the decade 1919–28 almost all the rise in net consumer capital expenditures as a proportion of total consumption expenditure was accounted for by automobiles. After 1929, the importance of housing, household furnishings, radios, and other household durable goods increased.[72] In terms of the significance of the automobile, the trends now underway in Europe mirror the era of increases in consumer capital formation in the United States that preceded World War II. There were 264 cars per thousand people in the United States in 1940, a figure that was approached by Sweden in 1968. The transition to an economy in which net consumer capital formation was paced by expenditures on consumer durable goods other than automobiles took place in the United States at a relatively slow rate in the 1930's and at an increasing tempo after 1950.

This suggests that Europe in the 1950's and 1960's telescoped into two decades a transition in patterns of consumption and resultant capital formation in business and private sectors that was spread over four decades in the United States, 1920–60. In terms of consumption expenditure patterns in Western Europe, the consumer durable goods revolution is overlapping the automobile revolution, and in Italy the two revolutions are not just overlapped but pyramided.

Where can the purchasing power be found to keep this consumer goods revolution rolling? From productivity increases in industrial sectors — perhaps. More immediate contributors to productivity increases on a scale that will have prompt and measurable impact on demand are food and other retail distribution sectors. Misuse of resources in most European countries is almost surely greatest in the food sector, from the farm to the consumer's table. If economic integration is to occur on a scale that will generate mass markets, one of the first requirements is to reduce the proportion of the labor force that is occupied at low levels of productivity in agriculture, marketing, food processing, livestock slaughter, and the storage and distribution trades.

The worst of the offenders are not on the farms but in the distribution chain. French farm prices, for example, have been among the lowest in Western Europe, while retail food prices have been among the highest. With less than 10 percent of her population employed in agriculture and over 50 percent in industry, manufacturing, and productive trades, the

Federal Republic of Germany is one of the most heavily industrialized nations of the world. Yet her population is devoting approximately the same proportion of total consumption expenditure to food that characterized the United States forty years earlier, in the mid-1920's.

Among countries, the range in marketing margins is great, and is compounded by tax policies. France, for example, collected 111.8 billion francs in public revenue in 1965, excluding social security taxes. Of this total, 81 billion francs or 72 percent represented indirect taxes, primarily on sales and transactions. These indirect taxes made up 21 percent of the entire French GNP in 1965. At the other extreme among Common Market countries, indirect taxes in the Netherlands in 1965 were only 44 percent of total tax collections (excluding social security taxes) and only 11 percent of GNP.[73] Variations of this magnitude in the extent to which tax and fiscal policies add to the margins between farm and retail food prices make it impossible to generalize about the relationship between farm-support programs and the proportion of consumer expenditures devoted to food. But it is obvious that high margins due to inefficient retailing are made worse by heavy reliance on indirect taxes that fall primarily upon sales. One conclusion seems clear. Continental Western Europe is rapidly approaching a point at which high food costs seem likely to retard the potentials for mass markets that can give economic meaning to the promise of integration.

Almost all the post-World War II proposals for a unified or integrated Europe have been launched with French leadership — and shot down by other Frenchmen. We may see a new variation of this phenomenon in the action ultimately taken on Common Market agricultural policies. There is no doubt that French farmers, in their support for the Common Market and its higher prices, were the main force that returned de Gaulle to the bargaining table in Brussels after his dramatic walkout in 1965. In this sense, French farmers "saved the Common Market." But it is France, among the countries of Western Europe, that could have the lowest food costs if she set out seriously to modernize her agricultural sector. And it is French taxpayers, and consumers, who will share heavily in the burden of high price supports and the resultant continuation of a structure of many small, inefficient producers and retail distributors.

If French farmers saved the Common Market in the 1960's, it may well be French taxpayers who threaten it most severely in the 1970's. Whether French-led or not, the European scene is increasingly ripe for a taxpayers' revolt.

The Seeds of Integration

In spite of clear evidence of an overcommitment to agriculture in Western Europe, and the growth of nonfunctional trade, it remains true that the prospects of trade expansion provide one of the most powerful accelerators for European integration. It is important to set these trends in a long-run perspective.

The development of a basis for international cooperation must begin with the facts as they are, not with some hypothetical base-point. And the acorns of international cooperation do not all grow into mighty oaks. But some do bear fruit. The negotiating process, in this respect, is much like the work of a mediator in a dispute between labor and management. The crucial first steps are to find some areas of common agreement with which to begin a dialogue.

The specification of "grades and standards" provided this common ground in the early history of most of the international agencies now active in Europe. This was true of the FAO in its earliest work immediately after World War II. It was true in the 1950's of the work of the United Nations Economic Commission for Europe, in Geneva. Work of this type provided most of the early examples of international cooperation between the countries of Eastern and Western Europe after 1950. The existence of this work on standardization unquestionably made it easier to develop the Common Agricultural Policy of the EEC. It is in this sense that the importance of these early agreements on seemingly minor items of common interest should not be underestimated.

Over the past decade, a series of agreements on international standards has developed, beginning with agreement in 1958 on the varietal certification of herbage seed moving in international trade.[74] This was followed in 1959 by a code for the testing of tractors in order to "facilitate trade by enabling an importing country to accept with confidence the tests carried out in another country." [75] Agreement was later reached on provisions for the certification of cereal seed, in 1966; on forest reproductive materials, in 1967; and on sugar and fodder beet seed, in 1968.[76] These supplement earlier agreements reached by the FAO on minimum standards for maize (corn) seed moving in international trade. Standard testing procedures for fertilizer distributors and combine harvesters were approved in 1967 and recommended to member countries.[77] Work was under way in 1968–69 on the preparation of a code of sanitary regulations for international trade in slaughter livestock and meat, a standard testing procedure for small internal combustion engines, and the harmonization of national safety regulations for tractors and farm machinery.

Another avenue of work has involved the standardization of trade specifications for fruits and vegetables. The initial agreements on this subject were developed by the United Nations Economic Commission for Europe. There were in 1969 some 27 standards for fruits and vegetables under these schemes, with the initial leadership in the United Nations now being supplemented by the OECD in devising methods for implementation.[78]

This is international cooperation at the grass-seed, if not the grass-root, level. It is mundane work, laborious and undramatic. But this is how foundation stones are laid for closer integration among nations. The work on specifications and standards is of growing importance, especially so in view of the increasing use of sanitary, safety, or health regulations to create nontariff barriers to trade.

Barriers to trade and closer integration rooted in lack of standardization are illustrated by the existence in Germany in 1966 of 28 recognized and approved varieties of domestic high-protein wheats (*Aufmischwei-zen*) that could be used to substitute for imported high-protein wheats in meeting baking standards. The number was so large that millers and dealers could not set up facilities to evaluate the wheats in the small quantities typically offered by farmers. It was impossible to pay the price premiums that would have been justified if there had been fewer varieties and larger quantities per variety.[79]

The all-night sessions that characterized the development of agricultural policies in the EEC, and the dramatic confrontation of top-level negotiators in the Kennedy Round, have diverted attention from the fact that the basis of a more rational international division of labor is agreement on common terms. Grades, standards, and specifications are the language of trade. In the same sense that the principle of interchangeable parts is the basis for the modern industrial factory, the development of agreement on grades and standards is the precondition for integration through trade. This is nowhere more clearly demonstrated than in the initiation of the dialogue between Eastern and Western Europe in the 1950's that yielded the greatly expanded trade contacts of the 1960's.

The Political Price and Promise of Community and Regional Government

The strains of the struggle for integration in Europe have begun to show. The most emphatic examples have been provided by the farmers of France. The revolts in Brittany in June and October 1967 were manifestations of violence and despair that contain a pregnant warning.[80] The Common Market has been presented in France as a solution to problems that are rooted in decades of underinvestment and structural lag, in agriculture and in industry. As the July 1, 1967, date for implementation of the common agricultural prices for grain approached, it became increasingly clear that the Common Market was no solution to the problem of the small farmers. Their reaction was elemental. It typifies in Europe the type of response that has been exhibited in American cities by the Negroes.

It would be a mistake to underrate the political hazard. The history of

Europe in modern times is a distressingly discouraging repetition of demagogic political movements fed by dissatisfied men from small farms and small towns. This history traces back through Poujadism in France, National Socialism in Germany, and on to the unpalatable peasant movements that convulsed the Balkans in the first decades of this century. This history seems to teach a clear lesson. It is that one of the greatest political dangers in Europe is not unrest in urban areas, or in industrial plants, or in strikebound ports. It is in reaction from the right led by dissatisfied and desperate small farmers and small-town men who see their way of life threatened and who strike out blindly.

This may be a real danger in Western Europe today. If true, it leads to some interesting speculation about the different processes of change in Eastern and Western Europe. In much of Eastern Europe the price of structural change on the scale necessary to accommodate industrial society has already been paid. This is not true in Poland, not completely true in Yugoslavia, but it is true for the rest of Eastern Europe. It was a very high price, it was almost surely an unjustified price, but it has been paid. It was paid by the generation that suffered through the changes that have created an agricultural structure in a substantial portion of Eastern Europe that is now in a form adapted to a realization of the benefits of modern revolutions in production, storage, transport, processing, and marketing. The structural base exists to enable Eastern Europe to take these benefits in stride. Western Europe has not yet paid this price.

This is not an argument for an Eastern European type of reform in Western European agriculture. It is rather an argument for a clear recognition of the scale of needed structural change. Western European farms are too small. Western European market structures are too fragmented. But the major thrust of the argument advanced in this chapter is against the conclusion that the only alternative is a structure of giant farms.

If an action program is to be mounted on the scale needed it will require a much greater investment in policies of structural change than anyone in Western Europe is now promoting. And if a program is scaled appropriate to the need, it will focus attention on one of the greatest defects in the European political structure. Europe, particularly in the Common Market version, is a collection of countries that have historically been dominated by strong capital cities. Paris has dominated France; Brussels was Belgium and never more emphatically so than in its recent factionalism and divisiveness. Berlin coerced Germany to 1945; and Rome dictated to Italy in political and ecclesiastic dimensions. In modern times these strongly centralized states have generated no viable units of government at the intermediate or regional level. There is a gap in the governmental structure in terms of the requirements placed upon it by modern society.

In the agricultural field one of the greatest needs is for reform in farm structures, not least in the marketing structure. But much more than that is needed. The goal of economic integration and a strong, supranational government in Europe will remain threatened until local government has been regenerated on a scale that can identify the desires of people with government more directly than they are now identified. There is a lesson to be read out of the accounts of rioting farmers in Brittany and out of threatened revolts in other countries of Europe. The lesson seems to be this: If an element of national sovereignty is passed up from national capitals to a supranational state, the experiment will not succeed unless at the same time some part of that national sovereignty is passed down the chain to regional units of government.

A fundamental weakness in the European Economic Community as now constituted lies in the sharply different political structures of its three strongest members, France, the Federal Republic of Germany, and Italy. The central governments of these nations do not negotiate from comparable positions of domestic political strength. Power in Germany is divided between Bonn and the *Länder*. But in this division there is a strength and stability that is absent in the rigid but fragile political structure of France, or in the unstable but still centralized power vacuum in Italy. It is this fragility, dramatized by the events of May and November 1968, that may deny to European leaders the freedom to contemplate political fulfillment of the Common Market idea.

Although the voters of France rejected de Gaulle's proposals for regional decentralization in the referendum of April 27, 1969, the pressures for decentralization are not likely to abate. France has been a prisoner of its highly centralized political structure. Given this outmoded and autocratic power system, it has been increasingly necessary to invoke a threat to national survival in order to silence internal dissention. And the process has been auto-generative. The existence of so autocratic a power structure has permitted its use for nationalistic purposes without the counterweight that strong regional and provincial political representation would have provided. This line of reasoning gives rise to an intriguing hypothesis: A devolution of political authority down from Paris may be a necessary condition for the future evolution of the political institutions of the EEC.

Seen in this light, the dissident farmers of Brittany may be forcing France upon a path that would lead ultimately to political fulfillment of the promise of the Common Market. What outside pressure failed to accomplish may yet be achieved through pressure from within. The French farmers have demonstrated in the streets of Brussels, but they want greater political and economic freedom from Paris. If this goal is achieved, it may create a greater regional sense of being "masters in their own houses," and this could build the sense of regional strength that would make tolerable some surrender of national sovereignty to a supranational body.

The present system has worked only because national governments could coerce their nationals. They could continue to do this into the twentieth century through wars and the threat of scarcity. Peace and abundance rob these governmental structures of their principal cohesive force. If problems once resolved in Paris or Rome or Berlin must now be resolved in Brussels the system becomes unworkable. The solution may be to focus the political thrust of integration in Europe not on a Brussels, but on the creation of new and viable units of regional government. The scale needed is a scale large enough to permit regional economic planning, with financial resources great enough to give the regions strength. Only then will those who rebel in Brittany or Bavaria against agreements made in Geneva or validated in Brussels feel that they possess viable means for redress of their grievances. And only then will the promise of a new economic base in Europe be fulfilled in its political dimensions.

CHAPTER 6

The Harmonization of Education

BY ROBERT H. BECK

IN THE twentieth century state-supported education in Western Europe has been characterized by a two-part system of schooling: compulsory education of the masses, ending at about ages 10–14, and a severely restricted secondary and higher education program oriented largely toward the humanities. Within this over-all pattern sharp differences between countries existed as each state's school system stressed the national language (or languages), history, art, literature, and so on, and developed its own standards and institutional forms. By the late 1960's, however, significant common changes were occurring, both programmatic and institutional, in response to the challenges of the modern world and to the general pressures for integration in Europe. This has led to a not inconsiderable "harmonization" of European education. Programmatically, harmonization is evident in the increasing emphasis on Europe in course-work and textbook content; examples of what may be called institutional harmonization are the establishment of the European Schools and the work toward a Europe-wide secondary-school leaving examination.

The factors bearing on harmonization interrelate and interact complexly, and they cannot be treated in an entirely discrete manner. But three lines of development may usefully be traced here: (1) the educational activities of organizations committed in some degree to European integration; (2) the Europeanization of textbooks; and (3) the common influence on European education of ideological and economic forces.

Organizations Promoting Harmonization

A number of organizations have been very influential in moving Western Europe in the direction of educational harmonization. These include three of the Continent's large-scale political and economic organizations (the Council of Europe, the European Economic Community, and the Organization for Economic Cooperation and Development); several smaller but significant groups (the Centre Européen de la Culture, the Centre International d'Etudes Pédagogiques at Sèvres, the Office Franco-Allemand pour la Jeunesse), two associations (the Comparative Education Society in Europe and the European Association of Teachers), and two teaching institutions (the European Schools and the College of Europe).

The Council of Europe, largely through its Council for Cultural Cooperation, has ranged widely in the educational activities in which it has been concerned.[1] It has worked closely with ministers of education in Western Europe, making it possible for the ministers to convene almost annually and supplementing the work of the regular ministerial staffs by furnishing to the ministers all-European data not always available in their home countries. It has developed a Documentation Center for Education in Europe. It maintains an up-to-date guide to European school systems and sponsors research on pupil guidance, examination systems, continued-education programs, teaching methods and techniques, teacher training, and technical and vocational education. It publishes and distributes to member countries reports prepared by educational experts, such as *Reform and Expansion of Higher Education in Europe* (1967) and *The Educational Aspects of Examinations* (1967). It also sponsored the *Dictionary of European Educational Terminology* (which greatly aids communication on a continent whose countries have their own idiosyncratic ways of describing educational facts and fancies) and has supported since 1965 an annual publication, *Paedagogica Europaea*, which reports on educational research being done in Europe. It has very actively encouraged textbook revision (this will be discussed separately in the next section of this chapter).

In order to promote a European orientation in the universities of member countries, the Council has encouraged free movement of academic personnel, payment of scholarships for students studying in nations other than their own, and exchange of faculty, students, and summer institutes and programs. To promote curricular equivalence a pilot study on the teaching of chemistry at the university level was undertaken, with others to follow in physics, biology, history, geography, and economics. The Council is doing research in the use of closed-circuit television in all types of schools, and it produces educational films. It is specially concerned with modern-language teaching, and it keeps member nations informed of developments and improvements.

Of special interest and importance are the Council's programs for out-of-school education, such as the European Experimental Youth Center to promote European awareness among youth leaders. Voluntary work camps are held to aid in preparing youth for civic, social, and family responsibilities. The idea of "lifelong education" (*l'éducation permanente*) is stressed as a necessary concomitant of the increased leisure brought by an industrialized society. To facilitate adjustment to technological changes the Council has sponsored studies of the cultural implications of regional planning and the relation of industrial design to everyday life. It has also been very concerned to preserve and protect objects of artistic and historical interest.

The Council of Europe tends to proceed cautiously in its activities, endeavoring never to embarrass nations or their officials. It must always keep in mind the practical problems of politicians seeking to balance educational needs with other demands on national resources. But it has nevertheless been very effective in pursuing its educational goals.

The arm of the OECD that has been primarily concerned with education is the Directorate for Scientific Affairs, established "to take charge of the activities of the Organisation relating to scientific research and to the expansion and rational utilization of the scientific and technical personnel available as to meet the needs arising from economic growth." [2] The economic need for highly qualified manpower, especially in technical and scientific fields, is one of the common problems facing the nations of Europe and its implications for education will be discussed at greater length later in this chapter; here it should be noted that the Directorate for Scientific Affairs has worked to focus attention on the problem and to stimulate action toward solutions.

The OECD has also encouraged each of its member countries to study educational policy and planning. It gives financial support to research teams from each country so that they can assess educational needs and goals and make recommendations for investment in education; then it sponsors meetings at which each nation's findings are presented to experts from other nations. This exchange permits a refinement of the material before release of a final report. Reports have been prepared for Sweden, Turkey, Italy, Spain, Greece, and Portugal. The OECD has no authority to insist on legislative implementation of a report in any nation; it can only recommend.

A Study Group on the Economics of Education, formed in 1962 under the sponsorship of the OECD, has produced a series of volumes exploring economic issues. Earlier, in 1961, the OECD sponsored a conference at Kungalv in collaboration with the Swedish Ministry of Education to discuss education as a principal means of social and economic progress, resulting in a report titled *Ability and Educational Opportunity*. The OECD has also supported studies by individuals on such subjects as modernizing schools, technical development and training, and the implications of enrollment expansion in education.

The interest of the EEC in education was clearly stated in section 260 of its *Ninth General Report* (1966): "The part played by the universities in training senior personnel and in cultivating and propagating ideas, has naturally led them to concern themselves more and more with problems of European unification. Being aware of the importance of these developments, the Commission has endeavored to encourage and in many cases to instigate them. Its co-operating with the universities has therefore gone on broadening. Several European documentation centers have been set up in faculties or institutes of law, economics or political science, and chairs have been founded. Many seminars have been organized, and more than 200 professors, assistant lecturers, and students preparing theses have been invited for individual one-week visits to the headquarters of the Communities. Sixty-five theses were submitted to the jury of the European Communities Prize, which was awarded in December for three works of great merit." [3]

The EEC agency responsible for carrying out these activities is the Bureau d'Information des Communautés Européennes, under the direction of Jean Moreau. The bureau also sponsors a small monthly journal, *Nouvelles Universitaires*, which lists courses and seminars on European themes. The journal is edited by F. De Fontaine, a leader in the reconstruction of French higher education.

Another agency closely associated with the EEC, although it has budgetary independence (its supporting funds are privately raised), is the European Community Institute for University Studies, founded in 1958. Its governing purpose is the initiation of teaching and research on European problems and European integration. It reported, for 1966, that 200 European courses and seminars were held — an increase of 70 over the previous year — and 503 doctoral theses on European integration were in preparation in five countries — an increase of 163 over 1965.[4] The institute's precise influence on these developments would be difficult to measure, but certainly it was not an insignificant factor. The chairman of the institute, Max Kohnstamm, and its directors, Louis Armand, Pietro Campilli, Dino Del Bo, André Donner, Paride Formentini, Walter Hallstein, Etienne Hirsch, and Jean Monnet, have all been prime movers of European integration. One of the institute's most important functions is publication of *University Research and Studies on European Integration* (the fourth volume of which appeared in 1967), the only compendium of studies on general Western European problems which exists.

The multivarious activities of large organizations like the Council of Europe, the OECD, and the EEC should not be allowed to overshadow the important work of smaller units.

One of these is the Centre Européen de la Culture in Geneva (which has ties with the Council of Europe's Council of Cultural Cooperation). Under Denis de Rougemont, one of the early European "federalists" and author of *Europe at Stake* (1948), the Centre Européen has been active in publishing for teachers text materials emphasizing Europeanness. It also issues *Civisme Européen*, a quarterly identifying bibliographical sources on European culture, civilization, and institutions such as the EEC and Euratom.

At Sèvres, on the outskirts of Paris, the Centre International d'Etudes Pédagogiques has helped European educators explore the idea of a European education. A number of educators from the United States have received at the Centre International their first briefing on education in Europe. While modest in size and not specializing in European education, the Centre International and its journal, *Les Amis de Sèvres*, have served as useful forums for the discussion of pan-European topics.

The Office Franco-Allemand pour la Jeunesse, with its German counterpart, Deutsch-Französisches Jugendwerk, has taken a fresh and direct approach to Europeanization by encouraging exchanges of young nationals of these traditionally hostile European nations. The motto of the organization runs across the top of its quarterly journal, published in Paris: "To appreciate one another, one must know one another; to know one another, one must meet." To that end, a quarter million young Frenchmen and Germans have visited each other's country under the auspices of the Office Franco-Allemand pour la Jeunesse since its founding in 1964. (This is of course only a fraction of the total visits exchanged by French and Germans.)

The European Association of Teachers (EAT; the French title is Association Européenne des Enseignants) was founded in 1956 at Paris. Its members are elementary and secondary school teachers and administrators, as well as staff members from colleges and universities for teacher training. It is organized in national sections: Austria, Belgium, France, West Germany, Greece, Ireland, Luxembourg, the Netherlands, Switzerland, and the United Kingdom. The outlook of the EAT is well summarized in its own statement: "As teachers we are concerned to bring up young people so that they will be able to become useful and happy members of their profession and their society. But the present is a time of rapid change in the world, and these changes impose upon us a double task. We must in our teaching take account of new developments and, further, we must endeavor through education to influence these developments. Perhaps the most important development of the present day is the emergence of a new harmony and the interdependence among the countries of Europe. A new community is developing and it is vitally necessary that we should equip young people to play their part in it as free men and women. This community is Europe." Therefore the aims of all the national sections of EAT are the same: "(a) to create among teachers an awareness of European problems and to disseminate information which has a bearing on the realization of European federation; (b) to work by all available means towards a deeper understanding of those essential qualities which are characteristic of European civilization and to ensure their preservation, notably by increasing the number of international contacts at the personal level; (c) to develop a similar understanding among the pupils and in all other fields where the teacher may exert an influence; (d) to support all activity directed to this end and to collaborate with other organizations which have similar international objectives." [5]

Founded in 1961, the Comparative Education Society in Europe held its first meeting at Sèvres, France, in 1963. It provides a sounding board for discussion of common educational issues. For example, secondary education was a theme at the second of its meetings, held in Berlin in 1965. Higher education in Europe was the theme of the 1966 conference in Ghent. And European curriculum development at the second level was the theme of its 1969 meeting at Prague. The questions taken to the floor of the society meetings have not been exclusively European, but the attention of the members has been on European solutions. While it is not possible to say just how effective the society has been, at least it permits the airing of issues by professors of comparative education and their advanced students, who attend the meetings. Conversations with the conferees suggest that almost all have been consulted by their governments about educational progress in other countries, including the United States.

Teaching institutions designed to foster Europeanization are still rare. But the European Schools (variously called Ecole Européenne, Europäische Schule, Scuola Europa, Europese School) are an important first step. [6] They were originally established in 1957 to solve the practical problem of providing education for the children of EEC officials. (They are not, however, institutions of the community but rather of the member states.) By 1966 there were six European Schools — at Luxembourg City; Brussels, Belgium; Varese, Italy; Mol, Belgium; Karlsruhe, West Germany; and Bergen, Holland. They enrolled 5592 students, with a mixture of nationalities in each school.

The twin objectives of the European Schools have been to promote Europeanness and at the same time not to erode national patriotism. To achieve the first of these goals the curriculum specifies "European hours" (six a week in primary school) during which all the pupils of a given grade, whatever their nationality, are grouped for singing, drawing, manual training, and gymnastics. In addition the children of each nationality are taught by fellow nationals only in courses on their native language. A German pupil, for example, would not study history, geography, or art with a German instructor teaching in German. Rather he would have a French instructor who would teach in French and his classmates would be Dutch and Italian. [7] While proficiency in a language other than the native one is stressed as a prerequisite to European community (French and German are the working languages in the Schools), the mother tongues of the students are not ignored; in the primary school twenty hours a week are programmed in German, French, Italian, and Dutch for the nationals of those languages. This attention to the mother tongue is not limited to instruction in vocabulary, grammatical rules, and other conventions of language study. Literature is an important part of the curriculum and the teachers help their pupils to understand the insights into society and conduct typical of their native country's literature. Their aim is to encourage students to develop a respect for their own country's literature without losing sight of the fact that the human condition cannot be isolated within any one country—that their own literature is most meaningful when viewed in the broader context of Western literature. It is in this way that the two objectives of the European Schools are constantly associated.

There are not yet very many European Schools but they are having an impact. They are encouraging children of various European nationalities to get to know one another, to respect one another's cultures, to learn common languages. And their impact will increase as the Schools multiply. They may even someday exist in socialist countries, in Yugoslavia perhaps first of all, although the socialist resistance to "contaminating" ideas will make this development slow.

The one pan-European institution of higher learning is the College of Europe at Bruges, established in 1949 as a "postgraduate institution for specialized study of the problems of European unification."[8] One of its founders was Henri Brugmans, author of *Panorama of Federalist Thought*.[9] This famous college has provided many staff members for pan-European organizations and for the well-known centers for European studies, such as that in Bologna, Italy. The college's alumni association now publishes, with the aid of the European Cultural Foundation, a quarterly journal, *Agenor*, "written for the new generation which must build and lead the united Europe of tomorrow," as stated on its masthead.

The EEC has advocated a University of Europe,[10] but none has as yet been established and not all are agreed that one is necessary. As one university faculty member said, "European universities are proud old ladies and moreover they think that the universities always have been institutions of higher learning without regard to national boundaries." That was certainly true of the medieval university and remains true of some European universities today, though probably not of the provincial universities. There have also been suggestions for regional centers specializing in certain kinds of study and drawing on the resources of all European nations: ventures in an "intellectual common market." One such was proposed by Joseph Ben-David, who commented on the "fragmentation of scientific endeavor in Europe into small units which make it impossible to concentrate sufficient resources for large-scale work in any one place." [11] He recommended coordination of scientific studies in regional centers. Nothing has so far been done to instrument this ideal.

The Europeanization of Textbooks

One activity of several organizations has been so significant in the harmonizing of European education that it requires separate discussion. This is the development of European rather than national textbooks, especially in history, geography, and civics.[12] Since the rise of nationalism in Europe the emphasis in textbooks has understandably been on national resources, national heroes, national needs and desires. A shift to recognition of common problems and goals, of interdependence, of the heritage and future of "Europe" has now begun. The EEC (through its Bureau d'Information), the Council of Europe, and UNESCO [13] have lent strong support to the movement to revise textbooks. This movement, incidentally, is not limited to Western Europe: the socialist countries have sent representatives to conferences on schoolbook revision. It would, however, be unrealistic not to acknowledge that there is still a long way to go before national bias in textbooks is eliminated.

It has been especially difficult to achieve objectivity in history texts. In this area the Council of Europe has made two important contributions. Between 1953 and 1959 it sponsored six conferences on periods of European history. The conferences examined the nature of a historian's largely unconscious bias, showing again and again how a particular interpretation simply reflected the origin or allegiance of the historian. They focused attention on the way historians of a larger European nation overlook the smaller nations, and the way a conventional or narrow reading of some event is perpetuated unthinkingly. These conferences did not result directly and immediately in new textbooks but rather set guidelines, clarified terms and concepts, and made recommendations helpful for teachers and authors.[14]

The Council of Europe also was responsible for publishing Edouard Bruley and E. H. Dance's *A History of Europe?* (1960) which is outstanding in showing how the idea of Europe can be central in a history text without that text either belittling any one nation — thus undermining patriotism — or denigrating the rest of the world.[15] Their section on "History Teaching Becomes International" is especially worthy of note.[16] One example of the fresh approach of Bruley and Dance is their insistence that an adequate reading of history would place Turkey within the development of Western Europe instead of casting her in the role of invader and plunderer of Western Europe's civilization and peoples.[17] A number of history textbooks following their precepts have been published, as well as a series of model lessons from a European perspective, prepared for and circulated by the Council of Europe.[18]

In 1967 a summary of what had been accomplished in twenty-five years of history textbook revision was published by the Council for Cultural Cooperation of the Council of Europe.[19] It is fitting that Otto-Ernst Schüddekopf wrote the book in collaboration with Edouard Bruley, E. H. Dance, and Haakon Vigander — the most distinguished names in a movement essential to the harmonization of European education. No one expected *History Teaching and History Textbook Revision* to blaze new trails; nor did it. But the four authors pulled together the results of the 146 conferences and important writing on the subject of history textbook revision, and then looked ahead.

The fourth chapter, written by Schüddekopf, is called "The Lesson Learned from History and History Textbook Revision." In it writers of textbooks are reminded that material presented must be well balanced in selection:

This is in fact the crucial aspect of textbook revision in our day. Many history textbooks make propaganda by unbalanced selection which by no means necessarily stems from ill will but can also be caused by a lack of knowledge and inherited prejudices which, however, are not recognized as such . . . Beside false or one-sided selections, omissions also frequently occur in history textbooks and constitute a serious problem, because when one is arriving at a judgment, historical and educational aspects conflict with one another and both can claim the support of weighty arguments.[20]

The other side of the coin requires Western Europeans to restrain the tendency "to distill from history a kind of 'European ideology' [of which Europeanists have to be especially wary!] . . . In addition the too one-sided attention paid by textbook work to Western Europe should be noted and if possible overcome." Schüddekopf recognized that a

start has already been made in this respect, for example the valuable Yugoslav-German contacts since 1953 and similar bilateral links between Western and Eastern Europe. In France, too, there has been criticism from time to time that contacts are restricted to the Occident. At the annual meeting in 1954 one member remarked: "He regards certain texts accepted at the time of the agreements between French and German historians in 1951 as an encouragement to the hostility of Western Germany towards the Soviet Union and the people democracies. He fears that participation at international gatherings organized mainly within the framework of Western Europe will force us to adopt an attitude or participate directly in a particular policy." . . . The talks between educationists of East and West European countries belong to the most promising features of our time and could possibly lead to the resumption of the efforts that for years had been attempted by the *Comité d'Entente* of the International Teachers' Associations and which the Cold War brought to an end.[21]

Other organizations have also sought to encourage cooperation among historians of Europe, among them the Norden Association in Scandinavia, the International Schoolbook Institute of Braunschweig, the English Historical Association, the French History and Geography Teachers' Association, and the Belgian Federation of History Teachers.[22]

Bias is not equally evident in civics texts, but as the Committee of Ministers of the Council of Europe noted in a resolution of October 6, 1964, there is in secondary education an "imperative duty . . . to inculcate an awareness of European facts and problems." Two years later the Council of Europe's Council of Cultural Cooperation published *Introducing Europe to Senior Pupils*, by René Jotterand, the secretary general of the Department of Education of the Canton of Geneva, which filled a serious gap that had existed in materials for teachers of civics.[23] Jotterand's book reflects the thought behind the words of Pierre Duclos, a historian of political aspects of harmonization in Europe: "Europe will only come into being when it exists in the hearts and consciousness of men." [24] *Introducing Europe to Senior Pupils* has to be taken as propaganda for integration of the European West. But it demonstrates that one can avow support for "one Europe" without a loss of national patriotism. Jotterand's text was the analogue of the ideal textbook on European history sketched out by Bruley and Dance. Jotterand made the simple suggestion that students think in terms of concentric circles to describe their allegiance. "In mounting progression from municipality to county or province, and then to country, the scope of syllabuses and textbooks should also extend to Europe and the world which form, as it were, the fourth and fifth concentric circles." [25]

In geography, distortion of texts is apt to lie in a patterning by national boundaries, in a failure to reveal the common problems, opportunities, and resources of the European community. In the mid-1960's Professor I. B. F. Kormoss of the College of Europe at Bruges was asked by the Bureau d'Information of the EEC to prepare community-wide maps of the administrative regions and units, density of population, land utilization and main crops, livestock and fishing, energy and steel, and aspects of industry, transportation, and external trade. The pupils and teachers who use Kormoss's *The European Community in Maps* (and by 1967 more than a quarter million of these maps had been requested by European schools) are exposed to thinking beyond a single nation to a region, to a larger, interdependent community — if only the community of the Six. For example, coal mined in one country is shown to be not only consumed by individuals and industries in that country but bought by another country to produce, say, steel — some of which may in turn be shipped back to the first country. The pupil sees how a coal and steel "community" developed because of the interdependence of countries.

The Council of Europe's Council for Cultural Cooperation has complemented Kormoss's publication with that of E. C. Marchant, *Geography Teaching and the Revision of Geography Textbooks and Atlases* (1968). Marchant showed that a regional approach to describing natural resources and their utilization was more realistic than the nationalistic one which had influenced so many geography textbooks and atlases.

There has been less emphasis on a Europeanizing of textbooks in other fields, but a conference held in 1966 by the Centre International d'Etudes Pédagogiques, devoted to aspects of teaching literature in European upper secondary schools, stressed that there is a European style in writing, painting, music. Denis de Rougemont commented there: "In this domain, everything is in common. Among other things we would cite: the epic, the novel, comedy . . . the ballad, sonnet, the rhymes, the strophes. . . . In painting: the use of the easel peculiarly European. . . . Analogous remarks could be made about music. . . . In brief, this basic structural similarity is not perceived simply because it is too evident." [26] When new textbooks are available they will certainly reflect de Rougemont's view.

Common Goals, Common Problems, Common Needs

The activities of pan-European organizations and the Europeanization of textbooks have been important factors in the movement toward harmonization of European education. But perhaps the most potent force has been a conjunction of ideological and economic motives throughout Europe that have had wide-ranging ramifications.

By the late 1960's European nations generally shared a commitment to ensure equal access to education for their young people whatever their social class, financial resources, race, sex, or place of birth, as well as a commitment to increase the years of compulsory schooling and the opportunity for advanced education so as to better prepare each citizen to fulfill his vocational potential, to exercise his civic responsibilities, and to enjoy a full life. At the same time there was recognition of the increasing need of all nations for more highly qualified manpower, especially in the technical and scientific fields, if economic development was to proceed as envisioned by the EEC and other such groups.[27] As a result European educators have been reassessing the organization of their schools and the traditional secondary-school leaving examinations; they have been giving more attention to guidance and to establishing "equivalence" of educational standards so that movement from one nation to another of those with needed skills is facilitated; and they have become concerned to increase the scope and prestige of technical studies at both the secondary and higher levels of education. The recognition of common goals and problems and the search for solutions, which have also often been common, have strengthened immeasurably the cross-national ties of European educators.

Their task has not been an easy one, nor will it become lighter in the near future. A major problem has been what many Europeans refer to as *l'explosion scolaire*.[28] The sharp rise in the birthrate after World War II led to mushrooming school enrollments that have now reached the secondary and university levels. Table 1 shows the growth indexes in secondary and higher education enrollment from 1955 to 1965, and Table 2 shows the actual increases in enrollment in higher education between 1950 and 1966. In Table 3 growth in the fifteen to nineteen age group by 1980 is projected. These numbers alone are an indication of the difficulties facing European educators. But along with these one must remember the steady increase in years of compulsory schooling, which puts an added strain on schools — both on the elementary schools the youngsters are required to attend and on the secondary schools and universities which a greater proportion of young people will now attend.[29]

The concept of universal public education is relatively new to Europe. In England, for example, compulsory attendance in state-supported schools was not introduced in legislation until 1876. The act covered children until the age of ten and based employment of children ten to fourteen years old on the attainment of certain educational standards. Not until the Education Act of 1921 was it obligatory for all English children to attend school to their fourteenth birthday. In 1882 a French law made

Table 1. Growth Indexes for Secondary and Higher Education in Thirteen European Countries from 1955 to 1965, with Indexes Based on 100 for 1955[a]

Country	Higher	Secondary
Austria	256	98
Belgium	197	159
Denmark	221	118
France	241	207
Germany (F.R.)	154	99
Italy	175	200
Netherlands	219	153
Spain	184	222
Sweden	263	134
Switzerland	195	...
Turkey	263	297
United Kingdom	...	148
Yugoslavia	182	213

SOURCE: Adapted from *Development of Secondary Education: Trends and Implications* (Paris: OECD, 1969), Table 5, p. 30.

[a] The comparable indexes for the United States are 208 for higher education and 155 for secondary.

Table 2. Enrollments in Higher Education for Thirteen European Countries in
Selected Years between 1950 and 1966

Country	Early 1950's	Mid-1950's	Early 1960's	Mid-1960's
Austria	20,710	19,124	38,533	48,895
	(1951–52)	(1955–56)	(1960–61)	(1965–66)
Belgium	35,033	38,393	51,999	75,468
	(1952–53)	(1955–56)	(1960–61)	(1964–65)
Denmark	19,946	22,797	33,275	50,493
	(1951–52)	(1956–57)	(1961–62)	(1965–66)
France	145,865	152,246	214,672	367,000
	(1950–51)	(1954–55)	(1959–60)	(1964–65)
Germany (F.R.)	246,090	332,795	408,616	512,208
	(1950)	(1956)	(1959)	(1965)
Netherlands[a]	29,736	29,642	40,727	58,361
	(1950)	(1955)	(1960)	(1964)
Norway[a]	7,000	5,600	9,600	19,637
	(1951–52)	(1955–56)	(1960–61)	(1965–66)
Portugal	16,152	18,838	24,060	29,000
	(1950–52)	(1955–56)	(1960–61)	(1964–65)
Spain	54,605	61,167	76,458	112,541
	(1950–51)	(1955–56)	(1960–61)	(1964–65)
Sweden	16,887	22,647	36,909	59,643
	(1950–51)	(1955–56)	(1960–61)	(1964–65)
Switzerland	16,501	17,881	24,648	34,846
	(1950–51)	(1955–56)	(1960–61)	(1964–65)
United Kingdom (England and Wales)...	...	106,000	151,000	...
		(1955–56)	(1960–61)	
Yugoslavia	45,041	58,181	94,769	106,050
	(1952–53)	(1955–56)	(1960–61)	(1964–65)

SOURCE: Adapted from *Development of Secondary Education*, Table 47, pp. 82–84.
[a] For these countries, higher education enrollments include university only.

Table 3. Expected Percentage of the 15–19 Age Group in
Eleven European Countries as of 1980, with a Base
of 100 for 1965 [a]

Country	Number	Country	Number
Austria	127.3	Ireland	117.9[b]
Denmark	89.4	Italy	106.1
France	101.9	Portugal	115.1[c]
Germany (F.R.)..	137.1	Sweden	84.8
Great Britain	110.1	Switzerland	101.0
Holland	103.0		

SOURCE: Adapted from *Development of Secondary Education*, Table 3, p. 27.
[a] The comparable index for the United States is 121.
[b] For 1981.
[c] The base of 100 was computed for 1966.

education compulsory for youngsters six to thirteen years of age. The Weimar Constitution of 1918 established compulsory full-time education for German youth of six to fourteen years; those from fourteen to eighteen were required to attend continuation schools part time. In Spain a general education act in 1857 declared education compulsory for children aged six to twelve.

Compare the situation in America, where compulsory education was introduced in the colony of Massachusetts in 1642 when parents and masters with apprentices were required to teach children to read. This requirement was stiffened by the famous "Old Deluder Satan" Act of 1647 which required each settlement of fifty families to appoint a teacher to give instruction in reading and writing. However, after the United States became a nation it was not until 1852 that one of the states legislated obligatory education — Massachusetts required attendance for twelve weeks of the year for youths between the ages of eight and fourteen. By 1889, twenty-five states had followed the example of Massachusetts, though the law was not enforced except in Massachusetts and Connecticut.

The number of years of compulsory schooling in Europe had shown an unmistakable upward trend by the 1960's. In Austria the eight years of obligatory education in 1955 had become nine in a decade. The same holds for France, and by 1975 the requirement there will be ten years of school. Portuguese law required only four years of common school in 1965, but by 1975 the period of obligatory education is to be increased 50 percent. The same trend appears in Eastern Europe. In the Soviet Union, Bulgaria, and Yugoslavia the seven-year had become the eight-year common school by 1960, and plans to make ten-year education universal in the Soviet Union were announced. In 1960 the Czechoslovak National Assembly voted to make school compulsory for all youth from six to fifteen years of age.

This increase in years of compulsory education reflects both the ideological and the economic motives mentioned above: Europeans have generally accepted the democratic philosophy that young people have a right to sufficient education to provide them with the knowledge, understanding, and training they need to find a satisfactory place for themselves in the modern world. At the same time the pressing needs of a highly industrialized society demand a relatively high level of education for its members if they are to function effectively to the benefit of society as a whole.

Obviously, if young people are to fulfill their own potential and meet the needs of society they require guidance, and beginnings in guidance programs have been made in most European countries.[30] In France use is made of a guidance council (*conseil d'orientation*) midway in secondary education. The experience of students is reviewed when they are about fifteen years old and have had four years in secondary school. The council, presided over by a full-time professional school guidance worker, discusses what might be the most suitable future for each student. All teachers who have had this student in class are present.[31] Depending on the recommendation of the council the student may enter the "long course" of the upper secondary school, a three-year sequence preparing students for the *baccalauréat*, or he may take the "short," two-year course, offering industrial, commercial, or administrative training.

Belgium and Denmark also have a *conseil d'orientation* or its equivalent. West Germany, Italy, Holland, Switzerland (the Canton of Geneva), and Turkey have plans to develop a council system. In Austria, Norway, and Sweden educators feel that guidance should not be left to a council but should be continuous throughout the grades.

An assumption underlying much of European vocational practice has been that the course of study from the beginning of the secondary school can be divided into several distinct curriculums, into which students can be appropriately steered in accordance with their interests and abilities. This assumption is related to the multilateral organization characteristics of schools in many European countries. At the age of ten or eleven—at the end of primary school — each pupil in a multilaterally organized school system is directed into one of a number of specific subject-matter curriculums. Some of these curriculums — classical languages, modern languages, mathematics and natural sciences — are designed to lead into the upper secondary school and on to higher education; others lead to one- or two-year vocational schools; still others are terminal and the students go from them directly to some kind of job. A pure type of multilateral organization has been typical of West Germany. A less pure type has been the French secondary school.[32]

In a comprehensive system, on the other hand, all pupils — of whatever social class, abilities, or expectations — are enrolled in a common curriculum for at least the first four years of secondary school. There is no differentiation among them until the age of fifteen or sixteen when some specialization usually occurs. Great Britain, Norway, Sweden, and the socialist countries of Eastern Europe have comprehensive secondary schools. (In 1968 the French Ministry of Education announced that there was to be a comprehensive organization of French schools at least during the period of compulsory education.)

This is not the place to detail the advantages and disadvantages of the two systems. There certainly has not been a consensus in Europe itself on which form is preferable.[33] It is likely, however, that with the increase in years of compulsory education the need for a longer period of general education for all children will become evident in multilateral systems. At the least it would seem that considerable shifting of students from one curriculum to another will have to be accommodated in multilateral systems as there is increased assessment of individual abilities and interests through counseling — either on a continuing basis or at specified periods as with the *conseil d'orientation* — rather than almost sole reliance on primary school grades and comprehensive examinations at age ten or eleven.

The increase in years of compulsory education for all young people and the subsequent increase in demand for upper secondary and higher education have been factors in the controversy over the traditional secondary-school leaving examination — the French *baccalauréat*, the German *Abitur*, the British GCE, and so on. Their prestige has been high but they have come under heavy criticism largely because they have been used as the sole determinant of university entrance (even though they have not predicted academic success with any high degree of accuracy) and they are designed so that a considerable number of candidates — already a select group — fail. In France, for example, the *baccalauréat* is divided into two parts and taken in successive years — the sixth year when the students generally are seventeen, and the terminal seventh year when most students are eighteen. In the decade 1950–60, 44 percent of the candidates failed Part I and 35 percent of those who survived Part I failed Part II.[34] Small wonder the *baccalauréat* has been called "terreur des familles . . . générateur des scènes de ménage." [35] In the 1960's the number of pupils who were successful increased: 60–65 percent passed the combined parts of the *baccalauréat*. Most European nations are contemplating reform of these examinations to make them less a qualification for university admission and more a certification of successful completion of a secondary course of general and specialized studies.[36]

There have also been concrete steps toward establishing a European *baccalauréat*. Clearly this would contribute significantly to the harmonizing of European education. The European ministers of education have given their blessing to the framing of a European *baccalauréat*, and research on it is being underwritten by the Council of Europe.[37] As indicated earlier, work is being done by the Council to establish pan-European standards in the various academic fields. There remains, however, a reluctance among several ministries of education to acknowledge that the system of education in other countries is as good as that in their own. This national pride has long been a stumbling block in the way of "freedom of establishment."

Most Americans will not have heard this phrase but it is common throughout Europe. It means simply that a trained person has the right to practice his occupation or profession in a country other than the one in which he received his education. It refers to "horizontal" freedom in contrast to "vertical" freedom, which is social. Vertical mobility has meant that a person could rise on the social ladder. Horizontal mobility would allow men to carry their occupational status across national boundaries.

The two forms of freedom are associated. Freedom to practice one's occupation or profession in a nation where it is needed, not just in the country where training was received, can make a real difference in income and social position for the individual. Freedom of establishment implies, of course, that the host country regards the educational standards of the home country as equivalent to its own.[38] Acceptance of this equivalence is important not only for the welfare of the individual but for the economic health of the European community. Shortages in this or that nation's reserves of some occupational category could hinder such a nation's economic development and hence the economic development of Europe as a whole if there is not relatively free cross-national movement of skilled manpower. This economic pressure is eroding the national barriers in education, but it cannot be said that freedom of establishment exists in Europe as yet.

Economic pressure also has been responsible for the larger and more prestigious role studies in technology and applied science are gradually coming to have at both the secondary and the university levels. Traditionally, the German *Gymnasium,* the French *lycée,* and the secondary schools of other Western European nations had the goal of training elite upper-middle-class and upper-class youths for university study, which in turn prepared them for the professions and for government service. To be sure, there was a sprinkling of lower-class and lower-middle-class youths in these secondary schools and in the universities, but no more than a sprinkling.[39] As late as World War II only about 5 percent of the college-age group were enrolled in institutions of higher education. With such a limited group it was possible to maintain a curriculum in both secondary schools and universities that gave classical languages and literature the greatest prestige, although mathematics, theoretical studies in science, and modern foreign languages had achieved a place by the twentieth century. It was not until after World War II that technological subject matter made its way into the curriculum.

Europe lagged far behind the United States in including coursework in the applied sciences in high school. With the late-eighteenth-century precedent of Benjamin Franklin's Academy, high school curriculums in vocational studies were common in the United States by 1900. Undoubtedly the college-preparatory curriculum, as it was called, had greater prestige than either the vocational or the general curriculum, but both the latter were widespread and well established long before their counterparts in Europe. In the higher education of the United States, too, technology and applied science early found a secure status. In 1862 President Lincoln signed the Land-Grant Act that provided for the donation by the federal government of public lands "to the several states and territories which may provide colleges for the benefit of agriculture and mechanic arts." Each state accepting title to these lands was obligated to establish "at least one college where the leading object shall be, without excluding other scientific and classical studies, and including military tactics, to teach such branches of learning as are related to agriculture and the mechanic arts . . . in order to promote the liberal and practical education of the industrial classes in the several pursuits and professions in life."

The acceptance of "mechanic arts" as well as liberal arts as a legitimate field of study at all levels of education in the United States — in other words, the emphasis in education upon the practical as well as the theoretical — has been an important element in creating the technology gap between America and Western European nations.[40] This is widely recognized in Europe, as is the urgent need for Europe to close this gap. Jean-Jacques Servan-Schreiber in writing of *The American Challenge* warned that Europe must reform its education if it wishes to compete successfully with the United States technologically.[41] Lord Butler of Saffrom Walden, master of Trinity College, Cambridge, told a 1968 Anglo-French Conference of political leaders and editors: "In Europe as a whole we are somewhat behind in our education. Europe has become the new frontier of American industry. American investment in Europe in many cases is found to be an outright takeover. If both Britain and France are to stand up to the American invasion we must improve our education. It is vital for Europe." [42]

Table 4 shows the pattern in secondary-school enrollments in the sciences and the humanities for five European countries from 1951–52 to 1965–66. There are obvious national differences (e.g., Austria), but over all a great increase in science enrollments is the trend. In Sweden and the United Kingdom, which are not shown in this table, the humanistic programs of history, literature, and languages have in the past enrolled a larger percentage of upper-secondary-school pupils than have the science curriculums; but this is unlikely to remain the case. Table 5 contrasts growth indexes over fifteen years for enrollment in vocational and technical schooling in nine countries. The most remarkable gains have been registered in Belgium, Sweden, Turkey, and Yugoslavia. Surprisingly, there appears to be a drop in enrollment indexes in Germany for technical education between the academic years 1960–61 and 1965–66. It is clear that there has been progress at the secondary level, especially in certain countries; it seems likely that there will be an acceleration in scientific and technological studies in the years to come.

There are no figures available to compare enrollments in scientific-technical and humanistic studies in higher education. European universities unquestionably have been slow in responding to the demands of society and of students themselves for needed reforms in curriculum — as evidenced most dramatically by the 1968 strike of French students, but also

Table 4. Enrollments from 1951–52 to 1965–66[a] in Humanities
and Science Programs in Academic General Secondary
Education in Five European Nations, with Growth
Indexes Based on 100 for 1955–56

Country and Program	1951–52	1955–56	1960–61	1965–66
Austria[b]				
Humanities	77	100	99	110
Sciences	77	100	103	59
Belgium[c]				
Humanities	87	100	112	145
Sciences	85	100	180	287
Italy[d]				
Humanities	84	100	103	128
Sciences	85	100	134	224
Switzerland[e]				
Humanities	70	100	111	148
Sciences	90	100	141	211
Turkey[f]				
Humanities	...	100	426	524
Sciences	...	100	581	676

SOURCE: Adapted from *Development of Secondary Education*,
Table 17, p. 48.

[a] For certain countries enrollments for the years selected were
not obtainable; therefore the nearest year available was used:
for Belgium 1952–53 rather than 1951–52; for Switzerland
1956–57 rather than 1955–56; for Belgium 1964–65 and for
Switzerland and Turkey 1961–62 rather than 1965–66. For
Turkey data for 1955–56 are incomplete.

[b] Humanities include Gymnasium, all grades; sciences include
Realgymnasium and Realschule (science-oriented gymnasium
and modern-language general secondary). Not included in the
table are Frauenoberschule (girls' general secondary school, now
called Wirtschaftskundliches Realgymnasium), Musisch-pädago-
gisches Realgymnasium (new type, of five years' duration), and
all "Sonderformen" (special types of gymnasium).

[c] Humanities include sections "Latin-Grec" of the "formation
générale" of the upper cycle of secondary school; sciences include sections "Latin-Mathématiques," "Latin-Sciences," "Scientifique," "Scientifique B," and "Classes de Soir Spéciales" of the
"formation générale" of the upper cycle of secondary school.

[d] Humanities include Liceo classico e ginnasio; sciences include Liceo scientifico.

[e] Humanities include sections "Classiques" in upper general
secondary schools; sciences include sections "Science" in upper
general secondary schools.

[f] Humanities include sections "Littérature" in lycée; sciences
include sections "Science" in lycée.

Table 5. Growth Indexes in General (Nontechnical) and Technical[a] Vocational
Secondary Education in Nine European Countries from 1950–51 to
1965–66,[b] with a Base Index of 100 for 1955

Country and Program	1950–51	1955–56	1960–61	1965–66
Austria				
General	78	100	105	117
Technical	58	100	94	100
Belgium				
General	91	100	158	181
Technical	93	100	157	214
Germany (F.R.)				
General	...	100	101	111
Technical	74	100	82	81
Netherlands				
General	74	100	152	163
Technical	82	100	135	144
Spain				
General	66	100	147	245
Technical	102	100	125	168
Sweden				
General	85	100	128	111
Technical	74	100	255	368
United Kingdom				
General	...	100	131	134
Technical	...	100	117	101
Turkey				
General	54	100	220	329
Technical	73	100	132	224
Yugoslavia[c]				
General	72	100	90	209
Technical	94	100	162	262

SOURCE: Adapted from *Development of Secondary Education*, Table 14, p. 41.

[a] The general includes commercial, domestic, etc.; the technical includes engineering, medical, etc.

[b] For certain countries data for the years selected were not obtainable; therefore the nearest year available was used: for Austria 1951–52 and for Belgium, Sweden, and Yugoslavia 1952–53 instead of 1950–51; for Germany 1959 instead of 1960–61; for Belgium, Spain, Sweden, and the United Kingdom 1964–65, and for the Netherlands 1964 instead of 1965–66; for Yugoslavia the figures for 1965–66 are provisional.

[c] Programs in upper primary school are not included.

in student riots in West Berlin, Italy, and elsewhere. Students increasingly have come to feel that the institutions of higher education in Europe are not addressing themselves to the great social problems of the day and are not preparing their students for the new careers developing in the wake of scientific and technological progress.[43]

Change must come. No longer can education "of the best in the best" mean that all those most able academically will study the humanities — more and more will turn their talents to science and technology.[44] European educators in accepting the challenge this offers — as well as the challenge of burgeoning enrollments generally — may well find their common labors binding them closer in a European educational community.

Conclusion

While even sophisticated and internationally minded Europeans will still describe systems of education in terms of their own or some other country, there are unmistakable signs of harmonization in European education. This harmonization has been in part a natural — that is, unplanned — outgrowth of common interests and efforts: the educators of all European nations have had many of the same goals, have faced many of the same problems, have reached in many instances similar solutions. In part the harmonization has been deliberately fostered by organizations like the EEC, the OECD, the Council of Europe, and numerous smaller groups, who have sponsored conferences, held seminars, published journals and books, constantly urged cooperation — and most notably, perhaps, encouraged the preparation and marketing of European-oriented textbooks.

One striking illustration of the move toward Europeanism in education may be cited, the case of Britain, long regarded by many as the least European of Europe's nations. In 1966 *University Research and Studies on European Integration* reported:

A remarkable phenomenon this year has been the tremendous growth of interest in European affairs in the various British universities. The number of European courses has leaped from eleven to thirty-two. They are particularly numerous and varied at the London School of Economics and the University of Sussex, where a post-graduate centre for European research has also been established. Five other universities (Exeter, Lancaster, Leicester, Manchester, and East Anglia) have instituted European study programmes, three of which constitute full degree courses in European studies and civilization: at Leicester and Reading the courses lead to Master's degrees and at Exeter to a Bachelor's degree. . . . Research into European problems is also steadily expanding, notably at the Center for Advanced European Studies of the Royal Institute of International Affairs and at the British Institute of International and Comparative Law. University teachers indicated their active interest in the study of European integration by holding two meetings in London (November 1965 and May 1966), when they discussed the organization of European teaching in British universities: the main question was at what stage in the university course European studies should be introduced.[45]

If communication, formal and informal, among European educators and students continues to broaden and deepen, the political, religious, linguistic, and other barriers that still divide Europe should become less formidable. The contribution education can make to progress toward the integration of Europe can hardly be overestimated.

CHAPTER 7

The Integration of People

BY ARNOLD M. ROSE

THE movement during the post-World War II era toward a more politically integrated Europe has been largely created by highly placed policy makers. Some were idealists, who believed that economic development and political stability could only be achieved in larger than national units. Others were opportunists, seeking more power for their relatively important nations or responding to American pressures to develop greater European strength. Probably both the idealists and the opportunists were reacting to the threat of Russian expansionism and sought safety by joining forces. These and other factors at first worked on a high level of leadership and made little impact on the broad masses of the Western European population. The economic benefits of reduced trade barriers and of the lesser efforts at economic collaboration were soon felt by the European "man in the street," and he generally came to approve of such international arrangements as the European Economic Community and the European Free Trade Association.[1] But in no sense could the development toward various international organizations in Europe be considered a mass movement with broad popular support.

Public opinion is developing on various aspects of European integration as a result of direct experience with them and publicity concerning them. The average European, as noted, has had direct experience with the economic aspects of integration agreements and has come to approve many of them. These economic aspects of integration involve an increasing transfer of goods and services across international borders. But the political and sociological aspects of integration — thus far less developed than the economic aspects — involve some kind of transferability of people themselves across international borders; indeed, full political and sociological integration entails one national group's regarding itself as interchangeable with another national group for such purposes as elections, granting powers over themselves, social participation in friendship, and so on. People need direct, personal contacts with others if they are to accept them as their "own kind," suitable for living with in a common political and social community. It is not that all such direct contacts lead to acceptance — other conditions must exist for this to happen; but direct contacts are a necessary requirement.

Some of this transfer or interchanging of peoples is now going on in Europe, and experience with it today can provide some clues to the probable reaction its more extensive and expanded forms will evoke tomorrow. The author suggests that the integration of people is just as important for the creation of "Europe" as the agreements of statesmen, that the agreements of statesmen will be able to go only so far without the further integration of people (although it must also be recognized that certain agreements of statesmen can facilitate the integration of people), and that the achievements to date in the creation of "Europe" will be reversed and nullified if there should be a large-scale rejection of the integration of people. The agreements among European nations so far have been more or less opportune for all the signatory powers; they have not yet had to face the test of making sacrifices for the benefit of their "brother" Europeans. Only the integration of a "European people" will get them over that hump. Without that basic integration, the promising international agreements of today will be as weak in the face of crisis as was the socialist ideology in 1914 in the face of war. All the talk about "class solidarity across national lines" did nothing to inhibit World War I, nor did the cross-national cousinly relationships among the aristocratic elite. In the face of challenge, the people of Europe did not think of themselves as the "people of Europe"; they thought of themselves as Frenchmen, Germans, Britons, and so on. Yet history shows that new nations *can* be born: the United States was born [2] out of these same Britons, Germans, Frenchmen; Germany was born out of Prussians, Bavarians, Hessians, etc.; and Italy was born out of Piedmontese, Tuscans, Calabrians, etc. [3] The question before us in whether Europe, in this sense, is being born today.

What is meant here by "the integration of people"? It means their acceptance of each other as members of a common nation, their having a sense of belonging to the same "community." It does not mean complete abandonment of self-identification as Greek or Swede or Frenchman, but it does mean a general tendency — for many purposes — to place self-identification as European *above* being Greek or Swedish or French. It does not mean the elimination of the old national cultures and institutions, but it does mean allowing a new cross-national culture and set of institutions to be built parallel to the old. Americans are not less loyal to their family or church or ethnic background for being loyal to the United States, and some are also loyal to their separate states. Germany, France,

Belgium, Norway, Spain, and the other nations will have to take on the psychological character of states in the American sense, or of ethnic groups, before there can be an integrated Europe. It is not necessary to go so far as to say that there must be the creation of a "United States of Europe," a new state, before there can be integration, but there must be a much stronger sense of mutual acceptance and of common Europeanness than Europe has ever had before, and probably some sort of political confederation.

Various other terms have been used which bear a close relationship to "integration." Eisenstadt[4] speaks of the "absorption" of Jewish immigrants of various national and cultural backgrounds into Israel; Zubrzycki[5] speaks of the "accommodation" of Polish refuges into Britain after World War II; and American sociologists for several generations have spoken of the "assimilation" of at least the white-skinned immigrants into the United States. This chapter will not get into a discussion of whether the "melting pot," "cultural pluralism," or "conformity to the dominant national culture" is the best relationship for nationality groups occupying the same territory to have toward each other, or even whether migration across national lines should be temporary or permanent. If there is to be an integration of people in Europe, economic factors will largely decide how temporary or how permanent a migration is to be, and sociological and psychological factors operating through individuals and families will decide whether there is to be "melting pot" or "cultural pluralism" or adherence to one dominant culture. Policies of government or private organizations can affect the outcome by modifying the influence of economic, sociological, or psychological forces. It is not intended here to suggest either the value premises for giving direction to such policies or the techniques by which one or the other set of goals can most effectively be reached.

Not only have European countries been politically and economically divided, but there are considerable differences of culture and "national character" among them. The medieval synthesis, provided by the Catholic Church and the Holy Roman Empire in much of Europe, has long since disappeared, and national differences have provided the outstanding facts about Europe during the past several centuries. Along with efforts at political and economic integration after World War II, efforts have been started toward social integration — cultural and educational exchanges, international meetings for all sorts of purposes, modification of school curriculums to orient children toward Europe and the world as well as toward their individual nations,[6] the encouragement of tourism, businessmen's collaboration on common enterprises,[7] special efforts to aid in the adjustment and assimilation of cross-national migrants, etc. Some of these were not entirely novel, and had antecedents going well back before World War I, but the considerable extent to which they were planned and effectuated was a distinctive characteristic of the post-World War II era. If Europe is to have internal peace, if it is to act even in small ways as a unified whole, it must integrate its culture and people to some extent — at least so it is felt by those who think in terms of "Europe." It is the purpose of this chapter to examine the most extensive of these efforts — the encouragement of migration of peoples across national lines — and to test certain hypotheses concerning its success or lack of success. That is, the chapter is limited to a consideration of the contribution which cross-national migration is or is not making to the integration of Europe.

Recent Cross-National Migration

In the discussion to follow, "migration" refers to situations in which individuals move across international boundaries and take employment, sometimes permanently but at least for a "season" (usually nine months). Thus excluded are tourism, study abroad, international meetings, diplomatic missions, daily frontier-crossing for work, and other situations in which there is usually no motive for the person who crosses the border to think of himself as a part of the country to which he travels. Most migrants in the sense used here expect to return to their home countries, but practically all of them also intellectually entertain the possibility that they will remain permanently in the country to which they move.

Cross-national migrations are not new in Europe, although their directions are somewhat so.[8] In the years before World War I not only was there the tremendous emigration from southern Europe overseas to the Americas, but numerous north Italians moved across the frontier to Switzerland and France; neighboring Spaniards, Belgians, and Swiss and more distant Poles also migrated to France; Austrians, Poles,[9] Serbians, Belgians, and Dutch went to Germany; Germans, Dutch, Italians, and Poles moved to Belgium. The early migration to France and Germany was mainly into agriculture; that to Belgium was mainly into mining. While many of the worker immigrants were seasonal rather than permanent, their numbers were substantial. In 1910 foreigners constituted some 15 percent of Switzerland's population, only slightly less than the 17 percent attained in 1964, and in 1907 the proportion of foreign workers in Germany's labor force was higher than that in 1965. The proportion of foreigners in France did not reach a peak until 1931, but then it was significantly higher than today. France was the leading country of immigration during the interwar years of 1919–31, with most of its economic immigrants coming from Poland and Italy, and refugees coming from White Russia and Armenia (in Turkey). With the partial exception of France, Europe in this period was much less permissive about cross-national migration than it had been before World War I. Part of this was due to poor

economic conditions, but part was due to growing nationalism and xenophobia.[10] The post-World War II years saw a resumption of the liberal
policy, and there was an increase of immigration — mainly of refugees at
first. For France this included a liberalization of the law on naturalization,
which caused the number of Frenchmen of foreign birth to rise sharply.
By 1962, there were 1,266,680 naturalized persons and 1,815,740 foreigners — respectively 2.72 percent and 3.90 percent of the French population.[11]

    The first decade after the end of World War II saw the relocation of
many refugees in Europe.[12] French, Belgian, Dutch, and other Allied nationals who had been forced into the German "work camps" during the
war now returned home, while Germans who lived in Prussia, the Sudetenland, and other eastern territories were now expelled into a narrower
Germany. There was little in the way of strictly economic migration within Europe, since most of the Continent was still recovering economically
from the war, although economic motives for migration were undoubtedly
mixed with political and ideological ones. The chief direction of economic
migration, and much of the refugee relocation also, was overseas. During
the decade 1945–55, "The chief countries of emigration have been Germany, Austria, Italy, Greece and the Netherlands; the chief countries of
reception, the United States, Australia, Canada, Argentina, and Brazil." [13]
Table 1 shows that Europe was not the major destination of most of the
European displaced persons or other migrants in the decade following
World War II. Some eight million Europeans moved across international
lines between 1946 and 1954, but only three of the ten countries leading
in their reception were European and these were at or near the bottom of
the list. The leading European country of immigration in that period was
the United Kingdom, which recovered economically from the war more
rapidly at first than the other war-involved nations of Europe.

Table 1. Leading Countries of Immigration, 1946 to 1954

Country	Number of Immigrants
United States	1,700,000
Canada	1,100,000
Australia	900,000
Israel	790,000
Argentina	760,000
Venezuela	500,000
United Kingdom	440,000
Brazil	410,000
France	390,000
Belgium	290,000

SOURCE: W. D. Borrie, *The Cultural Integration of Immigrants* (Paris: UNESCO, 1959), p. 17.

The chief sources of cross-national migration in Europe after 1955 were from within Europe itself, as shown by Table 2. West Germany drew from all labor-exporting countries of southern Europe, with the number from Greece, Spain, Turkey, and Yugoslavia growing each year. France, as noted, kept up a stream from Italy, but its immigration from Spain and Portugal [14] became even larger. France also had a major repatriation of its colonials, especially from Algeria, in the years 1962–63.[15] Switzerland kept its primary reliance for immigrant workers on Italy — although now they were from southern rather than northern Italy — but increasing numbers came from Spain. In 1963, Switzerland adopted a policy of forcing its employers to cut down on their number of foreign workers, and in the succeeding years it became an exporter, rather than an importer, of foreign (non-Swiss) labor. Immediately after World War II, Sweden was the beneficiary of immigrants — both skilled and unskilled — from the Baltic countries (now absorbed politically into the Soviet Union). Its continuing labor shortage led to an agreement among the Scandinavian nations for free movement of labor, and Sweden came to rely most heavily on Finland for unskilled labor, although significant numbers of workers came also from Italy, Greece, Yugoslavia, and Turkey. The Benelux countries drew on labor from all of southern Europe, as well as a small stream from Asia and Africa. The United Kingdom kept its traditional reliance on Ireland for unskilled labor but otherwise obtained very few workers from Europe; the United Kingdom also for a while relied heavily for labor on the colored Commonwealth countries of India, Pakistan, and the West Indies. For over a century after 1841, Ireland's emigration was larger than its natural increase so that the country reduced its total population from 6,529,000 in 1841 to 2,818,300 in 1961; even after 1961 emigration absorbed most of Ireland's natural increase.[16] Table 3 highlights emigration and immigration trends in the nations of Europe.

Although the official statistics (including those in Table 3) are inadequate and somewhat inaccurate, they permit us to draw the following conclusions: (1) While before World War II, France and Switzerland were the main immigrant countries of Europe, the Federal Republic of Germany had by 1960 surpassed them in the number of immigrants; these countries, then, are the ones to which the largest *number* of migrants go. The United Kingdom had a period of heavy immigration between 1960 and 1962. (2) In terms of *percentages* of foreigners in the active working force, Switzerland (with 32.3 percent) and Luxembourg (with 21.7 percent) are by far the highest ranking countries. Intermediate positions are held by Belgium, France, the United Kingdom, West Germany, and Sweden — in that order. Western European countries with low percentages of foreigners in their active working force are the Netherlands (with 1.6 percent), Austria (with 1.2 percent, mostly seasonal workers), Norway

Table 2. Origin of Foreign Labor Force in Immigrant Countries (in Thousands)

Country of Emigration	Belgium in 1964	France in 1962	Germany (F.R.) in 1965	Luxembourg in 1964	Netherlands in 1965	Sweden in 1966	Switzerland in 1965	United Kingdom 1960	United Kingdom 1966
Greece	6.0	4.4	181.7	...[b]	2.2	5.5	7.3	3.4	3.4
Italy	64.9	305.0	335.8	15.0	7.8	5.8	454.7	68.1	24.6
Portugal	0.7	30.1	10.5	0.5	0.9	0.4	...[b]	2.3	3.9
Spain	12.9	312.0	180.6	2.5	16.0	3.2	77.3	17.1	26.6
Turkey	5.3	7.5	121.1	...[b]	5.8	1.3	4.8	0.8	1.3
Yugoslavia	1.2	10.1	64.1	...[b]	1.1	11.9	5.3	8.9	1.4
EEC countries (except Italy)	45.2	68.4	116.9	13.5	29.0	18.7[c]	150.3[d]	...[e]	...[e]
Special countries	25.0[f]	219.3[g]	59.6[h]	...	5.2[i]	105.6[j]	39.8[h]	...[k]	...[k]
Stateless or uncertain	1.2	10.9	12.4	1.0	2.9	5.4[l]	12.3[m]	4.4	...[b]
Other European countries	5.4	117.6	34.0	0.5	4.4	17.0	58.4	239.5	57.4
Non-European countries (except special countries)	5.3	73.4	47.8	0.5	4.4	0.5	...[b]	66.6	45.9
Total[n]	172.9	1,065.2	1,164.4	33.5	79.6	175.4	810.2	405.9	164.5

SOURCE: For Belgium and France, estimated by OECD from census figures. For Germany and the Netherlands, semiannual tally of work permits. For Luxembourg, estimated on the basis of work permits issued and placements registered, but does not include frontier or detached workers. For Sweden, aliens registered as being gainfully employed. For Switzerland and the United Kingdom, census figures; for Switzerland figures do not include workers not under federal control. Since a variety of definitions, categories, and dates are used in calculating the labor force in various countries, the figures in the table are not strictly comparable.

[a] Figures reported are only for those registered with the police; since 1961 aliens have not been required to register after four years' residence in the United Kingdom. For this reason, the figures as of December 31, 1960, are also offered.
[b] Very small number; included in appropriate other category.
[c] Germans and Dutch only.   [d] Germans and French only.
[e] Included in other European countries; 1960 figures include Polish and Hungarian refugees.
[f] Mostly from Belgium's former colonies.
[g] Estimate of 200,000 Algerians and 19,300 Moroccans.
[h] From Austria.
[i] Mostly from the Netherlands' former colonies.
[j] Including 72,811 Finns, 19,379 Danes, 13,377 Norwegians.
[k] Estimate of 500,000–600,000 immigrants from other parts of the Commonwealth plus 350,000 from the Irish Free State in 1963, but these are considered citizens, not foreigners, and so are not included in the figures.
[l] Including 1937 Balts and 3466 Hungarians.   [m] Hungarians only.
[n] Because of rounding, columns do not add precisely to totals.

198

Table 3. Trends of Immigration (+) and Emigration (−) in European Countries, 1950 to 1965 (Net Migration in Thousands, with Statistical Adjustments)

Country	Annual Average		1960	1961	1962	1963	1964	1965
	1950–54	1955–59						
Countries of Immigration								
Belgium	+3.2	+10.6	+7.0	−1.0 a	+19.0	+34.0	+49.0	+31.0
France	+27.8	+156.0	+140.0	+180.0	+860.0	+250.0	+195.0	+141.0
Germany (F.R.)	+221.4	+297.2	+336.0	+419.0	+283.0	+224.0	+302.0	+344.0
Luxembourg	+0.9	+0.6	+0.6	+2.4	+2.8	+1.6	+3.1	+3.0
Netherlands	−20.6	−3.2	−13.0	+6.0	+17.0	−8.0	+14.0	+19.0
Sweden	+9.2	+9.8	+11.0	+14.0	+11.0	+12.0	+23.0	+33.0
Switzerland	+22.8	+32.0	+76.0	+101.0	+88.0	+57.0	+48.0	−1.0
United Kingdom b	−33.6	−3.2	+39.0	+198.0	+97.0	+43.0	+7.0	+10.0
Countries of Emigration								
Greece	−13.8	−25.0	−26.0	−19.0	−49.0	−56.0	−44.0	−43.0
Ireland	−34.8	−44.4	−41.0	−30.0	−16.0	−17.0	−24.0	−24.0
Italy	−100.8	−127.4	−192.0	−177.0	−137.0	−56.0	−81.0	−85.0
Portugal	−64.2	−68.0	−68.0	−32.0	−55.0	−47.0	−55.0	−53.0
Spain	−51.8	−104.0	−138.0	−133.0	−119.0	−126.0	−158.0	−135.0
Turkey c	…	…	…	−1.5	−11.2	−30.3	−66.2	−52.1
Yugoslavia	…	…	…		−34.0	−34.0	−56.0	−80.0

SOURCE: For all countries except Turkey and Yugoslavia, 1950–59 figures from ILO Automation Programme, *International Differences Affecting Labour Mobility* (Geneva: ILO, 1965), pp.12–14, and from OECD, *Manpower Statistics 1950–62* (Paris, 1963); 1960–64 figures from OECD, *Manpower Statistics 1954–1964* (Paris, 1965), corrected by unpublished OECD statistics; 1965 figures from unpublished OECD statistics. For Turkey, Turkish Employment Service. For Yugoslavia, 1965 figure from *Migration Today*, No. 5 (December 1965), p. 62; earlier figures from *Ekonomska Politika*, October 15, 1966, p. 1320.

a Not including correction from census.

b Figures for the United Kingdom do not include migrants from Ireland and, before 1962, do not include migrants from Commonwealth countries. Thus the data indicate a net emigration for Britain during the 1950's when in fact it was experiencing very heavy immigration from India, Pakistan, and the West Indies.

c Net immigration figures for Turkey are not available; reported here are the 161,300 persons aided by the Turkish Employment Service from 1961 through 1965. However, few Turkish emigrants had returned permanently by 1965, and for these five years only some 20,000 Turks emigrated without using the facilities of the Turkish Employment Service. Hence, the Turkish figures are roughly comparable to the OECD figures given for the other countries.

(with 1.0 percent), and Denmark (with 0.5 percent). Among the latter, only the Netherlands since 1960 has been receiving a steady, if small, flow of immigrants, and it will be considered a "country of immigration" for the purposes of this study, even though a significant small proportion of its own nationals emigrate overseas. (3) Spain has now surpassed Italy as the leading European "country of emigration" in terms of absolute *numbers*. (4) In terms of *proportions* of their total population emigrating, Ireland, Portugal, Greece, and Spain are leading in that order, with Yugoslavia and Turkey coming up. Italy has greatly reduced its net emigration, and Spain has begun a relative decline.

The Study of Adjustment to Migration

There has been a vast amount of literature, published and unpublished, on the subject of adjustment to cross-national migration, and a significant amount of this has been summarized in a separate volume by the author of this chapter.[17] That volume's original contribution to the study of cross-national migration rests on the use of a combination of approaches, not all of which have been utilized together even in the many superb monographic studies previously published. (1) This study is comprehensive and systematic, although it does not go into depth on all the many facets of the complicated problem. (2) This study is comparative, not for the purpose of making invidious distinctions among nations, but because comparison is the only satisfactory technique for making data on cross-national relations meaningful and measurable. It has not been possible to get every item of relevant information for every country studied, so there are a significant number of gaps, but nearly every fact is presented in a comparative context. (3) This study is couched in a framework of theory; that is, it is not purely descriptive, although description takes up the majority of its pages. (4) This study uses a great variety of data, including published and unpublished statistics, public opinion polls, direct and indirect case observations, historical and contemporary description from library materials, legal documents, interviews with specialists, and even some documents produced by the migrants themselves.

The economic factors of differential wages and differential opportunities for job mobility, twelve policies or programs which countries of immigration have adopted or practiced toward the migrants, public opinion toward immigration and immigrants, and six other non-policy factors facilitating the integration of foreign workers — all have been described and measured in the author's full-length work, insofar as data are available for measuring them, for each of the eight countries of immigration. Similarly, eight conditions prevailing in each of the seven European countries of emigration that facilitate or retard the adjustment to migration are described and measured there. And finally, five indexes of acceptance and adjustment are presented to give some idea of what is happening to the migrants themselves. Perhaps needless to say, systematic data on these subjects are incomplete and not always comparable among countries, but the author sought to make the best use of what was available to him.

In this chapter an attempt is made to give the high points of the longer analysis.

International Agreements for the Benefit of Cross-National Migrants

Several deliberate institutional arrangements, agreed to by various combinations of nations, to protect and otherwise benefit cross-national migrants will be the subject of this section. While not nearly as far-reaching in their implications as the NATO agreement on defense or the EEC agreement on trade, they are on the same order, relating to the institutional integration of Europe rather than to the integration of people which forms the central interest of this chapter. For lack of space, only the main facts will be presented here.

Two groups of nations, by multilateral treaties, have established completely free internal labor mobility, with no more required of the migrant than an identity card issued by his country of citizenship. These are the four Scandinavian countries plus Finland (in an agreement signed in 1954, called the Nordic Labor Zone Agreement, later called the Scandinavian Common Market for Labor) and the three Benelux countries (in an agreement signed in 1956). The United Kingdom once had a similar arrangement with Commonwealth nations throughout the world, but its unilateral statute of 1962 restricting immigration from all but a few remaining colonies ended that. However, the statute seems to be applied systematically only to the colored nations; migrants from the Irish Republic (and presumably from Australia, Canada, and New Zealand if they have ever wished to migrate) continue to enter freely into the United Kingdom, despite the law. In 1965, this law was strengthened so that now only a few hundred per year from the Commonwealth colored nations can migrate to the United Kingdom for work and permanent residence.

The EEC has had a three-stage plan for free labor mobility. Articles 48 and 49 of the 1957 Treaty of Rome specified that full freedom of labor mobility was to be achieved by the end of 1969.[18] The treaty looked forward to "the abolition of any discrimination based on nationality between workers of the Member States as regards employment, remuneration, and other working conditions," and stated that the individual rights which it includes shall be subject to limitations only where justified by reasons of public order, public safety, and public health. The first stage was inaugurated by EEC Council Regulation 15 issued August 16, 1961, which included five main provisions: labor permits are to be given automatically to member state nationals in the case of occupations in which there is a labor shortage; the domestic labor administration can restrict job opportunities to its own nationals for only three weeks, after which it must make the openings available to other member state nationals regardless of preexisting restrictive members or quotas; foreign workers for whom an employer has called by name will in certain cases be granted a permit without reference to the domestic labor market; member state nationals are to be given preference in filling jobs over other foreign workers; member state nationals are granted the right to renew their labor permits for the same occupation after one year of regular employment, for any other occupation for which they are qualified after three years, and for any kind of paid work after four years of regular employment.

The second stage, inaugurated by Regulation 38 issued March 25, 1964, restricted the priorities accorded to the domestic labor market to certain labor-surplus occupations and regions only, extended the rights and privileges of member state migrant workers, gave them the right to vote in factory elections after three years of employment by the same firm, gave them the right to bring in dependent forebears and descendants — in addition to spouse and children under age — if the worker could offer them satisfactory accommodation, and facilitated clearing offers of and applications for employment within the community. There remained a "safeguard clause" which enabled member states to reintroduce priority for national workers in certain occupations and areas where there is local unemployment. By November 1966, all the member states had renounced this opportunity except France.[19]

The third stage, scheduled for inauguration in 1968, is to be devoted to the abolition of the last obstacles standing in the way of free movement, so that workers of all member states will be assured of access to paid employment in each member state on the terms that apply to nationals of that state. They will have equal right of worker representation in the firm's organizations, will be able to bring in their families without proving that they have adequate housing, will be granted equal tax arrangements and social benefits. However, if unemployment occurs, member states are to discourage migration. On April 7, 1967, the EEC Commission proposed the institution of a community-wide identity card for all workers to replace the existing work permits given to foreign workers. This card — if adopted by the member states represented in the EEC Council — would eliminate all documentary distinctions among workers, nationals or foreign, if they are citizens of any of the Six.[20] Italians have been the main workers affected by all these provisions because, among the Six, they have been the most frequent migrants and because they are least likely — due to the geographic position of Italy — to be frontier workers with privileges obtained through earlier binational agreements. In the first six years, 1961 through 1966, during which EEC regulations on freedom of movement within the Six were operative, an average of 270,600 first work permits a year were issued to workers of the member states moving from one community country to another.[21] Of these, 80 percent were Italians. If the community-wide identity card should be adopted, all nationals of the Six would be benefited, and a portion of Europe would move a significant distance toward international integration.

The Organization for Economic Cooperation and Development — when it was still the Organization for European Economic Cooperation — on October 30, 1955, and December 20, 1955, made recommendations to its member states (twenty-one in number after 1960) to liberalize the international movement of workers. The OECD does not have the power to require the adoption of its recommendations, and its member states have adopted the recommendations only in part and gradually over a period of years. The OECD Council does, however, have the instrumentality of an annual report prepared by its staff to note the progress of each member state in accord with its recommendations, which are from time to time expanded on authorization of its Manpower Liberalization Group. The most important recommendation of the OECD, which is adhered to by most European countries, is that work permits must be issued as soon as it is established that no suitable workers are available on the home market, and that this determination should take place within a month. The OECD also has a labor exchange information system through which each country provides to all other member countries information about its labor market and working conditions, and this information can then be made available to workers.

The OECD recommendations have perhaps been useful in indicating possibilities to member states, but they are too general to cover all the special circumstances involved in the migration from one specific country to another. For that reason, various pairs of immigrant and emigrant countries among the OECD member states have agreed to bilateral treaties. Each of these treaties has somewhat different stipulations but touches on the same general points as all the others. They all provide a mechanism for getting migrants directly into a job in the country of immigration, for wages equal to those of national workers, for some vocational and language training, for transfer of earnings back to the home country, and for specification of the migrant's rights (e.g., to change jobs, to gain social security benefits, to get vacations).

National statutes restricting freedom of cross-national migration will not be dealt with here. Suffice it to say that Switzerland and the United Kingdom among the countries of immigration and Portugal and Spain among the countries of emigration had, in 1967, especially strong restrictions. Nor will the complex social security legislation governing foreign nationals be considered in this chapter.

The agreements among the Scandinavian countries and among the Benelux countries providing for the free flow of workers within these regions gave the workers from the other signatory countries all the rights and privileges of an economic and social nature which nationals of the countries of immigration have. These immigrants might just as well be in their native countries as far as their economic and social rights are concerned, except of course they do not have the right to vote in political elections (they can vote in firm or union elections) or hold political office. Language similarities often prevailing within each regional group make meaningful the provision for "equal access" to work information and training offered in the language of the immigrant country — which is seldom true for foreigners from outside the region who have different native languages.

The Common Market is working in the same direction as the regional pacts, and in these matters of social policy the Common Market has made consistent progress. This is because the Treaty of Rome gave a number of specific authorizations to the EEC Commission, and probably because the treaty requirements fit into trends within the nations making up the Common Market. Even during the years 1963–66, when it looked as if political and economic developments in the Common Market might be checked or reversed and when occasionally there was some pessimism about the future of the Common Market, steady progress was being made in extending and equalizing the social policies of the member states in regard to workers from other member states. Of course, it should be recalled that there was only one major country of emigration — Italy — in the Common Market, and Italy's rate of emigration was declining. Other cross-national migrants within the Six were largely frontier or seasonal workers who created few difficulties for the countries to which they migrated. Still, the application of the social security programs of member states for the benefit of workers from other member states covered about two million people and involved expenditures of about $80 million in 1964.[22] By July 1966, the EEC Commission had sent two recommendations to member states: one on social services for community nationals working in another community country and the other on housing for these workers and their families (although there is little evidence that the member states have acted on these recommendations). By the end of December 1965, the European Social Fund — set up by the Treaty of Rome, and one of the few examples of independent administrative activities of the EEC on a supranational basis — had allocated $31.7 million for the retraining and resettlement of 454,000 workers (275,000 of whom were Italians).[23] Plans are being formulated by the Commission for more independent and developmental use of the Social Fund, for a European-wide industrial health and safety system (including protection of young people and working women), and for harmonization of certain social security provisions but no action has yet been taken on these.

The EEC has made considerable progress in encouraging the improvement of working and living conditions, usually where the Treaty of Rome specified that certain things were to happen: The treaty set the end of 1964 as the date at which there should be equal pay for men and women, although some loopholes remain; the aforementioned steps toward free movement of workers and the training of workers have taken place; social security for migrant workers has been established under existing national laws. The EEC Commission lacks both legal powers and funds to go much further, however, and future developments will depend on authorization and funds that may be granted by member states acting through the Council.[24] Thus far, the member states have agreed to almost nothing beyond what was specified in the Treaty of Rome, even in regard to such matters as standardizing statistics collection and terminology. In sum, considerable progress in the social field — particularly in matters affecting migrating workers — has been achieved, mainly because of far-reaching commitments of the member states when they signed the Treaty of Rome, but this progress cannot be continued beyond 1969 unless the member states make further commitments. The major exception may be the Social Fund, since there is some flexibility in its use and it can set rules for granting aid, if one or more of the member states do not actively oppose extended uses for it. The exchanges of information, through conferences and Commission studies, are also likely to have a continuing influence on member states, even though no powers are inherent in them.[25] The best example of achievement through exchange of information has been some movement toward an alignment of national social security programs. Some alignment may also have come about as a result of the opening up of the economies of the Six to each other — a kind of "rub off" effect. It is hard to know whether the trend toward equalization of wages, hours of work, paid holidays, and other conditions of work actually has been influenced by a Common Market program (other than those developments which benefit the economies generally); equalization here might simply be due to the overcoming of economic backwardness in the relatively backward countries of the EEC.

There are many matters on which coordination among the Six in regard to migrant labor could yet take place, although to accomplish some of these would require more political authority than now exists in the community.[26] There is almost no coordination among the Six of manpower recruiting policies in non-EEC countries, and each country of immigration is in competition with every other one. Vocational guidance and training to meet the special needs of migrants is yet in its infancy except for notable spot achievements by the Germans and a retraining program in Italy under the European Social Fund. Since 1963, migrants from one EEC country to another can use the educational facilities of the country of immigration on the same terms as its own nationals. Reduction of differentials in social security, social assistance, and other welfare programs has a way to go. There is scope for much more imagination in the use of the Social Fund. Whether these things will or will not develop depends on the general political direction of the EEC, a matter which is considered elsewhere in this book.

The European Coal and Steel Community also created a Social Fund when it was established by the same six nations in 1952.[27] Its objective was to provide aids for workers whose employment was reduced or suspended as a result of the elimination of all barriers to the free flow of trade in coal or steel. Specifically, it offered assistance for occupational retraining, allowances for resettlement in the same country or any of the five other countries, and compensatory payments for workers whose employment was temporarily or wholly terminated as a result of closure or conversion of their enterprise to other production. Over 10 percent of the coal mines received some form of assistance from the inauguration of the program in 1954 up through 1964. But few used the aid for financing relocation — partly because the coal miners were reluctant to leave their home region and partly because the economic boom in their home countries allowed them to find other employment nearby. Two-thirds of the miners benefited were in West Germany (the nation with the most rapid economic expansion during 1954-64) and only 3.5 percent were in Italy (the only nation of emigration among the Six). The reason for this, of course, is that Germany has many more mines than Italy, but the differential benefit to these two countries shows that not all the Social Fund activities are equalizing.

The extensive cross-national migration of labor in Post-World War II Europe necessitated international agreements regarding social security.[28] A convention held among the Scandinavian countries in 1955 resulted in a unified program. One of the first actions of the Common Market — taken in 1958 and put into force from January 1, 1959 — was to coordinate national systems among the Six, replacing the eighty bilateral agreements (and several multilateral agreements) they had worked out between 1946 and 1958. Beginning in 1965, the Council of Europe, with the help of the International Labor Organization and the EEC, began to work on a European Social Security Convention, but by 1967 it was far from adoption.

The EEC agreement was based on three principles: (1) Equality of entitlement to social security — including family allowances, health care, old-age and unemployment benefits, and compensation in case of employment injury or occupational disease — for all nationals of the Six under the laws prevailing in the country of residence, except that family members domiciled in countries other than that of the insured worker receive medical and family allowance benefits at the level prevailing in their country of domicile (usually their country of birth). (2) Aggregation of periods of insurance and employment in more than one country, both for entitlement to benefit and for calculation of its amount. (3) Payment of most benefits in any community country. The third principle — which went beyond most of the earlier binational agreements — was a step toward the "harmonization" of social security systems among the Six, toward which the EEC has made some other advances. The implementation of the detailed regulations based on these principles presents many problems of interpretation, and a committee — composed of the directors of the six social security bodies with representatives of the EEC and the ECSC — meets monthly to settle these questions. Sometimes the committee calls in representatives of workers', employers', and farmers' organizations. Special regulations for seasonal workers and frontier commuters were adopted in 1963, and came into force on February 1, 1964. Special regulations are also being developed for seamen and for self-employed persons. The second major interest of the EEC in social security — that of "harmonization" or "leveling upwards" the diverse systems among the Six — generated an enormous amount of study, discussion, and differences of opinion, but by July 1963, an agreement was reached on general guidelines and a short-term program which goes only part way toward harmonization. The latter, in revised form, is now being implemented, but full harmonization had not been achieved by 1967.

There is another multilateral agreement — that of the Council of Europe — which supports free movement of workers, subject only to restrictions based on cogent economic and social reasons, and the right of migrant workers to protection and assistance for themselves and their families in the territory of any other contracting nation. This agreement, called the European Social Charter, includes these two points that affect migrants in a much larger framework of the rights of citizens to get various social benefits from their states without discrimination on grounds of color, race, sex, religion, political opinion, national extraction, or social origin. Most European countries signed the charter after it was drawn up in 1961, but it did not come into force until February 26, 1965, when the required five nations had ratified it. By January 1, 1966, it was ratified — and therefore presumably in operation — in the United Kingdom, Norway, Sweden, Ireland, Germany (F.R.), and Denmark. These countries "have undertaken to accept a number of broad aims of social policy, to observe a large proportion of the detailed provisions of the charter and to notify [*sic*] those they cannot immediately undertake to implement." [29] The difficulty with the Social Charter is that it leaves a number of loopholes and is not detailed: It is almost an expression of high ideals rather than a concrete agreement. However, it is an important step in that it indicates that the three major countries of immigration which are ratifying powers — the United Kingdom, Sweden, and Germany — have the intention of granting to all foreign workers the same kind of rights and privileges which the EEC nations grant to each other's nationals.

Another significant development of the same type — worked out jointly by the Council of Europe and the ILO — is the European Social Security Code, which was opened for signature on April 16, 1965. It sets out a series of standards (higher than those in the 1949 ILO convention) which member countries should apply to their national health schemes and social security provisions. It also provides for equal treatment of migrants and nationals.

The ILO has a convention ratified by France, West Germany, Italy, the Netherlands, and Norway as of June 1, 1964, recommending that signatory states facilitate the departure, journey, and reception of migrant workers by providing information, accommodation, food and clothing on arrival, vocational training and other access to schools, recreation and welfare facilities, equal employment conditions.[30] This recommendation is also unenforceable, but it indicates the intention of the ratifying immigrant countries of France, Germany, and the Netherlands to do what they can to aid immigrant workers. Northern Italy is in the process of becoming an immigrant territory — especially for Greek and Spanish workers — so Italy's signature to the ILO convention is also important.

Conclusions about the Acceptance of Cross-National Migrants

During the period from 1955 through 1966, at least eight million Europeans voluntarily left their homes to take up residence and work in some other country of Europe, most of these migrating from some southern country to some northern or central country. A couple of million among these have returned to their homelands, and another significant minority (perhaps a million) have become citizens of the country to which they had migrated (nearly all naturalizations of those migrating after 1955 have been in France, the United Kingdom, Sweden, and the Netherlands); at the end of the period there remained at least five million Europeans living and working as foreigners in European countries, plus their dependents. The economic recession in the winter and spring of 1966–67 sharply reduced the rate of migration, which might be presumed to have an upswing with the end of the recession. But for reasons too complex to consider here, the rate of migration will never return to what it was in the early 1960's. Some 4 percent of the people of Europe outside the Soviet bloc had voluntarily changed countries, and both economic and social-psychological factors were operating to reduce the rate of migration.

This movement has profound implications aside from the economic ones which largely stimulated it. (Since the economic impacts of the migration are not central to the problem here, they will not be considered further in this chapter.[31]) To mention some minor effects first, it should be noted that those who had special dissatisfactions in their native countries used migration to avoid these dissatisfactions, and presumably successfully so in the majority of instances. Among the dissatisfactions thus eliminated have been political repression, uncongenial dominant ideologies, obnoxious marital ties where divorce was legally impossible, repressive social customs (such as those restricting the freedom of women). The more libertarian and democratic countries of northern and central Europe provided sanctuaries from such kinds of political and sociological restrictions at the same time that they posed new social-psychological problems for the migrants.

The whole category of problems of adjustment to migration is the second set of effects that should be pointed out. The disruption of traditional patterns of behavior and accommodation to new ones — symbolized in such sociological concepts as culture shock, cultural conflict, and alienation — was probably experienced in one form or another by each of the migrants. Some of this was painful and damaging, especially to the tiny minority who manifested psychiatric symptoms, but in many cases it was just as constructive (in providing release from social constraints) as it was destructive. All change — including tourism — is disruptive; the question is what are the long-run and countervailing consequences of the disruption. Considering that most of the migrants were moving from a rural to an urban culture at the same time as they were crossing national (and cultural) lines, the disruption was considerable. But probably in only a small minority of cases did the long-run negative effects outweigh the long-run positive effects.

Table 4 summarizes the large amount of information gathered on the policies, programs, and practices of countries of immigration toward immigrants as indexes of "acceptance" and of facilitation of adjustment. Not included in the table is the very important policy toward admission of foreign workers, since this is a function of the economic needs of a country, of the proportion of foreign workers already present, and of the concern for "balance" of religious categories, linguistic groups, political parties, etc., rather than an index of "acceptance" and facilitation of adjustment of immigrants already admitted. (The only way it could be justified as the latter is in a psychological sense: If a country is open to further immigra-

Table 4. Policies of Countries of Immigration Favorable or Unfavorable to Immigrants [a]

Policy	Belgium	France	Germany (F.R.)	Luxembourg	Netherlands	Sweden	Switzerland	United Kingdom
Vocational training programs	2	1	1	2	2	1	2	2
Language training programs for adults	3	1	3	3	3	2	3	2
Orientation to work	2	2	1	1	1	1	2	2
Orientation to country	1	1	1	2	2	1	2	1
Social assistance programs	2	1	1	2	2	1	3	2
Educational programs for immigrant wives and children	2	1	2	2	3	2	2	1
Housing for single workers	2	1	1	1	2	2	2	2
Housing for families	1	1	2	1	2	1	3	2
Free-time programs	1	2	1	2	2	2	2	1
Openness to immigration of workers' families	1	1	2	1	3	1	3	1
Discouragement of segregation of immigrants	1	2	3	1	2	1	2	1
Openness to naturalization	2	1	1	3	1	2	3	1
Total	20	15	19	21	25	17	29	18

[a] The number 1 is used to characterize the most favorable policies toward immigrants, 3 the least favorable.

tion, it probably gives the present immigrants a feeling that they are wanted.) Here it will suffice to indicate that France seems to be the country of immigration most open to new immigration, while Switzerland and the Netherlands are the countries most closed to further immigration. The table does, however, provide ratings on the policy toward admission of the foreign worker's wife and children, since this is clearly an index of "acceptance" and of facilitation of the adjustment of immigrant workers.

Twelve policies are evaluated for each country in terms of a three-point scale. For seven of the policies — openness to immigration of foreign workers' families, avoidance of segregation, social security provisions, language training, special educational programs for immigrant wives and children, availability of housing for families, and openness to naturalization — there seemed to be enough information available about different policies and enough differences to use all three points in differentiating countries. For the other five policies — vocational training, orientation to work, orientation to country, availability of housing for single workers, free-time programs — there seemed to be smaller differences between countries or merely enough information available about different policies to justify using only two of the three possible points. In the table, number 1 is used to characterize a relatively favorable policy toward immigrants, number 3 to characterize a relatively unfavorable policy toward immigrants. Thus, the lower the total score, the more favorable is the country's policy toward immigrants.

The weaknesses in such a table are obvious: (1) The policies chosen and the number of points used in evaluating each policy are arbitrary, although arguments could be made in their support. (2) For many of the policies there was not sufficient information, and in all cases published and unpublished reports and arbitrarily chosen informants had to be relied on rather than direct observation and measurement. As mentioned, where information was sparse, only two points were used, rather than three, to differentiate countries. (3) The judgments are inevitably partly subjective, possibly even biased, although they do not conform to what the author anticipated when he began the study. The judgment of the degree of segregation encouraged by the country's policies is especially subjective. Because of these weaknesses the table is offered only tentatively, and it should be considered open to criticism and revision.

The advantages of having such a table are that (1) it permits a summary view of the many pages of description of policies that have been included in the author's full-length monograph cited earlier; (2) it permits a correlation — made elsewhere in this report — of policy with certain indexes of adjustment or integration of immigrants. Of course, the table also permits an invidious distinction to be made between countries. If the ratings are incorrect, an unfair slur has been cast on certain countries; if they are correct, an evaluation is being made of what is going on in Europe to-day. Many of those who have written reports on which the author has partly relied as source material are officials of international agencies and their position prevents them from making any invidious distinctions publicly. This limitation should not apply to an independent scholar. The evaluation, crude as it is, may be said to indicate the importance which the receiving country puts on facilitating adjustment of foreigners.

There were many more indexes of acceptance and adjustment that the author hoped to obtain when he began this study, such as the proportion speaking the language of the country of immigration, the proportion joining unions or other occupational associations, the proportion with close friends among nationals; but the data were not available. The relatively few indexes of dependent variables on which data were obtained are summarized in Table 5. Again, the low scores in the table indicate the greatest degree of acceptance and adjustment. While the data are not so adequate, nor the method so precise, as to permit incontrovertible conclusions, these are the findings: Sweden, the Netherlands, and the United Kingdom have the most adjusted immigrants; Switzerland has the least adjusted while those in Germany and Luxembourg are only a little better adjusted; immigrants in France and Belgium are in the middle ranges of adjustment.

Some of the specific findings of this study are here tentatively presented in summary form.[32]

1. Economic factors are the main ones in motivating individual workers to migrate, but policy factors seem to be most important in facilitating or retarding their acceptance in the country of immigration and their adjustment to that country. (This does *not* refer to policies excluding immigrants or reducing their number after they are in the country. It refers only to policies and practices toward foreigners already permitted to work in the country.)

2. There are gaps in each immigrant country's organized activities to aid in the acceptance and adjustment of its immigrants. A country may have an excellent program in several respects, but have little activity in other respects.

3. Nevertheless, it is possible to discern different central tendencies among countries in the intensiveness and extensiveness of their programs. France and Sweden lead in the variety and completeness of their organized efforts. At the other end, Switzerland does the least.

4. The multilateral international agreements — especially those of the EEC, the Council of Europe, the ILO, and the Scandinavian Common Market for Labor — have done a great deal to upgrade the programs and activities of their ratifying countries. While the benefits are specifically for the nationals of the member states, they tend to "spill over" and be applied to other migrants.

Table 5. Indexes of Acceptance and Adjustment in Countries of Immigration [a]

Index	Belgium	France	Germany (F.R.)	Luxem-bourg	Nether-lands	Sweden	Switzer-land	United Kingdom
Turnover of immigrants	1	1	1	2	1	1	3	2
Percentage of cross-national marriages	1	2	2	2	1	1	2	...
Ratio of naturalized foreigners to foreign labor force	3	2	3	2	1	1	3	2
Crime rate	3	2	2	2	1	1	1	1
Lag between repatriation peak and migration peak	1	2	3	3	3	...	3	1
Total	9	9	11	11	7	5–7	12	7–9

[a] Number 1 indicates the greatest degree of acceptance and adjustment, 3 the least.

213

5. Italy and Spain are the only emigrant countries to have significant programs to aid in the adjustment of their nationals going abroad, although Greece has also recently set up missions in several cities of Germany.

6. Private employers, trade unions, local governments, churches, and voluntary associations are significantly aiding the reception, training, and adjustment of foreigners.

7. While progress has been made in the past decade, the inadequacies of the programs to aid cross-national migrants make an adjustment — in the light of their initial handicaps of cultural limitations, rural background, low educational level, poor vocational preparation — suggest that, by and large, the life of the cross-national migrant is not a pleasant one. The inadequacies of housing and the exclusion of the family of the worker are probably the most unpleasant features. A large number of immigrant workers are being exploited economically without compensatory social advantages — or mistakenly think they are exploited because of insufficient orientation. Despite the progress, and despite the efforts of several countries and many groups throughout western and northern Europe, policies, programs, and practices toward migrant workers cannot be considered as generally favorable forces toward the future integration of Europe.

8. Sweden offers its workers the highest wages, for any given occupation, of any country in Europe, with Germany coming second. In occupational level, the immigrants to the United Kingdom rate the highest, mainly because that country no longer accepts many immigrants who are not skilled. Opportunities for upward occupational mobility are best for the immigrants into France and Sweden.

9. Public opinion polls indicate there is a good deal of dissatisfaction with the free migration policies now prevailing in most countries of northern and central Europe, as well as significant antagonism toward the migrants.

10. On the non-policy factors facilitating the integration of immigrants, France stands in the best position. These factors are ideology favoring integration of immigrants, flexibility of social structure, Catholic religion, Romance language, closeness to country of emigration, and attractiveness of climate.

11. Insofar as the culture and social structure of the countries of emigration facilitate the adjustment of their emigrants, Italians have the greatest likelihood of adjustment and Turks the least, among the seven European peoples studied.

12. The indexes used here, which are inadequate, suggest that the best adjustment has been made by immigrants to Sweden, the Netherlands, and the United Kingdom.

To turn now to a test of the main hypotheses of this chapter, the relevant facts have been assembled in Table 6. These hypotheses are that integration and adjustment of foreigners into a host society is a function of (1) the openness of the host society; (2) the degree of attachment of the immigrants to their society of origin (that is, the inverse of this should be correlated with measures of integration into the host society); (3) the similarity of the cultures, respectively, of the country of emigration and the country of immigration. As throughout this study, no attempt will be made to weight the diverse variables measured; instead a weight of 1 is arbitrarily assigned to each. In other words, they are all treated alike.[33] The dependent variables — that is, the measures of acceptance, integration, and adjustment — are important ones, but they may not be enough to cover what happens to the immigrants as they are intended to do. There may also be defects in the reliability of the data themselves, although they came from official government sources. Nevertheless, the summary index of dependent variables (item 6 in Table 6) was related to each of the summary indexes of independent variables (items 1–4).

The one significant correlation that appears is that between the summary index of dependent variables and the summary index of openness of a country's policies, practices, and programs in regard to immigrants (item 1). Using the rank-order coefficient of correlation for all eight immigrant countries, the author found a rho measure of .47, which means that there is a moderate relationship. This is a positive finding for the first hypothesis. One country is an obvious deviant in the relationship — the Netherlands. Its deviancy lies in the fact that immigrants make a good adjustment in the Netherlands, even though the country's policies, programs, and practices are not very open to them.[34] This seems easy to explain: the Netherlands is the poorest example of our immigrant countries — in fact, it is only marginally an immigrant country, having almost as many emigrants as immigrants. The Netherlands can afford to do very little for the immigrant, but Dutch public opinion is pro-immigrant, compared to that found in most other countries, and in this *informally* favorable atmosphere, immigrants make a relatively good adjustment. The author made no attempt to relate public opinion statistically to the dependent variables index, since the measuring instruments were noncomparable. If the Netherlands is left outside the correlation, rho jumps to .73, which is a fairly high correlation for complex data such as these. The author thus considers the first hypothesis confirmed — that integration and adjustment of immigrants is related to the openness of programs, policies, and practices of immigrant countries. The Dutch case indicates that if comparable measures of the openness of public opinion had been available, the indexes would be even more closely related.

But the other hypotheses do not hold up under correlation of the indexes. The findings give no reason to believe that the degree of attachment

Table 6. Summary Indexes for Independent and Dependent Variables Related to Acceptance and Adjustment of Immigrants [a]

Variable	Belgium	France	Germany (F.R.)	Luxem-bourg	Nether-lands	Sweden	Switzer-land	United Kingdom
1. Openness of policies of immigrant country [b]	5	1	4	6	7	2	8	3
2. Economic factors of immigrant country	2	2	1	1	3	1	2	1
3. Attachment to culture of emigrant country, according to distribution from various countries of emigration								
4. Differences between countries of emigration and countries of immigration [b]	2	2	3	2	1	1	1	3
5. Summary of rankings for independent variables	2	1	4	2	4	3	4	4
6. Summary of rankings for dependent variables	11	6	12	11	15	7	15	11
7. Summary of rankings for independent and dependent variables	4	4	5	5	2	1	6	3
	15	10	17	16	17	8	21	14

[a] The lower the number, the greater the degree of acceptance and adjustment.
[b] The indexes are rank orders based on the total score of 1–3 rankings for the variable.

216

of the immigrants to their society of origin inhibits good integration or adjustment to the immigrant country (rho $= 0$). And they give no reason to believe that similarity of cultures in the country of immigration and the country of emigration makes for better integration and adjustment of the immigrants (rho $= .10$). These hypotheses have *not* been disproved but there has been a failure to prove them. If the true relationships should be zero, as the crude indexes here suggest they are, this is indeed a most valuable finding, even if it does go against current sociological thinking: It would mean that the cultural and political background of the migrants — by country, not as individuals — has little or nothing to do with the kind of adjustment they make to the immigrant society, and that, in a significant sense, all cross-national migrant groups — on the average for their country — start off on the same foot when they migrate. The data here have shown that what is important for integration and adjustment is the openness of the *immigrant* country — certainly in its overt policies, programs, and practices and probably in its informal attitudes as well.

An important qualification needs to be made to these generalizations. The data being dealt with are macroscopic — that is, information applying to all national groups. No information is presented here on individual cases or on variations among individuals. It could still be true that *some* individual migrants are very much affected by their ties to their national and local backgrounds. It could still be true that a small number of immigrants find the different climate, language, or religion of the country of immigration to be such an obstacle that they cannot make an adjustment. And it could even be true that some immigrants make an excellent adjustment even when the immigrant country is least open and most hostile (within the range examined in this study). It is thus important to emphasize that the data here are *grouped*, macroscopic, that the correlations are of the type which have taken on the technical misnomer of "ecological," [35] and that the findings do not apply to all individuals.

The indexes which made up a measure of the openness of a country to immigrants as indicated by its formal policies, programs, and practices were summarized earlier in this report. There France, Sweden, and the United Kingdom, in that order, were found to be on the top, and the Netherlands and Switzerland to be on the bottom. In other portions of this report several other measures affecting or indicating the integration or adjustment of immigrants were presented. Drawing them all together makes for a theoretically meaningless index, but one which may have practical utility. Such a summary of summaries, presented in item 7 of Table 6, might be called an "index of favorable conditions" affecting immigrants. It shows where, among the eight countries of immigration studied, the immigrants are best off and where they are worst off. Sweden was ahead of France on this final measure, and the Netherlands and West Germany are, after Switzerland, the worst countries for the immigrant. These measures are all relative to each other: certainly no country is really very bad for immigrants; if it were, immigrants would soon cease to go or stay there. And certainly no country offers perfection for immigrants, although Sweden and France make a conscious national effort to do as well as they can.[36]

This "index of favorable conditions" for the countries of immigration harks back to one of the basic themes with which this chapter opened: To what extent are the people of Europe today changing their conception of themselves to think of themselves as Europeans and not merely as Frenchmen, Germans, Swedes, etc.? It was assumed at the outset that if this is not to be regarded as merely a verbal change, with no substance, it must take the form of European peoples accepting nationalities other than their own *as their own*. This applies to the total population of Europe, of course, but this chapter has concentrated on cross-national migrants and their hosts. In a very important sense, the migrants and their hosts are the best persons to test the question of acceptance: Their mutual presence is real, not academic or something to fill in on a questionnaire; it is of some duration, not for a few days of superficial tourism or convention going; the relationships occur under conditions of everyday living, not of the best behavior with which diplomats or experts confront each other at conferences. Cross-national migration provides an almost experimental situation for judging whether European peoples are accepting each other.

In this study the hosts have been examined to a greater extent than the migrants themselves, simply because there are more relevant data on them, and also the hosts provide a more critical test of the acceptance of others because they have more power and freedom than the migrants, who in a sense *must* accept the hosts. In speaking of the acceptance by the host peoples, the author does not refer to any hypothetical willingness to accept all foreigners under any and all conditions. Every nation has limits on its expansibility, and every nation must set limits on the rate of immigration, for economic reasons if no other. The purpose of this study was to find out whether the host people, who have invited the immigrants either to take the least desirable jobs in their countries or to fill in occupational gaps which their own nationals cannot fill, treat these migrants as they treat their fellow-nationals. This is what is meant by "acceptance" among the host people. All the host countries' policies, programs, and practices for which objective information could be obtained were examined, along with public opinion polls and indexes of the adjustability of the migrants. The author's conclusion is that there are gaps and faults in every country, but that France and Sweden have made significant formal efforts to accept the immigrants. "Formal" efforts are emphasized because the public opinion poll data show a considerable rejection even in those countries, and in

France the efforts seem to be conditioned on the immigrants' becoming "francisized." [37] The United Kingdom, Belgium, and Luxembourg follow behind the two leaders, with the British making an obvious effort to face up to their shortcomings, through studies, much public discussion, and legislation. Germany's policy apparently has been to be very formally correct in regard to the immigrants, to treat them well materially, but in no sense to accept them as equivalent peoples. The German policy is expressed in the term used to designate the migrants — "guest workers." The Netherlands represents almost a contrast-conception to France and Germany: It does little to help the immigrants formally, but its attitudes are more open than those in most countries and the immigrants generally find it easy to adjust to the Netherlands despite the lack of formal aids. Only Switzerland has chosen the conscious path of rejection to the point of overt and explicit chauvinism. To repeat, this is not because of Switzerland's restrictions on immigration, but because of the treatment which it metes out to the immigrants it has accepted into the country. While the "rejection" is clearest in Switzerland, it exists to some extent among all the immigration countries, and few nationals of these countries think of themselves as really interchangeable with their immigrants.

On the migrants there is less information. The naturalization and intermarriage rates presented offer important clues to the extent to which the migrants accept their hosts as interchangeable with people of their native nationalities, defined here as "acceptance." But clearly "acceptance" means something beyond assimilation, and both naturalization and intermarriage refer to acceptance only so far as it also means assimilation. Even if an immigrant returns to his home country and takes a spouse from among his native people, he can still accept his former hosts as "my own kind of people," as interchangeable with his own nationality for social and political purposes. It has not been possible to measure this kind of opinion, except very crudely by scattered references to such things as participation in cross-national voluntary associations. Very few emigrants leave their home countries with the intention of never coming back except maybe for a visit. But the fact that only a minority have returned is a crude index that the majority have accepted their host country as their adopted country, whether the law and those who apply it allow them to be naturalized or not. Except for those who return with bitterness or with psychological problems to their home countries, the migrants seem to show a great deal of tolerance, if not outright acceptance, toward their hosts.

This study lacks a real contrast or comparison, which probably could be best provided today by Canada, Australia, and some countries of Latin America. To make this comparison would take a separate study. But the author would guess that mutual acceptance is greater among migrants and their hosts in these countries than in Europe.

A few comparisons can be made with the migrants who came from Europe to the United States in the century and a half before the quota-restriction laws of the 1920's cut them off. The times were so different that the comparison is hardly appropriate: It was an era of laissez-faire for government, so the programs and practices toward immigrants were large-ly those of private organizations, which did much to aid the foreigners but not nearly as much as is done today by governments. It was a migration of much longer distance, and — although no information is available about whether the migrants initially dreamed of returning to their homelands — they found it much more difficult to return, even for a holiday. Other pro-found differences could be specified.

Mutual acceptance was dominant in the immigration to America in the pre-1921 period. There were those Americans who insisted that the immigrants adapt to an "American" cultural norm, those who looked for-ward to a more cosmopolitan "melting pot," and those who favored an equalitarian cultural pluralism. But — even at the height of the agitation for putting restrictions on further immigration, and even at the fever pitch of racist hatred — there was almost no one who insisted that the migrants return to their homelands after a period of labor in the United States. Dif-ferent conceptions prevailed about how the European immigrant was to become an American, but there was no doubt that he could become an American and that he should have full legal and political rights as an American. There was a norm of acceptance that made integration — de-spite many personal hardships attending the process — ultimately inevita-ble.

From the migrants themselves there are no comparative systematic data, but the historical studies of Marcus Hansen, Oscar Handlin, and others suggest that the immigrants to America also quickly thought of themselves as permanent Americans, not that many adopted assimilation as their personal goal, for many retained a sentimental and cultural loyal-ty to the "old country." But there was a transfer of political loyalty, which has yet to be measured among the intra-European migrants of today. Some of the American immigrants returned to their homelands, especial-ly the Italians, but there is no evidence that this involved repudiation of the United States: some returnees were trapped by European wars and new American immigration restriction laws into staying in the homelands when they originally had intended to go back to the United States after a holiday or a settlement of family affairs. The European immigration to the United States was a successful, integrative migration, if the evidence of history can be trusted. The study here raises a question whether there has been as much mutual acceptance among European migrants and their hosts in Europe today.

CHAPTER 8

The Changing Structure of Europe

THE age called "modern" has taken its character most largely from the thrust of European power and civilization onto the oceans and over the lands beyond. Europeans peopled North America and Australia, became the dominant social strata in South America, and made themselves masters of much of Asia and Africa. In this scarcely credible feat of self-assertion it was the nation-state that mobilized with such extraordinary effectiveness the cultural, economic, and military resources of the continent aptly called mother of empires. Yet within Europe itself again and again nation-state turned against nation-state; at length the capacity of European society to limit its internal conflicts was exhausted and within the space of a single generation two wars turned into orgies of self-destruction.

Since the early nineteenth century Europeans had become increasingly aware of the dangers of unrestrained nationalism. Yet they strove only feebly and intermittently to build international institutions which might bridle the conflict among themselves. Meanwhile a new major power center was growing across the Atlantic in an area largely peopled by integrated Europeans. With its development there came also an increasing cultural, economic, and political interdependence of the whole Atlantic area which was only dimly appreciated. In the twentieth century, despite its manifest reluctance to be involved, the United States — until then only a neophyte in greater Atlantic affairs — found itself drawn into two successive European wars. The disillusion with the results of World War I discouraged at that time any enduring commitment to participate in European affairs. As has been noted earlier, not even World War II succeeded in effecting a complete reversal of viewpoint, and it was only the bitter lessons of three years of aftermath which imposed acceptance of longer range responsibilities.

This study has traced the growth and partial erosion of European and Atlantic integrative movements and institutions during the two decades after 1948. Its second chapter has attempted some initial casting up of accounts which such landmarks of passing time as the twentieth anniversary of the Marshall Plan and the tenth of the EEC seemed to make particularly appropriate. The study has tried to identify what look like points of no return and to estimate the firmness of barriers that currently inhibit progress. At various stages it has stressed that the integrative process has been moving ahead on two fronts: (1) the building of international institutions or agreements that link two or more states along political, military, economic, and educational lines, and (2) a fusing in Western society that has continued inexorably, sometimes in conformity with understandings between states, sometimes quite independently of any official encouragement.

Perhaps the most noteworthy example of the contrasts to be found in the integrative movement is the special relationship between France and Germany: there has been a faltering implementation of the political and military sides of their alliance but at the same time an extraordinary advance in the "integration of peoples." This spread of "Europeanness," which perseveres on its own momentum even during phases of arrest or retreat in the efforts to make a "United States of Europe," both parallels and interlinks with the corresponding evolution of a *homo Atlanticus*. The American invasion of Europe after World War II has never moved forward more impressively along cultural, economic, scientific, and technological lines than since the enforced suspension early in 1963 of President John F. Kennedy's "grand design" for the development of a genuine transatlantic partnership. Somewhat paradoxically this contributes significantly to the more "European" tinge of life in the countries of the Continent. It is another example of how America, this time through educational, economic, and technological influences, preempts the most prominent place among the things Europeans have in common. There is no commensurate counter-penetration of European influences in the United States, though some such role is played by the backwash of the American waves that beat on Europe. The interaction is most difficult to measure, but at the same time that it tends to give a more "European" tinge to life on the eastern shores of the Atlantic it brings Europe close to its integrated children on the other side of that ocean.

Despite the forbidding walls that have been erected and curtains that have been dropped in the East in the past quarter century against the influences of the Western capitalist world, much of what has been said in the preceding chapters pertains also to developments within nations that lie in the Soviet sphere. The increasing industrialization of both blocks dictates similarities in the patterns of life in the two areas, and thus of the problems they face. On occasion these common problems and the solutions found make a mockery of the political barriers erected by the rulers of Eastern Europe. In view of the faster pace, greater affluence, and more sophisticated forms of social life in the West, it has been inevitable that the cultural thrust should be almost entirely in an eastward direction. In such matters as manners, styles, the amenities of life, and the aspirations of youth, the urge for emulation fuses with internal pressures that generate a wide range of demands in both the material and the spiritual spheres.[1] No doubt this is part of a worldwide phenomenon, but in the case of the other continents there is scarcely such a sense of common fate as prevails within Eastern Europe vis-à-vis Western Europe.

All aspects of East-West relations as well as relations within the two blocs themselves were bound to be profoundly affected by the Soviet intervention in Czechoslovakia in August 1968. Perhaps no event in the history of the post-World War II era is so easy to analyze in its more immediate and direct consequences and at the same time so difficult to assess for the full measure of its impact. At first glace, it is tempting to note some parallel with Hitler's seizure of rump Czechoslovakia in March 1939. At that time issues that had been blurred or indistinct emerged with startling clarity. Perception of the real drift of the Nazi dictator's policy was forced on millions who had been the victims of self-imposed illusions. Almost overnight indecision in many quarters hardened into purpose.

In 1968–69 it was not easy for international observers to discern the degree to which the Soviet action in the same country might be designated a true turning point in world affairs. At the very least, however, it was necessary to review and to some extent revise assumptions which had gained wide currency in the Atlantic world. October 1962 had witnessed the abandonment of the challenging posture that had been the imprint of Soviet policy since 1958. The Cuban missile affair had signified the end of the second Berlin crisis and of what we well may call the Second Cold War. During the following six years there was a tendency to assume a rising curve in East-West relations. It was logical to perceive a close correlation between this curve and the steadily declining one in the relationship between Moscow and Peking. Such evidences of a spirit of cooperation between Washington and Moscow as the nuclear test-ban and nonproliferation treaties were taken as the harbingers of an eventual détente involving the two superpowers. Nothing, also, was more natural than to think of the war in Vietnam as the central obstacle whose removal would definitely clear the way to rapid advance in that direction.

Particularly conducive to the spread of such hopes was the gathering impression of a much-reduced clash of interests in Europe, most notably in its Eastern countries. Soviet preoccupation with the problem of China and that of the United States with Southeast Asia seemed to dictate the relaxation of pressures in the European sphere generally. In Eastern Europe the competition between the Kremlin and Maoist China for Communist loyalties was visibly assisting in the erosion of the postwar satellite relationships.[2] Rumania pronounced a virtual declaration of independence

and there were numerous signs of restiveness under Soviet domination in
Poland, Czechoslovakia, and Hungary. To many Western observers, Moscow seemed to be more resigned to some limitation of its hegemony than
determined to keep it fully intact at whatever price. Also encouraging to
the West was the way in which its own Communist parties evidenced interest in somewhat greater autonomy and seemed generally less subservient
to Moscow. The eventual abandonment of the program of world revolution proclaimed and directed by Moscow for half a century no longer
seemed entirely beyond the realm of hope.

In response to such mellowing influences, the West in its turn was
bound to feel less need to be eternally on guard and was bound also to
abate the more combative aspects of its own policies. The year 1966 saw
the final repudiation of the goal of "liberation" of Eastern Europe that
had been proclaimed early in the first Eisenhower administration. The
change of direction was signaled in President Johnson's speech of October
7 in which he heavily stressed that the American aim of détente in relations with states of the Soviet orbit was not calculated as a device to split
the Moscow-controlled bloc. The United States also encouraged the Federal Republic to renounce the sterile clichés and doctrines which had fet-
tered German policy in building a bridge to Eastern Europe. The new
Kiesinger-Brandt government was fully prepared to move ahead on its
own. It immediately proceeded to establish diplomatic relations with Rumania and held out olive branches to Poland and Czechoslovakia. These
were struck out of its hands by Warsaw and Prague, but the Czechoslo-
vaks acted with obvious reluctance under Soviet pressure. Actually the
elements which soon were to make up the Dubček government were already determined to reverse gears at the earliest possible moment.[3] In
August 1968 well-informed quarters in Prague were anticipating diplomatic relations with West Germany by the end of the year.

All Western calculations regarding Eastern Europe formed before the
summer of 1968 were manifestly made invalid by the events of August.
When Czechoslovakia was jerked back into line, it meant for Poland and
Hungary that the heel of Moscow had also been set on their own necks.
In short, in the Soviet orbit the satellite relationship has been fully restored, Rumania hovering fearfully and Yugoslavia uneasily by. The
"Brezhnev doctrine," denying the right of self-determination to Communist countries other than the U.S.S.R. — at the very least to such as have
not already emancipated themselves — has now committed the Soviets to
a policy of enforced conformity. Before this it had been possible to hope
that the example of states, like Yugoslavia, Albania, and Rumania, which
had taken the plunge with relative impunity might be followed by others.
Such doors of escape have now been slammed shut.

It is the same story on any expectancy the Eastern nations might have had of escaping from Soviet economic bondage by cultivating commercial relations with Germany. For nearly a quarter century Moscow has exacted a heavy tribute from each of its Eastern European protectorates. Not only has this been costly in itself but the methods used prohibited any natural course of development. The extension of trade between Eastern European states and Germany had carried with it the prospect of loans and credits that would allow economic growth in directions that had previously been inhibited in the East. The Soviet occupation of Czechoslovakia was, among other things, intended to stop this drift toward economic independence. The rape of Prague blocked at least temporarily the program of détente in the East pursued by Bonn. It also created an altered set of relations within which the new German government of November 1969 could conduct its search for accommodation between East and West Germany.

Most central among the consequences of the Soviet move into Czechoslovakia was of course the effect on East-West relations. It dealt a heavy blow to the hope that the European freeze into two hostile camps would gradually yield to a general thaw. Rarely if ever in the history of our times were so many illusions so rudely shattered. There at last is hope that the increasing tendency of recent years to equate NATO with the Warsaw Pact is a thing of the past, the latter having emerged all too clearly for what it always was — "a treaty made by the Kremlin with itself." [4] Ironically, the pact's provisions for the use of military force have been invoked thus far only in relations among its members, things having reached a point where no political or economic pressure or even the threat of military action sufficed to maintain internal discipline.

For the time being this state of affairs should resolve any lingering doubts in the West about the wisdom of proceeding with as much dispatch as circumstances may permit to fortify its international institutions. The intervention in Czechoslovakia signaled once more that it is self-defeating to hold back with whatever steps toward European and Atlantic integration may be feasible in the hope of promoting the fusion of a larger, more inclusive Europe. There remain, of course, common European problems for which there should often be similar European solutions, however small may be the likelihood of dealing with them in the foreseeable future on a continent-wide basis. The approaches to these problems constitute the thin edge of Europeanization and, from a longer range view, can be seen in some relief against the divisive realities of the contemporary political, military, and economic scene.

One aspect of the Soviet mode of procedure that deserves close attention in the West is the way in which military intervention came only after agreement had been reached at Bratislava and Cierni and after the climax of tension had passed. There was no political step to precede what was equivalent to the launching of war operations. As one exceptionally keen Yugoslav observer put it:

It was believed that, in international relations, bolts struck only from a stormy sky on which clouds had gathered gradually. It was particularly not believed that they would strike out of a clear blue sky. This new, exceptionally momentous and dangerous element of uncertainty has been introduced into international relations by the occupation of Czechoslovakia. The threat to peace and mankind's very existence has thereby been intensified to an extent greater than it was by the invention of nuclear weapons. For, after all, man's behavior is more dangerous than the things he produces.[5]

If taken at its full face value, an even more ominous portent would be found in the Soviet assertion of a "right" to intervene in West Germany whenever they perceive a danger of the revival of fascism. Taken in conjunction with the procedure in Czechoslovakia delineated above, this would seem to set the stage for a surprise thrust westward whenever it should suit the Kremlin's policy. Nor is it possible to ignore the fact that at one sweep the Soviets have greatly altered the strategic line-up in Central Europe in their favor. By pushing forward their forces to the western borders of Bohemia, they have established an unbroken line from the Baltic to the southern frontier of Hungary. Thereby they have elongated by half the "front" on which they face West Germany and roughly tripled their direct contact with Austria. Overnight this created a new complex of problems for the makeup and deployment of NATO forces. It may be argued that, however reprehensible their procedure, the Soviets from their point of view were acting within the family and transgressed on no limits set them by Western statesmen. It can equally be maintained that their motivations lay more in internal than in bloc concerns and were, at least initially, unrelated to strategic military ones. But acceptance of these points cannot alter the real consequences in terms of the strategic situation in Central Europe and its unavoidable political impacts.

Time must now tell how the Western Alliance will respond to these new challenges. No doubt there has been an instinctive closing of ranks. National debates in 1969 on whether to remain with NATO were muted. France is no longer likely to leave the Alliance. There is much room for soul searching on whether these tragic events would have occurred if France had not left a gaping hole in the Western political and military front or the United States had not allowed itself to become so inextricably entangled in Southeast Asia. Perhaps all this gives hope that in many areas of European and Atlantic concern the participants will do better.

The Economic Scene

Greater shock absorbing capacity is needed in this world of instant communications. Economic integration yields risk-spreading effect, as the occupation of Czechoslovakia and the strikes and riots and other events of May–November 1968 dramatized. It has been true since at least the seventeenth century that each part of Europe is "a piece of the Continent, a part of the main," but this did not prevent two twentieth-century wars in a generation. It did not prevent a myopic nationalism from denying flatly that economic and political ill-health in one part of the Continent threatened all parts. And it has not yet destroyed the illusion that economic crises and business-cycle recessions can be treated by quarantine or by lifting the drawbridges. In the field of monetary policy, the conventional European response to a crisis in one country is still frighteningly reminiscent of reactions to the Black Death of the fourteenth century.

But this is changing. The scale and tempo of the communications revolution in Europe after 1950 have made it impossible to contain crises. And the response to the crises of the 1960's underlined the increasingly integrated nature of the European community.

Do the crises of 1968 confirm the integration of Europe? We think they do. The student protests of Italy, Germany, France, England, and, in a muted form, Spain — all of which had clear economic as well as ideological bases — all attest to the commonality of student aspirations and problem assessments. Anthony Sampson, reporting on a European seminar at Reading University in the first week of April 1968, concluded that "They clearly think they belong to some kind of single students' world . . ." [6] This is the more remarkable because of the clearly informal nature of contacts among student bodies of the principal European countries. In a previous generation a communications barrier might have slowed or deflected the chain-reaction effect of student strikes and protests. These shock waves are transmitted almost instantaneously today and this is as true of student sit-ins as it is of devaluation rumors.

The almost continuous monetary crisis of the late 1960's made it virtually impossible to ignore the interdependence of national economies in the Atlantic area. This negative lesson affected countries within the Common Market and those without. Although a French veto could block British entry through the front door in Brussels, it is increasingly clear that domestic events in Europe are leading to a back-door entry of Britain and the United States into economic ties with Europe that, in terms of impairment of conventional national sovereignty, are more "political" than any agreements yet implemented in the EEC. And the resignation of Charles de Gaulle had remarkably little impact on this trend.

Why did this happen in the 1960's? Economic crises in the past have often been divisive in their international impact. The breakdown of the international order after the London monetary talks of 1931 is only one of several examples that can be read out of the past. The divisive potential has been great in the almost continuous crisis atmosphere in which central bankers met in 1967 and 1968, and particularly in the critical meetings of August 1967 in London, September 1967 in Rio de Janeiro, March 1968 in Stockholm, and November 1968 in Bonn. On the record of 1967–69, the Western world's monetary system threatens to blow apart about every six months, yet it remains patched together. Why?

One reason, surely, is the communications revolution that now makes it all but impossible to avoid anticipating the chain reaction that would be set in motion by an excessively nationalistic approach to balance-of-payment problems. In chessboard terms, the international money players are now playing at least one move ahead, some of them two.

But instant communications is not the only reason. Another important one is that the leading European and Atlantic nations of the 1960's are all surplus producers in some important export sector. They are tied together by markets in a way that precludes a go-it-alone approach to international relations. And in this fact bankers and business communities can write "confirmed" to one of the major arguments that has supported moves toward closer union: trade integrates. This integrating effect is in theory more powerful if trade involves the supply of some goods that an importing country desperately wants. This seemed to be the lesson taught by colonial histories of the past, for which the British Commonwealth provided the best model. In practice, the lesson of the past decade is that the integrative effect of trade is still more powerful when it involves goods that exporting countries want to dump abroad. This can be seen in steel, in butter, in wood pulp, in grains, in textiles, and in a host of fabricated and manufactured articles. It is this dimension of trade that sets the 1960's apart from previous eras.

It is not hard to find a reason why. A country seeking imports typically has a deficit in the goods in question. The imports may compete with the domestic product, but that competition can be controlled. New domestic industries may be inhibited, but few domestic producers are likely to be thrown out of work by the imported products. Trade may be a threat to jobs, but that threat can be contained. A surplus-producing country needs export markets or some domestic producers must go unemployed. The lack of trade is a direct threat to jobs. The most stubborn surpluses are typically in sectors of low labor mobility, where the threat to jobs is felt most keenly: farming, forestry, fisheries, and the coal-and-steel complex.

One principle of modern economic behavior is emerging: In a society in which new technology has become an output rather than an input, the search for markets becomes the dominant driving force. It was this common search for markets, if not a search for common markets, that held Europe and the Atlantic states together in the 1960's. The then President de Gaulle dared not stay away from Brussels in 1966 — his surplus-producing farmers would not let him. Germany and Italy tolerated substantial internal strains in order to gain access to the wider EEC markets for their manufactured products. The attraction of the EEC for Britain is as a place to sell, not as a place to buy. And it was the struggle to retain access to markets that dominated United States behavior throughout the Kennedy Round.

Surpluses unite, shortages divide — this seems to be the lesson of the 1960's. This is not to deny the strains that surpluses put on the states of Europe at the end of the decade. Steel is sick, the butter surplus has preempted all available storage and shows no sign of falling, and the pulp and paper producers worry about excess capacity. But they still seek union.

The Common Market *is* having difficulties, some of its own creation, but most of them inherent in the present stage of postwar European development. This is especially true of its agricultural problems. Although the high prices and insulated market promise trouble for the future within the EEC, it is difficult to support the argument that the crippling surpluses of milk, soft wheat, and pork in 1967–68 were the result of EEC price policies. They were rather inherent in any system of prices and markets accompanied by a decade of peace and reasonably stable economic conditions.

After the mid-1950's European farmers were economically capable of applying new technology on an increasingly large scale. Tractors and combines, improved seeds, artificial insemination, nutritionally balanced animal feedstuffs, chemical herbicides and pesticides, and an indigenous fertilizer industry — all were available and in well-developed forms. The grain and milk surpluses, after 1965, were virtually inevitable. Although their magnitude in the late 1960's may have been influenced by EEC agricultural price policies, there would almost certainly have been embarrassing surpluses had there been no EEC.

The tractor and combine are the "first-stage" substitutes for labor in the process of agricultural modernization. Increasing emphasis on grain crops is the now-classic response of farmers who find labor rising in cost and short in supply. Given the institutional and structural characteristics of French and German agriculture in the 1960's, the resulting wheat surpluses in the EEC were the consequence of peace and relative stability of expectations rather than of higher prices or variable levies.

For somewhat different reasons the milk surplus is also to be debited more to technological advances and defects in the agrarian structure than to price policy. Between 1950 and 1962 bovine tuberculosis was virtually eliminated in Germany. And a sustained effort to introduce artificial insemination in France in the 1950's laid the foundation for the increase in output per cow that provides the principal explanation for the "white flood" of milk in the 1960's. The small size of European dairy farms makes it almost impossible to shift them out of dairying to other products. The options are to quit farming or to stay in dairying. And the only rational response of the small dairyman is to attempt to increase output. The bases for the resulting milk surplus of the 1960's werc laid in the 1950's, and the energizing force has been technology more than price.

Although agricultural price policies to the mid-1960's have not been the main cause of Europe's agricultural surpluses, the situation is changing rapidly. Major technological and structural changes are taking place in European agriculture. The rigid price policies of the EEC prevent the resultant increases in output from having any depressing effects on domestic prices. Producers are not receiving any price signals to warn them to cut back on output, and surpluses mount. This is reversing a century of trade relationships. For the first time in the industrial era, Western European food surpluses are being thrown on world markets.

While the search for these markets was an integrating force in Europe in the 1960's, the disruptive potential of the problems associated with disposing of food surpluses must not be underestimated. One of the most disturbing prospects concerns the protectionist sentiment that has been reawakened in the United States. The historical posture of the American farmer has been pro-free trade. The traditional bloc of export-oriented farmers — wheat, cotton, and tobacco growers — was augmentcd after 1945 by rice, sorghum, and soybean producers, for whom export markets have been taking 40 percent or more of total output in recent years. With the progressive closing off of markets in Western Europe and the appearance of heavily subsidized European grains and butter in world markets, the base is being laid for an American reaction. This threatens to undo the laborious efforts of the past thirty years to promote more liberal world trade policies. A retaliatory sentiment is building up that could realign traditional free-trade farmers with protectionist sectors of American industry. Europeans may protest that this is unrealistic — that the American farmer cannot escape the world-trade imperative forced upon him by his surplus position. Unrealistic or not, the cumulative irritation among American farmers resulting from the unloading of surpluses abroad by European surplus producers is a fact, of which there is ample evidence. And it must be expected that if this situation continues in the agricultural sectors of world trade, it will redound upon Europe's trade in manufactured goods.

The threatened drying up of Western European import markets for agricultural products has had a particularly unfortunate impact on Eastern Europe. Poland, Rumania, Bulgaria, and Yugoslavia have all gained desperately needed hard currencies from their agricultural trade with Western Europe. The retraction of these markets had begun in 1967 and was acutely evident in 1968. The political consequences are almost sure to be profound. At the moment when Eastern European political leaders needed the courage that only alternative export markets could give, they saw these markets contracting. Yugoslavia in particular has found the loss of Western European markets painful. "The Yugoslavs, for the first time since Stalin, now feel seriously threatened," Patrick Seale concluded in surveying Eastern Europe after the Czech crisis of 1968.[7] The economic root of this sense of insecurity can be traced in good part to the trade-diminishing consequences of the EEC.

With the exception of the Dutch and the Danes, European farmers have been characterized by parochial attitudes that have been one of the bulwarks of a narrow nationalism. Farmers producing for export cannot ignore what is going on in the world outside their village or their nation. Europe has had few of these internationally oriented farmers in the past, but this is changing. A new generation is being exposed to world market impacts, in terms of both potential outlets for surpluses and (more unfamiliar) potential competition for domestic markets. Although the EEC as a unit is insulated from world agricultural markets more completely than any nonsocialist nation, farmers within the EEC are being made emphatically aware of the competitive power of their national neighbors.

The first reaction is fright and a cry for protection. But this should not obscure the fact that the most insular sectors of European nations are now being forced to think in terms of market forces that transcend national boundaries. The educational value of this experience is enormous. It poses both a threat and a promise. The threat can be seen in the clustering of distressed farm people around radical leaders — of the Right, as in the neo-Nazi parties of Germany, or of the Left, as in France. The promise lies in the generation of an international awareness in sectors that have in the past been the hard-core repositories of nationalistic sentiment and political block-votes. The major manifestation of this awareness can be seen in attitudes toward the decline of rural populations.

French distress at the loss of a peasantry has led to a small library of books and monographs for which the theme was set by the title of one, *Une France sans Paysans*. The shock of this rapid decline in France was profound. An inquiry of June 1953 had disclosed that 57 out of every 100 sons of farmers stated that they intended to make farming their career. Nine years later, the census of 1962 disclosed that over half of all the sons of farmers had left the farms, or had abandoned agriculture as a career.[8]

The Italian labor force in agriculture was estimated at 8,500,000 in 1951; by 1966 it had fallen to 4,700,000. In the course of fifteen years it had declined by 3,800,000, or 45 percent.[9] The resulting impact on the age composition of rural families is indicated by a study of the 1,634,365 families registered with the Mutual Health Offices (the Casse Mutue) in

1965. In these farm families, which account for 11.6 of the total 13.2 million hectares of Italian farm land reported in the census of 1961, only 678,163 families, or 41.5 percent, had male members under age forty-nine at home.[10]

The full impact of these changes in European social structures is difficult for an American to appreciate. "We have communities where, for seven hundred years of record," a Polish sociologist pointed out to one of the authors, "farmers' sons have remained on the farm, barring wars. Now for the first time in our recorded history we find peasant sons who do not want to farm." Social stress and farm labor shortages are not the only consequences. The traditional peasant base for political parties is eroding away. Rural people are increasingly concerned with prospects for non-farm jobs. Their identification with real property is declining, their concern with job security in industry increasing.

Paralleling this rural change is an erosion of the traditional working class base for political parties of the Left. Industrial workers are acquiring cooperative apartments, or single-family houses, in increasing numbers. Their preoccupation with job security is accommodating to an unfamiliar identification with real property. The head-on clash of ideologies can be seen in the spectacle of Labour party-dominated city councils in England forced by their constituencies to sell public (council-built) houses to their working-class occupants, many of whom now demand and can pay for private housing. Jo Grimond, former leader of the British Liberal party, was led to observe that "The Labour Party has been busy sawing away the branch on which it used to sit. Its one certain achievement is to have devalued the trade unions."[11] The more relevant observation might have been to point out that social and economic changes were beating at the branches on which all the traditional political parties used to sit.

It is these changes that arouse uncertainty about the political future of European integration. The issue is not simply that of asking that national sovereignty give way to the demands of technology, trade, and the search for markets. The problem is rather that of an alteration in political structure so profound, and so recent, that the momentum of traditional political parties is prolonging their grasp on power long after the roots of that power have withered away.

The Integration of People and Institutions: Migrant Labor and Education

One may strongly suggest that Europeanization has been bolstered by the unplanned but mutually reinforcing developments in migration of labor across national boundaries and in formal education. Two dimensions are involved. One relates to types of manpower: the immigrant laborer, often unskilled, and the highly qualified or highly skilled person. The second dimension divides into two parts: essentially economic aspects of manpower development including "freedom of establishment" and non-economic activities in formal education.

The first decade after the end of World War II saw the relocation in Europe of many refugees — the French, Belgians, Dutch, and other Allied nationals who had been forced into German "work camps" during the war. In the next decade the flow of workers across boundaries was not the movement of captive peoples. Where Germany of the Third Reich had forcibly moved workers to serve industry, after 1955 West Germany attracted growing numbers who voluntarily moved from such labor-exporting countries of southern Europe as Greece, Spain, Turkey, and Yugoslavia. France did likewise, drawing primarily from Italy although large numbers of its migrant workers came from Spain and Portugal, while migrants came to Switzerland mainly from southern Italy and secondarily from Spain. Swedish industry employed immigrants, skilled and unskilled, who came from the Baltic countries now absorbed politically into the Soviet Union. A continuing labor shortage led to an agreement among the Scandinavian nations for free movement of labor, and they came to rely most heavily on Finland for unskilled labor, although significant numbers of workers came also from Italy, Greece, Yugoslavia, and Turkey. The Benelux countries drew on labor from all of southern Europe, as well as from Asia and Africa to a lesser degree. While most of these migrant workers think of themselves as moving only temporarily, as a means of accumulating savings or obtaining vocational experience, and expect to return to their home countries, most of them also intellectually entertain the possibility that they will remain permanently in the country to which they move.

An important influence on their Europeanization is the social services that are available in a host country. By 1966 the European Social Fund of the EEC had allocated $31.7 million for the retraining and resettlement of 454,000 workers. In 1967 and 1968 plans were being made to extend the fund's activities in establishing a European-wide system of industrial health care and safety. Although this has yet to be realized, the outlook is hopeful. In this same optimistic vein Europeanization can be said to be advanced by the progress the EEC has made in the over-all improvement of working and living conditions for migrant workers. The Treaty of Rome set the end of 1964 as the date at which there should be equal pay for men and women. Steps toward free movement of workers have taken place. Additionally, social security for migrant workers has been established under existing national laws, and there are plans for harmonization of certain social security provisions. A sobering note must, however, be registered for the immediate future. The EEC Commission lacks both legal powers and funds to go much further, and future developments will depend on authorization and funds that may be granted by member states acting through the Council.

Our guess is that the social objectives of the Treaty of Rome and the economic objectives of the EEC and OECD will be realized. So, too, the weakness that has existed in the vocational guidance programs for migrant labor will be repaired if for no other reason than that the manpower forecasting and vocational guidance applicable to any European nation's labor force, including the worker from abroad, will be improved. Norway and Sweden have pointed the way: a nation's economic posture and the welfare of the individual are bettered when manpower forecasting and vocational guidance become more effective. If a country wishes to be in a strong competitive position the usefulness of manpower planning and vocational-general guidance is a foregone conclusion.

One must face the question of the extent to which the people of Europe today are strengthening their conception of themselves as Europeans and not merely as Frenchmen, Germans, Swedes, and so on. In relation to migrant workers, the question might be phrased: to what extent do host people accept migrants on the same terms as fellow nationals? The answer is clear: there are deficiencies in every country. France and Sweden have made significant formal efforts to promote acceptance as public opinion poll data show, yet even in France the efforts seem limited by a proviso that the immigrant must become "francisized." While only Switzerland has chosen the conscious path of rejection to the point of overt and explicit chauvinism, frankness demands acknowledging that rejection exists to some extent in all the immigration countries. Few nationals of these countries think of immigrants as really interchangeable with themselves.

Those who seek Europeanness should take heart in the evidence that indicates migrants generally have come to feel at home in their host country. Relatively few so far have returned to the country from which they emigrated. Admittedly some do return with bitterness, but on the whole the migrants seem to tolerate and, at times, accept their hosts. And it may also be said that the host peoples on the whole tolerate and accept the migrants.

The free mobility of labor will continue. By the end of 1969 the workers of all EEC member states were to be assured access to paid employment in each member state on the same terms as nationals. The EEC Commission has proposed the institution of a community-wide identity card for all workers to replace the existing work permits given to foreign workers. The OECD has advocated the liberalization of worker movement. Although one cannot say that in the future there is likely to be as much migration of workers seeking positions in European countries other than their own,[12] it will almost certainly not become negligible.

When we turn to the question of free mobility and cross-national acceptance of those with highly developed skills or professional qualifications, the harmonization of education becomes an important issue. Many of the pan-European organizations have engaged vigorously in activities designed to bring about the harmonization of European education that would make "freedom of establishment" a reality. This has not yet come about. But economic pressures, as well as the influence of organizations, are forcing curricular and institutional reforms that are leading in the direction of equivalent educational standards.

The economic rationale for unrestricted movement within the European community of those with special skills should be obvious. Country A needs doctors in a center where there are a number of large industries — if adequate medical services are not provided the health of the workers will suffer, causing an increasing loss of manhours, and it will be difficult to attract to the area the new workers needed by the expanding industry. But this nation has few medical schools and they cannot turn out enough doctors to fill all the nation's needs. Country B on the other hand has excellent medical resources — both teachers and practitioners — but certain of its industries are faltering for lack of chemical engineers, which country C is training at a rate more rapid than its own industry can absorb efficiently. And so on. If those educated in one country are free to move to another where their particular skills are most needed, and are permitted to put their skills to work there without undue hindrance, there will be economic benefits not only for the host country but for the community of nations of which it is a part.

In some fields, of course, shortages of skills are characteristic of all or most European countries. This is true especially in the scientific and technological fields, putting the whole European community at a disadvantage in relation to the United States. Efforts to close the technology gap in education are being made throughout Europe. These efforts are part of a general movement toward more flexibility in educational curriculums and institutions — a movement driven by ideological as well as economic forces. Among the former are recognition of the right of all young people to equality of educational opportunity and acknowledgment of the need to lengthen the period of compulsory education to ensure better preparation for all citizens so that not only will they be able to make a living but they will lead a more rewarding life and fulfill adequately their civic responsibilities.

Forecasting is always hazardous but some educated guesses about the future integration of European peoples, educationally and occupationally, may be essayed. We think that there will be a falloff in the migration across national frontiers of unskilled laborers, semiskilled workmen, and skilled craftsmen or artisans. (Intracountry movement of the unskilled and semiskilled will see a continuing flow of workers and their families from rural to urban-suburban areas.) The demand for technicians in Europe will expand. Inevitably this will continue to stimulate growth in technical or applied-science studies in secondary and higher education and a lengthening of schooling for ever greater numbers of young people. Constraints of class, sex, or place of birth on educational opportunity will yield to the combined assault of these economic demands and the ideological demands of democratic society.

Concretely this will show up in at least five ways: (1) Such countries as Italy will develop middle schools to bridge primary and upper-secondary schooling, using the middle school to encourage pupils to remain in school. (2) There will be more vocational guidance to the end of having pupils who might succeed in technical education continue on into such studies. (3) The comprehensive school pattern will become increasingly prevalent in the nonsocialist countries of Europe. (4) The examination system in European education will be modified. Reform of the famous, or infamous, secondary-school leaving examinations probably will be in the direction of making them all-European instead of national and a certification of secondary-school accomplishment rather than a deliberately limiting mechanism for admission to a national university. In higher education there will be a move to increase the frequency of examinations within a single course, thus decreasing the effect on a student's academic career of failure on terminal comprehensive examinations. Reform of testing and examining in the European primary schools, secondary schools, and universities is long overdue. (5) Pedagogical research into the processes of learning and, then, into tests and measures will increase and will buttress reforms of the examination system. Some European countries, notably Germany, will probably try turning higher education into a series of ladders, some lasting only two years, any one of which a student might climb with the knowledge that completion of that particular ladder will give him a certificate of specialization useful in the job market of the highly qualified.

A guess is that revision of course examinations in higher education or the awarding of certificates at various stages along the way to completion of higher education will not fully allay student unrest. Why are so many European university students pressing for a greater degree of participation in the making of curricular policy? Primarily, they seem to want three things: greater prestige for applied science, more attention to training needed in the job market, and more opportunity for work in a department with several faculty of professorial rank instead of restriction to a project dominated by one or two senior professors. We think the students will succeed.

A Closing Note

The driving force for European integration has passed through distinct stages in the postwar years. Throughout the late 1940's and 1950's the Cold War clearly dominated. The West German currency reform of 1947 dramatized the separation of the two Germanys, leading as it did to the Berlin blockade of 1948–49, the airlift, and the subsequent chain of events that culminated in the erection of the Berlin wall in August 1961. Virtually all the transnational European institutions of the 1960's — the ECSC, the EEC, EFTA, the OECD — trace their birth to this time of tension between East and West.

This tension slackened but did not disappear in the 1960's. It was recycled by the invasion of Czechoslovakia by Warsaw Pact troops in August 1968. In the theater of Europe, this act appeared almost as if on cue. At a time when European preoccupation with national crisis was dampening the momentum of integration, the Soviets obligingly stepped in from the wings with a sword-rattling reminder of the genesis of European union.

But this shock to dreams of détente occurred in a Europe that had discovered in the meantime a new reason for integration: the technological gap. In retrospect, this motive force can be read into some of the arguments for European integration of the 1950's but did not then have driving power. It took on that power in the 1960's. The fear—real or imagined — of American dominance gave a new rationale to drives for educational reform, for the creation of truly European-wide businesses, and for the reduction of trade barriers.

These drives also generated new fears. How can cross-national integration promote cross-cultural understanding? How can one have economic integration without causing cultural disintegration? These questions loom large in a Europe in which tortured egos have both personal and national embodiment. It is these overstretched egos — French, Austrian, British, Italian, Spanish — that prevent much of the needed development in Europe today. "For in the great systems of conduct preceding that of modernity, it is precisely ego that had to be renounced," as Philip Rieff reminds us.[13] This process of renunciation is still in its infancy in strategic parts of Europe. And it is when viewed in this light that we can find much to admire in the political change that took place in England in the early 1960's. One of the most deeply rooted aspects of nationalism concerns the politics of a food supply. Guaranteeing a food supply has been a key element — perhaps the key element — of the national policies of England, France, and Germany since 1914. Of these three leading nations on the Western European scene, only England could not possibly survive on its own domestic food output. France could survive handily on its own food resources and West Germany too, though not without some

severe belt-tightening. But not England. The "renunciation of the national ego" reflected in the British bid to join the Common Market is thus
of a different order from that involved when six countries joined in signing the Treaty of Rome in 1957. In nationalistic terms, and in terms of
food politics, much greater risks are involved for the United Kingdom.

It may well require the combined force of threats from East *and* West
to weld an integrated Europe out of egocentric nations. The important
point in 1968–69 was that Europe was entering the next stage of the struggle for integration with an expanded catalogue of motive forces. And it
enters that stage without Charles de Gaulle in a position of power; there
is thus a lessened personal obstacle to integration. The pace should now
become faster, though along the way there are likely to be many hurdles.
In the conventional symbolism, the sticks have been augmented, that's
clear. It is not so clear that the carrots of integration have grown and multiplied. But that takes time, and peace. To provide both is the challenge
of the 1970's to those who would promote an integrated Europe — or for
that matter, a more nearly integrated world.

NOTES AND SELECTED READINGS

Notes

Chapter 2. Anniversaries and Balance Sheets

1. *New York Times,* June 6, 1947, p. 2.

2. A most useful general reference is P.E.P., *European Unity: A Survey of the European Organisations* (London: Allen and Unwin, 1968). This volume also provides information on European organizations not discussed here: the Economic Commission for Europe, the Council of Europe, the Western Economic Union.

3. Richard Mayne, *The Community of Europe* (London: Gollancz, 1963), p. 96.

4. From a speech given at Harvard University on May 22, 1961; reprinted in *Community Topics,* No. 2 (London: European Community Information Service, 1961).

5. An excellent discussion of different types of economic organization is found in U. W. Kitzinger, *The Politics and Economics of European Integration* (New York: Praeger, 1963). For an informative presentation of organizational structure and decision-making processes in the EEC, see Emile Nöel, *How the European Economic Community's Institutions Work,* in *Community Topics,* No. 11 (Brussels: European Community Information Service, 1963); Leon N. Lindberg, *The Political Dynamics of European Economic Integration* (Stanford, Calif.: Stanford University Press, 1963); and Henry G. Aubrey, *Atlantic Economic Cooperation: The Case of the OECD* (New York: Praeger, 1967).

6. When Jean Monnet, first president of the High Authority of the ECSC, resigned in 1955, he organized his Action Committee for the United States of Europe. This committee gathered together ". . . a solid and sober group of thirty-three leading representatives of all shades of authoritative political and trade-union opinion, except the extreme right and the Communists . . ." not all of whom were staunch backers of all integrative efforts. "By prodding governments and winning over parliamentary and trade-union opinion, there can be no doubt at all that Monnet and the Action Committee played a decisive part in securing the adoption and ratification of the Euratom and the Common Market Treaties." Mayne, *The Community of Europe,* p. 110.

7. See Emile Benoit, *Europe at Sixes and Sevens: The Common Market, the Free Trade Association, and the United States* (New York: Columbia University Press, 1961), p. 80. Differing views on bureaucracy are represented in the administrative apparatus of EFTA and the EEC. EFTA, with headquarters in Geneva, has remained a modest organization. The EEC (the much more complex nature of its operations must be admitted) has grown consistently, and the total number of its employees on March 31, 1968, was over 3500.

8. *Free Trade in EFTA,* U.K. Board of Trade Journal Supplement, January 6, 1967, p. 52.

9. See *Le Monde,* July 10 and 11, 1967, for comments on the French position. For a broader discussion see *The European Free Trade Association and the Crisis*

of European Integration (London: Michael Joseph for the Graduate Institute of International Studies, 1968). See also "Where Is EFTA Going," *EFTA Reporter*, November 29, 1968, p. 3.

10. See the discussion in the *ECSC Twelfth General Report* (Brussels, 1964), Chapter 3, "The Common Market for Coal and Steel."

11. The ECSC notes in *ibid.*, pp. 322–324 that labor market data are incomplete to the point where perhaps nothing is known about the destiny of at least a quarter of those whose employment has been terminated.

12. *Ibid.*, p. 123.

13. "Rationalization" has indeed taken place, in coal, in the phasing out of high-cost mines and in the emphasis upon technological innovation. For example, the underground output per man/shift in the community's hard-coal mines was 1413 kilograms in 1953; by 1963 it had risen to 2272. But United States mining technology has also kept pace so that, for example, American coal was as competitive in the mid-sixties as it was in 1955. "Rationalization" is also used, however, to refer to enterprise size as it relates to efficiency and cost. Here the charge has been that the ECSC competitive policy has, in steel at least, kept enterprise size below the optimal, and too many "inefficient" producers remain in production. The financial difficulties of a Belgian company — Cockerill-Ougrée — as reported in late 1966 epitomize this problem. A merger was approved between this company and Forges de la Providence. The total capacity of the new firm will be close to five million tons. It will be instructive to see if the situation improves with this more efficient-sized firm. See, for coal, "Ruhr Coal Mines Band Together in Attempt to Salvage Industry," *New York Times*, November 28, 1968, p. 75.

14. *The Economist*, Vol. 221, No. 6429 (November 18, 1966), p. 843.

15. The *Annual Reports* of Euratom seem to corroborate this. There is a wistful quality in the reports suggesting realization that much is going on with which its program should be concerned but which is falling outside its purview. See, for example, "Introduction" to *Euratom 1965: Eighth General Report* (Brussels).

16. From a speech before the European Parliament, December 20, 1961 (Doc. EUR/ C/ 4331/ 61–62, Euratom Commission).

17. Witness the 1966 dispute between Euratom and France on who would pay for the 180 kilograms of plutonium purchased from the United States. Etienne Hirsch in *Le Monde* (November 25, 1966) suggested that one of the real difficulties with Euratom was that it divided research monies among more research centers than were really efficient.

18. Don Cook, "Europe's Cooking with A-Power, but Who'll Watch the Pot?" *International Herald Tribune*, April 17, 1967, p. 5.

19. "Free Traders and Split Atoms," *The Economist*, Vol. 223, No. 6451 (April 15, 1967), p. 244.

20. For a discussion see Hans von der Groeben, *Competition Policy in the Common Market*, in *Community Topics*, No. 19 (Brussels: 1965), European Community Information Service, and D. L. McLachlan and D. Swann, *Competition Policy in the European Community* (Oxford: Oxford University Press, 1968). The following comments are based upon this source and upon the *General Reports* of the EEC Commission.

21. The best known example in this connection is the Grundig-Consten case, involving an exclusive dealing agreement and absolute territorial protection. The Commission found this agreement contrary to Article 85 of the Treaty of Rome. See, for details, the *EEC Eighth General Report on the Activities of the Community* (Brussels: EEC Commission, 1965), pp. 68–70.

22. Press release of the Commission of the EEC, Brussels, March 20, 1967.

23. The reader interested in analyses of the economic impacts of the formation of the EEC may refer to Alexander Lamfalussy, writing in *Lloyd's Bank Review*, October 1961; R. L. Major, "The Common Market: Production and Trade," *National Institute Economic Review*, August 1962, pp. 24–36; and *Intégration Européenne et Réalité Economique* (Bruges: College of Europe, 1964).

24. See *Preliminary Draft of the First Medium-Term Economic Policy Programme* (Brussels: EEC, March 25, 1966).

25. *EEC Eighth General Report*, p. 18.

26. Treaty of Rome, Article 75.

27. For critical comments see the articles by Paul Fabra in *Le Monde*, June 29 and 30, 1965.

28. One side effect, however, of American direct investment in the EEC countries — discussed later in Chapter 4 — is that the competitiveness of the "large" United States firm may force the development of multicountry enterprises. An excellent discussion of "industrial strategy" is found in a four-part series by Pierre Drouin which appeared in *Le Monde*, September 21–24, 1966.

29. See *The Sunday Times* (London), March 19, 1967, p. 25.

30. *The Economist*, Vol. 223, No. 6451 (April 15, 1967), p. 244.

31. Lindberg, *The Political Dynamics of European Economic Integration*, pp. 10–11.

32. Reproduced by the Commission of the EEC, mimeographed, 5569/PP/67-E.

33. Useful discussions of the crisis are found in Miriam A. Camps, *European Unification in the Sixties: From the Veto to the Crisis* (New York: McGraw-Hill, 1966), and John Newhouse, *Collision in Brussels: The Common Market Crisis of 30 June 1965* (London: Faber and Faber, 1967).

34. John Lambert writing in *The Sunday Times* (London), July 2, 1967.

35. *New York Times*, March 6, 1946, p. 4.

36. See Michael Kaser, *Comecon: Integration Problems of the Planned Economies* (London and New York: Oxford University Press, 1965).

37. An address by J. Robert Schaetzel, American ambassador to the European communities, to the Union International Club at Frankfurt, Germany, March 15, 1967. *U.S.A. Documents* (Public Affairs Office, United States Mission to the European Communities).

Chapter 3. The Western Crisis of the Sixties

1. In general this chapter will not offer citations to the rich literature about the affairs of the Atlantic world which has become available in recent years. These works are obviously indispensable to students of the problems dealt with in these pages and those most pertinent are listed in the Selected Readings. Citations will be confined to instances of direct quotation, the sources of polls, and some recent articles.

2. Experiences the writer had during visits to Germany from 1963 to 1966 confirmed this.

3. Alexander Werth, *De Gaulle* (New York: Harper and Row, 1965), p. 57.

4. *Major Addresses, Statements and Press Conferences of General Charles de Gaulle, May 1958–January 1964* (New York: French Embassy, Press and Information Division, 1964), p. 223.

5. *Ibid*, p. 123.

6. As related by Professor Carl J. Burkhardt, June 1958.

7. Marc Ullman, "De Gaulle's Secret Diplomacy," *Interplay*, Vol. I, No. 2 (August–September 1967), p. 41.

8. J. R. Tournoux, *La Tragédie du Général* (Paris: Plon, 1967), p. 575. The author is grateful to Professor James M. Erdmann of the University of Denver for making available to him an as yet unpublished study on de Gaulle and the Anglo-American leadership on the eve of D-Day.

9. The writer labors under the handicap of not being authorized to identify specifically a number of strategically placed persons whose comments seem to deserve quotation. He begs the indulgence of the reader when he presents such comment with no more than a general indication of the source.

10. Tournoux, *La Tragédie du Général*, p. 467.

11. This has been the experience, for example, of Alexandre Marc of the Comité International de Formation Européenne.

12. In illustration, Jacques Duhamel of the political Center related how six months before the election he had been in the Far East and had had long talks with Mao and Ho Chi Minh. When he talked to the voters about his experience, they listened like people who are told interesting things about a world that is far removed. Their questions almost without exception dealt with domestic problems. Another political figure, a senator, told how he simply could not get a crowd to come out to listen to him about *anything*. Yet he was reelected with a large majority.

13. Stefan Kisielewski, "De Gaulle Abroad . . . Poland," *Interplay*, Vol. I, No. 4 (November 1967), pp. 40–41.

14. As related in each instance by a French friend intimately associated with the affairs of several organizations working for such causes.

15. This conclusion is founded on the unanimous testimony of French, American, and German acquaintances of the author who had personal contact with de Gaulle in 1967. One German who was present at talks during de Gaulle's visit to Bonn in July stressed that, though he "disagreed with every word" he heard de Gaulle speak, there was every evidence of undiminished mental powers.

16. This survey involved a three-week tour of the provinces, talks with nearly one hundred persons representing every walk of life and political orientation, and the preparation of a substantial report which has been seen by the present writer.

17. As in an extensive discussion with some twenty French journalists in the spring of 1966.

18. Tournoux, *La tragédie du Général*, pp. 393, 432.

19. Karl W. Deutsch and others, *France, Germany and the Western Alliance: A Study of Elite Attitudes on European Integration and World Politics* (New York: Scribner's, 1967), p. 72. This set of polls involved 320 carefully selected French and German respondents, all "highly placed persons in public and private life." An argument for a considerable continued validity of the study is that it sought to concentrate on fundamental attitudes rather than on immediate concerns. Of course, even basic opinions can change rapidly and there is much to support the view that between 1964 and June 1967 French attitudes underwent much further accommodation to de Gaulle's specific policies, despite the fact that support for the idea of "Europe" increased. Still, it is the impression of the writer, based on conversations with many who had been polled in 1964, that the polls retained considerable significance. In the second half of 1967, of course, there was a shift to a more unfavorable estimate of Gaullist foreign policy.

20. The present writer did not visit Rumania and the statement above is based on the observations of Philip M. Raup, the member of the research group who spent considerable time in that country.

21. This issue was discussed with a number of German military men, of whom, since he is now retired, it is possible to mention General Heinz Trettner, until the summer of 1966 inspector general (commander-in-chief) of the Federal Army.

22. It is noteworthy that the author made this categorical statement in addresses before five French audiences, and often repeated it in discussion periods, and never encountered a word of contradiction, even the Gaullists present preferring to pass over it in silence.

23. The Soviet Union had always been exempt from the Hallstein Doctrine. This exemption was then extended to the states of the Warsaw Pact, when, in the debate over reestablishing diplomatic relations with Rumania at the end of 1966, it was argued that these nations had really had no choice but to follow the Soviet lead in their relations with East Germany. Thus the last real nail in the coffin of the Hallstein Doctrine was resumption of diplomatic relations with Yugoslavia, which acted under no such compulsion from Moscow.

24. As related to the writer by a member of Brandt's research group. The number of older expellees who would wish to return to their homes was reckoned to be at the most two to three hundred thousand of the ten million expelled.

25. Especially propagated by such nationally prominent pundits as James Reston and Walter Lippmann and such congressional figures as Senator Claiborne Pell, all of them naturally and properly eager to come up with prescriptions for the lessening of pressures at Berlin.

26. This was certainly one of the less practical proposals. Other considerations aside, a customs union between capitalist and Communist states would appear an economic anomaly.

27. Insofar as Schollwer's proposals did not leak to the press, this account is based on a confidential report made available to the author.

28. The issue of the SDP-SED debate aroused wide national interest and was closely covered in the German press. On Ulbricht's motives, the writer has had access to one confidential analysis by a specialist on the East German scene.

29. Tournoux, *La Tragédie du Général*, p. 390.

30. As one of Adenauer's ministers put it to the writer: "Adenauer had a veritable de Gaulle complex."

31. One member of the negotiating group, currently ambassador to a major European capital, said to the writer: "We were all shocked at how Adenauer was misleading de Gaulle." This reaction of Adenauer's associates was confirmed by another member of the group.

32. As related by a French cabinet minister who was present at the meeting.

33. Over recent years, many Germans have expressed the feeling that the estrangement between France and the United States was, after all, a lovers' quarrel which could be quickly forgotten. For France and Germany a new discordance would make matters worse than they had been before 1963.

34. Much of this conception was outlined by de Gaulle to André Philip in 1958 almost coincident with his return to power: "Relations with the East must be improved and we must continue to work toward German reunification. But this reunification cannot be achieved by American military pressure on Russia. With Russian consent, a détente must be initiated with Eastern Europe. The Rapacki Plan is not ripe but it is a step in the right direction." Tournoux, *La Tragédie du Général*, p. 284.

35. *Ibid.*, p. 462.

36. *Ibid.*, p. 499.

37. See also the discussion by Robert H. Beck of one organization's work, p. 175.

38. One top member of the NATO secretariat put it in this form in the autumn of 1966: "When Schröder says 'no' it can be like a slap in the face. In contrast, the French ambassador here says 'no' every day of the week and is the most popular man in the place."

39. Karl W. Deutsch and others, *France, Germany and the Western Alliance*, p. 67. The later conversations of the writer with many of the respondents to that survey confirmed these basic viewpoints, though the alliance had so much faded out in the two intervening years. By some it was described as no longer existing in any real sense.

40. *Ibid.*, p. 72.

41. The Italian Nenni Socialists did not join until after 1963.

42. For discussion from sharply different viewpoints of the current function and potential future of the Action Committee see the articles by Ian Davidson and François Duchene in *Interplay*, Vol. I, No. 4 (November 1967), pp. 11–14, and No. 5 (December 1967), pp. 17–19.

43. Karl W. Deutsch and others, *France, Germany and the Western Alliance*, p. 299.

44. The respective favorable percentages for polls taken in 1962, 1964, and 1966 were 34, 42, 55. Jacques-René Rabier, "The European Idea and National Public Opinion," *Government and Opposition*, Vol. 2, No. 3 (April–July 1967), p. 447.

45. Karl W. Deutsch and others, *France, Germany and the Western Alliance*, pp. 66–67, 71–72.

46. *Ibid.*, p. 150.

47. Tournoux, *La Tragédie du Général*, pp. 321–322. During the spring campaign of 1967, Couve de Murville professed to an interlocutor that he had known since 1958 that de Gaulle intended to leave NATO. *Ibid.*, p. 320n.

48. Thus a NATO "course conference" in January 1958 presented to the nowise reluctant Secretary General Spaak a resolution, drafted by the present writer, recommending a string of measures aimed at promoting this goal.

49. Karl W. Deutsch and others, *France, Germany and the Western Alliance*, p. 72.

50. One German general described as "moving" how the French officers sometimes seemed to cling to their German associates. A French political analyst who made a study of the breakdown of the vote in Paris districts after the 1967 spring election concluded that the trend was strongly anti-Gaullist in those in which there lived many officers, active or retired. It is, of course, impossible to differentiate between anti-Gaullist feeling of officers due to the NATO issue and that due to the General's renunciation of Algeria. One general of the writer's acquaintance, no less a personage than commander of the French NATO contingent, was dismissed and imprisoned for two years in the most arbitrary fashion following his expression of pro-NATO sentiments in personal conversation with de Gaulle.

51. These reflections are based on conversations with general and other officers from France, Germany, Norway, Denmark, and the United States. Perhaps the most helpful and enlightening was a meeting with General Trettner. May it be noted that the now abolished Standing Group, directly representing the national chiefs of staff, was not regarded by others in SHAPE as sharing the "integrated" spirit.

52. Général d'Armée Ailleret, "Défense 'Dirigée' ou Défense 'Tous Azimuts,' " in *Revue de Défense Nationale*, 23rd year (December 1967), pp. 1923–32.

53. The writer happened to be in Bonn the week after the appearance of the Ailleret article and was privileged to talk at some length with a highly placed military authority as well as with representatives of other German government agencies.

54. Hans Stercken, *De Gaulle hat gesagt . . . Eine Dokumentation seiner Politik* (Stuttgart: Seewald Verlag, 1967), p. 131.

55. Though it is hard to take seriously, there were some who feared that de Gaulle had his eyes on an independent Quebec for that purpose.

56. See the trenchant article by Alastair Buchan, "Battening Down Vauban's Hatches," *Interplay*, Vol. 1, No. 10 (May 1968), pp. 4–7. Of extraordinary interest for critical trends in French opinion is the article of Edmund Combaux, "Défense Tous Azimuts? Oui, mais . . ." *Revue de Défense Nationale*, 24th year (November 1968), pp. 1600–18.

Since these pages were written the erosion of Gaullist defense concepts has continued apace, signaled dramatically almost coincident with the General's departure from power by another article in the *Revue de Défense Nationale*, this time by Chief of Staff Michel Fourquet (it was reprinted in *Atlantic Quarterly*, Vol. 7, No. 2 (Summer 1969), pp. 241–254). There a renewed emphasis upon an "Eastern" enemy and a degree of accommodation to the doctrine of "flexible response" indicated virtual abandonment of the "défense à tous azimuts."

57. It is justifiable to ask, which Europe? There can be no doubt about the Common Market grouping, and then, by gravitational pull, the remaining states of Western Europe. Britain, to be sure, would have been more of a problem, but economic factors would have made it virtually impossible for her to stand aside.

58. See the discussion by John G. Turnbull, pp. 17–20.

59. *Newsweek*, March 11, 1968, p. 50.

60. See Chapter 2.

61. The principal reactions thus far have been in Italy. In France the government-controlled or government-influenced news media played these developments down as much as possible. The only evidence of concern in the summer of 1967 was a newspaper article by General Emile-Marie Béthouart.

Chapter 4. The Course of Economic Integration

1. Special issues will be treated in depth in separate monographs.

2. These three themes — the more favorable cultural attitudes in the United States, the greater amount of institutional integration, and the higher degree of policy harmonization — ran through interviews the writer had with several score Europeans, although of course there were variations of expression. He concluded that these forces are conducive to higher-level economic performance. For an analysis of other relevant factors — which some economists hold to be equally or more important — see Sidney Dell, "Economic Integration and the American Example," and Irving B. Kravis, "The U.S. Trade Position and the Common Market," both in Lawrence B. Krause, ed., *The Common Market: Progress and Controversy* (Englewood Cliffs, N.J.: Prentice-Hall, 1964).

3. Edward F. Denison, assisted by John-Pierre Poullier, *Why Growth Rates Differ: Postwar Experience in Nine Western Countries* (Washington, D.C.: Brookings, 1967). This volume, which compares the performance of the United States with that of eight European countries (Belgium, Denmark, France, Germany, Netherlands, Norway, the United Kingdom, and Italy, of which the first seven constitute northwest Europe), is a landmark of economic analysis and a most necessary source for anyone undertaking economic research on Europe.

4. *Ibid.*, p. 333.

5. A useful introduction to this topic is Peter M. Gutmann, ed., *Economic Growth: An American Problem* (Englewood Cliffs, N.J.: Prentice-Hall, 1964).

6. See OECD, *Economic Growth, 1960–1970* (Paris: OECD, 1966), p. 19. This volume, along with the work by Denison, is a basic source for anyone seeking full understanding of European developments. Another useful volume, which portrays a much longer historical time span, is Dudley Dillard, *Economic Development of the North Atlantic Community* (Englewood Cliffs, N.J.: Prentice-Hall, 1967). Also see Walter Krause and F. John Mathis, eds., *International Economics and Business: Selected Readings* (Boston: Houghton Mifflin, 1968).

7. The U.S. Council of Economic Advisers estimated (in reports made in 1965) that of the 4.7 percent annual increase in output for the United States, 1960–65, 3.5 to 3.75 percent came from underlying growth factors and .75 to 1.00 percent from an increase in the utilization of capacity — for example from a reduction in unemployment. In contrast, the EEC figure of 4.9 percent was almost entirely a consequence of the underlying growth rule; there was little in the way of expansion.

8. The level of unemployment may be used — with caution — as an indicator for the level of underutilization of capacity. See *Economic Growth, 1960–1970* for comments.

9. *Economic Report of the President* (Washington, D.C.: GPO, 1963), p. 28.

10. For comments relative to the American scene, see the *Economic Report of the President*, 1961 and subsequent years, and Walter W. Heller, *New Dimensions of Political Economy* (Cambridge, Mass.: Harvard University Press, 1966).

11. See Denison, *Why Growth Rates Differ*, pp. 7–11.

12. This is approximately the difference between indexes of national income for Europe and the United States respectively for 1960 (using European price weights). See Denison, *Why Growth Rates Differ*, p. 22. (Denison does not raise this percentage problem in his analysis, and other critics take an opposite point of view: that larger economies have been growing more rapidly than smaller ones. Since the author has not seen a definitive analysis of this problem he merely calls it to the reader's attention as a controversial issue.)

13. Denison, *Why Growth Rates Differ*, pp. 296–301. See also Chapter 20 in which Denison discusses "residual factors" relating to growth.

14. In his European research, the writer found no comprehensive analyses equivalent to those made by Denison. There were, however, many "qualitative" statements made to the effect that reductions in agricultural employment and self-employment contributed to output increases. In addition, some quantitative efforts

have been made to relate output increases to the formation of the EEC. One study suggests that output was higher by 15–20 percent because of the development of the EEC. See the papers by P. J. Verdoorn and F. J. M. Meyer Zu Schlochtern and by F. J. Clavaux in *Intégration Européenne et Réalité Economique* (Bruges: College of Europe, 1964).

15. Indeed, Donald D. Hornig, scientific adviser to Lyndon B. Johnson, noted in Paris, June 28, 1967, that "the series of [technological] differences that exist is not in innovation or ability . . . the technological disparity arises because these innovations are not properly exploited . . . it is almost a marketing problem." *International Herald Tribune*, June 29, 1967, p. 7. (One reader of this chapter in manuscript suggested that the definition of technology used here is too broad and blurred. The writer continues to feel, however, on the basis of his European exposure, that the broader view is the more helpful, given the European situation.)

16. See *Preliminary Draft of the First Medium-Term Economic Policy Programme* (Brussels: EEC Medium-Term Economic Policy Committee, March 25, 1966), pp. 5, 6, 7. See also *The Economist*, Vol. 222, No. 6441 (February 4, 1967), pp. 426–427.

17. *EEC Eighth General Report on the Activities of the Community* (Brussels: EEC Commission, 1965), p. 158.

18. Article by Henry R. Lieberman in *International Herald Tribune*, March 14, 1967, pp. 1, 10.

19. *Report of the Conference on Transatlantic Technological Imbalance and Collaboration* (sponsored by the Scientific/Technological Committee of the North Atlantic Assembly and the Foreign Policy Research Institute of the University of Pennsylvania, held at Deauville, France, May 25–28, 1967; *Report* dated June 1, 1967). See also, for a useful summary, James Brian Quinn, "Technological Competition: Europe vs. U.S.," *Atlantic Community Quarterly*, Winter 1966–67, pp. 549–572. Possibly the best general sources on technology this writer has come across are Edwin Mansfield, *The Economics of Technological Change* and *Industrial Research and Technological Innovation* (both New York: Norton, 1968).

20. Jean Piriac, "Des Réponses à Court Terme," in *Agenor: Revue Européenne*, 1967, No. 2, pp. 32–35. (This article is part of a feature series on the technological gap.)

21. See C. Freeman and A. Young, *The Research and Development Effort in Western Europe, North America and the Soviet Union* (Paris: OECD, 1965), pp. 33–34.

22. Jean-Michel Wagret, "Vers un Plan Marshall des Brevets d'Invention," *Revue de Marche Commun*, April 1967, p. 257. (Other tabulations in this article are worth inspection.)

23. *The Times* (London), June 22, 1967, p. 14. (The data were provided by the minister of technology; it was noted they should be "used with caution.")

24. C. T. Lanham, "Some Observations on the American Business Presence in Europe," paper given at the Brussels conference marking the twentieth anniversary of the Marshall Plan, Brussels, June 1967, p. 11.

25. "Competition" is, to be sure, a complex issue. At the same time the European is expressing his fears about the American thrust, the U.S. Congress is considering additional protective measures for American industry, the need for which is viewed as arising from the Kennedy Round tariff agreements.

26. For the view that research and development can, in certain instances, be conducted on a small scale, see "Comments" of F. M. Scherer in *Industrial Organization and Public Policy: Selected Readings*, ed. Werner Sichel (Boston: Houghton Mifflin, 1967), pp. 246–260.

27. *Report of the Conference on Transatlantic Technological Imbalance and Collaboration*, pp. 13–23.

28. See Agence Internationale d'Information pour la Presse, Daily Bulletin No. 2648, March 23, 1967.

29. Lanham, "Some Observations on the American Business Presence in Europe," p. 15.

30. Hendrik Casimir, quoted in *Time*, January 13, 1967, p. 31.

31. This hypothesis was first suggested by M. A. Lamfalussy, director and member of the Executive Committee, Banque de Bruxelles, Maitre de Conferences in the University of Louvain. The hypothesis was frequently referred to in interviews, sometimes being associated with his name, other times stated as the profit squeeze.

32. The first was *The Development of a European Capital Market*, with a "Summary" (Brussels: EEC, November 1966). This is the "Segré report," named for Claudio Segré who chaired the inquiry group. While the report was published by the EEC Commission, it was the result of an "independent" expert study group and hence reflects only the opinions and conclusions of the experts. The second was Sidney E. Rolfe, *Capital Markets in Atlantic Economic Relationships* (Boulogne-sur-Seine, France: Atlantic Institute, April 1967). This volume resulted from a capital markets conference held at Cannes, January 1967. It builds upon the OECD capital market study, the third of these works, *Report in Improvement of Capital Markets* (Paris: OECD, 1967). A summary of the latter is found in "Improving the Workings of Capital Markets," *The OECD Observer*, April 1967, pp. 3–7.

33. Rolfe, *Capital Markets in European Economic Relationships*, p. 40. Italics in original.

34. *The Development of a European Capital Market*, p. XII.

35. *Ibid.*, p. XIV.

36. But, as Rolfe notes, there is a paradoxical side to all this: "The rate of savings is greatest in Japan which offers no savings inducements, but there the cultural pattern — bonus payments and a lag in consumption habits compared to income — supports savings." Rolfe, *Capital Markets in European Economic Relationships*, p. 40.

37. *The Development of a European Capital Market*, "Summary," pp. XV–XVI.

38. Rolfe, *Capital Markets in European Economic Relationships*, p. 41.

39. *The Economist*, Vol. 222, No. 6439 (January 21, 1967), p. 244. On the increasing share of public sector demand in the EEC in 1961: net issues to public and local authorities and state enterprises totaled 18 percent of all issues; by 1965 this had risen to 36 percent. (At the same time private corporate bond issues fell from 11 to 4 percent of total security issuances.) See Rolfe, *Capital Markets in European Economic Relationships*, Table 4, Appendix.

40. And as the Segré report notes: "This trend, however, involves a risk of Member States moving further and further away from convertibility."

41. As an example of increasing national action, West Germany introduced in 1967 a program which included, among other elements, "more federal borrowing" to revive a flaccid economy. Thus: "An increased [government] investment program financed by borrowing and aimed at such infrastructure projects as road building. . . ." See *International Herald Tribune*, July 5, 1967, p. 7. Later references for 1968–69 highlight this for other countries such as France.

42. As *The Economist* pointed out: "The technical adjustments needed for a harmonization of Europe's capital markets, however difficult to hammer out, can only follow decisions on [the] major political issues, for if the Segré report had stuck safely but ineffectually to the technicalities alone, some of the ministers of The Hague might not have complained . . . that the report 'went too far and too deep.'" *The Economist*, Vol. 222, No. 6439 (January 21, 1967), p. 244. See also "Issues of Foreign Loans in the Republic of Germany," *Monthly Report of the Deutsche Bundesbank*, Vol. 20, No. 4 (April 1968), pp. 3–9.

43. This has nothing to do with "marketing" as such: a single-country company *can* sell its products in other countries. What is relevant is the inherent dimension of the enterprise: multinational as against national.

44. The description of the procedures utilized in the formulation of policies is found in Chapter 2 above.

45. *Information Memo* on the Tenth General Report of the Commission of the EEC (mimeo.; Brussels: EEC Commission, June 1967), "Summary," p. 9.

46. For critical comment, see the articles by Paul Fabra in *Le Monde*, June 29–30, 1966.

47. *Information Memo*, "Summary," p. 9.

48. See EEC press release IP (66) 132, November 15, 1966. (At the October 1966 meetings the decision was reached to defer discussion on the rate structure problem — really at the heart of negotiations since the beginning.) For an informative analysis see James R. Nelson, "Transport Policies for European Economic Integration," *American Economic Review*, Vol. 58, No. 2 (May 1968), pp. 378–392.

49. EEC press release IP (66) 132, November 15, 1966, p. 22.

50. Ian Davidson, "A Right Little, Tight Little Continent," *Agenor: Revue Européenne*, 1967, No. 2, pp. 68–69. For a gloomy 1969 evaluation of the state of affairs in the EEC see "The EEC: Why It Needs a New Treaty," *The Economist*, Vol. 230, No. 6549 (March 1, 1969), pp. 63–70.

51. Certainly the Kennedy Round trade negotiations could be regarded as another important example of interaction with the outer world. But they are past, agreement has been reached, and while structural readjustments will undoubtedly result from the new tariff levels, the problem is different in nature from the investment issues.

52. And, incidentally, with the same kind of criticism in the United States that one hears in Europe today.

53. See Lawrence B. Krause, *European Economic Integration and the United States* (Washington, D.C.: Brookings, 1968), p. 124.

54. See Christopher Layton, "European Pigmies, American Giants," *Encounter*, April 1967, p. 4. An informative analysis is to be found in Charles P. Kindleberger, *American Business Abroad* (New Haven, Conn.: Yale University Press, 1969).

55. *Monthly Report of the Deutsche Bundesbank*, Vol. 17, No. 5 (May 1965), p. 15. See subsequent issues for other data.

56. For a summary — in much greater detail than given above — of investment data, see Christopher Layton, *Trans-Atlantic Investments* (Boulogne-sur-Seine, France: Atlantic Institute, 1966), Chapter 1.

57. Krause, *European Economic Integration and the United States*, pp. 136–139, suggests that such direct investment was possibly one to two billions greater than it would have been had EFTA and the EEC not been created.

58. For a discussion of many of these issues see *Le Défi Américain* (Paris: Denoël, 1967) by Jean-Jacques Servan-Schreiber; published in English as *The American Challenge* (New York: Atheneum, 1968). This widely quoted volume portrays American business in Europe as both hero and villain.

59. For example, members of the EEC appearing in New York in 1958–60 indicated in strong terms the rapidly expanding market developments taking place on the Continent and the attractiveness of them for foreign investment.

60. But even the French seem consistently inconsistent. On June 29, 1967, French Finance Minister Michel Debré stated that France need not fear the foreign investments would compromise national independence. At the current 3–4 percent level he saw no takeover problem whatsoever — and he noted he did not expect this level to rise. News accounts during the summer indicated new U.S. direct investments were being made or contemplated in France in aluminum, biscuits, and nickel, to mention but a few.

61. *International Herald Tribune*, April 21, 1967, p. 9.

62. And caused some interesting shifts in banking "habits." A Brussels attorney, specializing in working with new American firms, noted that before 1966 local bankers had indicated to him they would welcome his recommending their firm(s) not only for general banking but as sources of funds. By 1966–67 the bankers no longer used this approach; they were having enough difficulties meeting demands from regular clients.

63. A classic example of this — at a higher level — occurred in 1963 when General Motors replaced the German directors of Opel with Americans. This, along with the detergent advertising war of the same period, raised a wave of criticism. On the other hand, some reversal of U.S. "centralization of control" is appearing. For example, the Ford Motor Company announced the creation in June 1967 of a subsidiary, Ford of Europe, Inc., to assume direction of the European automotive group of Ford: Henry Ford II noted that the increasing integration of European trade activity had made it apparent that the European automotive market could best be served from Europe. See *International Herald Tribune*, June 16, 1967, p. 7.

64. See Leo Model, "The Politics of Private Foreign Investment," *Foreign Affairs*, July 1967, pp. 639–651.

65. See, for example, Krause, *European Economic Integration and the United States*, pp. 140–141.

66. As noted earlier one of the most frequent statements the writer encountered in interviews in the European business community was that if the American wanted to invest, "he should bring his money with him." This is a new view, however, arising in 1966–67 as capital became tight in Europe.

67. Lawrence B. Krause and Kenneth W. Dam in *Federal Tax Treatment of Foreign Income* (Washington, D.C.: Brookings, 1964) suggest eight to ten years as the period required to turn a deficit to a surplus.

68. It is frequently suggested that Europe could undertake two steps that would be of assistance: increase its direct investment (new) in the United States and increase its assistance to underdeveloped nations. Both are valid contentions. But European firms (a few aside, such as Olivetti) view with some diffidence operating currently in the American market by the direct investment route. However, there is increasing U.S. interest in seeking out European firms to locate in this country. For example, in June 1967, a Pittsburgh banker met with a group in Paris for purposes of attracting European investors to the United States, particularly Pittsburgh. See the *New York Times*, Section 3, August 4, 1968, pp. 3 and 5, for accounts of French and German direct investments in the United States.

69. At about the same time that the Leo Model view reached the public, the United States Council of the International Chamber of Commerce issued a report urging President Johnson to encourage rather than restrict American investment abroad. The thesis was that only by means of expanding earnings from U.S. foreign investments would it be possible to meet the ever-growing foreign commitments of the United States.

70. One way to reduce the balance-of-payments gap would be through the travel-tourism route rather than through investment channels! If one suggests that U.S. direct investment is "too much," one can, by parity of reasoning, suggest that too many Americans go abroad. In a number of years in the late 1960's, for example, the excess of what Americans spent abroad in travel over what those from other countries spent in the United States was just about equal to the balance-of-payments deficit.

71. Servan-Schreiber's *The American Challenge* is ample evidence of this.

Chapter 5. Constraints and Potentials in Agriculture

1. Published originally in *L'Express* (Paris), September 2, 1967, and in excerpts in *The Times* (London), September 4, 1967, p. 4.

2. *Annual Review and Determination of Guarantees 1967*, Command 3229 (London: HMSO, March 1967), p. 40.

3. *Jordbruks Ekonomiska Meddelanden*, No. 4 (Stockholm, April 1968), Table 21.

4. See James H. Shideler, "Henry C. Wallace and Persisting Progressivism: A Comment," *Agricultural History*, Vol. 41, No. 2 (April 1967), p. 124.

5. *Kungl. Maj:ts proposition till riksdagen ångaende riktlinjer för jordbrukspolitiken m. m.*, No. 96 (Stockholm, March 31, 1967).

6. FAO, *The State of Food and Agriculture 1966* (Rome, 1966), p. 191, and OECD, *Agricultural Policies in 1966* (Paris, 1967), p. 259.

7. *Dritter Bericht der Bundesversammlung über die Lage der schweizerischen Landwirtschaft und die Agrarpolitik des Bundes* (Berne, December 10, 1965), and OECD, *Agricultural Policies in 1966*, p. 488.

8. Ministry of Agriculture, Fisheries, and Food, *Annual Review and Determination of Guarantees 1968*, Command 3558 (London: HMSO, March 1968), p. 31.

9. EEC, *Memorandum on the Reform of Agriculture in the European Economic Community* [the Mansholt Plan], Supplement to Bulletin No. 1, 1969, of the European Communities (Brussels, 1969), Annex 2, p. 52.

10. FAO, *The State of Food and Agriculture 1967* (Rome, 1967), p. 147.

11. F. Gerl, "Möglichkeiten und Grenzen der Deutschen Landwirtschaft in der Welternährungswirtschaft," *Archiv der DLG*, Vol. 37 (1966), pp. 128ff.

12. OECD, *Agricultural Policies in 1966*, p. 529.

13. U.S. Department of Agriculture, *World Agricultural Production and Trade* (Washington, D.C., April 1967), pp. 18–19.

14. Leonard Amey, "After the Harvest – A Twelve-Month Market," *The Times* (London), August 26, 1967, p. 17; U.S. Department of Agriculture, *Foreign Agricultural Circular*, FG 3-69 (Washington, D.C., February 1969).

15. Theodor Dams, "Agrarpolitische Entscheidungen der Europäischen Wirtschaftsgemeinschaft und ihre rechtliche Normierung," Inaugural Lecture, University of Freiburg (*Staatswissenschaftsfakultät*), December 5, 1966.

16. For a succinct and evocative account of this period see "The Politics of European Integration," *Government and Opposition*, Vol. 2, No. 3 (April–July 1967), especially "European Union in the Resistance" by Altiero Spinelli, pp. 321–329; "The Campaign of the European Congresses" by Denis de Rougemont, pp. 329–349; and "The Role of Jean Monet" by Richard Mayne, pp. 349–371.

17. John K. Fairbank, "Why Peking Casts Us as the Villain," *New York Times Magazine*, May 22, 1966, p. 31.

18. "Gaitskell Reassures Motorized Socialists," *The Observer* (London), April 8, 1962, p. 3.

19. Colin Buchanan, "Anarchy of the Road," Letter to the Editor, *The Times* (London), September 4, 1967, p. 9.

20. An excellent discussion of this development is contained in Charles Morazé, *Les Bourgeois Conquérants* (Paris: Armand Colin, 1957); published in English as *The Triumph of the Middle Classes* (London: Weidenfeld and Nicolson, 1966). See especially Chapter 8.

21. Data submitted by the Austrian delegation to the Working Party on Structural Change, European Commission on Agriculture, Food, and Agriculture Organization of the United Nations, Würzburg, Germany, September 5–10, 1966.

22. Interview with the staff of the Institut International du Froid, Paris, March 22, 1968; *Revue Générale du Froid*, Vol. 57, No. 11 (November 1966), pp. 1505–10.

23. See, for example, Franz Stahl, "Verbesserung oder Verschlechterung für den ländlichen Raum?" *Innere Kolonisation*, Vol. 17, No. 2 (February 1968), pp. 43–44.

24. Interviews with the staff of the Danish Agricultural Council and Danish Ministry of Agriculture at Copenhagen, August 15–19, 1967.

25. Commission of the European Communities, *Les Abattoirs dans la C.E.E.*, Part 2, Informations Internes sur l'Agriculture, No. 18 (Brussels, October 1967), p. 172.

26. Commission of the European Communities, *Les Abattoirs dans la C.E.E.*, Part 1, Informations Internes sur l'Agriculture, No. 17 (Brussels, June 1967), p. 80.

27. With the coming into force of the EEC Common Agricultural Policy, West Germany had over 6000 small flour mills of under 5 tons daily capacity, and only

56 mills with a daily capacity of over 80 tons. F. W. Hardach, "Getreidemühlen," *Handwörterbuch der Sozialwissenschaften*, Vol. 20 (Stuttgart, 1965), pp. 461–467.

28. F. E. Clements, *Plant Succession: An Analysis of the Development of Vegetation*, The Carnegie Institute Publication No. 242 (Washington, D.C., 1916).

29. For a review of this period see J. W. Burrow, *Evolution and Society: Study in Victorian Social Theory* (Cambridge: Cambridge University Press, 1967).

30. Emmanuel Le Roy Ladurie, *Histoire du Climat depuis l'An Mil* (Paris: Flammarion, 1967), p. 287.

31. Ulf Hafsten, "Application of Pollen Analysis in Tracing the First Farmer Culture," paper presented at University of Minnesota Symposium on Pollen Analysis, Minneapolis, 1958.

32. On the evolution of climax-crop thought see Rexford Daubenmire, *Plant Communities* (New York: Harper and Row, 1968), especially pp. 229–246.

33. Pierre Bourdieu, "The Attitude of the Algerian Peasant toward Time," in *Mediterranean Countrymen*, ed. Julian Pitt-Rivers (Paris: Mouton, 1963), p. 70.

34. A good example of this emphasis is provided by D. A. Chumichev, Ya. M. Berger, and L. A. Avdeichev, "The Natural-Historic Basis for the Development and Specialization of Agriculture in the Socialist Countries (Outside the USSR)," prepared for the Fourth Congress of the Geographical Society U.S.S.R., abstracted in English in *Soviet Geography* (American Geographical Society), Vol. 6, No. 1 (January 1965), pp. 43–47.

35. Michel J. Petit and Jean-Baptiste Viallon, *The Grain-Livestock Economy of France with Projections to 1970 and 1975*, Research Report No. 3, Institute of International Agriculture, Michigan State University (East Lansing, 1968), p. 23.

36. David Campbell, "Hazards Follow Intensive Cereal Farming," *The Times* (London), July 4, 1967, p. 25.

37. "Bigness in Industry: Not Always Best," *The Economist*, Vol. 222, No. 6438 (January 14, 1967), p. 137.

38. National Commission on Food Marketing, *Organization and Competition in the Livestock and Meat Industry*, Technical Study No. 1 (Washington, D.C., June 1966), p. 7.

39. Edward F. Denison assisted by Jean-Pierre Poullier, *Why Growth Rates Differ: Postwar Experience in Nine Western Countries* (Washington, D.C.: Brookings, 1967), Chapter 17.

40. Pearce Wright, "Programme for the Big Computer Prize," *The Times* (London), August 7, 1967, p. 17.

41. Nicholas Kaldor, *Causes of the Slow Rate of Economic Growth of the United Kingdom*, Inaugural Lecture of November 2, 1966, upon accession to a chair in economics, Kings College (Cambridge: Cambridge University Press, 1966). The argument is repeated and elaborated in Nicholas Kaldor, *Strategic Factors in Economic Development* (Ithaca: New York State School of Industrial and Labor Relations, Cornell University, 1967).

42. *The National Plan*, Command 2764 (London: HMSO, September 1965), pp. 136–137.

43. *Dritter Bericht der Bundesversammlung über die Lage der schweizerischen Landwirtschaft und die Agrarpolitik des Bundes* (Berne, December 10, 1965), p. 10.

44. M. A. Adelman, "Economic Policy," Letter to the Editor, *The Economist*, Vol. 221, No. 6434 (December 17, 1966), pp. 1200–2.

45. For the development of the idea, see George M. Foster, "Peasant Society and the Image of Limited Good," *American Anthropologist*, Vol. 67 (April 1965), pp. 293–315; Russell Langworthy, "The Peasant World View in Italy and India," *Human Organization*, Vol. 27, No. 3 (Fall 1968), pp. 212–219; F. G. Bailey, "The Peasant View of the Bad Life," *Advancement of Science*, Vol. 23 (1966–67), pp. 1–11. For critical responses see David Kaplan and Benson Saler, "Foster's 'Image of Limited Good': An Example of Anthropological Explanation," John W. Bennett, "Further Remarks on Foster's 'Image of Limited Good,'" and "Foster's Reply to Kaplan, Saler, and Bennett," *American Anthropologist*, Vol. 68 (1966), pp.

202–214. John G. Kennedy, " 'Peasant Society and the Image of Limited Good': A Critique," *American Anthropologist*, Vol. 68 (1966), pp. 1212–25.

46. See especially Danilo Dolci, *Chi Gioca Solo* (Turin: Guilo Einaudi, 1966), published in English as *The Man Who Plays Alone* (New York: Pantheon, 1969).

47. The author is indebted to P. J. H. Jonkman of The Hague for the reminder that this attitude is not confined to the very poor. A popular song in the Netherlands in the 1930's ran as follows: "Als je voor een dubbeltje geboren bent, Dan krijg je nooit een kwartje" ("If you have been born to have a dime, you will never get a quarter").

48. Michel Gervais, Claude Servolin, and Jean Weil, *Une France sans Paysans* (Paris: Seuil, 1965).

49. Claude Lévi-Strauss, *La Pensée Sauvage* (Paris: Plon, 1962); published in English as *The Savage Mind* (London: Weidenfeld and Nicolson, 1966).

50. Denis Bergmann, "Viande et Lait — Les Difficultés de la Politique Economique" (mimeo.; Paris: Institut National de la Recherche Agronomique, March 1968), p. 7.

51. C. J. Moss, "Machines to Overcome Labour Scarcity," *The Times* (London), Special Report, "Services to Industry," April 28, 1967, p. vi.

52. Ministère de l'Agriculture, *Situation Agricole en France*, Vol. 4, No. 43 (Paris, November 1, 1968), p. 9.

53. *Annuario Statistico Italiano, 1958* (Rome, 1958) and subsequent years; and U.S. Department of Agriculture, *Foreign Agriculture Circular*, FG 4-67 (Washington, D.C., April 1967).

54. See the series of studies coordinated by the Institute of International Agriculture, Michigan State University, under contract with the U.S. Department of Agriculture, on the grain-livestock economies of selected European countries, especially George E. Rossmiller, *The Grain-Livestock Economy of West Germany with Projections to 1970 and 1975*, Research Report No. 1; Fred A. Mangum, Jr., *The Grain-Livestock Economy of Italy with Projections to 1970 and 1975*, Research Report No. 2; Michel J. Petit and Jean-Baptiste Viallon, *The Grain-Livestock Economy of France with Projections to 1970 and 1975*, Research Report No. 3 (all East Lansing, 1968).

55. See F. Gerl, "Möglichkeiten und Grenzen der deutschen Landwirtschaft in der Welternährungswirtschaft," *Archiv der DLG*, Vol. 37 (1966), pp. 128ff; Romauld Ruf, "Vergleichende Darstellung Langfristiger Agrarprojektionen für die Bundesrepublik Deutschland" (mimeo.; Munich, IFO-Institut für Wirtschaftsforschung, e.V., 1967); George E. Rossmiller, *The Grain-Livestock Economy of West Germany, with Projections to 1970 and 1975*, pp. 175–176.

56. Vernon L. Sorenson and Dale E. Hathaway, *The Grain-Livestock Economy and Trade Patterns of the European Economic Community, with Projections to 1970 and 1975*, Research Report No. 5, Institute of International Agriculture, Michigan State University (East Lansing, 1968), Table 43, p. 103. Although a significant fraction of total milk output is fed to calves, averaging 19 percent of total milk output in 1965, it is clear that this manner of disposal will be inadequate to avoid burdensome surpluses.

57. J. Cranney and C. Servolin, "Les Causes des Excédents Laitiers" (mimeo.; Paris: Institut National de la Recherche Agronomique, 1968), pp. 1–2.

58. Bank of Finland, *Monthly Bulletin*, Vol. 41, No. 5 (May 1967), p. 21; Samuli Suomela, "Agricultural Policy Overshadowed by a Mountain of Butter," *Economic Review* (Helsinki), 1968, No. 4, pp. 143–152.

59. David R. Strobel, "World's Dairy Surplus Is Biggest in EEC," U.S. Department of Agriculture, *Foreign Agriculture* (Washington, D.C.), March 4, 1968.

60. These data and the data on French exports and Italian imports that follow are computed from EEC, *Newsletter on the Common Agricultural Policy*, No. 1 (Brussels, January 1967), p. 8 and Tables 11 and 13.

61. Statistical Office of the European Communities, *Agrarstatistik, 1968*, No. 1, p. 16; U.S. Department of Agriculture, *Grain Developments in the Common*

Market, Foreign Agriculture Service, FAS-M-202 (Washington, D.C., December 1968), p. 4 and *Foreign Agriculture*, September 29, 1969, p. 8.

62. U.S. Department of Agriculture, *Common Market Grain Statistics 1955–56 through 1965–66*, FAS-M-192 (Washington, D.C., September 1967), p. 17.

63. "Evaluation of Structural Policy Programs," the Swedish reply to questionnaire 29889/ E of the Working Party on Agrarian Structure, FAO (mimeo.; Solna, Sweden: National Board of Agriculture, March 14, 1966); Claes-Eric Norrbom, "The Future Extent and Localization of Arable Land in Sweden" (mimeo.; Solna, Sweden: National Board of Agriculture, May 27, 1968); H. Corver, "Der Niederländische Entwicklungs- und Sanierungsfonds für Landwirtschaft," *Agrarwirtschaft*, Vol. 16, No. 8 (August 1967), pp. 270–274; Karl Becker, "Zur Neuorientierung der landwirtschaftlichen Strukturverbesserung," *Berichte über Landwirtschaft*, Vol. 46, No. 3 (September 1968), pp. 465–502.

64. *European Community*, No. 118 (Brussels, November 1968), p. 20; EEC, *Memorandum on the Reform of Agriculture in the European Economic Community* [the Mansholt Plan], Supplement to Bulletin No. 1, 1969, of the European Communities (Brussels, 1969).

65. "Dr. Mansholt's Hair of the Dog," *The Economist*, Vol. 229, No. 6531 (October 26, 1968), p. 91.

66. "Net Budget Expenditures, Domestic Farm Programs and Foreign Programs Compared with Gross National Product" (mimeo.; Washington, D.C.: Office of the Secretary, U.S. Department of Agriculture, December 1968).

67. Data on food expenditures are from the United Nations, *Yearbook of National Accounts Statistics, 1966*, as consolidated in *National Food Situation*, U.S. Department of Agriculture, NFS-124 (Washington, D.C., May 1968), p. 9.

68. *National Food Situation*, U.S. Department of Agriculture, NFS-122 (Washington, D.C., November 1967), p. 5. The data from which these calculations were made refer to "disposable personal income." The percentage spent on food rises slightly if "private consumption expenditure" is taken as a base. For example, food expenditures in the United States were 18.2 percent of consumer disposable income in 1965, but 19.5 percent of private consumption expenditures, as shown in Table 9.

69. *Survey of Current Business* (U.S. Department of Commerce), Vol. 48, No. 6 (June 1968), p. S-1.

70. Donald W. Regier, "Projected Feed Grain Demand in the EEC," *Journal of Farm Economics*, Vol. 49, No. 5 (December 1967), p. 1357.

71. "The Freeze Britain Hasn't," *The Economist*, Vol. 224, No. 6473 (September 16, 1967), p. 1021.

72. See Harold G. Vatter and Robert L. Thompson, "Consumer Asset Formation and Economic Growth — The United States Case," *Economic Journal*, Vol. 76, No. 302 (June 1966), pp. 312–327, and the subsequent discussion by F. Thomas Juster and Robert E. Lipsey, "A Note on Consumer Asset Formation in the United States," and Harold G. Vatter, "Consumer-Asset Formation in the United States: A Rejoinder," *Economic Journal*, Vol. 76, No. 308 (December 1967), pp. 834–855.

73. OECD, *National Account Statistics, 1956–1965* (Paris, February 1967), pp. 122, 126.

74. OECD, *OECD Scheme for the Varietal Certification of Herbage Seed Moving in International Trade*, Documentation in Agriculture and Food, No. 76 (Paris, 1966).

75. OECD, *OECD Standard Code for the Official Testing of Agricultural Tractors*, Documentation in Agriculture and Food, No. 79 (Paris, 1966), replacing No. 20 (1959).

76. OECD, *Scheme for the Varietal Certification of Cereal Seed Moving in International Trade*, Documentation in Agriculture and Food, No. 88 (Paris, 1967); "Scheme for the Certification of Forest Reproductive Material Moving in International Trade," established May 30, 1967; "Scheme for the Varietal Certification of Sugar and Fodder Beet Seed Moving in International Trade," established February 20, 1968.

77. OECD, Paris, "Standard Testing Procedure for Fertilizer Distributors," Special Report AGR/T (66) 11, recommended in February 1967; "Standard Testing Procedures for Combine Harvesters," Special Report AGR/T (67) 12, recommended in December 1967.

78. United Nations Economic Commission for Europe, *The Standardization of Fruits and Vegetables in Europe* (Geneva, 1963); OECD, *International Standardization of Fruits and Vegetables*, Documentation in Agriculture and Food, Nos. 47 (Paris, 1961), 54 (Paris, 1962), 64 (Paris, 1964), and 89 (Paris, 1969); OECD, *Recommendations on the International Standardization of Packaging for Fruit and Vegetables*, Documentation in Agriculture and Food, No. 85 (Paris, 1966).

79. O. Strecker, H. W. Stinshoff, and W. Schüler, "Entwicklungslinien der Getreidepolitik in der EWG," *Agrarwirtschaft*, Vol. 15, No. 10 (October 1966), p. 350.

80. See F. H. de Virieu, "Terroirs sans Frontières," *Le Monde*, July 4, 5, 6, and 7, 1967.

Chapter 6. The Harmonization of Education

1. The best over-all statement of the Council's objectives may be found in the Council for Cultural Cooperation and Cultural Fund of the Council of Europe, *Annual Report, 1965* (Strasbourg: Council of Europe, 1966). Details on the Council for Cultural Cooperation are given in the *European Treaty Series*, No. 18 (Strasbourg: Council of Europe, n.d.), and are also available in a brochure titled *Council for Cultural Co-operation of the Council of Europe.*

2. Herbert S. Parnes, *Forecasting Educational Needs for Economic and Social Development* (Paris: OECD, 1962), p. 2.

3. *EEC Ninth General Report on the Activities of the Community* (Brussels: EEC Commission, 1966), Section 260, pp. 285–286.

4. *University Research and Studies on European Integration*, Vol. 4 (Brussels: European Community Institute for University Studies, 1967).

5. Quoted from the constitution governing the United Kingdom section.

6. For a careful and complete review of the European Schools see H. Hans Merten, *Rapport: Fait au Nom de la Commission de la Recherche et de la Culture sur les Ecoles Européennes et Leur Développement*, Parlement Européen Documents de Séance 1966–67, Document 8 (Brussels: EEC, March 7, 1966).

7. K. Voss, "The European Schools," *Forward in Europe* (Strasbourg: Directorate of Information, Council of Europe, April–May 1967), p. 9; interview with S. Sardo, director, Ecole Européenne, Brussels, October 5, 1966.

8. Catalogue of the college.

9. See David P. Calleo, *Europe's Future* (New York: Horizon Press, 1965), pp. 33ff.

10. *EEC Eighth General Report on the Activities of the Community* (Brussels: EEC Commission, 1965), Section 268; *Une Université Européenne?* (Geneva: Centre Européen de la Culture, 1958), Bulletin No. 8.

11. Joseph Ben-David, *Fundamental Research and the Universities: Some Comments on International Differences* (Paris: OECD, 1968), pp. 14, 66ff.

12. There is a good deal of reading relevant to this subject. The efforts at revising textbooks have been expertly chronicled by Otto-Ernst Schüddekopf, *20 Jahre Schulbuch Revision in Westeuropa* (Braunschweig: Albert Limbach Verlag, 1966). Two invaluable publications about attempts to introduce greater objectivity in history textbooks are E. H. Dance, *History the Betrayer: A Study in Bias* (London: Hutchinson, 1960); and Edouard Bruley and E. H. Dance, *A History of Europe?* (Leyden: A. W. Sythoff, 1960). In geography, reference should be made to I. B. F. Kormoss's *La Première Conférence sur la Révision des Manuels de Géographie: Résultats et Perspectives* (Bruges: Secrétariat, 1962); Association de Conférence des Régions de l'Europe du Nord-Ouest, *Conférence des Régions de l'Europe du Nord-Ouest* (Bruges: Secrétariat, 1965), which analyzes resources, population density and distribution, etc., in the Netherlands, the Federal Republic of Germany,

France, Luxembourg, and Belgium; and *The European Community in Maps* (Brussels: Press and Information Service of the European Communities, n.d.).

13. UNESCO has helped European organization of education by underwriting both educational planning and research on higher education, which are important for all European countries.

14. For the places at which the conferences were held and more about the discussions, see Bruley and Dance, *A History of Europe?* pp. 14ff. A "Glossary of Technical Terms in History" is found in Appendix I, pp. 57, 58.

15. The propriety of pride in one's nation is granted by Bruley and Dance, their plea being only for a balance. Bruley and Dance, *A History of Europe?* pp. 53ff.

16. *Ibid.,* pp. 46ff.

17. *Ibid.,* pp. 16, 20, 23, 63, 68–69.

18. "Enseignement de l'Histoire dans une Perspective Européenne," Association Européenne des Enseignements, 1966. The association writes, "Une série de 12 leçons-types, traitant des principaux aspects de l'histoire du XIXᵉ siècle dans une perspective européenne — français et anglais. Diffusé en 1966."

19. Otto-Ernst Schüddekopf in collaboration with Edouard Bruley, E. H. Dance, and Haakon Vigander, *History Teaching and History Textbook Revision*, Education in Europe, Section II — General and Technical Education, No. 8 (Strasbourg: Council of Europe, Council for Cultural Cooperation, 1967.)

20. Schüddekopf, *History Teaching*, p. 133. Almost twenty years earlier (1949) UNESCO had published its handbook containing eight criteria for textbook examination. Schüddekopf recognized these eight as necessary adjuncts of the criteria he would add: "1. How accurate is the information included? 2. Are the interpretations of events and the generalizations about them adequately supported by the facts presented? 3. Are important terms accurately and clearly defined? 4. Are the illustrations, charts, graphs and maps representative, accurate and up-to-date? 5. Are minority groups, other races, nations and nationalities treated fairly and justly? Is due representation and recognition given to their contributions? 6. Are the same standards of scholarship, justice and morality applied to other nations and groups as to one's own? 7. Are controversial issues presented objectively? 8. Are words and phrases which develop prejudice, misunderstanding and conflict avoided?" *Ibid.,* pp. 132–133.

21. *Ibid.,* pp. 160–161.

22. Georg Eckert, "International Textbook Revision," in *The Yearbook of Education: Education and International Life*, ed. George Z. F. Bereday and Joseph A. Lauwerys (London: Evans Brothers, 1964), pp. 319ff.

23. René Jotterand, *Introducing Europe to Senior Pupils*, in the series Education in Europe, Section II — General and Technical Education, No. 6 (Strasbourg: Council of Europe, Council for Cultural Cooperation, 1966). The Council of Europe's Council for Cultural Cooperation had published *Civics and European Education at the Primary and Secondary Level* in 1963. Teachers have available bibliographical help in *Books Dealing with Europe — A Bibliography for Teachers* (Strasbourg: Council of Europe, Council for Cultural Cooperation, 1965).

24. From the title page of Jotterand, *Introducing Europe to Senior Pupils.*

25. *Civics and European Education at the Primary and Secondary Level*, p. 12.

26. Denis de Rougemont, "Douze Langues, Une Littérature," *Les Amis de Sèvres*, September 1967, p. 11. Translation by the author.

27. See OECD Committee for Scientific and Technical Personnel, "Expansion in Secondary Education: Trends and Implication" (unpublished manuscript, March 14, 1968); Fabio L. Cavazza, "The European School System: Problems and Trends," and Ralf Dahrendorf, "Recent Changes in the Class of European Societies," in *A New Europe?* ed. Stephen R. Graubard (Boston: Houghton Mifflin, 1964); Michel Debeavais and others, "France," in *Access to Higher Education*, ed. Frank Bowles, Vol. II (Paris: UNESCO and International Association of Universities, 1965), pp. 94–95, 110ff, and Appendix 4, p. 165; Jean Floud and others, *Social Class and Educational Opportunity* (London: Heinemann, 1958); Henning Friis,

"Preface," Pierre Laderrière, "Regional Inequalities of Opportunity in French Education and the Measures Designed to Reduce Them," John Westergaard and Alan Little, "Educational Opportunity and Social Selection in England and Wales: Trends and Policy Implications," C. Arnold Anderson, "Sociological Factors in the Demand for Education," and Rose Knight, "Trends in University Entry: An Inter-Country Comparison," all in *Social Objectives in Educational Planning* (Paris: OECD, 1967); Mary Jean Bowman, "The Requirements of the Labour-Market and the Education Explosion," *The World Year Book of Education: The Education Explosion*, ed. George Z. F. Bereday and Joseph A. Lauwerys (London: Evans Brothers, 1965).

28. See Alfred Rosier, "The Explosion in World Population," in *The World Year Book of Education: The Education Explosion*, ed. Bereday and Lauwerys.

29. OECD Committee for Scientific and Technical Personnel, "Expansion in Secondary Education," pp. 3ff.

30. For a description of pupil guidance in Western Europe see Maurice Reuchlin, *Pupil Guidance: Facts and Problems*, in the series Education in Europe, Section II — General and Technical Education, No. 3 (Strasbourg: Council of Europe, Council for Cultural Cooperation, n.d.).

31. Y. Roger, *The Observation and Guidance Period*, in the series Education in Europe (Strasbourg: Council of Europe, Council for Cultural Cooperation, 1967).

32. In French secondary schools all the curriculums preparatory for higher education may be in the same building. It has been assumed by French educators that having the curriculums in one building would facilitate a pupil's moving out of one curriculum and into another, if he has an interest in transferring. The author is unaware of data on the number of actual transfers.

33. See Walter Schultze, "Die Begabtenforderung in ihrer Abhängigkeit vom Schulaufbau," *Die Deutsche Schule*, Vol. 2 (1967), pp. 61–77. The title of Schultze's essay has been translated as "The Encouragement of Ability, Insofar as It Depends on School Structure" in "Comprehensive School or Vertical Structure?" *Education in Germany* (Bad Godesberg: Inter Nationes, 1968), p. 2. See also Torsten Husén, "The Effect of School Structure upon Utilization of Ability: The Case of Sweden and Some International Comparisons," *Social Objectives in Educational Planning*, and Saul B. Robinsohn and J. Casper Kuhlman, "Two Decades of Non-Reform in West German Education," *Comparative Education Review*, Vol. 11, No. 3 (October 1967), p. 317.

34. Debeavais and others, "France," in *Access to Higher Education*, ed. Bowles, p. 107.

35. Jean Maquet, "Ces Faux Elèves Révolutionnent l'Université," *Paris Match*, November 26, 1966, pp. 53–54; Raymond Aron, "Que Valent les Etudes Françaises?" *L'Express*, October 31–November 5, 1966, p. 78.

36. Eugène Egger, in a study of such examinations, found that of nineteen countries, eleven said they were contemplating some change in the examinations. The question Egger asked was "Existe-t-il des projets de réformes de l'examen final? Si oui, quelles sont les grandes lignes de cette réformes de l'examen final?" ("Are there plans for the change of final examinations? If there are, what are the major lines of this change?") Only two countries said that they did not contemplate any change in the examinations. The other six countries could not describe their plans for another three or four years. Egger, *Les Examens de Fin d'Etudes Supérieures et l'Accession aux Etudes Universitaires* (Geneva: Reproduced privately, 1966), pp. 16–17.

37. A European *baccalauréat* is complemented by an international *baccalauréat*, which is being developed by the International Schools Association and its Examination Syndicate (since 1967 called the International Baccalaureate Office), Geneva. Both the European and the international *baccalauréat* are being standardized under the aegis of the Oxford University Department of Education. The history and activities of the International Schools are set forth in *The International Schools Association* (Geneva). A very interesting study of the international *baccalauréat*,

which includes material on the European Schools and the European *baccalauréat*, is Martin Mayer, *Diploma: International Schools and University Entrance* (New York: Twentieth Century Fund, 1968), Chapter 4.

38. "Equivalence" is stressed because it is highlighted in "Curricula and Equivalence," a report of the activities of the Committee for Higher Education and Research of the Council of Europe, in *Paedagogica Europaea*, Vol. 2 (1966), pp. 324–326. This issue of *Paedagogica Europaea*, pp. 318–319, has a notable review of educational research of the Council of Europe. Both the eighth and ninth general reports of the EEC, under the heading of "training," comment on the need for and the difficulty of achieving freedom of establishment. *EEC Eighth General Report*, Sections 265 and 266; *EEC Ninth General Report*, pp. 260ff. See also *Bulletin* of the International Association of Universities, Vol. 14 (May 1966), pp. 120, 124; and Jean Murat, "The Problem of the Equivalence of Degrees and Diplomas," in *The Year Book of Education: Education and International Life*, ed. Bereday and Lauwerys, p. 339.

39. On the influence of social class on education, see Jean Floud, "Social Class Factors in Educational Achievement," in *Ability and Educational Opportunity*, ed. A. H. Halsey (Paris: OECD, 1961); and Beresford Hayward, "Unequal Social Participation in Education: The OECD Programme and Implications for Policy," in *Social Objectives in Educational Planning*.

In the Soviet Union governmental and party leaders encourage the sociological study of the relation of the educational aspirations of young people to their social-class background. These studies have been similar to the social-class studies of education done in Western Europe. Although the Soviet research does not define upper, middle, and lower class, there is a transparent equivalence in the classification of specialists, employees, and urban and rural workers used in Soviet sociological studies of educational choice, which are reviewed in Murray Yanowitch and Norton Dodge, "Social Class and Education: Soviet Findings and Reactions," *Comparative Education Review*, Vol. 12, No. 3 (October 1968), pp. 268–280; and M. N. Rutkevich, ed., and M. Yanowitch, trans., *Career Plans of Youth: A Sociological Study* (New York: International Arts and Sciences Press, 1968).

40. See Chapter 4 above. Also see *Report of the Conference on Transatlantic Technological Imbalance and Collaboration* (dated June 1, 1967; sponsored by the Scientific/Technological Committee of the North Atlantic Assembly and the Foreign Policy Research Institute of the University of Pennsylvania, and held at Deauville, France, May 25–28, 1967); James Brian Quinn, "Technological Competition: Europe *vs* U.S.," *Atlantic Community Quarterly*, Winter 1966–67, pp. 549ff. One of the most searching recent studies of the gap both in technology (applied science) and in unapplied scientific research is Ben-David, "The Scientific Gap between the United States and Western Europe," *Fundamental Research and the Universities*, Chapter 1. Although Ben-David has written only of Western Europe, much of what he notes has been applicable to Eastern and Central Europe as well. Ben-David furnishes documentation for the existence of a gap and associates it with structural characteristics of higher education in Europe, e.g., one-man chairs instead of departments and inadequate investment both in basic and in applied research.

41. Jean-Jacques Servan-Schreiber, *Le défi américain* (Paris: Denoël, 1967); published in English as *The American Challenge* (New York: Atheneum, 1968).

42. "Lord Butler's Warning to Europe," *The Times* (London), March 26, 1968, p. 3.

43. The specific causes of student riots have, of course, varied from country to country and institution to institution, and not all have been directly related to curriculum. One motive of the 1968 riots at the University of Madrid was to register opposition to the control over Spanish higher education by the Franco government. At the Catholic University of Louvain, Belgium, in 1967 student activists focused on a linguistic issue: Flemish-speaking students wished to have a separate university set up for the French-speaking Walloons. Disturbances at the London School of Economics in 1968 seemed to have been motivated by a student desire to share

in administrative power. Even in the socialist countries, where control of all types of schools is impressive, there have been demonstrations by students, though without the violence that marked the French and Italian student riots; they have mostly been inspired by national patriotism, as in the Czech demonstrations of 1968–69.

44. In the 1960's the Council for Cultural Cooperation published a number of volumes promoting equivalence of natural science and technological studies at the university level: *Engineering Education* (1964), Guy Ourisson, *The Teaching of Chemistry at University Level* (1966), Jean Leclercq, *How to Qualify as a "Biologist" in the Universities of Europe* (1967), and W. Hanle and A. Scharmann, *The Teaching of Physics at University Level* (1967), all in the series Education in Europe, Section I — Higher Education in Europe.

45. "Introduction," *University Research and Studies on European Integration*, Vol. 3 (Brussels: European Community Institute for University Studies, 1966), p. XIV; see also *Formation des Cadres Européens* (Geneva: Centre Européen de la Culture, 1964), Bulletin No. 3.

Chapter 7. The Integration of People

1. Jacques-René Rabier, "L'Information de Européens et l'Intégration de l'Europe" (unpublished; Université Libre de Bruxelles, Institut d'Etudes Européennes, 1965); Jacques-René Rabier, "L'Opinion Publique et l'Europe" (unpublished; Université Libre de Bruxelles, Institut de Sociologie, 1966); Gallup International Poll, *L'Opinion Publique et l'Europe des Six* (Paris: Institut Français d'Opinion Publique, 1962); Reader's Digest Poll, "Products and People" (unpublished, 1963); "L'Opinion Publique et l'Europe," *Annuaire Européen*, Vol. 10 (1962), p. 46; International Research Associates, *L'Image de l'Europe Unie dans l'Opinion Publique* (Brussels, December 1966); *8000 Jeunes Ruraux Nous Disent . . .* (Louvain, Belgium: MIJARC, 1966); "Les Français et l'Entrée de la Grande-Bretagne dans le Marché Commun," *Le Monde*, January 24, 1967, p. 3; Gallup International Poll, "Big [British] Majority Keen on Joining Europe," *Daily Telegraph* (London), December 12, 1966, p. 18.

2. Seymour Martin Lipset, *The First New Nation* (New York: Basic Books, 1963).

3. Some Italians raise the question whether the Italian people have yet, by and large, accepted Italian nationality, or whether provincial and local loyalties are stronger. It is an interesting question, but no attempt will be made to answer it here. See *The Economist*, Vol. 222, No. 6447 (March 18, 1967), pp. 26–28.

4. S. N. Eisenstadt, *The Absorption of Immigrants: A Comparative Study Based Mainly on the Jewish Community in Palestine and the State of Israel* (London: Routledge and Kegan Paul, 1954).

5. Jerzy Zubrzycki, *Polish Immigrants in Britain* (The Hague: Martinus Nijhoff, 1956), pp. 165–175.

6. See Chapter 6 above.

7. See Chapter 4 above.

8. An excellent history of cross-national migrations is contained in Donald R. Taft and Richard Robbins, *International Migrations: The Immigrant in the Modern World* (New York: Ronald Press, 1955). For the specific period of World War II, see Joseph B. Schechtman, *European Population Transfers, 1939–1945* (New York: Oxford University Press, 1946). Also see W. D. Borrie, *The Cultural Integration of Immigrants* (Paris: UNESCO, 1959).

9. Germany allowed Poles to come as seasonal laborers and as miners. Poland, along with Italy, was a leading emigrant country in the pre-World War II era. Zubrzycki (*Polish Immigrants in Britain*, p. 27) states that there were 1,485,600 "permanent" emigrants between 1919 and 1938, of which 348,200 returned — leaving a permanent net emigration of 1,137,400. Many of these were dependents rather than workers only. The classic study by W. I. Thomas and F. Znaniecki, *The Polish Peasant in Europe and America* (Chicago: Badger Press, 1919), examines the causes

within Poland for the extensive emigration largely in terms of the breakdown of primary group controls.

10. For example, France returned some 117,000 Poles to their home country during the depression years 1931–35; see Zubrzycki, *Polish Immigrants in Britain*, p. 28. During the occupation years 1940–45, the Pétain government deported many foreigners, some of whom were sent to the slave-labor camps of Germany; see Taft and Robbins, *International Migrations*, p. 188. Probably under the influence of Hitlerism, some xenophobia developed in France during the 1930's and 1940's; see J. M. Domenach in *Esprit*, Vol. 34, No. 4 (April 1966), p. 529, and J. Doublet, "Les Mouvements Migratoires en Europe," *Revue Internationale des Sciences Sociales*, Vol. 17, No. 2 (1965), pp. 304–317.

11. La Documentation Française, *Les Travailleurs Etrangers en France, Notes et Etudes Documentaires*, No. 3057 (Paris, January 23, 1964), p. 15.

12. On the post-World War II refugees, see Taft and Robbins, *International Migrations*, Chapter 11; Jacques Vernant, *The Refugee in the Post-War World* (New Haven, Conn.: Yale University Press, 1953); H. B. M. Murphy and others, *Flight and Resettlement* (Paris: UNESCO, 1955); Louis W. Holborn, *The International Refugee Organization: Its History and Work, 1946–1952* (London and New York: Oxford University Press, 1956); Joint Statistical Project on European Migration (CIME, ILO, OEEC, and UN), *A Decade of Post-World War II European Migration* (Geneva, 1958).

13. Taft and Robbins, *International Migrations*, pp. 271–272. For general discussions of post-World War II international migration, besides Taft and Robbins, see Brinley Thomas, "International Migration," in P. M. Hauser and O. D. Duncan, *The Study of Population: An Inventory and Appraisal* (Chicago: University of Chicago Press, 1959), pp. 510–543; Anthony T. Bouscaren, *International Migrations since 1945* (New York: Praeger, 1963); Brinley Thomas, *Migration and Economic Growth* (Cambridge: Cambridge University Press, 1954).

14. "L'Immigration Portugaise," *Population*, Vol. 21, No. 3 (May–June 1966), pp. 575–576; "L'Immigration Portugaise," *Hommes et Migrations*, No. 105 (1966), p. 203.

15. J. L. Rognaut and J. Schultz, "Les Rapatriés d'Afrique du Nord dans l'Hérault (1954–1964)," *Société Languedocienne de Géographie. Bulletin Trimestrial*, 2nd series, Vol. 35 (July–December 1964), pp. 283–417; Christiane Toujas-Pinèda, "Les Rapatriés d'Algérie dans la Région Midi-Pyrénées," *Revue Géographique des Pyrénées et du Sud-Ouest*, Vol. 36 (December 1965), pp. 321–372.

16. John A. Jackson, "Experience with Emigrants Returning to the Home Country: Ireland," in *Supplement to the Final Report, Emigrant Workers Returning to Their Home Country, International Management Seminar, Athens, October 18–21, 1966* (Paris: OECD, 1967), p. 1.

17. Arnold M. Rose, *Migrants in Europe: Problems of Acceptance and Adjustment* (Minneapolis: University of Minnesota Press, 1969); the material in the balance of this chapter is adapted from this volume.

18. The treaty provisions and subsequent adaptations are summarized in Gordon L. Weil, *A Handbook on the European Economic Community* (New York: Praeger, 1965), pp. 259–265.

19. EEC press release No. 2549, November 8, 1966, p. 6.

20. *Le Monde*, April 8, 1967, p. 21. EEC press release, "Toward Complete Freedom of Movement for Workers," IP (67)53, Brussels, April 13, 1967.

21. EEC press release, April 13, 1967.

22. Lionello Levi Sandri, *Social Policy in the Common Market, 1958–65* (Brussels: European Community Information Service, 1966), p. 3.

23. *Ibid.*, p. 4. However, Sandri, a vice-president of the EEC Commission, states that the Social Fund has not had the impact expected and also has run into political opposition from the Council because of its supranational character. Vocational training is handled on a national basis, with the Social Fund paying 50 percent of the cost retroactively (the remaining 50 percent is often divided according to an

agreement between the country of emigration and the country of immigration). The Social Fund may also be used to pay for resettlement of workers whose firms have been adversely affected by modification of trade barriers and other development programs within the EEC. Most resettlement is within the country affected, not cross-national, and the country requesting Social Fund allocations for resettlement must pay half of the costs.

24. *Ibid.*, p. 7.

25. Exchanges of information have also been sponsored by ILO, through several conventions and resolutions, and by UNESCO, through its conference at Havana in 1956 (reported in W. D. Borrie, *The Cultural Integration of Immigrants*). The Office of Social Affairs of the European Office of the United Nations, in cooperation with Swiss authorities, convened an expert group at Mont-Pélerin in Switzerland in 1962 and a more extensive seminar at Madrid in 1964. The OECD held international conferences at Gröningen in 1960 (see H. Krier, *Rural Manpower and Industrial Development, Adaptation and Training* [Paris: OECD, 1961]); at Paris in 1961 (see G. Barbichon, *Adaptation and Training of Rural Workers for Industrial Work* [Paris: OECD, 1962]); at Wiesbaden in 1963 (see *Adaptation of Rural and Foreign Workers to Industry, Final Report, International Joint Seminar, Wiesbaden, December 10–13, 1963* [Paris: OECD, 1965]); and at Athens in 1966 (see *Emigrant Workers Returning to Their Home Countries, Final Report, International Management Seminar, Athens, October 18–21, 1966* [Paris: OECD, 1966]). The studies, conversations, reports, and periodicals of the International Catholic Migration Commission (see its periodical *Migration News*, and its Migration Informative Series No. 4, *Catholic Migration Activities*), the World Council of Churches (see its periodical *Migration Today*), and the Intergovernmental Committee for European Migration (see its periodical *International Migration*, and Paul Ladame, *Le Rôle des Migrations dans le Monde Libre* [Geneva: Droz, 1958]) have also had a considerable intellectual impact on those private persons and public authorities who provide various services to migrant workers. For information about these organizations, also see OECD Division of Social Affairs, "Etude de Politiques et Mésures d'Ordre Pratique: Organisations Internationales," MS/ S/ 2657/ 13 (Paris, October 23, 1964).

26. The point of view of this paragraph has also been guided by Sandri, *Social Policy in the Common Market*, p. 10.

27. Information for this paragraph has been taken from Martin Schnitzer, *Programs for Relocating Workers Used by Governments of Selected Countries*, U.S. Congress (89th) Joint Economic Committee (Washington, D.C.: GPO, 1966), pp. 70–73. Also see *Social Policy in the ECSC*, in *Community Topics*, No. 20 (Brussels: European Community Information Service, 1966).

28. This paragraph is based on Jacques Jean Ribas, *Social Security in the European Community* (Brussels: European Community Information Service, 1965), pp. 10–13.

29. British Information Services, *The Council of Europe* (London: Central Office of Information, 1966), p. 11.

30. I. Erixon, "Adaptation and Training of Rural Manpower Moving from Population Surplus Areas to Industrial Regions and Countries," MS/ S/ 65.128 (Paris: OECD, 1965), pp. 18–19.

31. See Rose, *Migrants in Europe*, for a discussion of the important economic impacts of the migration.

32. Further discussion and supporting data are to be found in *ibid*.

33. If there are a large number of variables, as is partly true in this study, there is mathematical support for using the arbitrary weight of 1. See Louis Guttman in Paul Horst, *The Prediction of Personal Adjustment* (New York: Social Science Research Council, 1941), pp. 251–364.

34. France is also somewhat of an exception — but to a smaller extent and of an opposite nature. France's immigrants do not have the highest integration and adjustment even though it is the most open country in terms of its policies, programs, and

practices. The reason would again appear to lie in public opinion – which in France is not always hospitable toward immigrants.

35. They should be known as "grouped-data" correlations. "Ecological" refers to a theoretical viewpoint which interprets social facts in terms of location and distance. It is true that ecology works with grouped data, but not all grouped data are ecological. There is nothing "ecological" about the present study, for instance. Ecology was a branch of sociology and geography for thirty years before the misnomer "ecological correlation" arose in the late 1940's.

36. Public opinion polls suggest that the Swedes cooperate more than the French with their government, big employers, and big trade unions in a conscious national effort to be pro-immigrant.

37. In the mid-1960's the Swedes were having a great debate about whether they should encourage the immigrants to be like Swedes or let them be like anyone they wanted to be. The very existence of such a debate indicates a degree of openness in Swedish society that no other European country had achieved at that time.

Chapter 8. Changing Structure of Europe

1. Three of the authors of this volume spent much of the summer of 1968 in Eastern Europe and the Soviet Union and were struck by the manner in which developments in these countries, notably in such areas as cultural life and education, reflected situations and problems familiar in the Western world.

2. It is worthy of note that references to the states of the Soviet orbit as "satellites" virtually passed out of the Western vocabulary by the mid-sixties.

3. One prominent Communist stated in the spring of 1967 that he expected this to take place "within a year."

4. An expression coined by Willy Brandt in alluding to one of the treaties between Moscow and its satellite in Pankow, East Germany.

5. Leo Mates, "Armed Force and Spheres of Influence," *Review of International Affairs*, Vol. 5, No. 19 (September 20, 1968), pp. 4–6.

6. Anthony Sampson, "Students of Europe 'Unite,' " *The Observer* (London), April 7, 1968, p. 3.

7. Patrick Seale, "De Gaulle: War in Europe Possible," *The Observer* (London), October 27, 1968, p. 2.

8. A. Brun, *Perspectives de Remplacement des Chefs d'Exploitation Agricole* (Paris: Institut National de la Recherche Agronomique, July 1967), p. 52.

9. Corrado Barberis, *Popolazione Agricola e Società Rurale* (Rome: Confederazione Nationale dei Coltivatori Diretti, January 1967), p. 7.

10. Federazione Nazionale delle Casse Mutue Malattia per i Coltivatori Diretti, *Famiglie senza Giovani*, Estratto dal Supplemento N. 5 a "L'Assistenza Malattia al Coltivatori Diretti," No. 4 (Rome, April 1966).

11. Jo Grimond, "Is the Party Game Finished?" *The Observer* (London), February 5, 1967, p. 10.

12. For one thing countries that have exported labor, including highly qualified manpower, are industrializing, developing advanced marketing structures and procedures, mechanizing, and otherwise making agricultural production scientific. All of this demands that more potentially qualified manpower remain at home. This demand also will help to create rewards that make "staying at home" possible.

13. Philip Rieff, "14 Points on Wilson," *Encounter*, April 1967, p. 86.

Selected Readings

General References

Aubrey, Henry G. *Atlantic Economic Cooperation: The Case of the OECD.* New York: Praeger, 1967.

Benoit, Emile. *Europe at Sixes and Sevens: The Common Market, the Free Trade Association, and the United States.* New York: Columbia University Press, 1961.

Camps, Miriam A. *European Unification in the Sixties: From the Veto to the Crisis.* New York: McGraw-Hill, 1966.

———. *What Kind of Europe? The Community since De Gaulle's Veto.* London: Oxford University Press, 1965.

Cleveland, Harold Van B., and Joan B. Cleveland. *The Atlantic Alliance: Problems and Prospects.* New York: Foreign Policy Association, 1966.

Cottrell, Alvin J., and James E. Dougherty. *The Politics of the Atlantic Alliance.* New York: Praeger, 1964.

Deniau, J. F. *The Common Market.* London: Barrie and Rockcliff, 1961.

European Community Information Service. *European Community* (a monthly publication). Washington, D.C.: European Community Information Service, 808 Farragut Building.

Haas, Ernst B. *The Uniting of Europe: Political, Social and Economic Forces, 1950–1957.* Stanford, Calif.: Stanford University Press, 1958.

Hallstein, Walter. *United Europe, Challenge and Opportunity.* Cambridge, Mass.: Harvard University Press, 1962.

Humphrey, Don D. *The United States and the Common Market: A Background Study.* New York: Praeger, 1963.

Krause, Lawrence B., ed. *The Common Market: Progress and Controversy.* Englewood Cliffs, N.J.: Prentice-Hall, 1964.

Lindberg, Leon N. *The Political Dynamics of European Economic Integration.* Stanford, Calif.: Stanford University Press, 1963.

Mayne, Richard. *The Community of Europe.* London: Gollancz, 1963.

Meyer, F. V. *The Seven.* London: Barrie and Rockcliff, 1960.

Newhouse, John. *Collision in Brussels: The Common Market Crisis of 30 June 1965.* London: Faber and Faber, 1967.

Nöel, Emile. *How the European Economic Community's Institutions Work.* Brussels: European Community Information Service, 1963.

Nourissier, François. *The French,* tr. Adrienne Foulke. New York: Knopf, 1968.

P.E.P. *European Unity: A Survey of the European Organisations.* London: Allen and Unwin, 1968.

Sampson, Anthony. *Anatomy of Europe.* New York: Harper and Row, 1968.

Servan-Schreiber, Jean-Jacques. *The American Challenge.* New York: Atheneum, 1968.

History and Politics

Amme, Carl H. *NATO without France: A Strategic Appraisal.* Stanford, Calif.: Hoover Institution, 1968.

Andren, Nils. *Power Politics and Non-Alignment: A Perspective on Swedish Foreign Policy.* Stockholm: Almquist and Wiksell, 1967.

Ball, George W. *The Discipline of Power.* Boston: Little, Brown, 1968.

Beaufre, André. *NATO and Europe.* London: Faber and Faber, 1966.

Beugel, Ernst H. van der. *From Marshall Aid to Atlantic Partnership: European Integration as a Concern of American Foreign Policy.* Amsterdam, London, New York: Elsevious Publishing Company, 1966.

Brugmans, Henri. *L'Idée Européenne.* Bruges: De Tempel, 1965.

Brzezinski, Zbigniew. *Alternatives to Partition: For a Broader Conception of America's Role in Europe.* New York: McGraw-Hill, 1965.

Calleo, David P. *Europe's Future: The Grand Alternatives.* New York: Horizon Press, 1965.

Carmoy, Guy de. *Les Politiques Etrangères de la France 1944–1966.* Paris: Editions de la Table Honde, 1967.

Cleveland, Harold van B. *The Atlantic Idea and Its European Rivals.* New York: McGraw-Hill, 1966.

Deutsch, Karl, and others. *France, Germany and the Western Alliance: A Study of Elite Attitudes on European Integration and World Politics.* New York: Scribner's, 1967.

Feld, Werner. *The European Common Market and the World.* Englewood Cliffs, N.J.: Prentice-Hall, 1967.

Finletter, Thomas K. *Interim Report.* New York: Norton, 1968.

Gordon, Kermit, ed. *Agenda for the Nation.* Washington, D.C.: Brookings, 1968.

Hess, John L. *The Case for De Gaulle.* New York: Morrow, 1968.

Kissinger, Henry A. *The Trouble Partnership: A Reappraisal of the Atlantic Alliance.* New York: McGraw-Hill, 1965.

Krause, Lawrence B. *European Economic Integration and the United States.* Washington, D.C.: Brookings, 1968.

Kulski, W. W. *De Gaulle and the World: Foreign Policy of the Third Republic.* Syracuse, N.Y.: Syracuse University Press, 1966.

Lindberg, Leon N. *The Political Dynamics of European Integration.* Stanford, Calif.: Stanford University Press, 1963.

Mayne, Richard. *The Institutions of the European Common Market.* London: Chatham House, 1968.

Richardson, James L. *Germany and the Atlantic Alliance: The Interaction of Strategy and Politics.* Cambridge, Mass.: Harvard University Press, 1966.

Tournoux, J. R. *La Tragédie du Général.* Paris: Plon, 1967.

Willis, F. Roy. *France, Germany, and the New Europe, 1945–1967.* Stanford, Calif.: Stanford University Press, 1968.

Economics: Policies and Practices

Adams, Walter, ed. *The Brain Drain.* New York: Macmillan, 1968.

Balassa, Bela. *The Theory of Economic Integration.* Homewood, Ill.: Richard D. Irwin, 1961.

Caves, Richard E., and associates. *Britain's Economic Prospects.* Washington, D.C.: Brookings, 1968.

Chase Manhattan Bank. *The European Markets: A Guide for American Businessmen.* New York: Chase Manhattan Bank, 1964.

Denison, Edward F., assisted by Jean-Pierre Poullier. *Why Growth Rates Differ: Postwar Experience in Nine Western Countries.* Washington, D.C.: Brookings, 1967.

Dillard, Dudley. *Economic Development of the North Atlantic Community.* Englewood Cliffs, N.J.: Prentice-Hall, 1967.

Frank, Isaiah. *The European Common Market: An Analysis of Commercial Policy.* New York: Praeger, 1961.

Freeman, C., and A. Young. *The Research and Development Effort in Western Europe, North America and the Soviet Union.* Paris: OECD, 1965.

Granick, David. *The European Executive.* New York: Doubleday, 1962.

Hinshaw, Randall. *The European Community and American Trade: A Study in Atlantic Economics and Policy.* New York: Praeger, 1964.

Kindleberger, Charles. *American Business Abroad: Six Lectures in Direct Investment.* New Haven, Conn.: Yale University Press, 1969.

Krause, Lawrence B. *European Integration and the United States.* Washington, D.C.: Brookings, 1968.

Kuznets, Simon. *Modern Economic Growth: Rate, Structure, and Spread.* New Haven, Conn.: Yale University Press, 1966.

Layton, Christopher. *Trans-Atlantic Investments.* Boulogne-sur-Seine, France: Atlantic Institute, 1966.

Mansfield, Edwin. *The Economics of Technological Change.* New York: Norton, 1968.

————. *Industrial Research and Technological Innovation.* New York: Norton, 1968.

Nelson, James R. "Transport Policies for European Economic Integration," *American Economic Review,* Vol. 58, No. 2 (May 1968), pp. 378–392.

OECD. *Economic Growth 1960–70: A Mid-Decade Review of Prospects.* Paris: OECD, 1966.

Rolfe, Sidney E. *Capital Markets in Atlantic Economic Relationships.* Boulogne-sur-Seine, France: Atlantic Institute, 1967.

Schmookler, Jacob. *Invention and Economic Growth.* Cambridge, Mass.: Harvard University Press, 1966.

Scitovsky, Tibor. *Economic Theory and Western European Integration.* Stanford, Calif.: Stanford University Press, 1958.

Statistical Office of the European Communities. *Basic Statistics of the Community.* Brussels: EEC, annual.

Agriculture

Ardagh, John. *The New French Revolution: A Social and Economic Survey of France, 1945–1967.* London: Secker and Warburg, 1968.

Ashton, J., and S. J. Rogers, eds. *Economic Change and Agriculture.* Edinburgh and London: Oliver and Boyd, for the Agricultural Adjustment Unit, University of Newcastle upon Tyne, 1967.

Butterwick, Michael, and Edmund Neville Rolf. *Food, Farming and the Common Market.* London: Oxford University Press, 1968.

Coppock, John O. *Atlantic Agricultural Unity: Is It Possible?* New York: McGraw-Hill, for the Council on Foreign Relations, 1966.

Dams, Theodor, Franz Gerl, Herbert Kötter, and Otto Strecker, eds. *Agrarpolitik in der EWG.* Munich: Bayerischer Landwirtschaftsverlag, 1968.

Denton, G. R., ed. *Economic Integration in Europe.* London: Weidenfeld and Nicolson, 1969.

Gervais, Michel, Claude Servolin, and Jean Weil. *Une France sans Paysans.* Paris: Seuil, 1965.

Graduate Institute of International Studies (Geneva). *The European Free Trade Association and the Crisis of European Integration.* London: Michael Joseph, 1968.

Hess, John L. *The Case for de Gaulle: An American Viewpoint.* New York: Morrow, 1968.

Lierde, Jacques Van. *Europese Landbouwproblemen en Europese Landbouwpolitiek.* Antwerp: Standard Wetenschappelijke Uitgeverij, 1967.

Mendras, Henri. *La Fin des Paysans, Innovations et Changement dans l'Agriculture Française*. Paris: S.E.D.E.I.S., Collection Futuribles, 1967.

Morazé, Charles. *Les Bourgeois Conquérants*. Paris: Armand Colin, 1957. Published in English as *The Triumph of the Middle Classes*. London: Weidenfeld and Nicolson, 1966.

OECD. *Agricultural Policies in 1966*. Paris, 1967.

————. *Agricultural Projections for 1975 and 1985: Production and Consumption of Major Foodstuffs*. Paris, 1968.

Sampson, Anthony. *The New Europeans: A Guide to the Workings, Institutions and Character of Contemporary Western Europe*. London: Hodder and Stoughton, 1968.

Tracy, Michael. *Agriculture in Western Europe: Crisis and Adaptation since 1880*. London: Jonathan Cape, 1964.

U.S. Department of Agriculture. *European Economic Community Agricultural Trade Statistics, 1961–67*. Economic Research Service, ERS-Foreign 247. Washington, D.C., February 1969.

Virieu, François-H. de. *La Fin d'un Agriculture*. Paris: Calman-Lévy, 1967.

Willis, F. Roy. *France, Germany, and the New Europe, 1945–1963*. Stanford, Calif.: Stanford University Press, 1965.

Education

Agazzi, Aldo. *The Educational Aspects of Examinations*. In the series Education in Europe, Section II — General and Technical Education, No. 10. Strasbourg: Council of Europe, Council for Cultural Cooperation, 1967.

Bereday, George Z. F., and Joseph A. Lauwerys, eds. *The World Year Book of Education: The Education Explosion*. London: Evans Brothers, 1965.

Billington, Roy A. "History Is a Dangerous Subject," *Saturday Review*, Vol. 49 (January 15, 1966), pp. 59–61, 80–81.

Bowles, Frank, ed. *Access to Higher Education*. Paris: UNESCO and International Association of Universities, 1965. 2 vols.

Brugmans, Henri. *Panorama à la Pensée Fédéraliste*. Paris: La Columbe, 1965.

Calleo, David P. *Europe's Future: The Grand Alternatives*. New York: Horizon Press, 1965.

Capedecombe, L. *Higher Education in France*. In the series Reform and Development of Higher Education in Europe. Paris: UNESCO, 1964.

Dance, E. H. *History the Betrayer: A Study in Bias*. London: Hutchinson, 1960.

Floud, Jean, and others. *Social Class and Educational Opportunity*. London: Heinemann, 1958.

Graubard, Stephen R., ed. *A New Europe?* Boston: Houghton Mifflin, 1964.

Halls, W. D., and Doreen Humphreys. *Mathematics*. European Curriculum Studies (in the Academic Secondary School), No. 1. Strasbourg: Council of Europe, Council for Cultural Cooperation, 1968.

Halsey, A. S., ed. *Ability and Educational Opportunity*. Paris: OECD, 1961.

Hanle, W., and A. Scharmann. *The Teaching of Physics at University Level*. In the series Education in Europe, Section I — Higher Education in Europe, No. 5. Strasbourg: Council of Europe, Council for Cultural Cooperation, 1967.

Hozelitz, Bert T., and Wilbert E. Moore, eds. *Industrialization and Society*. Paris: UNESCO-Mouton, 1966.

International Baccalaureate Office. *Semiannual Bulletin*, No. 1. International Schools Examination Syndicate, November 1968.

Marchant, E. C. *Geography Teaching and the Revision of Geography Textbooks and Atlases*. In the series Education in Europe, Section II — General and Technical Education, No. 9. Strasbourg: Council of Europe, Council for Cultural Cooperation, 1968.

Murat, Jean. "The Problem of the Equivalence of Degrees and Diplomas," in *The*

Yearbook of Education: Education and International Life. London: Evans Brothers, 1964.

OECD. *Development of Secondary Education: Trends and Implications.* Paris: OECD, 1969.

———. *Modernizing Our Schools.* Paris: OECD, 1966.

———. *Social Objectives in Educational Planning.* Paris: OECD, 1967.

Paedagogica Europaea, 1965–date.

Poignant, Raymond. *L'Enseignement dans les Pays du Marché Commun.* Paris: Institut Pedagogique National, 1965.

Reuchlin, Maurice. *Pupil Guidance: Facts and Problems.* In the series Education in Europe, Section II – General and Technical Education, No. 3. Strasbourg: Council of Europe, Council for Cultural Cooperation, 1964.

Robinson, E. A. G., and J. E. Vaizey, eds. *The Economics of Education* (proceedings of a conference held by the International Economic Association). New York: St. Martin's Press, 1966.

School Systems: A Guide. In the series Education in Europe, Section II – General and Technical Education, No. 5. Strasbourg: Council of Europe, Council for Cultural Cooperation, 1965.

Schüddekopf, Otto-Ernst, in collaboration with Edouard Bruley, E. H. Dance, and Haakon Vigander. *History Teaching and History Textbook Revision.* In the series Education in Europe, Section II – General and Technical Education, No. 8. Strasbourg: Council of Europe, Council for Cultural Cooperation, 1967.

Thut, I. N., and Don Adams. *Educational Patterns in Contemporary Societies.* New York: McGraw-Hill, 1964.

Western European Education, Vol. 1, No. 1 (Winter 1968).

Yanowitch, Murray, and Norton Dodge. "Social Class and Education: Soviet Findings and Reactions," *Comparative Education Review*, Vol. 12, No. 3 (October 1968), pp. 248–267.

Labor Markets, Labor Supplies, and Immigration

Barzanti, Sergio. *The Underdeveloped Areas within the Common Market.* Princeton, N.J.: Princeton University Press, 1965.

Bideberry, P. "Some Features of Immigration in France and in Europe," *International Migration*, Vol. 2 (December 1964), pp. 277–278.

Borrie, W. D. *The Cultural Integration of Immigrants.* Paris: UNESCO, 1959.

Bouscaren, Anthony T. *International Migrations since 1945.* New York: Praeger, 1963.

Economic Policy in Our Time, Vol. III in *Country Studies.* Chicago: Rand McNally, 1964.

Edding, Friedrich. *The Refugees as a Burden, a Stimulus and a Challenge to the West.* The Hague: Nijhoff, 1951.

Fei, John C. H., and Gustav Ranis. *Development of the Labor Surplus Economy: Theory and Policy.* Homewood, Ill.: Richard D. Irwin, 1964.

"Holland: How to Handle Immigrants," *The Economist*, Vol. 214, No. 6341 (March 6, 1965), p. 1008.

Kindleberger, Charles P. *Europe's Postwar Growth: The Role of Labor Supply.* Cambridge, Mass.: Harvard University Press, 1967.

OECD. *Adaptation of Rural and Foreign Workers to Industry.* Paris: OECD, 1965.

———. *Labor Market Policy in Sweden.* Paris: OECD, 1963.

Robertson, D. J. *A Market for Labor.* London: Institute of Economic Affairs, 1961.

Rundle, Stanley. *Language as a Social and Political Factor in Europe.* London: Faber and Faber, 1948.

Sandri, Lionello L. *Social Policy in the Common Market, 1958–65.* Brussels: European Community Information Service, 1966.

Schnitzer, Martin, for the U.S. Congress (89th), Joint Economic Committee. *Pro-*

grams for Relocating Workers Used by Governments of Selected Countries. Washington, D.C.: GPO, 1966.

Taft, Donald R., and Richard Robbins. *International Migrations: The Immigrant in the Modern World.* New York: Ronald Press, 1955.

Thomas, Brinley, ed. *Economics of International Migration.* London: Macmillan, 1958.

Vernant, Jacques. *The Refugee in the Post-War World.* New Haven, Conn.: Yale University Press, 1953.

Weil, Gordon L. *A Handbook on the European Economic Community.* New York: Praeger, 1965.

Wright, Gordon. *Rural Revolution in France: The Peasant in the Twentieth Century.* Stanford, Calif.: Stanford University Press, 1964.

INDEX

Index

Abelin, Pierre, 53
Ability and Educational Opportunity,
 173
"Ace Mobile Force" (NATO), 76
Acheson, Dean, 4
Action Committee for the United States
 of Europe, 14, 36, 71, 72, 241
Adelman, M. A., 148
Adenauer, Konrad, 56, 66, 245
Aerospace: U.S. and European expendi-
 tures in, 100, 103
Africa: migration from, 197, 233;
 mentioned, 221
Agenor, 177
Agfa-Gevaert Co., 26
Agricultural policy: affected by war,
 126–127; effect on economic and
 political institutions, 127, 129–130.
 See also Common Agricultural Policy
Agriculture: and EEC, 7, 21, 27, 28, 35,
 41, 55, 113, 114, 121, 122, 124, 130–
 133, 143, 146, 155–156, 157, 159,
 160, 166, 167, 229–230, 231; departure of labor from, 7, 93, 98, 128–129,
 147–148, 158–159, 231–232; and
 economies of scale, 7, 143–149; and
 EFTA, 14, 16, 130; surpluses in, 127–
 128, 151–155, 228, 229–231; and
 European integration, 130–133; affected by automobile, 134, 136–140;
 affected by research and development,
 140–141; and climax crop theory,
 141–143; reform of, 159–160, 168–
 170; self-sufficiency in, and nationalism, 237–238; mentioned, 11. *See
 also* Common Agricultural Policy
Ailleret, General, 79
Albania, 135, 224
Albert Lea, Minn., 139
Algeria, 55, 65, 79, 197
American Can Company, 114
Amis de Sèvres, Les, 175

Appalachian Mountains, 137
Arab-Israeli conflict (*1967*), 46, 49, 55
Aral, 117
Argentina, 196
Armand, Louis, 174
Armenia (Turkish), 195
Arms control: and NATO, 32. *See also*
 Nuclear nonproliferation treaty, Nu-
 clear test-ban treaty
Asia: migration from, 197, 233; men-
 tioned, 221
Asia, Southeast: U.S. involvement in,
 42–43, 56, 58–59, 74, 81, 223, 226
Association with Certain African Coun-
 tries and Madagascar, 125
Atlantic alliance. *See* Integration, At-
 lantic; Western Alliance
Atomic energy, 14, 26. *See also* Euro-
 pean Atomic Energy Community,
 Nuclear program
Austin, Minn., 139
Australia: migration to, 196, 219; mentioned, 201, 221
Austria: and EFTA, 14; and OECD, 15;
 and EEC, 16; affected by automobile,
 136–137; food expenditures in, 161,
 162; education in, 184, 185, 188, 189;
 migration from, 195, 196; migration
 to, 197; mentioned, 76, 175, 226, 237
Automobile: effect on European centers, 133–134; multiplication of, in
 Europe, 135–136; effect on rural
 Europe, 136–137; effect on marketing,
 138–140; European market for, 163,
 164; mentioned, 115

Baccalauréat: establishment of Euro-
 pean, 7, 171, 186–187, 258–259
Balance of payments. *See* Payments,
 balance of
Balkan Mountains, 136
Balkan States, 149, 168